Hands-On Time Series Analysis with R

Perform time series analysis and forecasting using R

Rami Krispin

BIRMINGHAM - MUMBAI

Hands-On Time Series Analysis with R

Commissioning Editor: Sunith Shetty
Acquisition Editor: Aditi Gour
Content Development Editor: Pratik Andrade
Technical Editor: Nilesh Sawakhande
Copy Editor: Safis Editing
Language Support Editor: Storm Mann
Project Coordinator: Namrata Swetta
Proofreader: Safis Editing
Indexer: Rekha Nair
Graphics: Jisha Chirayil
Production Coordinator: Aparna Bhagat

First published: May 2019

Production reference: 1310519

Published by Packt Publishing Ltd.
Livery Place
35 Livery Street
Birmingham
B3 2PB, UK.

ISBN 978-1-78862-915-7

www.packtpub.com

To Dana, Noa Gili, and Tal

`mapt.io`

Mapt is an online digital library that gives you full access to over 5,000 books and videos, as well as industry leading tools to help you plan your personal development and advance your career. For more information, please visit our website.

Why subscribe?

- Spend less time learning and more time coding with practical eBooks and Videos from over 4,000 industry professionals

- Improve your learning with Skill Plans built especially for you

- Get a free eBook or video every month

- Mapt is fully searchable

- Copy and paste, print, and bookmark content

Packt.com

Did you know that Packt offers eBook versions of every book published, with PDF and ePub files available? You can upgrade to the eBook version at `www.packt.com` and as a print book customer, you are entitled to a discount on the eBook copy. Get in touch with us at `customercare@packtpub.com` for more details.

At `www.packt.com`, you can also read a collection of free technical articles, sign up for a range of free newsletters, and receive exclusive discounts and offers on Packt books and eBooks.

Contributors

About the author

Rami Krispin is a data scientist at a major Silicon Valley company, where he focuses on time series analysis and forecasting. In his free time, he also develops open source tools and is the author of several R packages, including the TSstudio package for time series analysis and forecasting applications. Rami holds an MA in applied economics and an MS in actuarial mathematics from the University of Michigan—Ann Arbor.

I want to thank my beloved wife, Dana, for her help and support throughout the process of writing this book. I also want to thank Pratik Andrade and the Packt Publishing editing team for their support, guidance, and contribution to the creation of this book.

About the reviewers

Fernando C. Barbi (@fcbarbi) is a product manager at Analyx Labs in Switzerland, developing data analysis and risk management tools for the financial industry. He runs the Private Equity Lab, where he researches and teaches investment modeling. He has authored some R packages and, as a Python and R enthusiast, is often an instructor at tech conferences and online courses. He holds a PhD in economics from the São Paulo School of Economics (EESP) FGV.

Fiqry Revadiansyah is a data scientist at Bukalapak, where he provides insights and analytical strategies to enhance product quality by utilizing machine learning and any statistical experiment. He graduated from Universitas Padjadjaran, Bandung, with a BS in statistics. He is a statistician working in data science as a statistics researcher and as an academic consultant. His primary interests are research related to time series analysis and regression modeling, artificial intelligence, immersive computing, and gamification. He uses several programming languages, including R, Python, and C#.

I would like to express my sincere gratitude to the Almighty Allah for giving me the ability and opportunity to help complete this book.

I would like to thank the author of the book, Rami Krispin, who has worked brilliantly, day and night, to ensure the quality and quantity of the content is sky-high. Also, my gratitude extends to Zahid Ali as a Peer Reviewer Manager, and Namrata Swetta as my Project Coordinator.

Dr. Naftali Cohen is a research scientist at AI Research, JP Morgan. He has over 10 years of R&D work experience in numerical modeling, predictive analytics, machine learning, and AI in both academic and industrial settings.

Before joining JP Morgan, Dr. Cohen worked as an academic researcher at Yale University and Columbia University.

He holds a Ph.D. in applied mathematics from the Courant Institute of Mathematical Sciences—New York University. His academic research focused on climate science and storm formation. Dr. Cohen is a MacCracken fellow and an elected member of the International Space Science Institute.

Packt is searching for authors like you

If you're interested in becoming an author for Packt, please visit `authors.packtpub.com` and apply today. We have worked with thousands of developers and tech professionals, just like you, to help them share their insight with the global tech community. You can make a general application, apply for a specific hot topic that we are recruiting an author for, or submit your own idea.

Table of Contents

Preface

Time series analysis is the art of extracting meaningful insights and revealing patterns from time series data using statistical and data visualization approaches. These insights and patterns can then be utilized to explore past events and forecast future values in the series.

This book goes through all the steps of the time series analysis process, from getting the raw data, to building a forecasting model using R. You will learn how to use tools from packages such as **stats**, **lubridate**, **xts**, and **zoo** to clean and reformat your raw data into structural time series data. As you make your way through *Hands-On Time Series Analysis with R*, you will analyze data and extract meaningful information from it using both descriptive statistics and rich data visualization tools in R, such as the **TSstudio**, **plotly**, and **ggplot2** packages. The latter part of the book delves into traditional forecasting models such as time series regression models, exponential smoothing, and **autoregressive integrated moving average** (**ARIMA**) models using the forecast package. Last but not least, you will learn how to utilize machine learning models such as Random Forest and Gradient Boosting Machine to forecast time series data with the **h2o** package.

Who this book is for

This book is ideal for the following groups of people:

- Data scientists who wish to learn how to perform time series analysis and forecasting with R.
- Data analysts who perform Excel-based time series analysis and forecasting and wish to take their forecasting skills to the next level.

Basic knowledge of statistics (for example, regression analysis and hypothesis testing) is required, and some knowledge of R is expected but is not mandatory (for those who never use R, Chapter 1, *Introduction to Time Series Analysis and R*, provides a brief introduction).

What this book covers

Chapter 1, *Introduction to Time Series Analysis and R*, provides a brief introduction to the time series analysis process and defines the attributes and characteristics of time series data. In addition, the chapter provides a brief introduction to R for readers with no prior knowledge of R. This includes the mathematical and logical operators, loading data from multiple sources (such as flat files and APIs), installing packages, and so on.

Chapter 2, *Working with Date and Time Objects*, focuses on the main date and time classes in R—the Date and POSIXct/lt classes—and their attributes. This includes ways to reformat date and time objects with the **base** and **lubridate** packages.

Chapter 3, *The Time Series Object*, focuses on the ts class, an R core class for time series data. This chapter dives deep into the attributes of the ts class, methods for creating and manipulating ts objects using tools from the **stats** package, and data visualization applications with the **TSstudio** and **dygraphs** packages.

Chapter 4, *Working with zoo and xts Objects*, covers the applications of the zoo and xts classes, an advanced format for time series data. This chapter focuses on the attributes of the zoo and xts classes and the preprocessing and data visualization tools from the **zoo** and **xts** packages

Chapter 5, *Decomposition of Time Series Data*, focuses on decomposing time series data down to its structural patterns—the trend, seasonal, cycle, and random components. Starting with the moving average function, the chapter explains how to use the function for smoothing, and then focuses on decomposing a time series to down its components with the moving average.

Chapter 6, *Seasonality Analysis*, explains approaches and methods for exploring and revealing seasonal patterns in time series data. This includes the use of summary statistics, along with data visualization tools from the **forecast**, **TSstudio**, and **ggplot2** packages.

Chapter 7, *Correlation Analysis*, focuses on methods and techniques for analyzing the relationship between time series data and its lags or other series. This chapter provides a general background for correlation analysis, and introduces statistical methods and data visualization tools for measuring the correlation between time series and its lags or between multiple time series.

Chapter 8, *Forecasting Strategies*, introduces approaches, strategies, and tools for building time series forecasting models. This chapter covers different training strategies, different error metrics, benchmarking, and evaluation methods for forecasting models.

Chapter 9, *Forecasting with Linear Regression*, dives into the forecasting applications of the linear regression model. This chapter explains how to model the different components of a series with linear regression by creating new features from the series. In addition, this chapter covers the advanced modeling of structural breaks, outliers, holidays, and time series with multiple seasonality.

Chapter 10, *Forecasting with Exponential Smoothing Models*, focuses on forecasting time series data with exponential smoothing functions. This chapter explains the usage of smoothing parameters to forecast time series data. This includes simplistic models such as simple exponential smoothing, which is for time series with neither trend nor seasonal components, to advanced smoothing models such as Holt-Winters forecasting, which is for forecasting time series with both trend and seasonal components.

Chapter 11, *Forecasting with ARIMA Models*, covers the ARIMA family of forecasting models. This chapter introduces the different types of ARIMA models—the **autoregressive** (**AR**), **moving average** (**MA**), ARMA, ARIMA, and seasonal ARIMA (SARIMA) models. In addition, the chapter focuses on methods and approaches to identify, tune, and optimize ARIMA models with both autocorrelation and partial correlation functions using applications from the **stats** and **forecast** packages.

Chapter 12, *Forecasting with Machine Learning Models*, focuses on methods and approaches for forecasting time series data with machine learning models with the **h2o** package. This chapter explains the different steps of modeling time series data with machine learning models. This includes feature engineering, training and tuning approaches, evaluation, and benchmarking a forecasting model's performance.

To get the most out of this book

This book was written under the assumption that its readers have the following knowledge and skills:

- Basic knowledge of statistics or econometrics, which includes topics such as regression modeling, hypothesis testing, normal distribution, and so on
- Experience with R, or another programming language

You will need to have R installed (https://cran.r-project.org/) and it is recommended to install the RStudio IDE (https://www.rstudio.com/products/rstudio/).

Download the example code files

You can download the example code files for this book from your account at `www.packt.com`. If you purchased this book elsewhere, you can visit `www.packt.com/support` and register to have the files emailed directly to you.

You can download the code files by following these steps:

1. Log in or register at `www.packt.com`.
2. Select the **SUPPORT** tab.
3. Click on **Code Downloads & Errata**.
4. Enter the name of the book in the **Search** box and follow the onscreen instructions.

Once the file is downloaded, please make sure that you unzip or extract the folder using the latest version of:

- WinRAR/7-Zip for Windows
- Zipeg/iZip/UnRarX for Mac
- 7-Zip/PeaZip for Linux

The code bundle for the book is also hosted on GitHub at `https://github.com/PacktPublishing/Hands-On-Time-Series-Analysis-with-R`. In case there's an update to the code, it will be updated on the existing GitHub repository.

We also have other code bundles from our rich catalog of books and videos available at `https://github.com/PacktPublishing/`. Check them out!

Download the color images

We also provide a PDF file that has color images of the screenshots/diagrams used in this book. You can download it here: `https://www.packtpub.com/sites/default/files/downloads/9781788629157_ColorImages.pdf`.

Conventions used

There are a number of text conventions used throughout this book.

`CodeInText`: Indicates code words in text, database table names, folder names, filenames, file extensions, pathnames, dummy URLs, user input, and Twitter handles. Here is an example: "We will use the `Sys.Date` and `Sys.time` functions to pull date and time objects respectively."

A block of code is set as follows:

```
library(TSstudio)

data(USgas)
```

The output of the R code is prefixed by the ## sign:

```
ts_info(USgas)

##  The USgas series is a ts object with 1 variable and 227 observations
##  Frequency: 12
##  Start time: 2000 1
##  End time: 2018 11
```

Bold: Indicates a new term, an important word, or words that you see onscreen. For example, words in menus or dialog boxes appear in the text like this. Here is an example: "Select **System info** from the **Administration** panel."

Warnings or important notes appear like this.

Tips and tricks appear like this.

Get in touch

Feedback from our readers is always welcome.

General feedback: If you have questions about any aspect of this book, mention the book title in the subject of your message and email us at customercare@packtpub.com.

Errata: Although we have taken every care to ensure the accuracy of our content, mistakes do happen. If you have found a mistake in this book, we would be grateful if you would report this to us. Please visit www.packt.com/submit-errata, selecting your book, clicking on the Errata Submission Form link, and entering the details.

Piracy: If you come across any illegal copies of our works in any form on the Internet, we would be grateful if you would provide us with the location address or website name. Please contact us at copyright@packt.com with a link to the material.

If you are interested in becoming an author: If there is a topic that you have expertise in and you are interested in either writing or contributing to a book, please visit authors.packtpub.com.

Reviews

Please leave a review. Once you have read and used this book, why not leave a review on the site that you purchased it from? Potential readers can then see and use your unbiased opinion to make purchase decisions, we at Packt can understand what you think about our products, and our authors can see your feedback on their book. Thank you!

For more information about Packt, please visit packt.com.

Introduction to Time Series Analysis and R

Time series analysis is the art of extracting meaningful insights from time series data by exploring the series' structure and characteristics and identifying patterns that can then be utilized to forecast future events of the series. In this chapter, we will discuss the foundations, definitions, and historical background of time series analysis, as well as the motivation of using it. Moreover, we will present the advantages and motivation of using R for time series analysis and provide a brief introduction to the R programming language.

In this chapter, we will cover the following topics:

- Time series data
- Time series analysis
- Key R packages in this book
- R and time series analysis

Technical requirements

In order to be able to execute the R code in this book, you need the following requirements:

- You need R programming language version 3.2 and above; however, it is recommended to install one of the most recent versions (3.5 or 3.6). More information about the hardware requirements per operating system (for example, macOS, Windows, and Linux) is available on the CRAN website: `https://cran.r-project.org/`.

- The following packages will be used in this book:
  - **forecast**: Version 8.5 and above
  - **h2o**: Version 3.22.1.1 and above and Java version 7 and above
  - **TSstudio**: Version 0.1.4 and above
  - **plotly**: Version 4.8 and above
  - **ggplot2**: Version 3.1.1 and above
  - **dplyr**: Version 0.8.1 and above
  - **lubridate**: Version 1.7.4 and above
  - **xts**: Version 0.11-2 and above
  - **zoo**: Version 1.8-5 and above
  - **UKgrid**: Version 0.1.1 and above

You can access the codes for this book from the following link:

`https://github.com/PacktPublishing/Hands-On-Time-Series-Analysis-with-R`

Time series data

Time series data is one of the most common formats of data, and it is used to describe an event or phenomena that occurs over time. Time series data has a simple requirement—its values need to be captured at equally spaced time intervals, such as seconds, minutes, hours, days, months, and so on. This important characteristic is one of the main attributes of the series and is known as the frequency of the series. We usually add the frequency along with the name of the series. For example, the following diagram describes the four time series from different domains (power and utilities, finance, economics, and science):

- The UK **hourly** demand for electricity
- The S&P 500 **daily** closing values
- The US **monthly** unemployment rate
- The **annual** number of sunspots

The following diagram shows the (1) UK hourly demand for electricity, (2) S&P 500 daily closing values, (3) US monthly unemployment rate, and (4) annual number of sunspots:

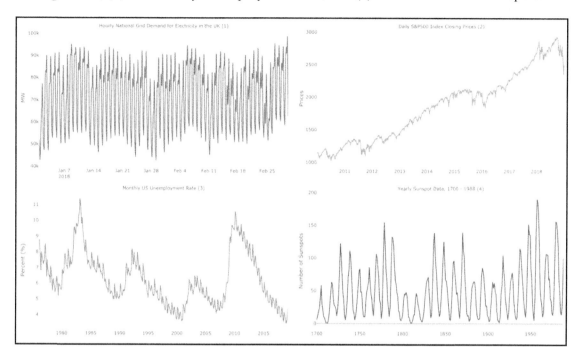

Taking a quick look at the four series, we can identify common characteristics of time series data:

- **Seasonality**: If we look at graph 1, there is high demand during the day and low demand during the night time.
- **Trend**: A clear upper trend can be seen in graph 2 that's between **2013** and **2017**.
- **Cycles**: We can see cyclic patterns in both graph 3 and graph 4.
- **Correlation**: Although S&P 500 and the US unemployment rate are presented with different frequencies, you can see that the unemployment rate has decreased since **2013** (negative trend). On the other hand, S&P 500 increased during the same period (positive trend). We can make a hypothesis that there is a negative correlation between the two series and then test it.

Don't worry if you are not familiar with these terms at the moment. In `Chapter 5`, *Decomposing Time Series Data*, we will dive into the details of the series' structural components—seasonality, trend, and cycle. `Chapter 6`, *Seasonality Analysis*, is dedicated to the analysis of seasonal patterns of time series data, and `Chapter 7`, *Correlation Analysis*, is dedicated to methods and techniques for analyzing and identifying correlation in time series data.

Historical background of time series analysis

Until recently, the use of time series data was mainly related to fields of science, such as economics, finance, physics, engineering, and astronomy. However, in recent years, as the ability to collect data improved with the use of digital devices such as computers, mobiles, sensors, or satellites, time series data is now everywhere. The enormous amount of data that's collected every day probably goes beyond our ability to observe, analyze, and understand it.

The development of time series analysis and forecasting did not start with the introduction of the stochastic process during the previous century. Ancient civilizations such as the Greeks, Romans, or Mayans researched and learned how to utilize cycled events such as weather, agriculture, and astronomy over time to forecast future events. For example, during the classic period of the Mayan civilization (between 250 AD and 900 AD), the Maya priesthood assumed that there are cycles in astronomy events and therefore they patiently observed, recorded, and learned those events. This allowed them to create a detailed time series table of past events, which eventually allowed them to forecast future events, such as the phases of the moon, eclipses of the moon and the sun, and the movement of stars such as Venus, Jupiter, Saturn, and Mars. The Mayan's priesthood used to collect data and analyze the data to identify patterns and cycles. This analysis was then utilized to predict future events. We can find a similarity between the Mayan's ancient analytical process and the time series analysis process we use now. However, the modern time series analysis process is based on statistical modeling and heavy calculations that are possible with today's computers and software, such as R.

Now that we defined the main characteristics of time series data, we can move forward and start to discuss the main characteristics of time series analysis.

Time series analysis

Time series analysis is the process of extracting meaningful insights from time series data with the use of data visualization tools, statistical applications, and mathematical models. Those insights can be used to learn and explore past events and to forecast future events. The analysis process can be divided into the following steps:

1. **Data collection**: This step includes extracting data from different data sources, such as flat files (such as CSV, TXT, and XLMS), databases (for example, SQL Server, and Teradata), or other internet sources (such as academic resources and the Bureau of Statistics datasets). Later on in this chapter, we will learn how to load data to R from different sources.

2. **Data preparation**: In most cases, raw data is unstructured and may require cleaning, transformation, aggregation, and reformatting. In Chapter 2, *Working with Date and Time Objects*; Chapter 3, *The Time Series Object*; and Chapter 4, *Working with zoo and xts Objects*, we will focus on the core data preparation methods of time series data with R.

3. **Descriptive analysis**: This is used in summary statistics and data visualization tools to extract insights from the data, such as patterns, distributions, cycles, and relationships with other drivers to learn more about past events. In Chapter 5, *Decomposition of Time Series Data*; Chapter 6, *Seasonality Analysis*; and Chapter 7, *Correlation Analysis*, we will focus on descriptive analysis methods of time series data.

4. **Predictive analysis**: We use this to apply statistical methods in order to forecast future events. Chapter 8, *Forecasting Strategies*; Chapter 9, *Forecasting with Linear Regression*; Chapter 10, *Forecasting with Exponential Smoothing Models*; Chapter 11, *Forecasting with ARIMA Models*; and Chapter 12, *Forecasting with Machine Learning Models*, we will focus on traditional forecasting approaches (such as linear regression, exponential smoothing, and ARIMA models), as well as advanced forecasting approaches with machine learning models.

It may be surprising but, in reality, the first two steps may take most of the process time and effort, which is mainly due to data challenges and complexity. For instance, companies tend to restructure their **business units** (**BU**) and IT systems every couple of years, and therefore it is hard to identify and track the historical contribution (production, revenues, unit sales, and so on) of a specific BU before the changes.

In other cases, additional effort is required to clean the raw data and handle missing values and outliers. This sadly leaves less time for the analysis itself. Fortunately, R has a variety of wonderful applications for data preparations, visualizations, and time series modeling. This helps to reduce the time that's spent on the preparation steps and lets you allocate more time to the analysis itself. Throughout the rest of this chapter, we will provide background information on R and its applications for time series analysis.

Learning with real-life examples

Throughout the learning journey in this book, we will use real-life examples of time series data in order to apply the methods and techniques of the analysis. All of the datasets that we will use are available in the **TSstudio** and **UKgrid** packages (unless stated otherwise).

The first time series data we will look at is the monthly natural gas consumption in the US. This data is collected by the US **Energy Information Administration (EIA)** and measures the monthly natural gas consumption from January 2000 until November 2018. The unit of measurement is billions of cubic feet (not seasonally adjusted). The following graph shows the monthly natural gas consumption in the US:

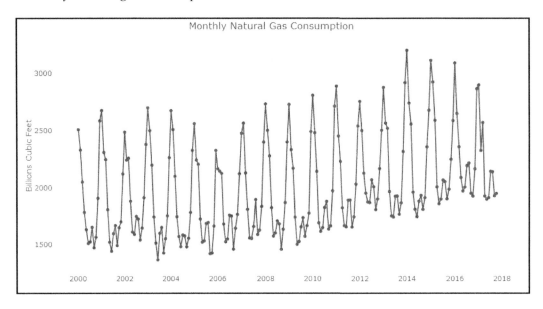

The following series describe the total vehicle sales in the US from January 1976 until January 2019. The units of this series are in thousands of units (not seasonally adjusted). The data is sourced from the **US Bureau of Economic Analysis**. The following graph shows the total monthly vehicle sales in the US:

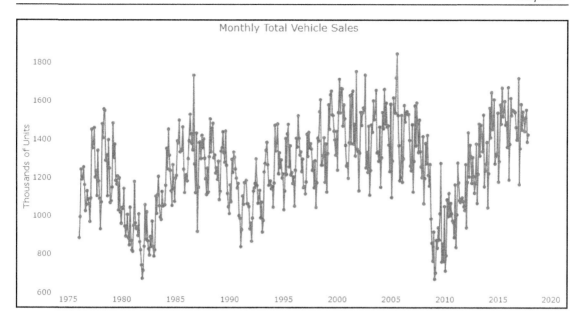

Another monthly series that we will use is the monthly US unemployment rate, which represents the number of unemployed as a percentage of the labor force. The series started in January 1948 and ended in January 2019. The data is sourced from the **US Bureau of Labor Statistics**. The following graph shows the monthly unemployment rate in the US:

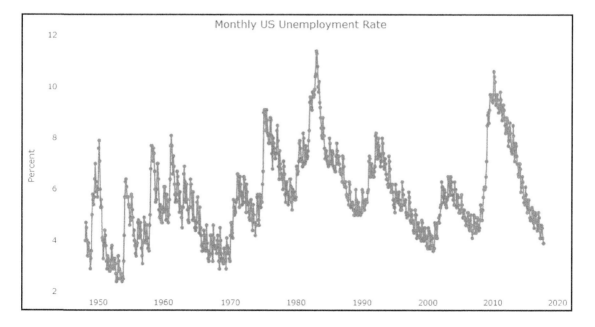

Last but not the least, we will use the national demand for electricity in the UK (as measured on the grid systems) between 2011 and 2018, since it provides an example of high-frequency time series data with half-hourly intervals. The data source is the UK National Grid website, and the information is shown in the following graph:

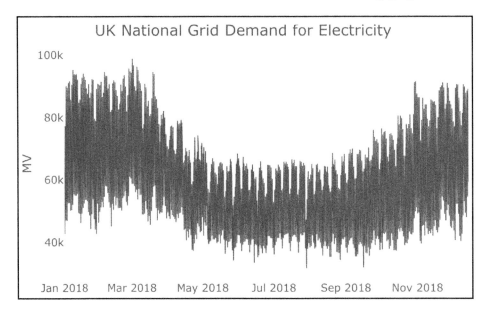

Let's start by installing R.

Getting started with R

R is an open source and free programming language for statistical computing and graphics. With more than 13,500 indexed packages (as of May 2019, as you can see in the following graph) and a large number of applications for statistics, machine learning, data mining, and data visualizations, R is one of the most popular statistical programming languages. One of the main reasons for the fast growth of R in recent years is the open source structure of R, where users are also the main package developers. Among the package developers, you can find individuals like us, as well as giant companies such as Microsoft, Google, and Facebook. This reduces the dependency of the users significantly with any specific company (as opposed to traditional statistical software), allowing for fast knowledge sharing and a diverse portfolio of solutions.

The following graph shows the amount packages that have been shared on CRAN over time:

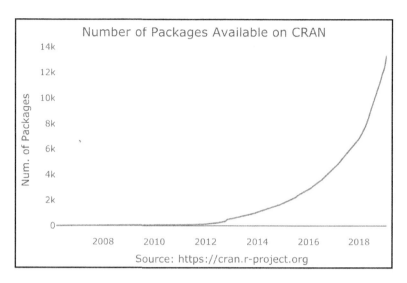

You can see that, whenever we come across any statistical problem, it is likely that someone has already faced the same problem and developed a package with a solution (and if not, you should create one!). Furthermore, there are a vast amount of packages for time series analysis, from tools for data preparations and visualization to advance statistical modeling applications. Packages such as **forecast**, **stats**, **zoo**, **xts**, and **lubridate** made R the leading software for time series analysis. In the *A brief introduction to R* section in this chapter, we will discuss the key packages we will use throughout this book in more detail.

Now, we will learn how to install R.

Installing R

To install R on Windows, Mac, or Linux, go to the **Comprehensive R Archive Network** (**CRAN**) main page at `https://cran.r-project.org/`, where you can select the relevant operating system.

For Windows users, the installation file includes both the 32-bit and the 64-bit versions. You can either install one of the versions or the hybrid version, which includes both the 32-bit and 64-bit versions. Technically, after the installation, you can start working with R using the built-in **Integrated Development Environment** (**IDE**).

However, it is highly recommended to install the **RStudio** IDE and set it as your working environment for R. **RStudio** will make your code writing and debugging and the use of visualization tools or other applications easier and simple.

RStudio offers a free version of its IDE, which is available at
`https://www.rstudio.com/products/rstudio/download/`.

A brief introduction to R

Throughout the learning process in this book, we will use R intensively to introduce methods, techniques, and approaches for time series analysis. If you have never used R before, this section provides a brief introduction, which includes the basic foundations of R, the operators, the packages, different data structures, and loading data. This won't make you an R expert, but it will provide you with the basic R skills you will require to start the learning journey of this book.

R operators

Like any other programming language, the operators are one of the main elements of programming in R. The operators are a collection of functions that are represented by one or more symbols and can be categorized into four groups, as follows:

- Assignment operators
- Arithmetic operators
- Logical operators
- Relational operators

Assignment operators

Assignment operators are probably the family of operators that you will use the most while working with R. As the name of this group implies, they are used to assign objects such as numeric values, strings, vectors, models, and plots to a name (variable). This includes operators such as the back arrow (<-) or the equals sign (=):

```
# Assigning values to new variable
str <- "Hello World!" # String
int <- 10 # Integer
vec <- c(1,2,3,4) # Vector
```

We can use the `print` function to view the values of the objects:

```
print(c(str, int))
## [1] "Hello World!" "10"
```

This is one more example of the `print` function:

```
print(vec)
## [1] 1 2 3 4
```

While both of the operators can be used to assign values to a variable, it is not common to use the = symbol to assign values other than within functions (for reasons that are out of the scope of this book; more information about operator assignment is available on the `assignOps` function documentation or `?assignOps` function).

Arithmetic operators

This family of operators includes basic arithmetic operations, such as addition, division, exponentiation, and remainder. As you can see, it is straightforward to apply these operators. We will start by assigning the values 10 and 2 to the x and y variables, respectively:

```
x <- 10
y <- 2
```

The following code shows the usage of the addition operator:

```
# Addition
x + y
## [1] 12
```

The following code shows the usage of the division operator:

```
x/ 2.5
## [1] 4
```

The following code shows the usage of the exponentiation operator:

```
y ^ 3
## [1] 8
```

Now, let's look at the logical operators.

Logical operators

Logical operators in R can be applied to numeric or complex vectors or Boolean objects, that is, TRUE or FALSE, where numbers greater than one are equivalent to TRUE. It is common to use those operators to test single or multiple conditions under the if...else statement:

```
# The following are reserved names in R for Boolean objects:
# TRUE, FALSE or their shortcut T and F
a <- TRUE
b <- FALSE

# We can also test if a Boolean object is TRUE or FALSE
isTRUE(a)
## [1] TRUE
isTRUE(b)
## [1] FALSE
```

The following code shows the usage of the AND operator:

```
# The AND operator
a & b
## [1] FALSE
```

The following code shows the usage of the OR operator:

```
# The OR operator
a | b
## [1] TRUE
```

The following code shows the usage of the NOT operator:

```
# The NOT operator
!a
## [1] FALSE
```

We can see the applications of those operators by using an if...else statement:

```
# The AND operator will return TRUE only if both a and b are TRUE
if (a & b) {
        print("a AND b is true")
} else {
    print("a And b is false")
```

The following code shows an example of the OR operator, along with the `if...else` statement:

```
# The OR operator will return FALSE only if both a and b are FALSE
if(a | b){
        print("a OR b is true")
} else {
         print("a OR b is false")
## [1] "a OR b is true"
```

Likewise, we can check whether the Boolean object is TRUE or FALSE with the isTRUE function:

```
isTRUE(a)
## [1] TRUE
```

Here, the condition is FALSE:

```
isTRUE(b)
## [1] FALSE
```

Now, let's look at relational operators.

Relational operators

These operators allow for the comparison of objects, such as numeric objects and symbols. Similar to logical operators, relational operators are mainly utilized for conditional statements such as if...else, while:

```
# Assign for variables a and b the value 5, and 7 to c
a <- b <- 5
c <- 7
```

The following code shows the use of the if...else statement, along with the output:

```
if(a == b){
    print("a is equal to b")
    } else{
        print("a is not equal to b")
    }
## [1] "a is equal to b"
```

Alternatively, you can use the `ifelse` function when you want to assign a value in an `if...else` structure:

```
d <- ifelse(test = a >= c,
            yes = "a is greater or equal to c",
            no = "a is smaller than c" )
```

Here, the `ifelse` function has three arguments:

- `test`: Evaluates a logical test
- `yes`: Defines what should be the output if the test result is `TRUE`
- `no`: Defines what should be the output if the test result is `FALSE`

Let's print the value of the `d` variable to check the output:

```
print(d)
## [1] "a is smaller than c"
```

As a core function of R, the operators are defined on the base package (one of R's inherent packages), where each group of operators is defined by a designated function. More information about the operators is available in the function documentation, which you can access with the `help` function (`?` or `help()`):

```
# Each package must have documentation for each function
# To access the function documentation use the ? or the help(function)
?assignOps
?Arithmetic
?Logic
?Comparison
```

Now, let's look at the R package.

The R package

The naked version of R (without any installed packages) comes with seven core packages that contain the built-in applications and functions of the software. This includes applications for statistics, visualization, data processing, and a variety of datasets. Unlike any other package, the core packages are inherent in R, and therefore they load automatically. Although the core packages provide many applications, the vast amount of the R applications are based on the uninherent packages that are stored on CRAN or in GitHub repository.

As of May 2019, there are more than 13,500 packages with applications for statistical modeling, data wrangling, and data visualization for a variety of domains (statistics, economics, finance, astronomy, and so on). A typical package may contain a collection of R functions, as well as compiled code (utilizing other languages, such as C, Java, and FORTRAN). Moreover, some packages include datasets that, in most cases, are related to the package's main application. For example, the **forecast** package comes with a time series dataset, which is used to demonstrate the forecasting models that are available in the package.

Installation and maintenance of a package

There are a few methods that you can use to install package, the most common of which is by using the `install.packages` function:

```
# Installing the forecast package:
install.packages("forecast")
```

You can use this function to install more than one package at once by using a vector type of input:

```
install.packages(c("TSstudio", "xts", "zoo"))
```

Most of the packages frequently get updates. This includes new features, improvements, and error fixing. R provides a function for updating your installed packages. The `packageVersion` function returns the version details of the input package:

```
packageVersion("forecast")
[1] '8.5'
```

The `old.packages` function identifies whether updates are available for any of the installed packages, and the `update.packages` function is used to update all of the installed packages automatically. You can update a specific package using the `install.packages` function, with the package name as input. For instance, if we wish to update the **lubridate** package, we can use the following code:

```
install.packages("lubridate")
```

Last but not least, removing a package can be done with the `remove.packages` function:

```
remove.packages("forecast")
```

When updating or removing an installed package with the `install.packages` or `remove.packages` functions, make sure that the package is not loaded to the working environment. The following section explains how to check whether a package has been loaded.

Loading a package in the R working environment

The R working environment defines the working space where the functions, objects, and data that are loaded are kept and are available to use. By default, when opening R, the global environment is loaded, and the built-in packages of R are loaded.

An installed package becomes available for use on the R global environment once it is loaded. The `search` function provides an overview of the loaded packages within your environment. For example, if we execute the `search` function when opening R, this is the output you expect to see:

```
search()
## [1] ".GlobalEnv"         "package:stats"     "package:graphics"
## [4] "package:grDevices"  "package:utils"     "package:datasets"
## [7] "package:methods"    "Autoloads"         "package:base"
```

As you can see from the preceding output, currently, only the seven core packages of R are loaded. Loading a package into the environment can be done with either the `library` or the `require` function. While both of these functions will load an installed package and its attached functions, the `require` function is usually used within a function as it returns `FALSE` upon failure (compared to an error that the `library` function returns upon failure). Let's load the **TSstudio** package and see the change in environment:

```
library(TSstudio)
```

Now, we will check the global environment again and review the changes:

```
search()
```

We get the following output:

```
##  [1] ".GlobalEnv"         "package:TSstudio"  "package:stats"
##  [4] "package:graphics"   "package:grDevices" "package:utils"
##  [7] "package:datasets"   "package:methods"   "Autoloads"
## [10] "package:base"
```

Similarly, you can unload a package from the environment by using the `detach` function:

```
detach("package:TSstudio", unload=TRUE)
```

Let's check the working environment after detaching the package:

```
search()
## [1] ".GlobalEnv"         "package:stats"     "package:graphics"
## [4] "package:grDevices"  "package:utils"     "package:datasets"
## [7] "package:methods"    "Autoloads"         "package:base"
```

The key packages

Here is a short list of the key packages that we will use throughout this book by topic:

- Data preparation and utility functions. These include the following::
    - **stats**: One of the base packages of R, this provides a set of statistical tools, including applications for time series, such as time series objects (`ts`) and the window function.
    - **zoo and xts**: With applications for data manipulation, aggregation, and visualization, these packages are some of the main tools that you use to handle time series data in an efficient manner.
    - **lubridate**: This provides a set of tools for handling a variety of dates objects and time formats.
    - **dplyr**: This is one of the main packages in R for data manipulation. This provides a powerful tool for data transformation and aggregation.
- Data visualization and descriptive analysis. These include the following:
    - **TSstudio**: This package focuses on both descriptive and predictive analysis of time series data. It provides a set of interactive data visualizations tools, utility functions, and training methods for forecasting models. In addition, the package contains all the datasets that are used throughout this book.
    - **ggplot2 and plotly**: Packages for data visualization applications.

- Predictive analysis, statistical modeling, and forecasting. These include the following:

  - **forecast**: This is one of the main packages for time series analysis in R and has a variety of applications for analyzing and forecasting time series data. This includes statistical models such as ARIMA, exponential smoothing, and neural network time series models, as well as automation tools.
  - **h2o**: This is one of the main packages in R for machine learning modeling. It provides machine learning algorithms such as Random Forest, gradient boosting machine, deep learning, and so on.

Variables

Variables in R have a broader definition and capabilities than most typical programming languages. Without the need to declare the type or the attribute, any R object can be assigned to a variable. This includes objects such as numbers, strings, vectors, tables, plots, functions, and models. The main features of these variables are as follows:

- **Flexibility**: Any R object can be assigned to a variable, without any pre-step (such as declaring the variable type). Furthermore, when assigning the object to a new variable, all the attributes of the object transform, along with its content to the new variable.
- **Attribute**: Neither the variable nor its attributes are needed to be defined prior to the assignment of the object. The object attribute passes to the variable upon assignment (this simplicity is one of the strengths of R). For example, we will assign the `Hello World!` string to the `a` variable:

```
a <- "Hello World!"
```

Let's look at the attributes of the `a` variable:

```
class(a)
```

We get the following output:

```
## [1] "character"
```

Now, let's assign the `a` variable to the `b` variable and check out the characteristics of the new variable:

```
b <- a
b
```

We get the following output:

```
## [1] "Hello World!"
```

Now, let's check the characteristics of the new variable:

```
class(b)
```

We get the following output:

```
## [1] "character"
```

As you can see, the `b` variable inherited both the value and attribute of the `a` variable.

- **Name**: A valid variable name could consist of letters, numbers, and the dot or underline characters. However, it must start with either a letter or a dot, followed by a letter (that is, `var_1`, `var.1`, `var1`, and `.var1` are examples of valid names, while `1var` and `.1var` are examples of invalid names). In addition, there are sets of reserve names that R uses for its key operations, such as `if`, `TRUE`, and `FALSE`, and therefore cannot be used as variable names. Last but not least, variable names are case-sensitive. For example, `Var_1` and `var_1` will refer to two different variables.

Now that we have discussed operators, packages, and variables, it is time to jump into the water and start working with real data!

Importing and loading data to R

Importing or loading data is one of the key elements of the work flow in any analysis. R provides a variety of methods that you can use to import or load data into the environment, and it supports multiple types of data formats. This includes importing data from flat files (for example, CSV and TXT), web APIs or databases (SQL Server, Teradata, Oracle, and so on), and loading datasets from R packages. Here, we will focus on the main methods that we will use in this book—that is, importing data from flat files or the web API and loading data from the R package.

Flat files

It is rare to find a type of the available common data format that isn't possible to import directly to R from CSV and Excel formats to SPSS, SAS, and STATA files. RStudio has a built-in option that you can use to import datasets either from the environment quadrant or the main menu (**File** | **Import Dataset**). Files can be imported from your hard drive, the web, or other sources. In the following example, we will use the `read.csv` function to import a CSV file with information about the US monthly total vehicle sales from GitHub:

1. First, let's assign the URL address to a variable:

```
file_url <-
"https://raw.githubusercontent.com/PacktPublishing/Hands-On-Time-Se
ries-Analysis-with-R/master/Chapter%201/TOTALNSA.csv"
```

2. Next, we will use the `read.csv` function to read the file and assign it to an object named `df1`:

```
df1 <- read.csv(file = file_url, stringsAsFactors = FALSE)
```

3. We can use `class` and `str` to review the characteristics of the object:

```
class(df1)
## [1] "data.frame"
```

4. The following code block shows the output of the `str` function:

```
str(df1)
## 'data.frame':    504 obs. of  2 variables:
##  $ Date : chr  "1/31/1976" "2/29/1976" "3/31/1976" "4/30/1976"
...
##  $ Value: num  885 995 1244 1191 1203 ...
```

The file path is stored in a variable for convenience. Alternatively, you can use the full path directly within the `read.csv` function. The `stringsAsFactors` option transforms strings into a categorical variable (factor) when `TRUE`; setting it to `FALSE` prevents this. The CSV file is stored in an object name, that is, `df1` (`df` is a common abbreviation for data frame), which is where the `read.csv` file stores the table content in a data frame format. The `str()` function provides an overview of the key characteristics of the data frame. This includes the number of observations and variables, the class, and the first observation of each variable.

Be aware that some of your data attributes may get lost or change during the import process, mainly when working with non-numeric objects such as dates and mixed objects (numeric and characters). It is highly recommended to check data attributes once they are imported into the environment and reformat the data if needed. For example, a common change in the data attribute occurs when importing date or time objects from a TXT or CSV file. Since those objects are the key elements of the time series data, the following chapter focuses on handling and reformatting date and time objects. In `Chapter 2`, *Working with Date and Time Objects*, we will discuss how to handle the loss of the attributes of date and time objects when importing from external sources.

Web API

Since the ability to collect and store data has improved significantly in recent years, the use of the web API became more popular. It opens access for an enormous amount of data that is stored in a variety of databases, such as the **Federal Reserve Economic Data (FRED)**, the Bureau of Labor Statistics, the World Bank, and Google Trends. In the following example, we will import the US total monthly vehicle sales dataset (`https://fred.stlouisfed.org/series/TOTALNSA`) again, this time using the `Quandl` API to source the data from FRED:

```
library(Quandl)

df2 <- Quandl(code = "FRED/TOTALNSA",
              type = "raw",
              collapse = "monthly",
              order = "asc",
              end_date="2017-12-31")
```

Source

U.S. Bureau of Economic Analysis, Total Vehicle Sales [TOTALNSA], retrieved from FRED, Federal Reserve Bank of St. Louis; https://fred.stlouisfed.org/series/TOTALNSA, May 19, 2019.

The main arguments of the `Quandl` function are as follows:

- `code`: This defines the source and name of the series. In this case, the source is FRED and the name of the series is TOTALNSA.
- `type`: This is the data structure of the input series. This could be either `raw`, `ts`, `zoo`, `xts`, or `timeSeries` objects.

- `collapse`: This sets the aggregation level of the series frequency. For example, if the raw series has a monthly frequency, you can aggregate the series to a quarterly or annually frequency.
- `order`: This defines whether the series should be arranged in ascending or descending order.
- `end_date`: This sets the ending date of the series.

Now, let's review the key characteristics of the new data frame:

```
class(df2)
## [1] "data.frame"
```

This is the output when we use `str(df2)`:

```
str(df2)
## 'data.frame':    504 obs. of  2 variables:
##  $ Date : Date, format: "1976-01-31" "1976-02-29" ...
##  $ Value: num  885 995 1244 1191 1203 ...
##  - attr(*, "freq")= chr "monthly"
```

The `Quandl` function is more flexible than the `read.csv` function we used in the previous example. It allows the user to control the data format and preserve its attributes, customize the level of aggregation, and be a time saver. You can see that the structure of the `df2` data frame is fairly similar to the one of the `df1` data frame—a data frame with two variables and `504` observations. However, we were able to preserve the attribute of the `Date` variable (as opposed to the `df1` data frame, where the `Date` variable transformed into character format).

R datasets

The R package, in addition to code and functions, may contain datasets that support any of the R designated formats (data frame, time series, matrix, and so on). In most cases, the use of the dataset is either related to the package's functionalities or for educational reasons. For example, the **TSstudio** package, which stores most time series datasets, will be used in this book. In the following example, we will load the US total monthly vehicle sales again, this time using the **TSstudio** package:

```
# If the package is not installed on your machine:
 install.packages("TSstudio")
# Loading the series from the package
 data("USVSales", package = "TSstudio")
```

The `class(USVSales)` function gives us the following output:

```
class(USVSales)
## [1] "ts"
```

The `head(USVSales)` function gives us the following output:

```
head(USVSales)
## [1]   885.2   994.7 1243.6 1191.2 1203.2 1254.7
```

 Note that the `data` function is not assigning the object. Rather, it is loading it to the environment from the package. The main advantage of storing a dataset in a package format is that there is no loss of attributes (that is, there is no difference between the original object and the loaded object).

We used the `data` function to load the `USVSales` dataset of the **TSstudio** package. Alternatively, if you wish to assign the dataset to a variable, you can do either of the following:

- Load the data into the working environment and then assign the loaded object to a new variable.
- Assign directly from the package to a variable by using the `::` operator. The `::` operator allows you to call for objects from a package (for example, functions and datasets) without loading it into the working environment. For example, we can load the `USVSales` dataset series directly from the **TSstudio** package with the `::` operator:

  ```
  US_V_Sales <- TSstudio::USVSales
  ```

Note that the `USVSales` dataset series that we loaded from the **TSstudio** package is a **time series (ts)** object, that is, a built-in R time series class. In `Chapter 3`, *The Time Series Object,* we will discuss the `ts` class and its usage in more detail.

Working and manipulating data

R is a vector-oriented programming language since most of the objects are organized in vector or matrix fashion. While most of us associate vectors and matrices with linear algebra or other mathematics fields, R defines those as a flexible data structure that supports both numeric and non-numeric values. This makes working with data easier and simpler, especially when we work with mixed data classes. The matrix structure is a generic format for many tabular data types in R.

Among those, the most common types are as follows (the function's package name is in brackets):

- `matrix (base)`: This is the basic matrix format and is based on the numeric index of rows and columns. This format is strict about the `data` class, and it isn't possible to combine multiple classes in the same table. For example, it is not possible to have both numeric and strings at the same table.
- `data.frame (base)`: This is one of the most popular tabular formats in R. This is a more progressive and liberal version of the `matrix` function. It includes additional attributes, which support the combination of multiple classes in the same table and different indexing methods.
- `tibble (tibble)`: It is part of the tidyverse family of packages (RStudio designed packages for data science applications). This type of data is another tabular format and an improved version of the `data.frame` base package with the improvements that are related to printing and sub-setting applications.
- `ts (stats) and mts (stats)`: This is R's built-in function for time series data, where `ts` is designed to be used with single time series data and **multiple time series (mts)** supports multiple time series data. Chapter 3, *The Time Series Object*, focuses on the time series object and its applications.
- `zoo (zoo) and xts (xts)`: Both are designated data structures for time series data and are based on the matrix format with a timestamp index. Chapter 4, *Decomposition of Time Series Data*, provides an in-depth introduction to the `zoo` and `xts` objects.

If you have never used R before, the first data structure that you will meet will probably be the data frame. Therefore, this section focuses on the basic techniques that you can use for querying and exploring data frames (which, similarly, can be applied to the other data structures). We will use the famous `iris` dataset as an example.

Let's load the `iris` dataset from the **datasets** package:

```
# Loading dataset from datasets package
data("iris", package = "datasets")
```

Like we did previously, let's review the object structure using the `str` function:

```
str(iris)
## 'data.frame':    150 obs. of  5 variables:
##  $ Sepal.Length: num  5.1 4.9 4.7 4.6 5 5.4 4.6 5 4.4 4.9 ...
##  $ Sepal.Width : num  3.5 3 3.2 3.1 3.6 3.9 3.4 3.4 2.9 3.1 ...
##  $ Petal.Length: num  1.4 1.4 1.3 1.5 1.4 1.7 1.4 1.5 1.4 1.5 ...
```

```
##  $ Petal.Width : num  0.2 0.2 0.2 0.2 0.2 0.4 0.3 0.2 0.2 0.1 ...
##  $ Species     : Factor w/ 3 levels "setosa","versicolor",..: 1 1 1 1 1
1 1 1 1 1 ...
```

As you can see from the output of the str function, the iris data frame has 150 observations and 5 variables. The first four variables are numeric, while the fifth variable is a categorical variable (factor). This mixed structure of both numeric and categorical variables is not possible in the normal matrix format. A different view on the table is available with the summary function, which provides summary statistics for the data frame's variables:

```
summary(iris)
##   Sepal.Length    Sepal.Width     Petal.Length    Petal.Width
##   Min.   :4.300   Min.   :2.000   Min.   :1.000   Min.   :0.100
##   1st Qu.:5.100   1st Qu.:2.800   1st Qu.:1.600   1st Qu.:0.300
##   Median :5.800   Median :3.000   Median :4.350   Median :1.300
##   Mean   :5.843   Mean   :3.057   Mean   :3.758   Mean   :1.199
##   3rd Qu.:6.400   3rd Qu.:3.300   3rd Qu.:5.100   3rd Qu.:1.800
##   Max.   :7.900   Max.   :4.400   Max.   :6.900   Max.   :2.500
##        Species
##   setosa    :50
##   versicolor:50
##   virginica :50
##
##
##
```

As you can see from the preceding output, the function calculates the numeric variables' mean, median, minimum, maximum, and first and third quartiles.

Querying the data

There are several ways to query a data frame. This includes the use of built-in functions or the use of the data frame rows and columns index. For example, let's assume that we want to get the first five observations of the second variable (Sepal.Width). We will take a look at four different ways that we can do this:

- We can do so using the row and column index of the data frame with the square brackets, where the left-hand side represents the row index and the right-hand side represents the column index:

```
iris[1:5, 2]
## [1] 3.5 3.0 3.2 3.1 3.6
```

- We can do so specifying a specific variable in the data frame using the `$` operator and the relevant row index. This method is limited to one variable as opposed to the previous method, which supports multiple rows and columns:

```
iris$Sepal.Width[1:5]
## [1] 3.5 3.0 3.2 3.1 3.6
```

- Similar to the first approach, we can use the row index and column names of the data frame with square brackets:

```
iris[1:5, "Sepal.Width"]
## [1] 3.5 3.0 3.2 3.1 3.6
```

- We can do so using a function that retrieves the index parameter of the rows or columns. In the following example, the `which` function returns the index value of the `Sepal.Width` column based on the following argument:

```
iris[1:5, which(colnames(iris) == "Sepal.Width")]
## [1] 3.5 3.0 3.2 3.1 3.6
```

When working with R, you can always be sure that there is more than one way to do a specific task. We used four methods, all of which achieved similar results. The use of square brackets is typical for any index vector or matrix format in R, where the index parameters are related to the number of dimensions. In all of these examples, besides the second one, the object is the data frame, and therefore there are two dimensions (rows and columns index). In the second example, we specify the variable (or the column) we want to use and, therefore, there is only one dimension, that is, the row index. In the third method, we used the variable name instead of the index, and in the fourth method, we used a built-in function that returns the variable index. Using a specific name or function to identify the variable index value is useful in a scenario where the column name is known, but the index value is dynamic (or unknown).

Now, let's assume that we are interested in identifying the key attributes of `setosa`, one of the three species of the Iris flower in the dataset. First, we have to subset the data frame and use only the observations of `setosa`. Here are three simple methods to extract the `setosa` values (of course, there are more methods):

- We can use the `subset` function, where the first argument is the data that we wish to subset and the second argument is the condition we want to apply:

```
Setosa_df1 <- subset(x = iris, iris$Species == "setosa")
```

Let's use the head(Setosa_df1) function:

```
head(Setosa_df1)
##   Sepal.Length Sepal.Width Petal.Length Petal.Width Species
## 1          5.1         3.5          1.4         0.2  setosa
## 2          4.9         3.0          1.4         0.2  setosa
## 3          4.7         3.2          1.3         0.2  setosa
## 4          4.6         3.1          1.5         0.2  setosa
## 5          5.0         3.6          1.4         0.2  setosa
## 6          5.4         3.9          1.7         0.4  setosa
```

- Similarly, you can use the filter function.
- Alternatively, you can use the index method we introduced previously with the which argument in order to assign the number of rows where the species is equal to setosa. Since we want all of the columns, we will leave the columns argument empty:

```
Setosa_df2 <- iris[which(iris$Species == "setosa"), ]
```

Let's use the head(Setosa_df2) function:

```
head(Setosa_df2)
##   Sepal.Length Sepal.Width Petal.Length Petal.Width Species
## 1          5.1         3.5          1.4         0.2  setosa
## 2          4.9         3.0          1.4         0.2  setosa
## 3          4.7         3.2          1.3         0.2  setosa
## 4          4.6         3.1          1.5         0.2  setosa
## 5          5.0         3.6          1.4         0.2  setosa
## 6          5.4         3.9          1.7         0.4  setosa
```

You can see that the results from both methods are identical:

```
identical(Setosa_df1, Setosa_df2)
## [1] TRUE
```

Using the subset data frame, we can get summary statistics for the setosa species using the summary function:

```
summary(Setosa_df1)
##   Sepal.Length    Sepal.Width     Petal.Length    Petal.Width
## Min.   :4.300   Min.   :2.300   Min.   :1.000   Min.   :0.100
## 1st Qu.:4.800   1st Qu.:3.200   1st Qu.:1.400   1st Qu.:0.200
## Median :5.000   Median :3.400   Median :1.500   Median :0.200
## Mean   :5.006   Mean   :3.428   Mean   :1.462   Mean   :0.246
## 3rd Qu.:5.200   3rd Qu.:3.675   3rd Qu.:1.575   3rd Qu.:0.300
## Max.   :5.800   Max.   :4.400   Max.   :1.900   Max.   :0.600
##       Species
```

```
##   setosa     :50
##   versicolor: 0
##   virginica : 0
##
##
##
```

The `summary` function has broader applications beside the summary statistics of the `data.frame` object and can be used to summarize statistical models and other types of objects.

Help and additional resources

It is not a matter of *if* but rather *when* you will get your first error or try to solve a problem. You can be sure that dozens of people faced a similar problem before you did, and you should look for answers on the internet. Here are some good resources to look at for some help or information about R:

- **Stack Overflow**: This is an online community website for developers of any programming language. You can ask your question or look for answers to similar questions by visiting `https://stackoverflow.com/`.
- **GitHub**: This is known as a hosting service for version control with Git, but it is also a great platform for sharing code, reporting errors, or getting answers. Each R package has its own repository that contains information about the package and provides a communication channel between the users and the package maintainer (to report errors).
- **Package documentation and vignettes**: This provides information about the package's functions and examples of their uses.
- **Google it**: If you couldn't find the answer you were looking for in the preceding resources, then Google it, and try to find other resources. You will be surprised by the amount of information that's available for R out there.

Summary

This chapter provided an overview of time series analysis with R. We started with the basic definition of time series data and the analysis process, which we will use throughout this book. In addition, we discussed the uses of R for time series analysis. This included the packages and the datasets we will use in this book. Last but not least, we provided a brief introduction to the R programming languages so that we could align them with the R prerequisites of this book.

In the next chapter, we will focus on the date and time object, one of the core elements of the time series object.

Working with Date and Time Objects

The main attribute of time series data is its timestamp, which could be a date object, time object, or other index format depending on the series frequency. Typically while loading raw data, it is not trivial to have the date or time object formatted and ready to use. Therefore, it is most likely that the raw data may require some reformatting before you are able to transform your data into time series format. The ability to work with time and date objects is an essential part of the data preparation process. In this chapter, we will introduce a set of tools and applications for dealing with those objects, starting with R's built-in tools and classes from the **base** package and moving to the advanced applications of the **lubridate** package.

In this chapter, we will cover the following topics:

- The date and time formats
- Date and time objects in R
- Creating a date or time index
- Manipulation of date and time with **lubridate** package

Technical requirements

The following packages will be used in this chapter:

- **lubridate**: Version 1.7.4 and above
- **base**: Version 3.6.0 and above

You can access the code for this book from the following link:

```
https://github.com/PacktPublishing/Hands-On-Time-Series-Analysis-with-R/tree/
master/Chapter02
```

The date and time formats

One of the main challenges of working with date and time objects is the variety of formats that can be used for representing date and time. For example, most of the common calendar systems use an alphabetical form to represent the three date components:

- Y: Refers to the year, which can display either using the yy (two-digits year, for example, 18) or yyyy (four-digit year, for example, 2018) formats.
- M: Refers to the month. Here there are four methods to display the month:
    - m: One-digit month (the first 9 months represented by a single digit, for example, 1 for January, 2 for February, and so on)
    - mm: Two-digit month (the first 9 months represented by two digits, for example, 01 for January, 02 for February, and so on)
    - mmm: Three-letter abbreviation for a month (for example, Jan for January, Feb for February, and so on)
    - mmmm: Full month name (for example, January, February, and so on)

- D: Refers to the day. In a similar fashion to the month, there are four methods for displaying it:
    - d: One-digit day (the first 9 days of the months represented by a single digit, for example, 1, 2, 3, and so on)
    - dd: Two-digit month (the first 9 days of the months represented by two digits, for example, 01, 02, 03, and so on)
    - ddd: Three-letter abbreviation for the day of the week (for example, Mon for Monday, Tue for Tuesday, and so on)
    - dddd: Full name of the day of the week (for example, Monday, Tuesday, and so on)

In addition, each country or region uses a different order to represent the date components, as seen in the following table:

Order styles	Main regions and countries	Approximate population in millions
DMY, YMD	Afghanistan, Albania, Austria, the Czech Republic, Germany, Kenya, Macau, the Maldives, Montenegro, Namibia, Nepal, Singapore, South Africa, Sri Lanka, and Sweden	225
DMY	Asia (Central, South East, West), Australia, New Zealand, parts of Europe, Latin America, North Africa, India, Indonesia, Bangladesh, and Russia	3,565
YMD	Bhutan, Canada, China, Korea, Taiwan, Hungary, Iran, Japan, Lithuania, and Mongolia	1,745
DMY, MDY	Malaysia, Nigeria, the Philippines, Saudi Arabia, and Somalia	380
MDY	The United States, the Federated States of Micronesia, and the Marshall Islands	325

Table 1: Date format style by region/country

This creates a large number of possible combinations to represent a single date, for example, October 14, 2014 would be displayed as follows:

- 10/14/2015 or Oct 14th, 2015 in the US
- 14/10/2015 or 14th Oct 2015 in Europe
- 2015/10/14 in Canada or China
- Either 14/10/2015 or 2015/10/14 in Sweden or South Africa

With so many types of formats, working with date and time objects can be cumbersome and challenging in any programming language. Luckily, R provides good tools to handle those types of objects in a seamless and effective way. Among the many types of date and time objects, this chapter focuses on R's built-in classes, as they are the core of most of the other classes. In Chapter 4, *Working with zoo and xts Objects*, we will discuss the **zoo** package, which provides more advanced and friendly classes for date and time objects.

Date and time objects in R

The **base** package, one of R's core packages, provides two types of date and time classes:

1. `Date`: This is a simple representation of a calendar date following the ISO 8601 international standard format (or the Gregorian calendar format) using the `YYYY-m-d` date format. Each date object has a numeric value of the number of days since the origin point (the default setting is `1970-01-01`). In the *Handling numeric date objects* section in this chapter, we will discuss the usage of the origin in the reformatting process of date objects in more detail. It will make sense to use this format when the frequency of the data is daily or lower (for example, monthly, quarterly, and so on) and the time of the day doesn't matter.

2. `POSIXct/POSIXlt`: Also known as the `DateTime` classes (that is, they represent both date and time), these are two POSIX date/time classes that represent the calendar date, the time of the day, and the time zone using the ISO 8601 international standard format of `YYYY-m-d H:M:S`. The main difference between the two is the form in which the values are stored internally. The `POSIXct` class, similar to the `Date` class, represents the (signed) number of seconds since the origin point (1970-01-01, UTC time zone) as a numeric vector. On the other hand, the `POSIXlt` class stores each one of the date and time elements as a list.

In `Chapter 3`, *The Time Series Object*, and `Chapter 4`, *Working with zoo and xts Objects*, we will see the applications of the `Date` and `POSIXct/POSIXlt` objects as an index or timestamp of time series objects.

> For naming convenience throughout this chapter, date object refers to the `Date` class and time object refers to the `POSIXct/POSIXlt` class (unless stated otherwise).

It makes sense to use a time object (either `POSIXct` or `POSIXlt` objects) only if the series frequency is higher than daily (such as hourly, half-hourly, by minute, or by second). Otherwise, for simplicity reasons, it is recommended that you use the date object. Let's review the differences between date and time objects. We will use the `Sys.Date` and `Sys.time` functions to pull date and time objects respectively:

```
date <- Sys.Date()
date
## [1] "2019-02-10"

time_ct <- Sys.time()
time_ct
## [1] "2019-02-10 20:57:45 PST"
```

Let's check the `class` of the two objects:

```
class(date)
## [1] "Date"

class(time_ct)
## [1] "POSIXct" "POSIXt"
```

By default, the `Sys.time` function returns an object of the `POSIXct`, `POSIXt`, or `POSIXct` class. We can use the `as.POSIXlt` function to convert the object to a `POSIXlt` object:

```
time_lt <- as.POSIXlt(time_ct)

time_lt
## [1] "2019-02-10 20:57:45 PST"

class(time_lt)
## [1] "POSIXlt" "POSIXt"
```

While both the `POSIXct` and `POSIXlt` objects have the same representation, the key difference between the two is in the method in which each object is stored internally in the time details. We will use the `unclass` command to strip down the object to the format it is stored internally:

```
unclass(time_ct)
## [1] 1549861066
```

The `POSIXct` object stored the numeric distance of the time object from the origin point. On the other hand, `POSIXlt` returned a detailed list with the different time components:

```
unclass(time_lt)

## $sec
## [1] 45.81006
## $min
## [1] 57
## $hour
## [1] 20
## $mday
## [1] 10
## $mon
## [1] 1
## $year
## [1] 119
## $wday
## [1] 0
## $yday
```

```
## [1] 40
## $isdst
## [1] 0
## $zone
## [1] "PST"
## $gmtoff
## [1] -28800
## attr(,"tzone")
## [1] ""     "PST" "PDT"
```

Here, the POSIXct object returned the following components:

- sec: The seconds of the time object.
- min: The minutes of the time object.
- hour: The hours of the time object (24-hour military time).
- mday: The day of the month.
- month: The month of the year.
- year: Defines the number of years since 1900 (for example, 119 for 2019).
- wday: The day of the week represented by an integer between 0 and 6 (where 0 is Sunday).
- isdst: Daylight saving time flag.
- yday: The day of the year, an integer between 0 and 365.
- zone: The time zone. Note that the time zone is defined by the defined time zone of the machine.
- gmtoff: The offset in seconds from GMT.

The following additional feature of the POSIXlt class is very useful when you want to query for a specific element of the time object. For instance, we can pull the second value of the object using the following command:

```
unclass(time_lt)$sec
## [1] 45.81006
```

Or we can pull the day of the year:

```
unclass(time_lt)$yday
## [1] 40
```

Creating date and time objects

R has a structural method to assign values to a specific class or object, which is usually the combination of as.[the class name]. For example, as.character assigns or converts an object to the character class. Similarly, creating a new object or converting the existing object to Date, POSIXlt, or POSIXct can be done with as.Date, as.POSIXlt, or as.POSIXct respectively.

As long as the assigned object follows the relevant format, the creation of the object is fairly simple. For instance, we can convert the "2014-5-12" string into a Date object using the as.Date function:

```
date <- as.Date("2014-5-12")

date
## [1] "2014-05-12"

class(date)
## [1] "Date"
```

The as.POSIXct or as.POSIXlt function works in a similar manner:

```
time_ct <- as.POSIXct("2014-5-12 20:05:35", tz = "EST")

time_ct
## [1] "2014-05-12 20:05:35 EST"

class(time_ct)
## [1] "POSIXct" "POSIXt"
```

The format of both the classes is well defined by the ISO 8601 international standard. This is really helpful, as it leaves no room for interpretation once the object is created and therefore reduces the ambiguity when working with this type of objects. However, the main challenge remains: the import process of data with the date or time objects from external sources such as flat files, databases, or web API. Unlike numeric values that automatically get assigned to the numeric object, date and time objects may require additional reformatting and conversion efforts before they can be assigned into one of the date or time classes. In the next section, we will start to dive into the reformatting process of date and time objects.

Importing date and time objects

Importing date and time objects to any programming language can be a challenging process for several reasons:

- Firstly, unlike other fields of programming language, there is no single format or a clear standard for date or time objects. While R adopted the ISO 8601 format, it is not necessarily true that other software use the same format.
- Moreover, the setting of the origin point (or the reference point) varies between the software. While in R it is set to January 1, 1970, in SAS it is set to January 1, 1960, and in Excel, it is set to January 1, 1900. If the source of your data is coming from other software and converted to a numeric value, then you modify the default origin point accordingly.
    - Last but not least, even if your objects are already reformatted to the ISO 8601 standard, in some cases, the attributes are lost and R will automatically classify it as a string or categorical variable (if the `stringsAsFactors` function is set to `TRUE`).

Once the date or time object is imported to R, the process of reformatting and converting date and time objects to `Date` or `POSIXct`/`POSIXlt` classes, respectively, is fairly similar. For reasons of simplicity, we will start first with the reformatting methods of date objects and then generalize the process to time objects.

Reformatting and converting date objects

Reformatting or converting date objects is the process of transforming a non-date (or `POSIXct/lt`) object such as character or numeric to a `Date` format (or `POSIXct/lt`). The next example demonstrates the complexity of working with different `Date` formats. The `dates_formats.csv` file contains a representation of a date sequence using seven different formats. The file is available on the book's GitHub repository and can be loaded using the following URL:

```
url <-
"https://raw.githubusercontent.com/PacktPublishing/Hands-On-Time-Series-Ana
lysis-with-R/master/Chapter%202/dates_formats.csv"

dates_df <- read.csv(url, stringsAsFactors = FALSE)
```

Before starting with the reformatting process, let's review the structure of the data frame using the `str` function:

```
str(dates_df)
## 'data.frame': 22 obs. of 7 variables:
## $ Japanese_format : chr "2017/1/20" "2017/1/21" "2017/1/22" "2017/1/23"
...
## $ US_format : chr "1/20/2017" "1/21/2017" "1/22/2017" "1/23/2017" ...
## $ US_long_format : chr "Friday, January 20, 2017" "Saturday, January 21,
2017" "Sunday, January 22, 2017" "Monday, January 23, 2017" ...
## $ CA_mix_format : chr "January 20, 2017" "January 21, 2017" "January 22,
2017" "January 23, 2017" ...
## $ SA_mix_format : chr "20 January 2017" "21 January 2017" "22 January
2017" "23 January 2017" ...
## $ NZ_format : chr "20/01/2017" "21/01/2017" "22/01/2017" "23/01/2017"
...
## $ Excel_Numeric_Format: num 42755 42756 42757 42758 42759 ...
```

The data frame contains 7 columns, where each represents a different representative of the same date sequence. The first six columns are character objects and the seventh object is numeric. In the following examples, we will convert each one of the columns to a date object by identifying the date structure and reformat it accordingly.

The first variable in the data frame represents Excel's Japanese format for date. Since this format has a similar structure to the ISO 8601 there is no need to reformat them and the conversion from `character` to `Date` format is straightforward with the `as.Date` function:

```
dates_df$Japanese_format_new <- as.Date(dates_df$Japanese_format)
```

You can notice that the converted object looks exactly like the original input object:

```
head(dates_df[, c("Japanese_format", "Japanese_format_new")])
## Japanese_format Japanese_format_new
## 1 2017/1/20 2017-01-20
## 2 2017/1/21 2017-01-21
## 3 2017/1/22 2017-01-22
## 4 2017/1/23 2017-01-23
## 5 2017/1/24 2017-01-24
## 6 2017/1/25 2017-01-25
```

Although both visually look the same, each has its own unique attribute, and they are not identical:

```
identical(dates_df$Japanese_format, dates_df$Japanese_format_new)
## [1] FALSE

class(dates_df$Japanese_format)
```

```
## [1] "character"

class(dates_df$Japanese_format_new)
## [1] "Date"
```

If the format of the input object is different from the ISO 8601 standard, using the `as.Date` function without declaring the object format structure would return incorrect results (and, in some instances, an error). For example, let's try to convert the `31-01-2018` date to `Date` format without reformatting it:

```
as.Date("31-01-2018")
## [1] "0031-01-20"
```

This is totally wrong! One way to solve this issue is by adding the `format` argument in the `as.Date` function in order to map the different components of the input object to the structure of the `Date` object. Going back to the previous example, the mapping should be according to the date components order of the input object:

```
as.Date("31-01-2018", format = "%d-%m-%Y")
## [1] "2018-01-31"
```

That looks much better! The following table provides a summary of the main arguments for date objects. The full list is available in the documentation of the `strptime` function (`?strptime`) at `https://www.rdocumentation.org/packages/base/versions/3.6.0/topics/strptime`:

Symbol	Meaning	Example
%a	Abbreviated weekday name in the current locale on this platform	Sun, Mon, Thu
%A	Full weekday name in the current locale	Sunday, Monday, Thursday
%b	Abbreviated month name in the current locale on this platform	Jan, Feb, Mar
%B	Full month name in the current locale	January, February, March
%d	Day of the month as a decimal number	01, 02, 03
%m	Month as a decimal number	01, 02, 03
%y	A year without a century (two-digit)	18
%Y	A year with a century (four-digit)	2018
%r	For a 12-hour clock defined by the AM/PM indicator	AM

Table 2: The main arguments for reformatting date objects with the format argument

Using these arguments is fairly easy, and we need to follow a simple logic:

- The order of the arguments needs to match the order of the input object
- The argument type needs to be aligned with the date component type (for example, %Y for 2018, %y for 18, and so on)
- The separators between the arguments must match the ones in the input object

Going back to the `dates_df` data frame, we will use the `format` argument to reformat and convert the other date objects in the table. The second column represents the US date format, which is MDY:

```
dates_df$US_format[1]
## [1] "1/20/2017"
```

Since this format is different from the ISO 8601 format, we will add the `format` argument to map the date component properly:

```
dates_df$US_format_new <- as.Date(dates_df$US_format, format = "%m/%d/%Y")
```

Similarly, we will apply this logic to the next columns:

```
dates_df$US_long_format[1]
## [1] "Friday, January 20, 2017"

dates_df$US_long_format_new <- as.Date(dates_df$US_long_format, format =
"%A, %B %d, %Y")

dates_df$CA_mix_format[1]
## [1] "January 20, 2017"

dates_df$CA_mix_format_new <- as.Date(dates_df$CA_mix_format, format = "%B
%d, %Y")

dates_df$SA_mix_format[1]
## [1] "20 January 2017"

dates_df$SA_mix_format_new <- as.Date(dates_df$SA_mix_format, format = "%d
%B %Y")

dates_df$NZ_format[1]
## [1] "20/01/2017"

dates_df$NZ_format_new <- as.Date(dates_df$NZ_format, format = "%d/%m/%Y")
```

Handling numeric date objects

As discussed previously, date objects are stored internally in R as numeric values that represent the number of days from the origin point. You can easily retrieve the numeric value of the object by using the `as.numeric` function. To demonstrate how this system works, we will store two variables with the following date:

- January 1, 1970, which also represents the origin point in R
- The current date, by capturing it from the system using the `Sys.Date` function:

```
date1 <- as.Date("1970-01-01")
date2 <- Sys.Date()

print(c(date1, date2))
## [1] "1970-01-01" "2019-02-10"
```

Now let's get the numeric representation of the two objects using the `as.numeric` function:

```
as.numeric(date1)
## [1] 0

as.numeric(date2)
## [1] 17937
```

Not surprisingly, the numeric value of `date1` (which is also the origin date) is equal to `0`, and the numeric value of `date2` is equal to `17937`, which is the number of seconds between `date2` and the origin (which is represented by `date1`).

This attribute could be very useful when importing data from other software that uses a similar approach (that is, setting the origin point) such as Python, SAS, Stata, and Excel. The conversion of a numeric-date input to a date object in R is fairly simple and could save you some time and effort if utilized correctly. For example, the last variable in the `dates_df` table is an example of the numeric formation of date in Excel:

```
head(dates_df$Excel_Numeric_Format)
## [1] 42755 42756 42757 42758 42759 42760
```

In Excel, the numeric value of the origin point (that is January 1st, 1900) set to `1`, as opposed to other programming languages such as R which define the origin point as `0`. Therefore, when importing a date or time objects from Excel, in order to align to R origin point definition, the origin point should be set as December 31st, 1899 (which equivalent to `0` numeric value).

Since Excel is using a different origin point than R (December 30, 1899 versus January 1, 1970), we will have to add the `origin` argument and specify the original date that is used to generate the data:

```
dates_df$Excel_Numeric_Format_new <- as.Date(dates_df$Excel_Numeric_Format,
origin = as.Date("1899-12-30"))

head(dates_df$Excel_Numeric_Format_new)
## [1] "2017-01-20" "2017-01-21" "2017-01-22" "2017-01-23" "2017-01-24"
## [6] "2017-01-25"
```

The following table provides some examples for the origin point of commonly used software and the numeric value of the January 1, 2020 date:

Software	Origin date	January 1, 2020 numeric value
Excel	12/30/1899	43,831
Python	1/1/1970	18,262
R	1/1/1970	18,262
SAS	1/1/1960	21,915
Stata	1/1/1960	21,915

Table 3: The origin point setting of common software

After reformatting and converting all the seven variables in `dates_df`, let's check again the structure of the data frame and compare the reformatted variables with their origin versions:

```
str(dates_df)
## 'data.frame': 22 obs. of 14 variables:
## $ Japanese_format : chr "2017/1/20" "2017/1/21" "2017/1/22" "2017/1/23"
...
## $ US_format : chr "1/20/2017" "1/21/2017" "1/22/2017" "1/23/2017" ...
## $ US_long_format : chr "Friday, January 20, 2017" "Saturday, January 21,
2017" "Sunday, January 22, 2017" "Monday, January 23, 2017" ...
## $ CA_mix_format : chr "January 20, 2017" "January 21, 2017" "January 22,
2017" "January 23, 2017" ...
## $ SA_mix_format : chr "20 January 2017" "21 January 2017" "22 January
2017" "23 January 2017" ...
## $ NZ_format : chr "20/01/2017" "21/01/2017" "22/01/2017" "23/01/2017"
...
## $ Excel_Numeric_Format : num 42755 42756 42757 42758 42759 ...
## $ Japanese_format_new : Date, format: "2017-01-20" "2017-01-21" ...
## $ US_format_new : Date, format: "2017-01-20" "2017-01-21" ...
## $ US_long_format_new : Date, format: "2017-01-20" "2017-01-21" ...
## $ CA_mix_format_new : Date, format: "2017-01-20" "2017-01-21" ...
```

```
## $ SA_mix_format_new : Date, format: "2017-01-20" "2017-01-21" ...
## $ NZ_format_new : Date, format: "2017-01-20" "2017-01-21" ...
## $ Excel_Numeric_Format_new: Date, format: "2017-01-20" "2017-01-21" ...
```

Looking at the output of the `str` function, you can see that no matter what the format type of the inputs variables or their classes (character or numeric) was, the converted variables (any variable with `format_new` extension) are all date objects using the same formation. We can now move forward and start to discuss the reformatting process of time objects.

Reformatting and conversion of time objects

After we dived into the small details of the reformatting and conversion process of the date objects, it is time to generalize the process for time objects by using the `as.POSIXct` or `as.POSIXlt` functions. Similar to the `as.Date` function, the `as.POSIXct` or `as.POSIXlt` functions are the **base** package applications for reformatting and conversion of any time input to a `POSIXct` or `POSIXlt` objects, respectively. The `POSIX` classes are an extension of the `Date` class, with the addition of four elements (in addition to the date elements): hours, minutes, seconds, and time zone. This makes the reformatting process a bit more cumbersome as the mapping now includes seven elements instead of four elements, as was previously the case.

We will start with a simple example, where the input is following the ISO 8601 international standard:

```
time_str <- "2018-12-31 23:59:59"

class(time_str)
## [1] "character"
```

The input object is assigned to the `time_str` variable as a `character` object. We can now use the `as.POSIXct` function to convert the input variable to a `POSIXct` object:

```
time_posix_ct1 <- as.POSIXct(time_str)

class(time_posix_ct1)
## [1] "POSIXct" "POSIXt"
```

While the objects look alike, each has a different attribute and they are not identical, as one is a string and the other one is a `POSIXct` object:

```
time_str
## [1] "2018-12-31 23:59:59"

time_posix_ct1
```

```
## [1] "2018-12-31 23:59:59 EST"

identical(time_str, time_posix_ct1)
## [1] FALSE
```

The structure of the `time_str` object is set according to the ISO 8601 standard for time objects, therefore the conversion to a time object is straightforward. Alternatively, you can convert the numeric value of the time object to one of the time classes. The numeric value of the time object represents the number of seconds since the origin point (that is, January 1, 1970). For example, let's convert the number `1546318799` to a time object using the `as.POSIXct` function with the `origin` argument:

```
time_numeric <- 1546318799

class(time_numeric)
## [1] "numeric"

time_posix_ct2 <- as.POSIXct(time_numeric, origin = "1970-01-01")
```

We can now compare the two time objects we converted:

```
print(c(time_posix_ct1, time_posix_ct2))
## [1] "2018-12-31 23:59:59 EST" "2018-12-31 23:59:59 EST"

identical(time_posix_ct1, time_posix_ct2)
## [1] TRUE
```

Those are fairly simple examples, which do not require a reformatting step. However, whenever the format of the input object does not follow a `YYYY-m-d H:M:S` structure, you will have to use the format argument to map the object's elements. Let's use a full date and time pattern (US format) to represent the same input we used previously: that is, `Monday, December 31, 2018 11:59:59 PM`.

Firstly, you probably notice that the time format is a 12-hour clock (as opposed to the 24-hour clock of the `POSIX` classes). Thus, in addition to the data and time mapping, we will have to identify and map the cycle of the day (AM or PM). The next thing that should catch your attention is that the number of elements in the input objects is higher than the expected output (eight in the input versus six in the output). The two extra elements are the day of the week (`Monday`), which is redundant, and the cycle of the day indicator, which is crucial for the mapping. However, all elements, including the two extra elements, must be included in the `format` argument. The following example demonstrates the transformation process of this type of time object to a `POSIX` class. First, let's assign the input object into a variable:

```
time_US_str <- "Monday, December 31, 2018 11:59:59 PM"
```

Next, we will use the `format` argument to declare the structure of the input object:

```
time_posix_ct3 <- as.POSIXct(time_US_str, format = "%A, %B %d, %Y %I:%M:%S
%p")

time_posix_ct3
## [1] "2018-12-31 23:59:59 EST"#
  identical(time_posix_ct1, time_posix_ct2, time_posix_ct3)## [1] TRUE
```

The new output has the same attributes as the previous two objects we created:

```
time_posix_ct3
## [1] "2018-12-31 23:59:59 EST"

identical(time_posix_ct1, time_posix_ct2, time_posix_ct3)
## [1] TRUE
```

The following table is an extension of *Table 2*, which provides the most common arguments for reformatting time objects. The full arguments list can be found in the `strptime` documentation:

Symbol	Meaning	Example
%H	Hours as a decimal number (00-23)	17:00:00
%I	Hours as a decimal number (01-12)	5:00:00 PM
%M	Minutes as a decimal number (00-59)	17:15:00
%S	Seconds as an integer (00-61), allowing for up to two leap-seconds	17:15:45
%p	AM/PM indicator in the locale	AM, PM
%r	Equivalent to %I:%M:%S %p for 12-hour clock time	9:35:00 PM
%T	Equivalent to %H:%M:%S	17:15:00
%Z	Time zone abbreviation as a character string	GMT, EST, PDT

Table 4: The main arguments for reformatting POSIXct/lt objects with the format argument

Time zone setting

The time zone is the seventh element of the `POSIX` classes and can be set by either the `tz` argument of the `as.POSIXct/as.POSIXlt` functions or by the `format` argument. Those functions synchronize and automatically calculate the time differences between two different time zones in a similar manner to an electronic calendar. For example, if you are working in London, UK, and your colleague from New York, US, sends you an invite for a meeting for 10 AM EST, your calendar will automatically transform the time of the meeting to 3 PM GMT (assuming that the time zone on your calendar is set to GMT). What will happen if you receive an invite for a call from a different time zone and the time zone in your calendar is not set properly? You will either be too early or miss the call. You get a sense of where it is going: working with time objects from multiple time zones without adjusting the time differences could yield bad errors. The `Sys.timezone` function returns the time zone according to the setting of your system:

```
Sys.timezone()
## [1] "America/Los_Angeles"
```

Since the time zone in my computer is set to US **Pacific Standard Time** (**PST**), loading a date object from different time zone without specifying it would yield a different output:

```
time_str <- "2018-12-31 23:59:59"

time_default_tz <- as.POSIXct(time_str)

time_assign_tz <- as.POSIXct(time_str, tz = "GMT")

print(c(time_default_tz, time_assign_tz))
## [1] "2018-12-31 23:59:59 EST" "2018-12-31 18:59:59 EST"

identical(time_default_tz, time_assign_tz) ## [1] FALSE
```

A full list of the 592 time zones available in R (both location and abbreviation formats) can be found in the `OlsonNames` function:

```
head(OlsonNames(), 20) ## [1] "Africa/Abidjan" "Africa/Accra"
"Africa/Addis_Ababa"
## [4] "Africa/Algiers" "Africa/Asmara" "Africa/Asmera"
## [7] "Africa/Bamako" "Africa/Bangui" "Africa/Banjul"
## [10] "Africa/Bissau" "Africa/Blantyre" "Africa/Brazzaville"
## [13] "Africa/Bujumbura" "Africa/Cairo" "Africa/Casablanca"
## [16] "Africa/Ceuta" "Africa/Conakry" "Africa/Dakar"
## [19] "Africa/Dar_es_Salaam" "Africa/Djibouti"
```

Creating a date or time index

So far, our focus in this chapter was mainly on the attributes of the date and time classes. Let's now connect the dots and see some useful applications of time series data. As introduced in `Chapter 1`, *Introduction to Time Series Analysis and R*, the main characteristic of time series data is its time index (or timestamp), an equally spaced time interval. The **base** package provides two pairs of functions, `seq.Date` and `seq.POSIXt`, to create a time index vector with `Date` or `POSIX` objects respectively. The main difference between the two functions (besides the class of the output) is the units of the time interval. It will make sense to use the `seq.Date` function to generate a time sequence with daily frequency or lower (for example, weekly, monthly, and so on) and `as.POSIXt` in other instances (for higher frequencies than daily, such as hourly, half-hourly, or by minutes). As you can see in the following example, the use of these functions is straightforward:

```
daily_index <- seq.Date(from = as.Date("2016-01-01") # Starting date
                        to = as.Date("2018-12-31"), # Ending date
                        by = "day") # Defining the time intervals

head(daily_index)
## [1] "2016-01-01" "2016-01-02" "2016-01-03" "2016-01-04" "2016-01-05"
## [6] "2016-01-06"
```

We used the `from` and `to` arguments of the `seq.Date` function to set the range of the sequence, and the `by` argument to set the time intervals of the sequence. Alternatively, you can use the `length.out` (number of observations to create) argument instead of the `to` argument in order to set the range of the sequence. Each function has a set of possible options for the `by` argument (for example, day, week, month, and so on), which can be found in the functions documentation. In addition, it is possible to mix integers with those arguments to create a new time interval combination. For example, if you wish to create a series with 3-day time intervals (as opposed to a 1-day interval), you can simply define the `by` argument to `3 days`:

```
daily_3_index <- seq.Date(from = as.Date("2016-01-01"),
                          to = as.Date("2018-12-31"),
                          by = "3 days")

head(daily_3_index)
## [1] "2016-01-01" "2016-01-04" "2016-01-07" "2016-01-10" "2016-01-13"
## [6] "2016-01-16"
```

The `to` argument is optional: you can instead use the `length.out` argument if you know the length of the series. For example, let's create an hourly sequence with a length of 48 hours, using the `seq.POSIXt` function:

```
hourly_index <- seq.POSIXt(from = as.POSIXct("2018-06-01"), by = "hours",
length.out = 48)

str(hourly_index)
## POSIXct[1:48], format: "2018-06-01 00:00:00" "2018-06-01 01:00:00" ...
```

The following table summarizes the possible time interval arguments of each function:

Function	Interval argument
seq.Date	"day", "week", "month", "quarter", "year"
seq.POSIXt	"sec", "min", "hour", "day", "DSTday", "week", "month", "quarter", "year"

Table 5: Optional time interval for the by argument

In addition to the `seq.Date` and `seq.POSIXt` functions, the **base** package provides additional applications for processing and handling date and time objects. Since those functions have a fairly similar structure to the previous ones, we will not get into the details. However, it is worth going over the documentation of the `Date` and `POSIXt` classes and checking the related functions of each class (in the *See Also* section of the function document).

Manipulation of date and time with the lubridate package

The title of the **lubridate** package documentation in CRAN is **Make Dealing with Dates a Little Easier**. In my mind, this is a very modest title for a package that makes work with date and time objects more effective, simple, and time efficient. This section introduces alternative tools and applications with the **lubridate** package for reformatting, converting, and handling date and time objects.

Reformatting date and time objects – the lubridate way

To understand how simple it is to reformat date and time objects with the **lubridate** package, let's go back to the complex time object (Monday, December 31, 2018 11:59:59 PM) we converted earlier to a POSIXct class:

```
time_US_str <- "Monday, December 31, 2018 11:59:59 PM"

class(time_US_str)
## [1] "character"

time_US_str
## [1] "Monday, December 31, 2018 11:59:59 PM"
```

Recall that the format of the input object is not following the ISO 8601 standard, therefore, when we used the as.POSIXct function earlier, we added the format argument to map the input components to the POSIXct class:

```
time_base <- as.POSIXct(time_US_str,
                        format = "%A, %B %d, %Y %I:%M:%S %p")

class(time_base)
## [1] "POSIXct" "POSIXt"

time_base
## [1] "2018-12-31 23:59:59 EST"
```

Now, let's use the ymd_hms (which stands for a year, month, day, hour, minute, and second) conversion function from the **lubridate** package to convert the object to a POSIXct object:

```
library(lubridate)

time_lubridate <- mdy_hms(time_US_str, tz = "EST")

class(time_lubridate)
## [1] "POSIXct" "POSIXt"

time_lubridate
## [1] "2018-12-31 23:59:59 EST"
```

This is much simpler than the `as.POSIXct` conversion. The `ymd_hms` function is able to automatically map the different time components of the input object, even when some components are redundant (such as the full weekday name in the example previously).

 Note that if the `tz` (time zone) argument of the `mdy_hms` function is not defined, the function will set UTC as the main time zone.

Unlike the manual mapping process of the `as.POSIXct` function (or the `as.POSIXlt` function), the `mdy_hms` function parses the string components and aligns them according to the order of the function letters. There are 12 possible combinations of letters, which cover most of the common methods of representing date with time together. Likewise, the `ymd` (which stand for the year, month, and day) function converts date objects to a `Date` class. We can now go back and load `dates_df` again and convert the first six variables into date objects with the `ymd` function:

```
url <-
"https://raw.githubusercontent.com/RamiKrispin/Hands-On-Time-Series-Analysi
s-with-R/master/dates_formats.csv"

dates_df <- read.csv(url, stringsAsFactors = FALSE)

str(dates_df)
## 'data.frame': 22 obs. of 7 variables:
## $ Japanese_format : chr "2017/1/20" "2017/1/21" "2017/1/22" "2017/1/23"
...
## $ US_format : chr "1/20/2017" "1/21/2017" "1/22/2017" "1/23/2017" ...
## $ US_long_format : chr "Friday, January 20, 2017" "Saturday, January 21,
2017" "Sunday, January 22, 2017" "Monday, January 23, 2017" ...
## $ CA_mix_format : chr "January 20, 2017" "January 21, 2017" "January 22,
2017" "January 23, 2017" ...
## $ SA_mix_format : chr "20 January 2017" "21 January 2017" "22 January
2017" "23 January 2017" ...
## $ NZ_format : chr "20/01/2017" "21/01/2017" "22/01/2017" "23/01/2017"
...
## $ Excel_Numeric_Format: num 42755 42756 42757 42758 42759 ...

#Conversion with ymd functions
dates_df$Japanese_format_new <- ymd(dates_df$Japanese_format)
dates_df$US_format_new <- mdy(dates_df$US_format)
dates_df$US_long_format_new <- mdy(dates_df$US_long_format)
dates_df$CA_mix_format_new <- mdy(dates_df$CA_mix_format)
dates_df$SA_mix_format_new <- dmy(dates_df$SA_mix_format)
dates_df$NZ_format_new <- dmy(dates_df$NZ_format)
```

The ymd function easily handles the different types of date formats; however, it is not designed to convert numeric values of date objects. This type of conversion can be done with the as_date function for date objects (or as_datetime for time objects), which works in the same manner as as.Date (or the as.POSIXct/as.POSIXlt functions) works with date numeric values:

```
dates_df$Excel_Numeric_Format_new <- as_date(dates_df$Excel_Numeric_Format,
                                      origin = ymd("1899-12-30"))
```

Let's review the data frame with the changes we applied in the preceding code:

```
str(dates_df)## 'data.frame': 22 obs. of 14 variables:
## $ Japanese_format : chr "2017/1/20" "2017/1/21" "2017/1/22" "2017/1/23"
...
## $ US_format : chr "1/20/2017" "1/21/2017" "1/22/2017" "1/23/2017" ...
## $ US_long_format : chr "Friday, January 20, 2017" "Saturday, January 21,
2017" "Sunday, January 22, 2017" "Monday, January 23, 2017" ...
## $ CA_mix_format : chr "January 20, 2017" "January 21, 2017" "January 22,
2017" "January 23, 2017" ...
## $ SA_mix_format : chr "20 January 2017" "21 January 2017" "22 January
2017" "23 January 2017" ...
## $ NZ_format : chr "20/01/2017" "21/01/2017" "22/01/2017" "23/01/2017"
...
## $ Excel_Numeric_Format : num 42755 42756 42757 42758 42759 ...
## $ Japanese_format_new : Date, format: "2017-01-20" "2017-01-21" ...
## $ US_format_new : Date, format: "2017-01-20" "2017-01-21" ...
## $ US_long_format_new : Date, format: "2017-01-20" "2017-01-21" ...
## $ CA_mix_format_new : Date, format: "2017-01-20" "2017-01-21" ...
## $ SA_mix_format_new : Date, format: "2017-01-20" "2017-01-21" ...
## $ NZ_format_new : Date, format: "2017-01-20" "2017-01-21" ...
## $ Excel_Numeric_Format_new: Date, format: "2017-01-20" "2017-01-21" ...
```

As you can see from the output, we received the same results with the ymd and the as_date functions as the results we received earlier with as.Date.

Before moving to the next topic, it is important to add the caveat that those functions (both ymd and ymd_hms) are not able to handle rare or extreme cases where one of the separators is a double string (such as a double apostrophe, "") or some of the formats are not written well in a specific format of year, month, and day, such as 201811-01, 201811-1, or 111-2018 (as opposed to 2018-11-01 or 01-11-2018).

Utility functions for date and time objects

In some cases, you may want to extract a specific component from a date or a time object. The **lubridate** package provides a set of functions for extraction and modification of the elements of time and date objects. In most cases, those functions carry the name of the element (that is, the second, minute, and hour functions for extracting the seconds, minute, and an hour respectively). However, in other cases, a single function may have several applications. For example, the day has several reference points in a calendar year: the day of the week (1-7), month (1-31), quarter (1-92), or year (1-365). The day function contains a set of functions for this type of querying, which we will use in the following example:

```
time_obj <- mdy_hms(time_US_str, tz = "EST")

class(time_obj)
## [1] "POSIXct" "POSIXt"

time_obj
## [1] "2018-12-31 23:59:59 EST"
```

This extracts the day of the year:

```
yday(time_obj)
## [1] 365
```

This extracts the day of the quarter:

```
qday(time_obj)
## [1] 92
```

This extracts the day of the month:

```
day(time_obj)
## [1] 31
```

This extracts the day of the week:

```
wday(time_obj, label = TRUE)
## [1] Mon
## Levels: Sun < Mon < Tue < Wed < Thu < Fri < Sat
```

In addition to the extraction functionality, you can use this function to modify any of the object elements such as the hour, minute, or even second. For example, if you wish to modify the hour of the object from 11 PM to 11 AM, you can use the hour function to assign the value to the object:

```
hour(time_obj) <- 11

time_obj
## [1] "2018-12-31 11:59:59 EST"
```

Another useful application from the **lubridate** package is the round_date function. This set of functions includes three applications:

- round_date: A function that, as you might expect, rounds date or time object to the nearest value of a specific time unit
- floor_date: Rounds the object down according to a specific time criterion (second, minute, hour, and so on)
- ceiling_data: Rounds the object up according to a specific time criterion (second, minute, hour, and so on)

We will again use the time_obj time object and demonstrate the uses of those functions:

```
time_obj <- mdy_hms(time_US_str, tz = "EST")

time_obj
## [1] "2018-12-31 23:59:59 EST"
```

Rounding the time object by the minute, hour, and day looks like this:

```
round_date(time_obj, unit = "minute")
## [1] "2019-01-01 EST"

floor_date(time_obj, unit = "hour")
## [1] "2018-12-31 23:00:00 EST"

ceiling_date(time_obj, unit = "day")
## [1] "2019-01-01 EST"
```

Those sets of functions are very useful when extracting mainly time objects from a different type of format. For example, the time index of a time series object (or ts class) is stored as the cycle units over a sequence of time (for example, months over a sequence of years). Conversion of this type of object may suffer from rounding errors, and the correction can be done with one of those functions.

Summary

Date and time objects are one of the foundations of the time series data. Thus, the ability to import, reformat, and convert this type of object in R seamlessly is an essential part of the time series analysis process. In this chapter, we introduced the primary date and time objects in R, the `Date` and `POSIXct/POSIXlt` classes, and their main attributes. Furthermore, we introduced two main approaches in R to handle and process those objects, with the **base** and **lubridate** packages. While the work with the **base** functions is more technical (or hardcore coding), the work with the **lubridate** package is based on common English language communication with the objects and therefore is much simpler to use. I personally found that deep understanding of the **base** package approach makes working with the **lubridate** package much smoother and more straightforward, as date and time objects play a pivotal role in time series analysis.

In the following chapters, you will see the use of the applications that we learned in this chapter. Our next chapter focuses on presenting the time series objects with their attributions and uses. It teaches how to utilize functions for time series objects and how to create, manipulate, and visualize a `ts` object and identify the object's attributes.

The Time Series Object

3

Time series data has unique features and a special signature that distinguishes it from other types of data. Among those features, you can find the series timestamp (or the series index), the series frequency and cycle, and the time interval in which the data was captured. We will discuss these features in detail in this chapter. These sets of features, as you will see throughout this book, are more than just a convenient data structure, as they have a meaningful statistical application for both a descriptive and predictive analysis of time series data. R provides several classes for representing time series objects for a variety of applications. Among those classes, `ts` is one of the main formats for time series data in R, mainly due to its simplicity and the wide adoption of this class by the main packages in R for time series analysis, for example, the **forecast** and **stats** packages. In this chapter, we will focus on the `ts` class and the set of supporting functions from the **stats** package (the R core package for statistical applications).

In this chapter, we will cover the following topics:

- Using the attributes of the `ts` class
- Creating, manipulating, and extracting data from a `ts` object
- Visualizing a `ts` object

Technical requirement

The following packages will be used in this book:

- **forecast**: Version 8.5 and above
- **stats**: Version 3.6.0 and above
- **Quandl**: Version 2.9.1 and above

You can access the codes for this chapter from the following link:

```
https://github.com/PacktPublishing/Hands-On-Time-Series-Analysis-with-R/tree/
master/Chapter03
```

The Natural Gas Consumption dataset

In this chapter, and generally throughout this book, we will use the **Natural Gas Consumption** (**NGC**) dataset as an example of time series data. This dataset represents the quarterly consumption of natural gas in the US between 2000 and 2018. We will use the **Quandl** package to load the data from the **Federal Reserve Bank of St. Louis database** (**FRED**) and store it as a `ts` object:

```
library(Quandl)

NGC <-Quandl(code = "FRED/NATURALGAS",
             collapse="quarterly",
             type = "ts",
             end_date = "2018-12-31")
```

The class of the output can be defined by the `type` argument, which, in this case, was set to the `ts` object:

```
class(NGC)
## [1] "ts"
```

Typically, when loading a new dataset, it is recommended that you plot the series before moving to the next step in the analysis. This allows you to have a quick look at the series to observe whether the data has been appropriately transformed and get a general understanding of the series' structure. The simplest method to plot a `ts` object is with the `plot` function, the R built-in plotting function from the **graphics** package:

```
plot.ts(NGC,
        main = "US Quarterly Natural Gas Consumption",
        ylab = "Billion of Cubic Feet")
```

The following diagram shows us the quarterly consumption of natural gas in the US between 2000-2017:

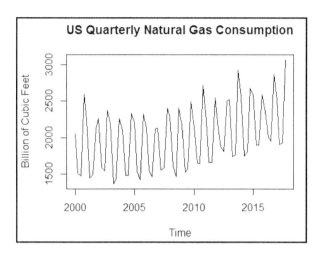

Don't worry if you are not familiar with this function; we will discuss the methods of visualizing ts objects in detail later in this chapter.

The attributes of the ts class

The ts class is R's built-in format for a regular univariate time series object. Before we dive into the attributes of this class, let's pause and define regular time series data and its main characteristics.

At regular time series is defined as an ordered sequence of observations over time, which is captured at equally spaced time intervals (that is, every day, week, month, and so on). Whenever this condition ceases to exist, the series becomes an irregular time series. Since this book's main topic is time series analysis and the forecasting of regular time series data, the term *time series*, or *series*, refers to regular time series data unless stated otherwise.

The main characteristics of regular time series data is as follows:

- **Cycle/period**: A regular and repeating unit of time that split the series into consecutive and equally long subsets (for example, for monthly series, a full cycle would be a year).
- **Frequency**: Defines the length or the number of units of the cycle (for example, for quarterly series, the frequency is four).
- **Timestamp**: Provides the time each observation in the series was captured, and can be used as the series index. By definition, in a regular time series the time difference (or delta) between two consecutive observations must be equal.

A ts object is composed of two elements—the series values and its corresponding timestamp. In addition, it also has several attributes, such as the series, cycle, frequency, and the time interval between each consecutive observation. Let's go back to the NGC dataset that we loaded earlier and look at the data structure of the ts object. After loading new data into the environment, it is always recommended that you check and verify whether the data structure is aligned with your expectations. A fast and recommended check to start with would be to verify the data class and length, which can be done with the is.ts and length functions:

```
is.ts(NGC) # Test if the object is a "ts" class
## [1] TRUE

length(NGC) # Get the number of observations
## [1] 76
```

The structure of the ts object is a bit different from most data structures in R (matrix, data.frame, data.table, tibble, and so on). While the ts object is a two-dimensional dataset (time/index and the series observations), it doesn't share the common attributes of most of the regular tables in R (such as matrix or data.frame) since the series index is embedded within the object itself. Therefore, some of the common functions for R's tables won't work with a ts object (such as the dim function). We can observe the structure of the NGC with the head function:

```
head(NGC, 32)

## Qtr1 Qtr2 Qtr3 Qtr4

## 2000 2050.6 1513.1 1475.0 2587.5

## 2001 2246.6 1444.4 1494.1 2120.2

## 2002 2258.4 1591.4 1542.2 2378.9
```

```
## 2003 2197.9 1368.4 1428.6 2263.7

## 2004 2100.9 1483.7 1482.2 2327.7

## 2005 2205.8 1534.1 1422.5 2326.4

## 2006 2126.4 1550.9 1462.1 2122.8

## 2007 2128.8 1555.2 1590.5 2399.2
```

The `ts` class transforms the series elements into table format, where the rows represent the number of the cycle and the columns represent the cycle units.

In the case of the NGC dataset, each calendar year is a full cycle and the quarters are the cycle units. Similarly, the `cycle` and the `time` functions from the **stats** package provide the cycle units and the timestamp of each observation in the series:

```
head(cycle(NGC), 32)
##      Qtr1 Qtr2 Qtr3 Qtr4
## 2000    1    2    3    4
## 2001    1    2    3    4
## 2002    1    2    3    4
## 2003    1    2    3    4
## 2004    1    2    3    4
## 2005    1    2    3    4
## 2006    1    2    3    4
## 2007    1    2    3    4
```

Similarly, you can see the structure of the `time` function output in the following code snippet:

```
head(time(NGC), 32)

##           Qtr1      Qtr2      Qtr3      Qtr4
## 2000 2000.00 2000.25 2000.50 2000.75
## 2001 2001.00 2001.25 2001.50 2001.75
## 2002 2002.00 2002.25 2002.50 2002.75
## 2003 2003.00 2003.25 2003.50 2003.75
## 2004 2004.00 2004.25 2004.50 2004.75
## 2005 2005.00 2005.25 2005.50 2005.75
## 2006 2006.00 2006.25 2006.50 2006.75
## 2007 2007.00 2007.25 2007.50 2007.75
```

As you can see, the timestamp is a decimal number that is aligned with the cycles of the series. The values on the left-hand side of the decimal point represent the cycle number (in this case, the calendar year), and the values on the right-hand side represent the cycle units, where the count of the units start from 0. A more practical and concise method to get the characteristics of the series is with the `frequency` and `deltat` functions from the **stats** package, which provide the series frequency and the time interval between the observations:

```
frequency(NGC)
## [1] 4
deltat(NGC)
## [1] 0.25
```

Other useful utility functions are the `start` and `end` functions, which, as their names imply, return the series timestamp's starting and ending point, respectively:

```
start(NGC)
## [1] 2000    1
end(NGC)
## [1] 2017    4
```

The `ts_info` function from the **TSstudio** package provides a concise summary of most of the preceding functions. This includes the object class, the number of observations, the frequency, and the starting and ending of the series. Let's load the **TSstudio** package and use this function to get a summary of the NGC object:

```
library(TSstudio)

ts_info(NGC)
## The NGC series is a ts object with 1 variable and 76 observations
## Frequency: 4
## Start time: 2000 1
## End time: 2018 4
```

Let's now look at *multivariate time series objects*.

Multivariate time series objects

In some instances, such as correlation analysis, you may need to work with multivariate time series objects. In those cases, working with `ts` objects (assuming that all the series have the same frequency and overlap between their indices) may be cumbersome, as each series is required to be processed individually. Alternatively, you can use the `mts` (**multiple time series**) class, an extension of the `ts` class. The `mts` class is a combination of the `ts` and `matrix` classes, and its advantage is that it shares the attributes of both those classes.

The `Coffee_Prices` dataset from the **TSstudio** package is an example of an `mts` object. This `mts` object represents the monthly prices (USD per kg) between 1960 and 2018 of Robusta and Arabica, two popular coffee species:

```
data(Coffee_Prices)

ts_info(Coffee_Prices)

## The Coffee_Prices series is a mts object with 2 variables and 701
observations
## Frequency: 12
## Start time: 1960 1
## End time: 2018 5
```

Generally, the `mts` object is also a `ts` and `matrix` object, as you can see in the following output:

```
class(Coffee_Prices)
## [1] "mts"    "ts"      "matrix"
```

As the `mts` class inherited the `matrix` class attributes, the output of the `mts` object is a `matrix`-like table:

```
head(Coffee_Prices)
##           Robusta Arabica
## [1,] 0.6968643  0.9409
## [2,] 0.6887074  0.9469
## [3,] 0.6887074  0.9281
## [4,] 0.6845187  0.9303
## [5,] 0.6906915  0.9200
## [6,] 0.6968643  0.9123
```

Moreover, you can utilize and apply any designated function for a `matrix` object (when applicable) on an `mts` object. Similarly, the `mts` object also supports the `ts` objects functions, such as the `frequency`, `time`, `start`, or `end` functions. For example, we will use the `frequency`, `deltat`, `time`, and `cycle` functions to extract the series' characteristics:

```
frequency(Coffee_Prices)
## [1] 12
deltat(Coffee_Prices)
## [1] 0.08333333
head(time(Coffee_Prices))
## [1] 1960.000 1960.083 1960.167 1960.250 1960.333 1960.417
head(cycle(Coffee_Prices))
## [1] 1 2 3 4 5 6
```

Two or more series can be merged to an `mts` object only if all the following prerequisites are met:

- All inputs are regular time series
- All inputs have exactly the same frequency or time interval between the observations
- All inputs start at the same cycle number and cycle unit (unless missing values are filled with NAs)

Creating a ts object

The `ts` function from the **stats** package allows you to create a `ts` object by assigning sequential observations and mapping their attributes. Let's start with a simple example, and set an arithmetic progression series with the `1` to `60` values as a monthly series beginning on January 2010. This series would have the following attributes:

- **Frequency**: This is a `12` month period, where each frequency unit represents a specific month of the year
- **Cycle**: The units of the series are in years, where a full cycle is derived from the frequency units of the series and is defined as `12` months
- **Start**: The starting point of the series is January 2010, or, in other words, the beginning point of the series is on frequency unit `1` (assuming that the mapping of the month is aligned to the calendar order of the months), and the cycle unit is defined as the year
- **End**: The end point of the series is December 2014, or frequency unit `12` and cycle unit `2014`

Let's define those attributes on this arithmetic progression series and transfer the data into a `ts` object:

```
my_ts1 <- ts(data = 1:60, # The series values
           start = c(2010, 1), # The time of the first observation
           end = c(2014, 12),  # The time of the last observation
           frequency = 12) # The Series frequency
```

```
ts_info(my_ts1)
##   The my_ts1 series is a ts object with 1 variable and 60 observations
##   Frequency: 12
##   Start time: 2010 1
##   End time: 2014 12
```

The output of the `my_ts1` object can be seen as follows:

```
my_ts1
##        Jan Feb Mar Apr May Jun Jul Aug Sep Oct Nov Dec
## 2010    1   2   3   4   5   6   7   8   9  10  11  12
## 2011   13  14  15  16  17  18  19  20  21  22  23  24
## 2012   25  26  27  28  29  30  31  32  33  34  35  36
## 2013   37  38  39  40  41  42  43  44  45  46  47  48
## 2014   49  50  51  52  53  54  55  56  57  58  59  60
```

The `start` and `end` arguments of the `ts` functions define the time of the first and the last observations respectively, in terms of cycle and frequency units. Those arguments can be defined by either a single integer or by a vector of two integers:

- Using a two-integer vector to define the start or end of the series is the most convenient method, as it allows the user to be explicit about the cycle and frequency units. It is sufficient to define either the `start` or `end` arguments, as the end or start value of the series can be derived from the length of the series and its frequency. For example, we can redefine the `my_ts1` series by setting only the `end` argument:

  ```
  my_ts2 <- ts(data = 1:60,
               end = c(2014, 12),
               frequency = 12)

  start(my_ts2)
  ## [1] 2010    1
  ```

- When setting the `start` or `end` arguments as a single integer input, the value of the integer represents the cycle number. In this case, by default, the value of the frequency unit is defined as `1`. For example, we can define the starting point of the series as `2010`, which is equivalent to the cycle and frequency units of `2010` and `1`, respectively:

```
my_ts3 <- ts(data = 1:60,
             start = 2010,
             frequency = 12)

start(my_ts3)
## [1] 2010    1
```

As you can see from the output of the following `identical` function, all the three series are identical:

```
identical(my_ts1, my_ts2, my_ts3)
## [1] TRUE
```

It is most likely that your raw data won't come in `ts` format and some preprocessing steps may be required before transforming the input to a `ts` object. Those preprocessing steps may include the following:

- Exporting the data from an external source, for example, an Excel or CSV file, SQL database, GitHub, and so on
- Reformatting the timestamp of the series or defining the series index
- Reordering the series according to its chronological order

In the following example, we will demonstrate a typical process of converting data from a `data.frame` object to a `ts` object, applying the following steps:

1. Let's load the `US_indicators` dataset from the **TSstudio** package. This dataset is a `data.frame` with two series—the monthly total vehicle sales and the unemployment rate in the US. In addition, the data includes the timestamp of the two series in `Date` format. Let's load the series and view its structure:

```
data(US_indicators)

str(US_indicators)
## 'data.frame':     517 obs. of  3 variables:
##  $ Date             : Date, format: "1976-01-31" "1976-02-29"
...
##  $ Vehicle Sales    : num  885 995 1244 1191 1203 ...
##  $ Unemployment Rate: num  8.8 8.7 8.1 7.4 6.8 8 7.8 7.6 7.4 7.2
...
```

As you can see from the `str` function output, this series has `517` observations and the following three variables:

- `Date`: The monthly timestamp of the two series in `Date` format
- `Vehicle Sales`: A numeric object that represents the total monthly amount of vehicle sales (in thousands)
- `Unemployment Rate`: A numeric object that represents the unemployment rate (a percentage)

For now, we will only convert the vehicle sales series into a `ts` object; therefore, for the sake of simplicity, we will extract the first two columns of the series and assign them to a new `data.frame` named `tvs`, which denotes the total vehicle sales:

```
tvs <- US_indicators[, c("Date", "Vehicle Sales")]

str(tvs)
## 'data.frame':    517 obs. of  2 variables:
##  $ Date         : Date, format: "1976-01-31" "1976-02-29" ...
##  $ Vehicle Sales: num  885 995 1244 1191 1203 ...
```

An important pre-step before converting a `data.frame`, or generally any other R table format (such as `tibble` and `data.table`) to a `ts` object is to arrange the data in chronological order. We will use the `arrange` function from the **dplyr** package to sort the data:

```
library(dplyr)

tvs <- tvs %>% arrange(Date)

head(tvs)
##         Date Vehicle Sales
## 1 1976-01-31         885.2
## 2 1976-02-29         994.7
## 3 1976-03-31        1243.6
## 4 1976-04-30        1191.2
## 5 1976-05-31        1203.2
## 6 1976-06-30        1254.7
```

The `ts` function will set the order of the series according to the original order of the input series. Thus, if the input series is not sorted according to the chronological order of the series, the output won't be mapped correctly to the actual index of the series, which yields a false result. Therefore, whenever the input series is not ordered by the series index, you must sort it before applying the `ts` function (and, to be on the safe side, it is always recommended that you sort the series, even if it is already in order).

2. Next, we want to define the `start` (or `end`) argument of the series. Since the input series is monthly, we need to define the cycle (`year`) and frequency (`month`) units of the first observation of the series. This can be done manually, by observing the first date of the series and set the start point accordingly. In this case, the series started in January 1976, and therefore we can define it as `start = c(1976, 1)`. Alternatively, we can write a code to capture the starting point of the series. This is useful when working with multiple series and/or when the starting point is changing over time. We will use the **lubridate** package to extract the year and month of the first observation with the `year` and `month` functions:

```
library(lubridate)

start_point <- c(year(min(tvs$Date)), month(min(tvs$Date)))

start_point
## [1] 1976    1
```

We can now define the series with the `ts` function, utilizing the `start_point` variable to define the beginning of the series:

```
tvs_ts <- ts(data = tvs$`Vehicle Sales`,
             start = start_point,
             frequency = 12)
```

One of the main limitations of the `ts` class is that its timestamp or index supports only two input elements, which represents the cycle and frequency units. This creates two problems:

- It doesn't support timestamps with multiple seasonality or cycles, such as daily time series, which can have both weekdays and yearly cycles
- In cases where the timestamp of the series is more than two elements, such as date or time, it is not possible to retrieve the original value of the series timestamp, as one or more elements are lost during the transformation process

For example, once we transformed the `tvs` dataset to a `ts` object, the `day` component was lost, as we were able to store only the month and year:

```
head(tvs$Date, 5)
## [1] "1976-01-31" "1976-02-29" "1976-03-31" "1976-04-30" "1976-05-31"
head(time(tvs_ts), 5)
## [1] 1976.000 1976.083 1976.167 1976.250 1976.333
```

On the other hand, the series' values do not change during the transformation and can therefore be retrieved from the `ts` object:

```
head(tvs$`Vehicle Sales`)
## [1]  885.2  994.7 1243.6 1191.2 1203.2 1254.7

head(tvs_ts)
## [1]  885.2  994.7 1243.6 1191.2 1203.2 1254.7

identical(tvs$`Vehicle Sales`, as.numeric(tvs_ts))
## [1] TRUE
```

Let's now create an `mts` object.

Creating an mts object

The process of converting a multiple time series object from a data frame to `ts` format is fairly similar to that of the `ts` object. We will now go back to the `US_indicators` dataset and join both the vehicle sales and the unemployment rate series to an `mts` object. First, let's make sure that the series is sorted in chronological order with the `arrange` function:

```
US_indicators <- US_indicators %>% arrange(Date)
```

Similarly, as we defined earlier, the `ts` object we will create is the `mts` object by using the `ts` function, where the input data includes two columns (as opposed to a single one for the `ts` object):

```
US_indicators_ts <- ts(data = US_indicators[, c("Vehicle Sales",
"Unemployment Rate")],
                        start = c(year(min(tvs$Date)),
month(min(tvs$Date))),
                        frequency = 12)
```

We can review the transformed object with the `ts_info` and `head` functions:

```
ts_info(US_indicators_ts)
##  The US_indicators_ts series is a mts object with 2 variables and 517
observations
##  Frequency: 12
##  Start time: 1976 1
##  End time: 2019 1

head(US_indicators_ts)
##       Vehicle Sales Unemployment Rate
## [1,]         885.2               8.8
## [2,]         994.7               8.7
## [3,]        1243.6               8.1
## [4,]        1191.2               7.4
## [5,]        1203.2               6.8
## [6,]        1254.7               8.0
```

Let's now set the series frequency.

Setting the series frequency

The frequency of the series has an important role in defining the series attributes, as it sets (along with the time interval between the series observations) the length of the cycle. Moreover, it defines the cycle units; for example, the units of a series with a frequency of 12 is 1 to 12. Generally, the most common length of a cycle is a calendar year. The calculation of the series frequency, in this case, can be divided into two groups:

- A daily frequency or any other frequency that is derived from the number of days in a calendar year (such as the number of the weeks, hours, or minutes in a year)
- Any other frequency that is not derived from the number of days in a year (such as monthly, quarterly, or half-year)

The frequency setting of the last group is straightforward and is derived from the number of periods per cycle. In most cases, the cycle length is one year, and we will therefore set the frequency of monthly, quarterly, and half-year to 12, 4, and 2 respectively. Moreover, you can generalize this calculation for an R series with different cycle lengths:

Frequency = cycle length / time interval between observation

For the first group (daily and its subsets) the calculation is fairly similar, with a small transformation that is required due to leap years. A leap year contains one additional day (hence, 366 days instead of 365 days in a common year), by extending February to 29 days. This occurs every 4 years (with some exceptions), in order to synchronize the calendar year with the astronomical year. Hence, if you are setting the frequency of a daily series to 365, you will have a day gap every 4 years. Therefore, in order to avoid this gap, we will have to add a quarter of a day every year and set the frequency to 365.25. The leap year effect also affects the series so that their frequency units are derived from the number of calendar days per year. For example, a weekly series will be set to 52.178 instead of 52 (or 365.25 / 7). The following table summarizes the frequencies of the most common series:

Time interval	Cycle length	Frequency
Half-year	Year	2
Quarterly	Year	4
Monthly	Year	12
Weekly	Year	52.179 (or 365.25 / 7)
Daily	Year	365.25 (or (365 * 3 + 366) / 4)
Daily	Weekly	7
Hourly	Daily	24
Hourly	Weekly	168 (or 24 * 7)
Hourly	Yearly	8,766 (or 24 * 365.25)
Minutes	Hourly	60
Minutes	Daily	1,440 (or 60 * 24)
Minutes	Weekly	10,080 (or 60 * 24 * 7)
Minutes	Yearly	525,960 (or 60 * 24 * 365.25)

Table 1: Common frequency types

The downside of including the leap year effect on the frequency setting (for example, setting series with a daily frequency of 365.25 as opposed to 365) is that it may shift some of the seasonal patterns of the series, such as holidays, as we are shifting each year by a quarter of a day. In addition, some forecasting models do not support non-integer series.

In the following example, you can see how setting the frequency impacts the structure of the `ts` object output. First, we will simulate close to ten years of daily data. We will use the `seq.Date` method to create a sequence of 3,650 days (or 365 times 10, which is 10 years excluding the extra day during leap years) starting on January 1, 2010. We will then use the `rnorm` function to generate the corresponding values of the series following a normal distribution with a `mean` of 15 and a standard deviation (`sd`) of 2:

```
daily_df <- data.frame(date = seq.Date(from = as.Date("2010-01-01"),
                length.out = 365 * 10, by = "day"),
            y = rnorm(365 * 10, mean = 15, sd = 2))
```

We now have a `data.frame` object with date and numeric objects:

```
str(daily_df)
```

We will get the following output:

```
## 'data.frame':    3650 obs. of  2 variables:
##  $ date: Date, format: "2010-01-01" "2010-01-02" ...
##  $ y   : num  14.25 10.79 9.82 11.71 15.48 ...
```

We will assign the first date of the series to a variable (`start_date`) and use it to set the start point of the series:

```
start_date <- min(daily_df$date)
```

For a daily series with weekly cycles, the frequency of the series should be set to seven (for example, Monday to Sunday) as can be seen in the following example:

```
days_week_ts <- ts(daily_df$y,
                start = c(1, wday(start_date)),
                frequency = 7)
```

Note that we utilized the `wday` function from the **lubridate** package to extract the day of the week from the first date of the series. Using the `ts_info` function, you can see the attributes of the series:

```
ts_info(days_week_ts)
```

We will get the following output:

```
##   The days_week_ts series is a ts object with 1 variable and 3650
observations
##   Frequency: 7
##   Start time: 1 6
##   End time: 523 1
```

If the dominant cycle of the series is yearly (for example, a full cycle is 365 days), then you have two options. The first option is to set the `frequency` to `365`, if you are ignoring the leap year effect:

```
daily_ts <- ts(daily_df$y,
               start = c(year(start_date), yday(start_date)),
               frequency = 365)

ts_info(daily_ts)
```

We will get the following output:

```
##   The daily_ts series is a ts object with 1 variable and 3650
observations
##   Frequency: 365
##   Start time: 2010 1
##   End time: 2019 365
```

Alternatively, we can set the `frequency` as `365.25` to smooth the effect of the leap year:

```
daily_leap_ts <- ts(daily_df$y,
                    start = c(year(start_date), yday(start_date)),
                    frequency = 365.25)

ts_info(daily_leap_ts)
```

We will get the following output:

```
##   The daily_leap_ts series is a ts object with 1 variable and 3650
observations
##   Frequency: 365.25
##   Start time: 2010
##   End time: 2019.99041752225
```

As can see in the two preceding examples, we used the `year` and `yday` functions from the **lubridate** package as well to set the start point of the series. In the case of daily series, the year is used as the cycle number and the day of the year as the frequency unit of the series. The setting of both `start` and `frequency` can be determined, as shown in the output of the `ts_info` function in the preceding three cases.

Data manipulation of ts objects

The data preprocessing does not complete once the series is transformed into a `ts` object because, in many cases, you may be required to apply some additional transformation or preprocessing steps. This includes steps such as extracting or subsetting a specific element of the series or aggregating the series to a different frequency (for example, from monthly to quarterly). A typical example of such a step is splitting the series into training and testing partitions when training a forecasting model. Due to the unique structure of the `ts` object, in most cases, the common extraction methods for `data.frame` do not apply to `ts` objects. In this section, we will introduce methods and designated functions for data manipulation of `ts` objects by using the `window`, `aggregate`, and other functions.

The window function

One of the main functions associated with the `ts` class is the `window` function from the **stats** package. The main purpose of the `window` function is to subset a `ts` object based on a time range. It is fairly similar to the famous `subset` function from the **base** package, where the input of the function is a `ts` object, and the output is a subset of that object, based on the `window` time setting. Let's go back to the `NGC` dataset we loaded earlier and see how these functions work:

```
start(NGC)
## [1] 2000    1
end(NGC)
## [1] 2018    4
frequency(NGC)
## [1] 4
```

The main arguments of the `window` function are the `start` and `end` arguments, which define the range of time to extract from the input object. For example, let's use the `window` function to extract all the observations of the year 2005 from the NGC series:

```
window(NGC, start = c(2005,1), end = c(2005, 4))
##        Qtr1   Qtr2   Qtr3   Qtr4
## 2005 2205.8 1534.1 1422.5 2326.4
```

Similarly, we can extract a specific frequency unit from the series. For example, let's assume that we are interested in extracting all the observations of the series that occurred in the third quarter of the year. This can be done by setting the starting point at the third quarter of the first year and the `frequency` to `1` (which will set the output to a yearly series):

```
window(NGC, start = c(2000, 3), frequency = 1)
## Time Series:
## Start = 2000
## End = 2018
## Frequency = 1
##   [1] 1475 1494 1542 1429 1482 1422 1462 1590 1461 1575 1638 1656 1807
1767
## [15] 1809 1901 1948 1923 2156
```

Setting the starting and ending point of the subset series is done with the `start` and `end` arguments of the `window` function. It is sufficient to use either the `start` or `end` argument when you wish to subset the series from or up to a specific point, respectively. The use of both arguments is required whenever you wish to bind the series between two points of time. For example, extracting the third quarter of the series between the years 2006 and 2012 can be done by doing the following:

- Setting the start and end cycles of the subset series as the years 2006 and 2012, respectively
- Setting the start and end frequency unit as the third quarter (for example, 3)
- Defining the `frequency` of the series as 1

The following code snippet demonstrates this process:

```
window(NGC, start = c(2006, 3), end = c(2012, 3),frequency = 1)
## Time Series:
## Start = 2006.5
## End = 2012.5
## Frequency = 1
## [1] 1462.1 1590.5 1460.9 1575.0 1637.5 1655.6 1807.2
```

The output of this function is a yearly series (that is, a series with a frequency of one), with the third quarter values of the series during the selected time range.

Let's now learn how to aggregate `ts` objects.

Aggregating ts objects

The `aggregate` function from the **stats** package is a generic function for aggregating `ts` and `data.frame` objects. This splits the data into subsets, computes specific summary statistics (based on the user's choice), and then aggregates the results to a `ts` or `data.frame` object (depending on the input type). In the context of the `ts` object, it is a handy application, as it provides the ability to collapse the series' frequency to a lower frequency (for example, from monthly to quarterly). For example, let's use the `aggregate` function to transform the NGC series from a quarterly frequency to yearly:

```
NGC_year <- aggregate(NGC, nfrequency = 1, FUN = "sum")
```

The `FUN` argument defines the calculation method to apply to each subset. The most common method (and the default) is the `sum` function, which sums each of the subsets and joins the output into a new series, as shown in the preceding example.

Alternatively, you can apply other functions on the aggregate data with the `FUN` argument, such as `mean`, `sd`, and `median`. By setting the `nfrequency` argument to `1`, the function aggregates the series from a quarterly series with a frequency of four to a yearly series with a frequency of one:

```
NGC_year
## Time Series:
## Start = 2000
## End = 2018
## Frequency = 1
##  [1] 7626 7305 7771 7259 7394 7489 7262 7674 7743 7765 8144 8085 8307
8952
## [15] 8792 8981 9171 9430 9811
```

Handling missing values, if these exist, can be done by using the `na.action` argument of the `aggregate` function, which, by default, ignores missing values.

Let's now learn how to create lags and leads for `ts` objects.

Creating lags and leads for ts objects

The use of lags in time series analysis is widespread because, typically, a time series is correlated with some of its previous lags. We can generally distinguish between two types of lags:

- Past lags, or simply lags, represent a shift in the series by n steps back, with respect to the original series. For a series with t observations, the n lag of the series begins at time $n+1$ and ends at time $t+n$ (where the first n observations are missing).
- Lead or negative lags represent a shift in the series by n steps forward, with respect to the original series. In this case, for a series with t observations, the lead n of the series begins at the time n and end at time $t-n$ (where the last n observations are missing).

The following table demonstrates the relationship between a series and its first lag and lead. You can note that for **Lag-1** and **Lead-1** of the series, the first and last observations are missing:

Timestamp	Lag-1	Series	Lead -1
Jan-18	NA	3	5.5
Feb-18	3	5.5	4.7
Mar-18	5.5	4.7	3.6
Apr-18	4.7	3.6	2.5
May-18	3.6	2.5	4.3
Jun-18	2.5	4.3	2.8
Jul-18	4.3	2.8	2.2
Aug-18	2.8	2.2	1.9
Sep-18	2.2	1.9	3.6
Oct-18	1.9	3.6	4.3
Nov-18	3.6	4.3	2.9
Dec-18	4.3	2.9	NA

Table 2: An example of the lag and lead of a series

The `lag` function from the **stats** package (this should not be confused with the `lag` function from the **dplyr** package) can be used to create lags or leads for `ts` objects. This function has one argument, `k`, which defines the number of lags or leads to be created for a given input series. The n lag of the series is defined by `k = -n` and, similarly, the n lead of the series is defined by `k = n`. For example, if we wish to create a seasonal lag (seasonal lag is defined as $n = frequency\ of\ the\ series$) of the NGC series, we need set `k` to -4:

```
NGC_lag4 <- stats::lag(NGC, k = -4)
```

You can see that, in the preceding function, we added the package name with double colons (`::`), or `stats::lag`, before the `lag` function. Using this method ensures that we are calling the `lag` function from the **stats** package and not from the **dplyr** package. Generally, you should apply this method whenever the function name exists in two different packages that are loaded to the working environment.

We will get the following data when we use `ts_info(NGC_lag4)`:

```
ts_info(NGC_lag4)
##  The NGC_lag4 series is a ts object with 1 variable and 76 observations
##  Frequency: 4
##  Start time: 2001 1
##  End time: 2019 4
```

As you can see in the preceding output, the series shifted by four observations, and each observation of the new series represents the fourth lag of the original series (for example, the first quarter of 2001 is the lag of the corresponding quarter in 2000).

Visualizing ts and mts objects

One of the first things that you probably want to do once you create or convert your data to a `ts` or `mts` format is to visualize it. This step is a quick sanity check to make sure that your data looks like you expect it would and to identify outliers, seasonality, and other patterns within your data. There are two approaches for visualizing a time series object:

- **Direct**: This approach uses a visualization function to plot the object without any data transformation or conversion to another class. There are few packages that provide direct tools for visualizing time series objects. In this chapter, we will focus on three packages:
  - `stats`: In addition to the `ts` objects, this provides the `plot.ts` function for visualizing time series objects. This function is an extension of the `plot` function, which is an R built-in visualization function.
  - `dygraphs`: This R package is an interface for the `dygraphs` JavaScript visualization library. It provides an interactive application for visualizing `ts` objects.

- `TSstudio`: This is a designated package for descriptive and predictive analysis of time series data. This includes rich and interactive visualization applications for time series objects, such as `ts`, `mts`, `zoo`, `xts`, and other table-based formats (such as `data.frame` and `tibble`). Like the previous package, the **TSstudio** package is uses the **plotly** package engine.
- **In-direct**: This approach involves applying some data transformation steps to restructure the data as a numeric two-dimensional structure (values over time). This includes the use of packages such as **ggplot2**, **plotly**, **highcharter**, and **rbokeh**. Using these packages for a time series object is not in the scope of this book.

The main difference between the direct and indirect approaches is that the former was designed to work with the `ts` objects and it therefore automatically transfers the value of the series and timestamp onto a *y*-axis and *x*-axis respectively. On the other hand, in the indirect approach, you will have to define those two dimensions (values versus time) manually.

Let's now look at the `plot.ts` function.

The plot.ts function

The `plot.ts` function from the **stats** package is built-in R function for visualizing of a `ts` object. It is straightforward to plot a `ts` object with this function, as it based on the `plot` function. Therefore, most of the arguments of the `plot` function (such as title and labeling options) can be used with the `plot.ts` function (generally, using the `plot` function with a `ts` object is the equivalent of using the `plot.ts` function). For instance, let's use the function to visualize the `tvs_ts` series we created earlier:

```
plot.ts(tvs_ts,
  main = "US Monthly Total Vehicle Sales",
  ylab = "Thousands of Vehicle",
  xlab = "Time"
  )
```

This will give us the following graph:

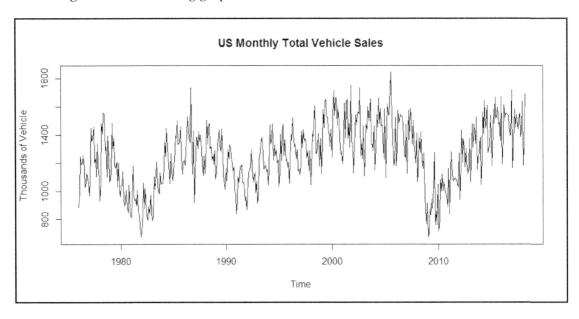

We used the `main` argument to add to the plot title, and the `ylab` and `xlab` variables to add labeling for the *y* and *x*-axis, respectively. Similarly, we can use the function to plot an `mts` object:

```
plot.ts(US_indicators_ts,
        plot.type = "multiple",
        main = "US Monthly Vehicle Sales vs. Unemployment Rate",
        xlab = "Time")
```

The following is the output:

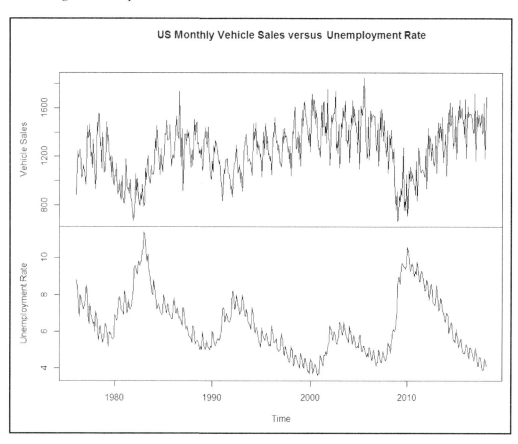

When plotting an `mts` object, you can choose to plot all the series in a single plot or to separate them on multiple plots (one for each series) with the `plot.type` argument. The `single` mode is more applicable when all the series are on the same scale. On the other hand, when the series are in a different scales (as in the preceding example), it will make more sense to use the `multiple` option. Let's now look at the **dygraphs** package.

The dygraphs package

The **dygraphs** package is an R interface to the `dygraphs` JavaScript charting library, and it is completely dedicated to visualizing time series objects, including the `ts` class. In addition, it is highly customized, interactive, and supports HTML implementation (for example, the **rmarkdown** and **Shiny** packages).

Let's plot the `tvs_ts` and `US_indicators_ts` series again with the `dygraph` function:

```
library(dygraphs)

dygraph(tvs_ts,
        main = "US Monthly Total Vehicle Sales",
        ylab = "Thousands of Vehicle") %>%
    dyRangeSelector()
```

We will get the following output:

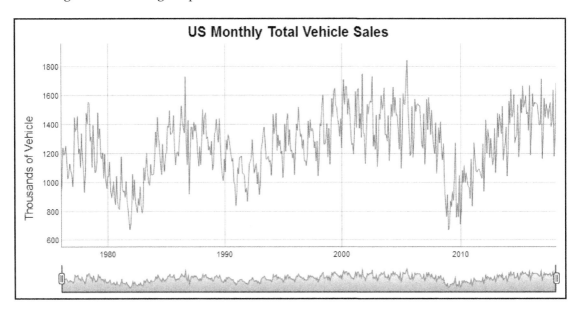

You can see that the main `dygraph` arguments are fairly similar to the `plot.ts` function arguments (titles and labeling options). We used the `dyRangeSelector` argument to add a time slider, which allows the user to change the time frame of the plot. For the `US_indicators_ts` series, we will add a second *y*-axis, which allows us to plot and compare the two series that are not on the same scale (for example, thousands of units versus percentage):

```
dygraph(US_indicators_ts,
        main = "US Monthly Vehicle Sales vs. Unemployment Rate") %>%
    dyAxis("y", label = "Vehicle Sales") %>%
    dyAxis("y2", label = "Unemployment Rate") %>%
    dySeries("Vehicle Sales", axis = 'y', color = "green") %>%
    dySeries("Unemployment Rate", axis = 'y2', color = "red") %>%
    dyLegend(width = 400)
```

We will then get the following plot:

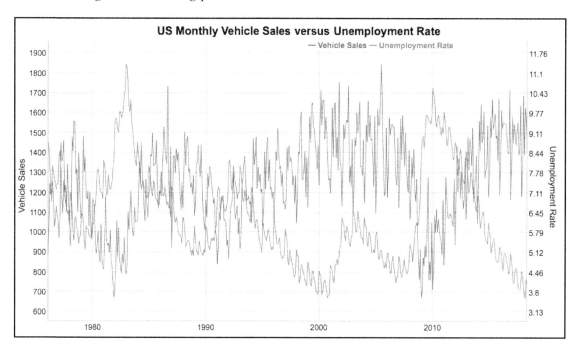

The `dygraph` argument is using an object-oriented approach, which allows you to add a different component to the plot with the pipe operator (`%>%`). This allows the user to add additional arguments for the plot, as opposed to a large amount of arguments in one function. Looking at the plot of the `US_indecator_ts` series when using two *y*-axes, you can see that it is easier to identify the relationship between the two series as opposed to plotting them on a separate plot (as we did with the `plot.ts` function earlier). With a quick glance at the graph, you can see that, generally, unemployment increases when vehicle sales decrease. Although this is not conclusive evidence about the relationship between the two, it provides you with a directional path when starting the analysis. Let's now look at the **TSstudio** package.

The TSstudio package

The **TSstudio** package provides us with a set of interactive applications for descriptive and predictive analysis of time series. This includes the `ts_plot` function for visualizing time series objects using the **plotly** package visualization engine. In addition, this function supports both time series objects, such as `ts`, `mts`, `zoo`, and `xts`, and also data frame types such as `data.frame`, `data.table`, and `tibble`. Let's now plot the `tvs_ts` series with the `ts_plot` function:

```
library(TSstudio)

ts_plot(tvs_ts,
        title = "US Monthly Total Vehicle Sales",
        Ytitle = "Thousands of Vehicle",
        slider = TRUE
)
```

This gives us the following graph:

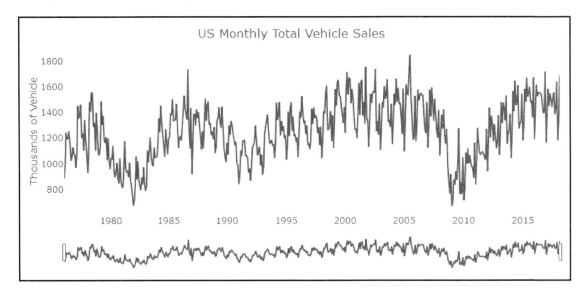

As with the `dygraph` function, you can add an interactive slider for the *x*-axis. Similarly, the `ts_plot` function supports `mts` objects:

```
ts_plot(US_indicators_ts,
  title = "US Monthly Vehicle Sales vs. Unemployment Rate",
  type = "multiple")
```

This will give us the following graphs showing `Unemployment.Rate` and `Vehicle.Sales`:

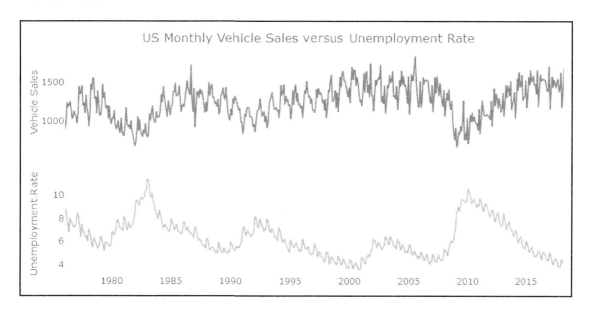

We will extensively use the **TSstudio** package throughout this book for a descriptive analysis of time series with data visualization.

Summary

The `ts` class is one of the most common formats for time series data and is widely used in the domain of forecasting. In this chapter, we focused on the main attributes of the `ts` class and its associated functions from the **stats** package. Those attributes will be handy when we dive more into time series analysis in the advanced chapters of this book. In addition, we introduced common methods for visualizing a `ts` object with the basic `plot` function, as well as advanced visualization tools from the **dygraph** and **TSstudio** packages.

The main advantage of the `ts` class is that it sets a clear standard about both the structure and attributes of the time series object in R. On the other hand, due to the unique structure of the `ts` object, preprocessing and working with it could be cumbersome, with respect to other data classes in R, such as `data.frame`.

In the next chapter, we will introduce the `xts` and `zoo` classes, formats that are flexible and easy to work with for time series data.

4
Working with zoo and xts Objects

In the previous chapter, we introduced the core class in R for time series data, the `ts` object. In this chapter, we will focus on another common data structure for time series data—the `zoo` class and its extension and the `xts` class, from the **zoo** and **xts** packages respectively. Those two classes are popular in the domain of financial time series analysis (that is, stock prices, indices, and so on), mainly due to their index format, which can store external date and time objects such as the `Date`, `POSIXct/lt`, `yearmon`, and `yearqtr` classes. Throughout this chapter, we will introduce methods and techniques for creating, manipulating, and visualizing `zoo` and `xts` objects.

In this chapter, we will cover the following topics:

- Creating, working with, and manipulating `zoo` and `xts` objects
- The attributes of the `zoo` and `xts` classes
- The `yearmon` and `yearqtr` time classes
- Visualizing `zoo` and `xts` objects

Technical requirement

The following packages will be used in this chapter:

- **xts**: Version 0.11-2 and above
- **zoo**: Version 1.8-5 and above

You can access the codes for this chapter from the following link:

```
https://github.com/PacktPublishing/Hands-On-Time-Series-Analysis-with-R/tree/
master/Chapter04
```

The zoo class

The **zoo** package provides a framework for working with regular and irregular time series data. This includes the zoo class, an indexed object for storing time series data, and a set of functions for creating, preprocessing, and visualizing time series data. Similar to the ts and mts classes, the zoo class is comprised of two components:

- **Data structure**: A vector (for univariate time series data) or matrix (for multivariance time series data) format
- **Index vector**: This stores the series observation's corresponding index

On the other hand, unlike the ts class, the index of the zoo class has a flexible structure, as it can store different date and time classes, such as Date, POSIXct/lt, yearmon or yearqtr, as indices.

 yearmon and yearqtr are two index classes for regular time series data. The yearmon class is suitable for representing a monthly time series when there is no meaning for the day or time for which the observations were captured. Similarly, the yearqtr class is suitable for representing quarterly time series data. In this case, the class describes the year and quarter in which the observations were captured.

The Brent Crude Oil Prices series from the **TSstudio** package is an example of a zoo object. Let's load and review the main characteristics of the series:

```
library(TSstudio)

data(EURO_Brent)
library(zoo)
```

The ts_info function from the **TSstudio** package, which we introduced in the previous chapter, also supports the zoo and xts classes. We will utilize this to get a summary of the EURO_Brent dataset:

```
ts_info(EURO_Brent)
##  The EURO_Brent series is a zoo object with 1 variable and 380
observations
##  Frequency: monthly
##  Start time: May 1987
##  End time: Dec 2018
```

As you can see from the output of the `ts_info` function, the `EURO_Brent` series is a monthly series with `380` observations. In addition, the index of the series uses the month and the year of the observation. We will discuss the attributes of the `zoo` object and its index in the following section.

The zoo class attributes

The `zoo` class can handle both regular (where the time intervals between the observations are equally spaced) and irregular time series data. The `zoo` object automatically identifies whether the series is regular or not based on the index of the object, and will classify it accordingly.

The classification of the `zoo` object to regular or irregular can be observed by the class of the object:

```
class (EURO_Brent)

## [1] "zooreg" "zoo"
```

In this case, you can see that the object has two classes: `zoo` and `zooreg`. The `zooreg` class is the indication that the object was classified as a regular time series.

 You should note that, in some cases, the `zoo` function won't be able to identify that the object is regular time series data due to the index structure. For example, if the input series is monthly and is captured on the first of each month, it won't necessarily be classified as regular, although we could consider it regular. This is mainly because the number of days in each month varies (28 days in February and 30 or 31 days in the rest of the year), which will cause the index to be unequally spaced over time.

The `zoo` class supports some of the **stats** package functions, which were introduced in `Chapter 3`, *The Time Series Object*, in retrieving the different attributes of the object. Those functions, such as the `frequency` or `cycle` functions, are applicable only if the object was classified as `zooreg`. For example, we can pull the frequency and cycle units of the series with the `frequency` and `cycle` functions:

```
frequency(EURO_Brent)
## [1] 12

head(cycle(EURO_Brent), 12)
## May 1987 Jun 1987 Jul 1987 Aug 1987 Sep 1987 Oct 1987 Nov 1987 Dec 1987
##        5        6        7        8        9       10       11       12
```

```
## Jan 1988 Feb 1988 Mar 1988 Apr 1988
##       1         2        3        4
```

Similarly, we can retrieve the starting, ending, and index units of the `zoo` object with the `start`, `end`, and `time` functions:

```
start(EURO_Brent)
## [1] "May 1987"

end(EURO_Brent)
## [1] "Dec 2018"

head(time(EURO_Brent), 12)
##  [1] "May 1987" "Jun 1987" "Jul 1987" "Aug 1987" "Sep 1987" "Oct 1987"
##  [7] "Nov 1987" "Dec 1987" "Jan 1988" "Feb 1988" "Mar 1988" "Apr 1988"
```

You can see that the output of those functions is consistently aligned to the structure of the index, which, in this case, is the `yearmon` class.

The index of the zoo object

One of the main features of the `zoo` class is the unique structure of its index. Unlike the index of the `ts` class, the `zoo` index supports the use of external date and time objects as the series index. The main advantage of this method is that it allows us to preserve the original index format (for example, `Date`, `POSIXct/lt`, and so on) when transforming a time series object from a different format, such as `data.frame`. Furthermore, it can store more granular information about the timestamp of the series as opposed to the `ts` index, which is limited to two elements. This will become handy when you are working with high-frequency (that is, a high number of observations per cycle unit) time series data, such as the `hourly` series. We will continue to use the `EURO_Brent` series to review the main features of the `index` function. We will start by using the `index` function from the **zoo** package to view the first observations of the series index:

```
head(index(EURO_Brent))
## [1] "May 1987" "Jun 1987" "Jul 1987" "Aug 1987" "Sep 1987" "Oct 1987"
```

Generally, you can see that the output of the `index` function is similar to the output of the `time` function that we used before. However, the `zoo` index is an independent object, therefore it has its own `attributes` and `class` functions. We will use these `class` and `attributes` functions to review the characteristics of the series index:

```
class(index(EURO_Brent))
## [1] "yearmon"
```

```
attributes(index(EURO_Brent))
## $class
## [1] "yearmon"
```

As the `zoo` index is an independent object, you can convert it to other classes as long as it is applicable. Since the `EURO_Brent` series has a monthly frequency, we can transform the index from a `yearmon` object to a `Date` object:

```
index(EURO_Brent) <- as.Date(index(EURO_Brent))

head(EURO_Brent)
## 1987-05-01 1987-06-01 1987-07-01 1987-08-01 1987-09-01 1987-10-01
##      18.58      18.86      19.86      18.98      18.31      18.76

class(index(EURO_Brent))
## [1] "Date"
```

Working with date and time objects

Date and time objects are some of the core elements of the time series object, as they set series attributes (that is, frequency, cycle, and so on) and help to index series observations. The **zoo** package provides us with a set of utility functions for handling and preprocessing date and time objects. In addition, the package provides us with two types of `date` objects, `yearmon` and `yearqtr`, for indexing a monthly and quarterly series, respectively. `as.yearmon` and `as.yearqtr` are two conversion functions that allow us to convert `Date` objects to `yearmon` and `yearqtr` objects, respectively. The following example demonstrates the conversion of a `Date` object to a `yearmon` object with the `as.yearmon` function. First, let's create a sequence of 12 dates, representing the beginning of each month in 2019, with the `seq.Date` function:

```
monthly_dates <- seq.Date(from = as.Date("2019-01-01"), length.out = 12, by
= "month")

head(monthly_dates)
```

We will get the following output:

```
## [1] "2019-01-01" "2019-02-01" "2019-03-01" "2019-04-01" "2019-05-01"
## [6] "2019-06-01"
```

Next, we will use the `as.yearmon` function to convert the `monthly_dates` object to a `yearmon` object:

```
monthly_yearmon <- as.yearmon(monthly_dates)

head(monthly_yearmon)
```

We will get the following output:

```
## [1] "Jan 2019" "Feb 2019" "Mar 2019" "Apr 2019" "May 2019" "Jun 2019"
```

In a similar manner, you can convert a sequence of dates spaced by three months (that is, a quarter) to a `yearqtr` object with the `as.yearqtr` function. The use of the `yearmon` and `yearqtr` classes, in my mind, provides a more concise representation of the monthly or quarterly data, assuming that there is no meaning for the day element of the date.

 When converting a `Date` object to either the `yearmon` or `yearqtr` class, the day element of the original object is lost. Conversion back to a `Date` object can be done with the `as.Date` function, which, by default, will assign the first day of the month as the day element of the object.

Another useful function is the `as.Date.ts` function, which allows us to convert the timestamp (or index) of a `ts` object to a `Date` object when applicable (for example, in a monthly series). For example, let's load the `USgas` series, which represents the US monthly consumption of natural gas, from the **TSstudio** package and convert the series timestamp to a `Date` object:

```
data(USgas)

head(time(USgas))
```

We will get the following output:

```
## [1] 2000.000 2000.083 2000.167 2000.250 2000.333 2000.417
```

Let's now use the `head` function to view the output of the `as.Date.ts` function for the `USgas` series:

```
head(as.Date.ts(USgas))
```

We will get the following output:

```
## [1] "2000-01-01" "2000-02-01" "2000-03-01" "2000-04-01" "2000-05-01"
## [6] "2000-06-01"
```

Creating a zoo object

Creating a zoo object is relatively simple and follows the same logic as the ts function we introduced in the previous chapter. Generally, there are two methods for creating a zoo object:

- Convert an existing time series object from a different class by using the as.zoo function. This function supports a variety of time series classes, such as ts and xts.
- Create a zoo object with the zoo function, using a numeric vector as an input.

We will start with a simple example of converting a data.frame object to a zoo object with the zoo function. We will use the US_indicators dataset as an input object. Let's load the US_indicators series from the **TSstudio** package again, and review its structure:

```
data(US_indicators)

str(US_indicators)
```

We will get the following output:

```
## 'data.frame':    517 obs. of  3 variables:
## $ Date             : Date, format: "1976-01-31" "1976-02-29" ...
## $ Vehicle Sales    : num  885 995 1244 1191 1203 ...
## $ Unemployment Rate: num  8.8 8.7 8.1 7.4 6.8 8 7.8 7.6 7.4 7.2 ...
```

You should recall that this dataset represents the monthly vehicle sales and the unemployment rate in the US since 1976. Next, we will use the zoo function to convert the second column of the data.frame object (Vehicle Sales) to a zoo object. Since this is a monthly series, we will set the frequency argument of the zoo function to 12:

```
Vehicle_Sales1 <- zoo(x = US_indicators$`Vehicle Sales`,
                      frequency = 12)
```

We can review the characteristics of the new object with the `class`, `frequency`, and `head` functions:

```
class(Vehicle_Sales1)
## [1] "zooreg" "zoo"

frequency(Vehicle_Sales1)
## [1] 12

head(Vehicle_Sales1)
## Jan 0001 Jan 0002 Jan 0003 Jan 0004 Jan 0005 Jan 0006
## 885.2 994.7 1243.6 1191.2 1203.2 1254.7
```

By default, if not assigning an index with the input object, the `zoo` function sets the object's index based on the `frequency` setting. In the case of a monthly or quarterly series, the `zoo` function sets the index as `yearmon` or `yearqtr`, respectively. Otherwise, it will define a sequence of ordered integers as the index (that is, *1, 2, ..., t*, for a series with *t* observations).

The `order.by` argument of the `zoo` function can be used to set the `index` operator of the output object. In the case of the vehicle sales series, we can assign the `Date` object with the `order.by` argument as the series index:

```
Vehicle_Sales2 <- zoo(x = US_indicators$`Vehicle Sales`,
                      order.by = US_indicators$Date,
                      frequency = 12)
```

As we can see in the following output, the `order.by` argument persevered with the attributes of the original series and set the series index as an original `Date` object:

```
head(Vehicle_Sales2)
## 1976-01-31 1976-02-29 1976-03-31 1976-04-30 1976-05-31 1976-06-30
##      885.2      994.7     1243.6     1191.2     1203.2     1254.7

class(index(Vehicle_Sales2))
## [1] "Date"
```

In addition to the `zoo` function, the package provides the `as.zoo` function, a transformation function of a variety of time series classes (such as `ts`, `fts`, and `xts`), to a `zoo` class. For instance, we can use the `as.zoo` function to convert the `USgas` series from a `ts` object to a `zoo` object.

You should recall that the `USgas` series represents the US monthly natural gas consumption since January 2000, and this series is available in the **TSstudio** package. The conversion process with the `as.zoo` function is straightforward:

```
data(USgas)

USgas_zoo <- as.zoo(USgas)
```

We will use the `ts_info` function to compare the main characteristics of the original and the transformed objects:

```
ts_info(USgas)
##   The USgas series is a ts object with 1 variable and 227 observations
 ##   Frequency: 12
 ##   Start time: 2000 1
 ##   End time: 2018 11

ts_info(USgas_zoo)
##   The USgas_zoo series is a zoo object with 1 variable and 227
observations
 ##   Frequency: monthly
 ##   Start time: Jan 2000
 ##   End time: Nov 2018
```

You will notice from the output of the original and transformed objects that the `as.zoo` function is automatically mapped and transformed from the original index of the `ts` object to the `yearmon` object.

As previously mentioned, the `zoo` class supports both regular and irregular time series data, where the `zooreg` class indicates that the `zoo` object is a regular time series. Generally, the **zoo** package defines three types of time series structures:

- **The irregular time series**: This is any time series data where the time intervals between the series observations are unequally spaced
- **The strictly regular time series**: This is any time series where all the observations of the series are equally spaced
- **The underlying regularity time series**: This is any time series object that is created from a regular time series, such as a subset of a regular series

While all three types are defined as a `zoo` class, only the last two have the additional attribute of the `zooreg` class.

If an object has only the `zoo` attribute, this does not necessarily imply that the object is an irregular time series data object. On the other hand, whenever an object has both of the attributes (`zoo` and `zooreg`), this implies that the object is a regular time series object (according to the definition of the **zoo** package).

The `zoo` function can identify whether the input series has the characteristics of a regular time series data object only if the following two inputs occur:

- The index defines a date or time object with the `order.by` argument that does not leave room for ambiguity (for example, a `yearmon` class for a monthly frequency)
- The frequency of the series is appropriately set with the `frequency` argument

Using those two inputs, the `zoo` function can identify the characteristics of the series and classify it accordingly.

The `is.regular` function can be used for identifying whether a `zoo` object is regular or not. If the `strict` argument of the function is set to `TRUE`, the function will test whether the object is strictly regular. For example, we can examine the `zoo` objects that we have used so far with the `is.regular` function and test whether they are strictly regular:

```
is.regular(EURO_Brent, strict = TRUE)
## [1] FALSE

is.regular(Vehicle_Sales1, strict = TRUE)
## [1] TRUE

is.regular(Vehicle_Sales2, strict = TRUE)
## [1] FALSE

is.regular(USgas_zoo, strict = TRUE)
## [1] TRUE
```

Both the `EURO_Brent` and `Vehicle_Sales2` are not strictly regular, as their index is a `Date` object (as opposed to a `yearmon` object). The use of a `Date` object as an index creates some ambiguity, as the distance between each observation could be either 28 or 29 (on a leap year) days during February, and 30 or 31 days throughout the rest of the year. On the other hand, since the frequency of those objects is well defined, they will be considered to be regular (but not strictly regular):

```
is.regular(EURO_Brent, strict = FALSE)
## [1] TRUE
```

```
is.regular(Vehicle_Sales2, strict = FALSE)
## [1] TRUE
```

Working with multiple time series objects

Creating a multivariate time series `zoo` object is straightforward and is fairly similar to the process of creating a univariate time series object, as shown previously. The main distinction between the two object types is that, in the case of a multivariate time series object, the input contains a multiple columns object (as opposed to a single vector). In the following example, we will use the `US_indicators` dataset again, but this time we will transform both the vehicle sales and unemployment rate into a single `zoo` object:

```
US_indicators_zoo <- zoo(x = US_indicators[,c("Vehicle Sales",
"Unemployment Rate")],
                          frequency = 12,
                          order.by = US_indicators$Date)
```

We will use the `ts_info` and `head` functions to review the characteristics of the new object:

```
ts_info(US_indicators_zoo)
##   The US_indicators_zoo series is a zoo object with 2 variables and 517
observations
##   Frequency: monthly
##   Start time: 1976-01-31
##   End time: 2019-01-31

head(US_indicators_zoo)
##             Vehicle Sales Unemployment Rate
## 1976-01-31          885.2               8.8
## 1976-02-29          994.7               8.7
## 1976-03-31         1243.6               8.1
## 1976-04-30         1191.2               7.4
## 1976-05-31         1203.2               6.8
## 1976-06-30         1254.7               8.0
```

Similarly, the new object is a regular time series object (but not `strict`, as it has a `Date` index):

```
is.regular(US_indicators_zoo, strict = FALSE)
## [1] TRUE
```

The xts class

The eXtensible time series, **xts** package is an extension of the **zoo** package. It provides the `xts` class and a set of functions and tools for preprocessing, manipulating, and visualizing time series data. The `xts` class is a `zoo` object with additional attributes. Therefore, by default, any `xts` object carries `zoo` class attributes, and any of the `zoo` functions can be applied to the `xts` object. In the following examples, we will use the `Michigan_CS` series, which is an `xts` object that represents the famous consumer sentiment index of the University of Michigan since 1980. This series is available on the **TSstudio** package. We will start by loading the series and will review its main characteristics:

```
data(Michigan_CS)

ts_info(Michigan_CS)
##  The Michigan_CS series is a xts object with 1 variable and 468
observations
##  Frequency: monthly
##  Start time: Jan 1980
##  End time: Dec 2018

class(Michigan_CS)
## [1] "xts" "zoo"
```

You can see from the preceding class function output that the class of the series is both `xts` and `zoo`, which is the standard attribute of the `xts` object. Therefore, any of the functions from either the `zoo` or the `stats` functions we used before can also be applied on the `xts` objects. An example of this is shown in the following code snippet:

```
class(index(Michigan_CS))
## [1] "yearmon"

frequency(Michigan_CS)
## [1] 12

is.regular(Michigan_CS, strict = TRUE)
## [1] TRUE
```

One of the main improvements of the `xts` class with respect to the `zoo` class is the matrix format structure of the object (as opposed to the vector representation of the `zoo` class):

```
head(Michigan_CS)
##            [,1]
## Jan 1980 67.0
## Feb 1980 66.9
## Mar 1980 56.5
```

```
## Apr 1980 52.7
## May 1980 51.7
## Jun 1980 58.7
```

This is more than just an aesthetic representation of the object; it is easier to extract or subset data from this code. Creating a univariate or multivariate time series object with the **xts** package follows the same process as in the **zoo** package. For example, we can transform the US_indicators data.frame object to an xts object with the xts function:

```
library(xts)

US_indicators_xts <- xts(x = US_indicators[,c("Vehicle Sales",
"Unemployment Rate")],
                         frequency = 12,
                         order.by = US_indicators$Date)

head(US_indicators_xts)
```

We will get the following output:

```
##            Vehicle Sales Unemployment Rate
## 1976-01-31         885.2               8.8
## 1976-02-29         994.7               8.7
## 1976-03-31        1243.6               8.1
## 1976-04-30        1191.2               7.4
## 1976-05-31        1203.2               6.8
## 1976-06-30        1254.7               8.0
```

The xts class attributes

Generally, as the xts object is also a zoo object, it automatically inherits all the attributes and functionality of the zoo class. Therefore, all the attributes of the zoo object that we have introduced can also be applied to the xts object. The main distinction between the two classes is related to the structure of the univariate time series object. While the zoo object has a vector structure, the xts object has a matrix structure. The uniqueness of the xts object is related to the rich functionality of the **xts** package.

The xts functionality

The **xts** package provides us with a set of utility functions that make working with the xts object seamless. In the following examples, we will apply some of the main utility functions to the Michigan_CS series.

We will start with the `periodicity` function.

The periodicity function

The output of the function is a combination of the `frequency`, `start`, and `end` functions which we used with the `ts` and `zoo` objects, as this returns text with a short description of those attributes:

```
periodicity(Michigan_CS)
## Monthly periodicity from Jan 1980 to Dec 2018
```

Manipulating the object index

The **xts** package provides us with a set of functions for handling the index of the `xts` object. The `indexClass` family of functions (use `?indexClass` to get the full list of functions) provides us with a set of tools for extracting or replacing the `xts` class index. The `indexClass` function itself returns the index class of the object:

```
indexClass(Michigan_CS)
## [1] "yearmon"
```

The `converIndex` function, as its name implies, converts the object index class. For instance, we can utilize the function to convert the index of the `Michigan_CS` series from `yearmon` to `Date`:

```
Michigan_CS <- convertIndex(Michigan_CS, "Date")

indexClass(Michigan_CS)
## [1] "Date"
```

In addition, the `indexClass` function provides a set of functions for extracting the date or time component of the object index. For example, the `.indexmon` function returns the corresponding months of the index:

```
head(.indexmon(Michigan_CS), 12)
## [1]  0  1  2  3  4  5  6  7  8  9 10 11
```

You will notice that the count of the index starts at 0, which, in this case, corresponds to the month of January. Another useful function is `indexFormat`, which allows us to modify the index format.

In the next example, we will utilize the function to modify the index format from **year, month, day (y-m-d)** to **month, day, year (m-d-y)**:

```
indexFormat(Michigan_CS) <- "%m-%d-%Y"

head(Michigan_CS)
```

We will get the following output:

```
##              [,1]
## 01-01-1980 67.0
## 02-01-1980 66.9
## 03-01-1980 56.5
## 04-01-1980 52.7
## 05-01-1980 51.7
## 06-01-1980 58.7
```

Subsetting an xts object based on the index properties

In many instances, you may want or need to extract or subset some elements or parts of your series. A typical example of this would be extracting the first or last 12 months of the series, or splitting it into the training and testing partitions. One of the strengths of the xts class is the ability to extract data from an object in a seamless way without the need for a window or any other function (as opposed to the ts class we saw in the previous chapter). As the xts class is a semi-data frame, it is relatively simple to manipulate or extract data by using a data.frame style. Moreover, it is possible to retrieve data based on a specific time range using the series index. For example, let's say that you wish to extract the first 12 months of the vehicle sales data from the US_indicators dataset that we created. We will start with the data frame style extraction of the first 12 months:

```
Vehicle_Sales_xts1 <- US_indicators_xts$`Vehicle Sales`[1:12]

ts_info(Vehicle_Sales_xts1)
```

We will get the following output:

```
##  The Vehicle_Sales_xts1 series is a xts object with 1 variable and 12
observations
##  Frequency: monthly
##  Start time: 1976-01-31
##  End time: 1976-12-31
```

The `xts` object supports text-based queries for subsetting the series. For instance, we can extract the first year of the series by specifying the year value (that is, `1976`):

```
Vehicle_Sales_xts2 <- US_indicators_xts$`Vehicle Sales`["1976"]

ts_info(Vehicle_Sales_xts2)
```

We will get the following output:

```
##   The Vehicle_Sales_xts2 series is a xts object with 1 variable and 12
observations
##   Frequency: monthly
##   Start time: 1976-01-31
##   End time: 1976-12-31
```

Furthermore, it is possible to have a more granular subset by using other elements of the `index` object. For instance, if you wish to extract the first 6 months of the year 1976, you can use the following structure:

```
Vehicle_Sales_xts3 <- US_indicators_xts$`Vehicle Sales`["1976-01/06"]

ts_info(Vehicle_Sales_xts3)
```

We will get the following output:

```
##   The Vehicle_Sales_xts3 series is a xts object with 1 variable and 6
observations
##   Frequency: monthly
##   Start time: 1976-01-31
##   End time: 1976-06-30
```

Manipulating the zoo and xts objects

One of the main advantages of the `zoo` class and, in particular, the `xts` class (with respect to the `ts` object), is their friendly and simple structure. This allows us to preprocess and manipulate these types of objects in a seamless manner. Both the **zoo** and the **xts** packages provide a variety of utility functions for working with these types of objects. In this section, we will introduce some of the main functions for manipulating the `zoo` and `xts` objects.

Merging time series objects

In some instances, you may want to join or merge different series into a single object. Both the **zoo** and **xts** packages provide functions for merging a time series object (including merging mixed classes, such as zoo or xts).

The merging process is based on identifying any overlap between the input indices. Therefore, the first step is to identify the type or structure of the input indices before starting the merging process. If the indices do not follow the same structure, a transformation of the indices is required. The main difference between the merge.xts and merge.zoo functions is that the first provides the ability to set the type of join in a SQL-like style. This includes the common join options, such as outer, inner, left, or right, which are defined by the join argument.

For example, let's assume that you want to merge the Michigan_CS series (an xts object) with the EURO_Brent series (a zoo object). The first step is to identify the structure of the indices of both of the objects:

```
indexClass(Michigan_CS)
## [1] "Date"

class(index(EURO_Brent))
## [1] "Date"
```

As both of the indices are Date objects, we can move forward to the next step and observe whether there is any overlap between the indices of those two objects, as it makes sense to merge time series objects whenever there is some level of overlap between the series. We will utilize the ts_info function to observe the date range of the indices:

```
ts_info(Michigan_CS)
##   The Michigan_CS series is a xts object with 1 variable and 468
observations
##   Frequency: monthly
##   Start time: 1980-01-01
##   End time: 2018-12-01

ts_info(EURO_Brent)
##   The EURO_Brent series is a zoo object with 1 variable and 380
observations
##   Frequency: monthly
##   Start time: 1987-05-01
##   End time: 2018-12-01
```

You can see in the preceding output that both of the series have an overlap between their indices, as the `Michigan_CS` series starts in January 1980 and ends in December 2018, while the `EURO_Brend` series starts in May 1987 and ends in December 2018.

Therefore, in this case, the merge process is straightforward. The next step is to set the `merge.xts` function and merge those objects:

```
xts_merge_outer <- merge.xts(Michigan_CS = Michigan_CS,
  EURO_Brent = EURO_Brent,
  join = "outer" )

ts_info(xts_merge_outer)
```

We will get the following output:

```
##  The xts_merge_outer series is a xts object with 2 variables and 468
observations
##  Frequency: monthly
##  Start time: 1980-01-01
## End time: 2018-12-01
```

Since we applied an outer join, the merged object will start at the earliest starting point (January 1980) and end at the latest (December 2018) of the two series timestamps. As the starting point of the `EURO_Brent` series is about 7 years after the ones in the `Michigan_CS` series (May 1987 versus January 1980), all those missing observations will be filled by an `NA` value:

```
head(xts_merge_outer["1987"])
##              Michigan_CS EURO_Brent
## 01-01-1987         90.4         NA
## 02-01-1987         90.2         NA
## 03-01-1987         90.8         NA
## 04-01-1987         92.8         NA
## 05-01-1987         91.1       18.58
## 06-01-1987         91.5       18.86
```

Similarly, when setting the `join` argument to `inner`, the merged object will be bound by the overlapping period of the two series:

```
xts_merge_inner <- merge.xts(Michigan_CS = Michigan_CS,
                          EURO_Brent = EURO_Brent,
                          join = "inner" )

ts_info(xts_merge_inner)
```

We will get the following output:

```
##  The xts_merge_inner series is a xts object with 2 variables and 380
observations
##  Frequency: monthly
##  Start time: 1987-05-01
##  End time: 2018-12-01
```

Let's now use the head function to check the output:

```
head(xts_merge_inner)
```

We will get the following output:

```
##             Michigan_CS EURO_Brent
## 05-01-1987         91.1      18.58
## 06-01-1987         91.5      18.86
## 07-01-1987         93.7      19.86
## 08-01-1987         94.4      18.98
## 09-01-1987         93.6      18.31
## 10-01-1987         89.3      18.76
```

Rolling windows

In some instances, you may want to apply some mathematical calculations to consecutive observations of a series with a rolling window. A typical application for the use of a rolling window is the moving average or smoothing functions. Those functions are based on the use of a rolling window to calculate the average of each observation with its n consecutive observations. We will discuss the moving average and its applications in detail in the next chapter. The rollapply function from the **zoo** package provides this functionality, as it applies a mathematical function with a rolling window on a series. The function's main arguments are:

- data: This defines the input series
- width: This is an integer that sets the width of the rolling window
- align: This defines the structure of the rolling window; the argument is set to center by default
- FUN: This is a function to apply along with the rolling window

For a series with *t* observations, a rolling window with a width of *n* is defined as a function that subsets each observation of the series (when applicable) with its *n-1* neighbors' observations. The subset of the neighbors' observations is defined by the window structure. Common types of window structure are as follows:

- **Center**: The subset of the *t* observation of the series includes the *t* observation and its *n-1/2* preceding and following observations (assuming that *n* is an odd number). For example, for a window of size 3, the rolling window of the *t* observation of the series includes the observations *t-1*, *t*, and *t +1*.
- **Left/Right**: The subset of the *t* observation of the series includes the *t* observation and its *n-1* preceding/following observations, respectively.

For example, we can calculate the 3 months, moving average for the EURO_Brent series by using the rollapply function. By default, the rollapply function uses a center window. Therefore, for a 3-month rolling window, the function subsets the *t* observation of the series along with the preceding observation, *t-1*, and the next observation, *t+1*:

```
EURO_Brent_3ma <- rollapply(EURO_Brent,
                            width = 3,
                            FUN = mean)
```

Let's review the characteristics of the new series with the ts_info function:

```
ts_info(EURO_Brent_3ma)
```

We will get the following output:

```
##  The EURO_Brent_3ma series is a zoo object with 1 variable and 378
observations
##  Frequency: monthly
##  Start time: 1987-06-01
##  End time: 2018-11-01
```

You will note that the new series is missing the first and last observations of the original series. This is related to the window size and structure. In this case, as we used a rolling window of size 3, we cannot create a window for the first and last observations.

Creating lags

As with the `ts` object, creating lags for the `zoo` and `xts` objects can be done with the `lag` function from the **stats** package. You may recall that the function's main parameter is the `k` parameter, which sets the number of lags (for negative values) or the number of leading observations (for positive values). For example, we can create a 3-month lag with the `lag` function for the `EURO_Brent` series and merge it with the original series:

```
EURO_Brent_lag3 <- lag(EURO_Brent, k = -3)

EURO_Brent_merge <- merge.zoo(EURO_Brent, EURO_Brent_lag3)

head(EURO_Brent_merge)
```

We will get the following output:

```
##              EURO_Brent EURO_Brent_lag3
## 1987-05-01       18.58              NA
## 1987-06-01       18.86              NA
## 1987-07-01       19.86              NA
## 1987-08-01       18.98           18.58
## 1987-09-01       18.31           18.86
## 1987-10-01       18.76           19.86
```

Aggregating the zoo and xts objects

Aggregating the `zoo` and `xts` objects is straightforward with the `aggregate` function. The aggregation process can be done by defining the aggregate level with the `by` argument (that is, the new frequency unit of the `aggregate` object), and by setting the `FUN` argument to the `sum` function. For example, let's aggregate the `USgas_zoo` series we created previously from monthly to quarterly:

```
USgas_zoo_qtr <-  aggregate(USgas_zoo,
                            by = as.yearqtr,
                            FUN = sum)
```

As you can see, we set the index of the new series as quarterly with the `as.yearqtr` function from the **zoo** package. We can review the `aggregate` object characteristics with the `ts_info` function:

```
ts_info(USgas_zoo)
```

We will get the following output:

```
##  The USgas_zoo series is a zoo object with 1 variable and 227
observations
##  Frequency: monthly
##  Start time: Jan 2000
##  End time: Nov 2018
```

In a similar manner, we can aggregate the USgas_zoo object to a yearly frequency by using the year function from the **lubridate** package as the new object index:

```
library(lubridate)

USgas_zoo_yr <- aggregate(USgas_zoo,
 by = year,
 FUN = sum)

head(USgas_zoo_yr)
```

We will get the following output:

```
##     2000     2001     2002     2003     2004     2005
## 22538.6 22238.8 23027.0 22276.5 22402.5 22014.5
```

Plotting zoo and xts objects

As we discussed in the previous chapter, there are two main approaches for plotting time series objects such as the zoo and xts objects:

- **Direct**: Using built-in or customized functions to visualize either the zoo or xts objects, such as plot.zoo and plot.xts functions, or other visualization tools from the **TSstudio** or **dygraph** packages
- **Indirect**: By transforming or reformatting the structure of the object and using some data visualization packages, such as **ggplot2**, **plotly**, and **rbokeh**

 Note that plotting the zoo or xts objects with the **TSstudio** or **dygraph** packages follows the exact same process as we demonstrated in the previous chapter with the ts object. Therefore, to avoid redundancy, we will focus in this section only on the built-in visualization functions of the **zoo** and **xts** packages.

The use of either approach depends on the user's needs and preferences, but the direct approach is simple to use, as no preprocessing or transformation steps are required.

The plot.zoo function

The `plot.zoo` function is based on the `plot` function (R has built-in plotting functions from the **graphics** package). Therefore, it is straightforward to utilize this function along with any of the `plot` function arguments (it generally makes no difference whether you are using `plot` or `plot.zoo`). For example, let's use this function to plot the `EURO_Brent` function:

```
plot.zoo(EURO_Brent,
         main = "Crude Oil Prices: Brent - Europe",
         ylab = "USD per Barrel",
         col = "blue")
```

The following graph shows the plot for the crude oil prices for the `EURO_Brent` series:

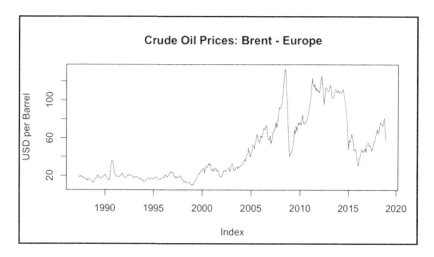

You can see that we have added the `main` and `ylab` arguments to set the plot and *y*-axis titles, respectively. The `col` argument is used to set the color of the plot. In a similar manner, you can apply the `plot.zoo` function to plot a multiple time series object.

The following example demonstrates the use of the function for plotting the `US_indicators` dataset that we transformed before into a `zoo` object:

```
plot.zoo(US_indicators_zoo,
         main = "Monthly Vehicle Sales and Unemployment Rate in the US",
         ylab = c("Vehicle Sales (Thousands of Units)", "Unemployment Rate
(%)"),
         col = c("blue", "red"))
```

We will get the following output plot:

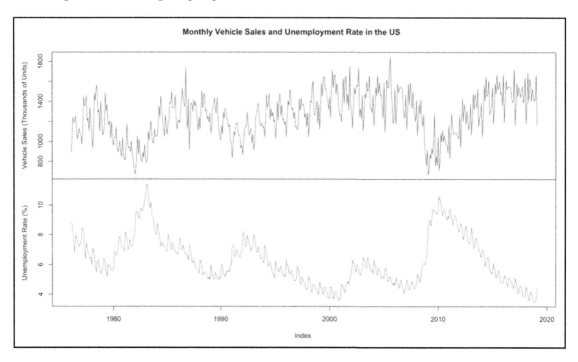

As shown in the preceding output, you can customize each plot by setting each argument with the corresponding setting for each plot.

The plot.xts function

The `plot.xts` function is also based on the `plot` function, yet it provides additional built-in functionality (with respect to the `plot.zoo` function) that makes the customization of the plot simpler. We will start with a simple plot and then demonstrate how to customize it and create additional features. Let's plot the `Michigan_CS` series:

```
plot.xts(Michigan_CS)
```

We will get the following output plot:

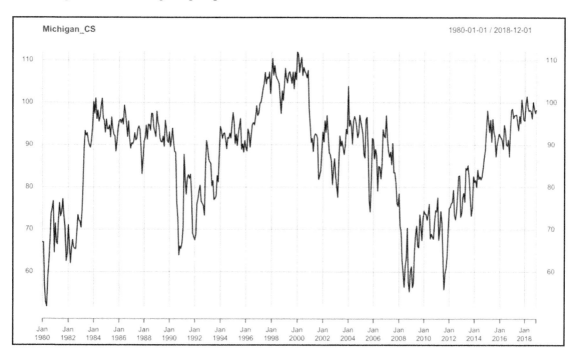

By default, the `plot.xts` function returns the index range of the series on the top right, and in the top left it returns the series name. In addition, it automatically set the x-axis ticks and provides the y-axis values from both sides of the plot. We can modify the range of the plot with the subset argument, and adjust the x-axis grid lines and the ticks intervals with the `grid.ticks.on` and `minor.ticks` arguments, respectively. We will set the interval of the x-axis grid and ticks for a year:

```
plot.xts(Michigan_CS,
         subset = "2010/",
         main = "University of Michigan Consumer Sentiment Index",
         col = "blue",
         grid.ticks.on = "years",
         minor.ticks = "years")
```

We will get the following output plot:

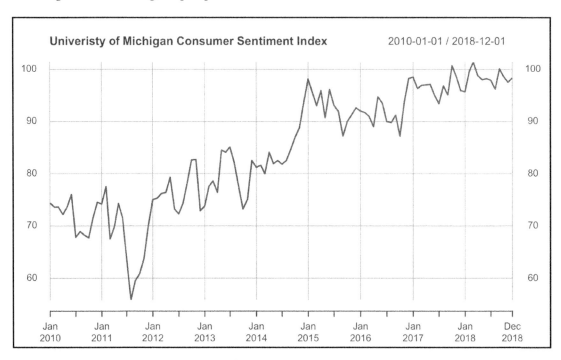

The functionality of plot.xts becomes handy when working with multiple time series objects, as it is more straightforward to customize or modify the plot's parameters. Let's plot the US_indicators dataset again; this time, we will use the xts version we created before:

```
plot.xts(US_indicators_xts,
        multi.panel = 2,
        yaxis.same = FALSE,
        grid.ticks.on = "years",
        minor.ticks = FALSE,
        main = "Monthly Vehicle Sales and Unemployment Rate in the US")
```

We will get the following output plot:

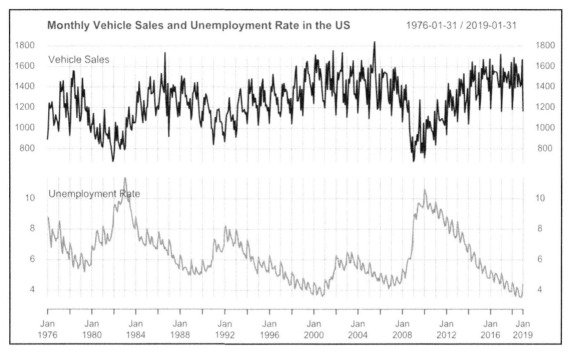

For multiple time series objects, you can either plot all the series in a single object or dedicate a separate panel for each series. The `multi.panel` argument allows you to set the number of panels to use in the plot. It would make sense to set all the plots in a single panel when all the series are within the same range.

In the preceding case, as the two series have different scales of units (the units of the vehicle sales series are in thousands, whereas the unemployment rate is in percentages), we used a separate panel for each plot by setting the `multi.panel` argument to 2.

In the last example, we will connect all the elements we learned about in this chapter and create a summary plot of the `USgas` dataset. The summary plot will include the following features:

- A plot of the series itself.
- A moving average of the series. This will provide a rough estimate about the trend of the series (don't worry if, at this point, you are not familiar with those terms; we will discuss trend estimation and smoothing methods in detail with the moving average in the next chapter). We will use the `rollapply` function to calculate the moving average of the series.

- The monthly percentage change of the series. We will use the `lag` function to calculate the first lag of the series and use that to calculate the monthly change of the series over time.
- The year-over-year percentage growth of each observation of the series, by using the yearly lag (that is, lag 12) of the series to calculate it.

We will start by converting the `USgas` series from a `ts` object to an `xts` object with the `as.xts` function:

```
USgas_xts <- as.xts(USgas)

indexClass(USgas_xts)
```

We will get the following output:

```
## [1] "yearmon"
```

You can see that the index of the transformed object is a `yearmon` object. The next step is to calculate the moving average of the series with the `rollapply` function. We will set the width of the rolling window to `12`:

```
USgas_xts_ma <- rollapply(USgas_xts,
                          width = 12,
                          FUN = mean)
```

We can now merge the two series (`USgas_xts` and `USgas_xts_ma`) to a multiple time series object with the `merge.xts` function:

```
USgas_merge <- merge.xts(USgas = USgas_xts,
                         USgas_Smooth = USgas_xts_ma)
```

Last but not least, we will calculate the monthly percentage difference and the year-over-year growth by utilizing the `lag` function:

```
USgas_month_diff <- 100 * (USgas_xts / lag(USgas_xts, n = 1) - 1)
USgas_yoy_diff <- 100 * (USgas_xts / lag(USgas_xts, n = 12) - 1)
```

Now, one we have prepared all the required inputs for the summary plot, we can start to build it. One of the downsides of the `plot` function is that it does not support pipes (that is, `%>%`), therefore, the plot and its additional features must run step by step in a sequential order. The first step is to create the main plot, which will include both the main series, the US natural gas consumption, and its moving average (using the merged data of both of these series). As we wish to overlay the moving average of the series on top of it, we will set the `multi.panel` argument to `FALSE`:

```
plot.xts(USgas_merge,
         main = "US Natural Gas Consumption Summary",
         multi.panel = FALSE,
         col = c("black", "blue"),
         ylim = c(1400, 3700))
```

Note that the `col` argument automatically aligns the colors input according to the order of the input series (that is, black for the first series and blue for the second). Generally, the setting of the *y*-axis range with the `ylim` argument is not required, as it automatically adjusts it. However, in order to be able to fit the plot legend, we will slightly increase the *y*-axis range. The next step is to add the graphs of the monthly percentage change and the year-over-year growth to the plot by using the `lines` function:

```
lines(USgas_month_diff ,
      col = "red",
      type = "h",
      on = NA,
      main = "Monthly Difference (%)")

lines(USgas_yoy_diff ,
      col = "purple",
      type = "h",
      on = NA,
      main = "YoY Growth (%)")
```

As both of those features (monthly percentage change and year-over-year growth) represent a percentage change, we will plot each feature on a separate panel using a barchart. Setting the `type` argument to `h` sets the plot as a barchart. Setting the `on` argument as `NA` adds a new panel to the existing plot. Last but not least, we will utilize the `addLegend` function from the **xts** package to add a legend to the plot:

```
addLegend("topleft",
          on=1,
  legend.names = c("Gas Consumption", "Moving Average", "Monthly Diff. (%)",
  "YoY Change (%)"),
  lty=c(1, 1), lwd=c(2, 1),
  col=c("black", "blue", "red", "purple"))
```

The final output of the plot is as follows:

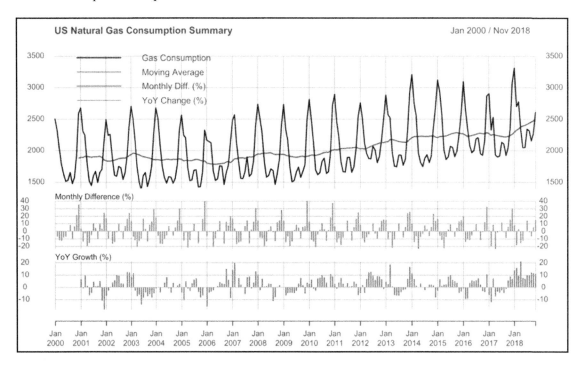

xts, zoo, or ts – which one to use?

It depends.

There is no doubt that out of the three objects we have introduced so far (ts, zoo, and xts), the xts class is the most advanced and friendly to use. Moreover, since the xts class is also a zoo class with additional functionalities and improvements, the question actually should be xts or ts—which one to use? This mainly depends on the type of packages and applications you are using for time series analysis. However, in my mind, working with xts objects has more benefits compared to ts objects, since most of the forecasting models in R support only ts objects.

On the other hand, if you're not bound by requirements or if you just want to slice and dice a time series object, it is highly recommended that you use the xts (or zoo) object. The good news here, as we saw in some instances, is that both the **xts** and **zoo** packages provide tools for transforming and working with ts objects.

Summary

In this chapter, we introduced two of the most advanced classes for time series data in R, the zoo and xts classes, and their applications. It is safe to claim that working with those objects, in particular, the xts class, is more friendly and convenient than the ts class. Their unique structure of data frames and well-organized time indices gives users seamless preprocessing and faster data querying. Furthermore, the **zoo** and **xts** packages have rich functionality and applications; more than we can cover in one chapter. Therefore, it is highly recommended that you look at the documentation and vignettes of the packages for more information.

In the next chapter, we will look at the decomposition of time series data process.

5
Decomposition of Time Series Data

Our primary focus in the previous chapters has been on the attributes and structure of time series data. Starting from this chapter, we are shifting gears and moving toward the analysis phase of time series data. This chapter focuses on one of the essential elements of time series analysis—the decomposition process of time series data to its components: the trend, seasonal, and random components. We will start with the moving average function and see its applications for smoothing time series data, removing seasonality, and estimating a series trend. In addition, we will introduce the `decompose` function and look at its applications. The topics in this chapter are an introduction to more advanced time series analysis topics that will be introduced later in the book.

In this chapter, we will cover the following topics:

- The moving average function
- Identifying time series components
- Decomposing a series down to its components

Technical requirement

The following packages will be used in this chapter:

- **forecast**: Version 8.5 and above
- **TSstudio**: Version 0.1.4 and above
- **plotly**: Version 4.8 and above
- **xts**: Version 0.11-2 and above

You can access the codes for this chapter from the following link:

```
https://github.com/PacktPublishing/Hands-On-Time-Series-Analysis-with-R/tree/
master/Chapter05
```

The moving average function

The **moving average** (**MA**) is a simple function for smoothing time series data. This function is based on averaging each observation of a series, when applicable, with its surrounding observations, that is, with a past, future, or a combination of both past and future observations, in chronological order. The output of this transformation process is a smoothed version of the original series. The MA function has a variety of applications, such as data smoothing, noise reduction, and trend estimation. Also, with some small modifications, this function can be used as a forecasting model. In `Chapter 10`, *Forecasting with Exponential Smoothing Models*, we will discuss the forecasting applications of the MA function in detail. The main components of the MA function are as follows:

- **The rolling window**: This is a generic function that slides across the series in chronological order to extract sequential subsets
- **Average function**: This is either a simple or weighted average, which is applied on each subset of the rolling window function

The characteristics of the MA function are defined by those components, and we will discuss their applications in detail.

The rolling window structure

The rolling window function plays a pivotal role in the smoothing of time series data process with the MA function, as its structure defines the sub-setting method of series observations. The most common types of window structures are as follows:

- **The one-sided window**: This is a sliding window with a width of n, which groups each observation of the series (when applicable) with its past consecutive $n-1$ observations. The following diagram demonstrates the smoothing of time series data process with a one-sided rolling window:

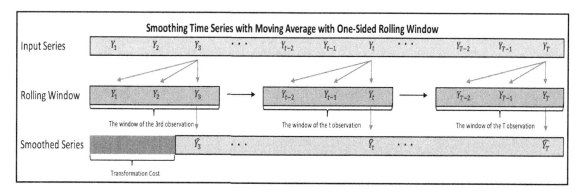

The preceding diagram shows the smoothing process of Y, time series data with T observations, with the use of a one-sided rolling window function. In this case, the rolling window function has a width value of three, and it therefore groups each observation of the series with its past consecutive observations, starting with the third observation of the series. As the previous two consecutive observations are not available for the first and second observations of the series, we cannot smooth the first and the second observations of the series. Therefore, the output of the MA function (marked in green), is missing the first two observations (marked in red), which are considered to be the cost of the transformation process when using a one-sided rolling window.

- **The two-sided window**: This defines a rolling window with a width of n, which groups each observation of the series (when applicable) with its past n_1 and future n_2 observations. If n is an odd number and n_1 is equal to n_2, we can define the two-sided rolling window as centered. Similarly, the following diagram demonstrates the smoothing of time series data process with a two-sided rolling window:

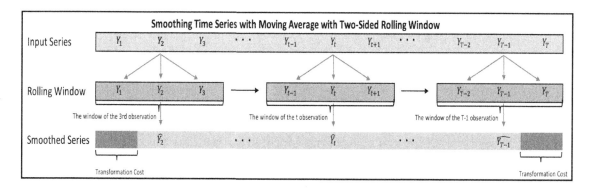

Similar to the first diagram, the second diagram describes the smoothing process of Y, time series data with T observations, but this time with the use of a two-sided rolling window function. Note that, in this case, as the window width is set to three, the `window` function groups each observation with its preceding and leading observations. You should also note that, in the case of a two-sided window with a width of three, we cannot transform the first and last observations of the series (marked in red).

Using these two examples, we can generalize the characteristics of both the one-sided and two-sided rolling window structure functions. In the following equation, $\hat{Y}_t$ represents the smoothed value of Y_t, the t observation of series Y with the use of a one-sided rolling window function with a width of n, and an arithmetic average:

$$\hat{Y}_t|n = \frac{Y_{t-n+1} + Y_{t-n+2} + \ldots + Y_t}{n}, \text{ where } t = n, \ldots, T \text{ and } n \leq T$$

Similarly, for a two-sided `window` function with a width of of n, using past n_1 and future n_2 observations, we will use the following equation:

$$\hat{Y}_t|n_1, n_2 = \frac{Y_{t-n_2} + \ldots + Y_{t-1} + Y_t + Y_{t+1} + \ldots + Y_{n2}}{n_1 + n_2 + 1}, \text{ where } t = n_1 + 1, \ldots, T - n_2, \ n = n_1 + n_2 + 1, \text{ and } n \leq T$$

The average method

The second element of the MA function, besides the window structure, is the averaging method of the window's subset. There are two types of averaging methods:

- **The arithmetic average**: This is the most common and basic method for averaging a sequence of observations. It is based on summing all the observations and dividing them by the number of observations. This method is also known as the arithmetic mean or simple average, and can be formalized with the following expression:

$$\bar{Y} = \frac{\sum_{i=1}^{n} Y_i}{n}$$

- **The weighted average**: This method is based on applying weight to each observation of the series, and can be formalized with the following equation:

$$\bar{Y}_t = \sum_{i=1}^{n} w_i Y_i$$

Here, w_i represents the corresponding weight of the i observation of Y.

A weighted average should be used with time series data when there is a systematic relationship between some observations in the series based on their timestamp distance. Chapter 7, *Correlation Analysis*, focuses on the identity of this type of systematic relationship based on correlation analysis.

The MA attributes

In addition, the MA function has two primary attributes that are derived directly from the window structure:

- **Order**: This defines the magnitude of the MA and is equal to the length of the window. In the case of the one-sided window, the width of the window is defined by n, as we are using the current observation with the past n -1 consecutive observation. (In the case of forecasting, we are using the past n observations to predict the current one. Don't worry about it now, we will return to discuss this in detail in Chapter 10, *Forecasting with Exponential Smoothing Models*). Likewise, if we are using a two-sided window function, using past n_1 and future n_2 observations, then the length of the window is $n_1 + n_2 + 1$, or $2_n + 1$ when using an equal number of past and future observations.
- **Cost**: There are no free lunches; the use of the MA comes at a cost. This cost is the loss of observations during the transformation of the origin series to the smoothed series by the MA process. This process shaves the first n observations in the case of the one-sided window, and the first n_1 and last n_2 observations in the case of the two-sided window, where n or n_1 and n_2 refer to the use of past and future observations by the window, as defined previously.

Once the parameters of the function (the window structure and average type) are set, the function starts to roll the window over the series observations (when applicable) in chronological order, to calculate the series, MAs. The observations of the new series represent the corresponding MAs of the original series in chronological order. Where the new series inherits the main characteristics of the origin series, such as the frequency and timestamp, the main applications of the MA function are the following:

- **Noise reduction**: The use of the MA method creates a smoothing effect that reduces the series variation, smoothing the random noise and outliers.

- **De-seasonalize**: In addition to the noise reduction, MAs can be used to remove the seasonal component (if any). This process has a pivotal role in the classical decomposing process, as it provides an estimation for the trend component, which is then utilized to estimate the seasonal component.
- **Forecasting**: With some small modifications, the MA function can be used to forecast the future observations of the series by averaging the past observations to estimate future values of the series. The averaging method varies from a simple average to more advanced averaging methods.

In this chapter, we will focus on the smoothing applications of the MA function. Just one word of caution before we delve into the MA function, in time series analysis, the term MA refers to two common, yet distinct methods. The MA as defined refers to the use of a smoothing function to smooth or forecast time series data. On the other hand, the second definition refers to the process of establishing a relationship between the error term of the forecasting model and the use of regression analysis.

 Throughout this book, unless stated otherwise, the term MA refers to the smoothing function, and the term MA model or MA process refers to the regression analysis of the error term (which will be one of the topics of `Chapter 11`, *Forecasting with ARIMA Models*).

The interesting thing about MA functions is their simplicity. The main two parameters to set are the window size and average type; it is relatively easy to customize a function and set it according to the user's requirements. Those unique combinations of different window structures, along with different averaging methods, create multiple types of MA functions.

In the following section, we will introduce the most common MA methods—a one-sided MA with an arithmetic average, also known as a simple MA, a two-sided MA, and, last but not least, a weighted MA.

In the following examples, we will use the US monthly vehicle sales to demonstrate the applications of each method. Let's load the dataset from the **TSstudio** package:

```
library(TSstudio)

data(USVSales)
```

Let's recall the essential characteristics of this series using the `ts_info` and `ts_plot` functions:

```
ts_info(USVSales)
```

We will get the following output:

```
##  The USVSales series is a ts object with 1 variable and 517 observations
##  Frequency: 12
##  Start time: 1976 1
##  End time: 2019 1
```

Let's now plot USVSales:

```
ts_plot(USVSales,
        title = "US Monthly Total Vehicle Sales",
        Ytitle = "Thousands of Units",
        Xtitle = "Years",
        Xgrid = TRUE,
        Ygrid = TRUE)
```

We will get the following graph:

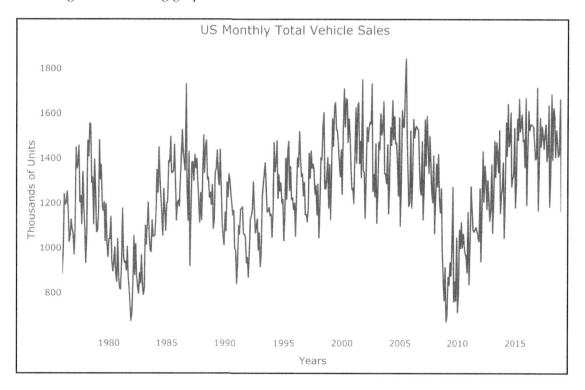

Let's now look at the simple moving average.

The simple moving average

The **simple moving average (SMA)** is one of the common MA functions, and, as the name implies, it is also one of the simplest MA functions. This transformation method is based on applying an arithmetic average on a one-sided rolling window. Hence, the rolling window groups each observation in the series (when applicable) with its previous n consecutive observations in order to calculate their arithmetic average. We can formalize the transformation process of Y_t, the t observation of the Y series, that is, a time series with T observations, with the use of an SMA function with a window width, n, by using the following formula:

$$\hat{Y}_t | n = \frac{Y_{t-n+1} + \ldots + Y_{t-1} + Y_t}{n}, \ where \ n \leq t \leq T$$

Shifting this window across all the observations in the series, in chronological order, yields a new time series, $\hat{Y}$. Where $\hat{Y}_t$ represents the corresponding average of the original series observation at time (or index) t with its past n-1 consecutive observations. The length of the window, as mentioned previously, defines the MA order and the cost of the function. In the case of SMA, the order is n, and the cost is the first n -1 observation of the series.

You can be sure that there is more than one package in R that provides an MA transformation function. Throughout this chapter, we will use the `ts_ma` function from the **TSstudio** package to demonstrate the different types of MAs. However, there is added value to building a MA function from scratch in order to get a better understanding of the mechanics of this method.

Let's dedicate a few lines of code to creating an SMA function for the time series objects. We will code the logic of the MA method by constructing the following functions:

- **The rolling window**: For simplicity, we won't use the `window` function but will mimic its applications by adding the series, its n lags to it (according to the order of the function)
- **The average function**: This returns the average of each window and constructs a new series

We will start with the rolling window `lags` function:

```
# The lags function return the series with its l lags
lags <- function(ts.obj, l){
  ts_merged <- NULL
  # Creating n lags
  for(i in 1:l){
    ts_merged <- ts.union(ts_merged, stats::lag(ts.obj, k = -i))
  }
  # Merge the lags with the original series
  ts_merged <- ts.union(ts.obj, ts_merged)
  # Set the columns names
  colnames(ts_merged) <- c("y", paste0("y_", 1:i))
  # Removing missing values as results of creating the lags
  ts_merged <- window(ts_merged,
                      start = start(ts.obj) + l,
                      end = end(ts.obj))
  return(ts_merged)
}
```

The input of this function is a `ts` object and the number of lags to construct. It then utilizes the `ts.union` and `lag` functions from the **stats** package to create `l` lag and then unites them with the original series.

The output of this function is a multiple time series object (`mts` class):

```
head(lags(USVSales, l = 3))
##            y      y_1     y_2     y_3
## [1,] 1304.6 1483.8 1148.7 1077.5
## [2,] 1373.0 1304.6 1483.8 1148.7
## [3,] 1183.8 1373.0 1304.6 1483.8
## [4,] 1164.4 1183.8 1373.0 1304.6
## [5,] 1207.2 1164.4 1183.8 1373.0
## [6,] 1029.6 1207.2 1164.4 1183.8

ts_info(lags(USVSales, l = 3))
##  The lags(USVSales, l = 3) series is a mts object with 4 variables and
478 observations
##  Frequency: 12
##  Start time: 1979 4
##  End time: 2019 1
```

The output of the `lags` function illustrates the cost associated with the MA method. In this case, we lost the first three observations as a result of creating three lags for the `USVSales` series (since we cannot create lags for the first three observations). The `lags` function automatically drops the first `l` observation (where `l` is the `lag` setting argument in the preceding `lags` function) of the original series. Therefore, the first observation of `USVSales` is April 1974 (as opposed to January 1974 in the original series).

The second and last step of this process is to calculate the arithmetic average of the series with its *n* lags. We will utilize the `ts_sum` function from the **TSstudio** package, which sums up the rows of the `mts` objects and returns a `ts` object:

```
ts_mean <- function(mts.obj){
  ts_avg <- ts_sum(mts.obj) / dim(mts.obj)[2] # Simple average calculation
  return(ts_avg)
}
```

We can now finalize the `sma` function by linking the lags and the average functions. Note that the input parameters of the `sma` function are the series and the order of the SMA:

```
sma <- function(ts.obj, order){
  l <- order -1
  l <- lags(ts.obj = ts.obj, l = l)
  m <- ts_mean(l)
  u <- ts.union(ts.obj, m)
  colnames(u) <- c("original", "transformed")
  return(u)
}
```

Let's utilize this function to smooth the US vehicle sales series. We will set the order of the `sma` function to 4 (hence, we will calculate the average price of each month with the past 3 consecutive months):

```
sma_4 <- sma(USVSales, order = 4)

ts_plot(sma_4, type = "multiple",
        title = "US Vehicle Sales - SMA (Order 4)",
        Ytitle = "Thousands of Units",
        Ygrid = TRUE,
        Xgrid = TRUE,
        Xtitle = "Year")
```

We will get the following graph:

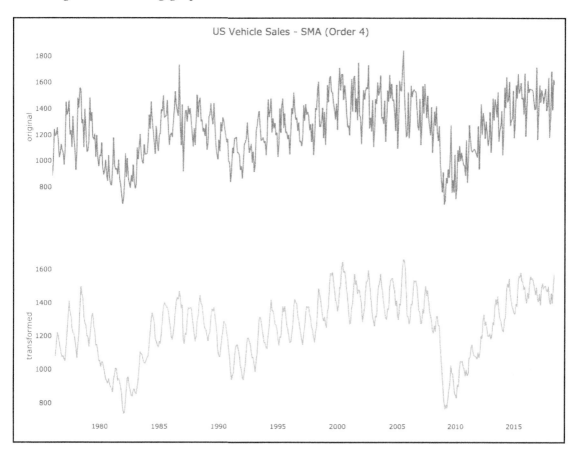

The immediate effect of this transformation process, as you can see in the preceding graph, is noise (or oscillation) reduction. The use of a relevantly lower-order (with respect to the frequency of the series) SMA reduces some of the oscillation in the series that can be related to random noise.

The remaining oscillation of the series is mainly related to the seasonality pattern of the series and to the trend and cycle of the series (for now, don't worry if you are not familiar with the terms seasonality, trend, and cycle; we will define them later on in this chapter). The use of the more aggressive order of the SMA function will reduce the series oscillation further. For example, let's increase the order from 4 to 12:

```
sma_12 <- sma(USVSales, order = 12)

ts_plot(sma_12, type = "multiple",
```

```
title = "US Vehicle Sales - SMA (Order 12)",
Ytitle = "Thousands of Units",
Ygrid = TRUE,
Xgrid = TRUE,
Xtitle = "Year")
```

We will get the following graph:

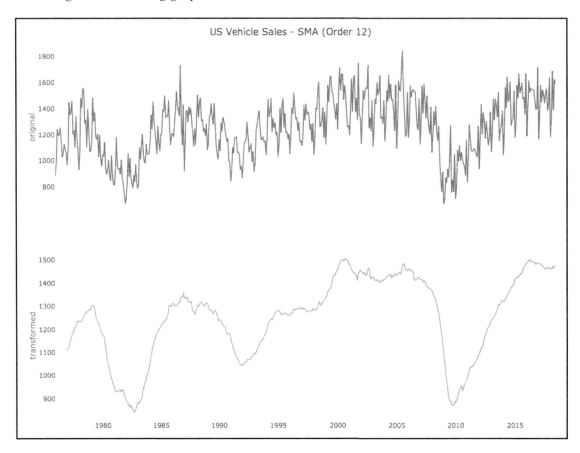

The change in the order of the SMA function from 4 to 12 reduces the remaining oscillation of the series, which is mainly related to the seasonal patterns of the USVSales series. The removal of both the seasonal patterns and random noise by the SMA with the order of 12 provides an estimation of the trend and cycle of the series. This use of an MA to estimate the series trend and then to estimate the seasonal pattern is part of the decomposition process of the time series and we will discuss this later on in this chapter.

Two-sided MA

The two-sided MA method, as its name implies, is based on a two-sided rolling window function. As mentioned previously, the two-sided rolling window function groups each observation of the series with the past n_1 and future n_2 consecutive observations (as opposed to the SMA or one-sided MA, which use only past *n-1* observations). The term two-sided MA refers to the use of the two-sided window function with an arithmetic average unless mentioned otherwise.

Let's now dive into the formula of the two-sided MA function as previously defined:

$$\hat{Y}_t|n_1, n_2 = \frac{Y_{t-n_2} + \ldots + Y_{t-1} + Y_t + Y_{t+1} + \ldots + Y_{n2}}{n_1 + n_2 + 1}, where\ t = n_1 + 1, \ldots, T - n_2,\ n = n_1 + n_2 + 1,\ and\ n \leq T$$

Here, $\hat{Y}_t|n_1, n_2$ represents the average of the *t* observation of the original series along with its past n_1 and future n_2 consecutive observations. Similar to the SMA function, the order and cost of this function are derived from the length of the window, which in this case are $n_1 + n_2 + 1$ and $n_1 + n_2$ respectively.

On the other hand, the loss of observation when using a two-sided window is from both sides of the series (the beginning and end of the series). This is related to the use of both past and future observations in the `window` function. The function shaves both the first n_1 observations and the last n_2 observations. The output of the two-sided MA function could be either of the following:

- **Centered**: This is when n_1 and n_2 are equal, which ensures that the function output at time *t* is centered around the *t* observation of the original *y series*
- **Uncentered**: This is when the length of n_1 is different from the length of n_2, or the order of the MA is an even number

Typically, the default option of the two is the centered output. However, for a variety of reasons, in some instances, you may choose to use an uncentered MA.

A typical example of this is classic trend estimation with the two-sided MA method. In this case, the order is set to the value of the frequency of the series. Hence, whenever you use a series with an even frequency, such as quarterly or monthly, the order value will also be an even number. As a result, the MA output will be uncentered.

For instance, if the input series has a monthly frequency, we will use a 12-order two-sided MA function. Whenever the value of the series frequency is an even number, the order of the MA will be even and, as a result, will be uncentered. This type of order can be defined as follows:

$$n = n_1 + n_2 + 1 = 12, \ or$$

$$n_1 + n_2 = 11$$

In this case, to keep the MA as centered as possible, you can set the number of past and future periods to use in the window (n_1 and n_2) to either five and six or six and five, respectively.

Let's return to the US vehicle sales dataset and look at the effect of a different order two-sided MA using the `ts_ma` function. The `ts_ma` function from the **TSstudio** package allows us to generate and plot multiple MA outputs simultaneously, using different orders and methods (SMA, two-sided MA, and so on). The main parameters of this function are as follows:

- n: This sets the length of the past and future observations to be used in a two-sided MA function. For example, if n is set to three, the `window` function will group each observation with its past and future three consecutive observations, which will yield a 7 order MA. In addition, it is possible to set this parameter with multiple values in order to generate multiple two-sided MA functions simultaneously using a different order.
- n_left/n_right: These are used to customize the MA function by setting the length of the past (n_left) manually and/or the future (n_right) side of the `window` function. If both parameters are defined, the output is a two-sided MA function, either centered or uncentered. If only one of those parameters is set, the function output is a one-sided MA.

The following code generates three versions of two-sided MA outputs with an order of 5, 11, and 12, using the `ts_ma` function. The first two outputs with an order of 5 and 11 are defined by setting the n parameter to 2 and 5. This yields a centered output, as the window of this function is symmetric. The third output of an order of 12 is uncentered, as its window is set to the past 6 and future 5 observations, using the n_left and n_right parameters:

```
two_sided_ma <- ts_ma(ts.obj = USVSales,
              n = c(2,5),# Setting an order 5 and 11 moving average
              n_left = 6, n_right = 5, # Setting an order 12 moving
average
              plot = TRUE,
```

```
multiple = TRUE,
margin = 0.04)
```

We will get the following graphs:

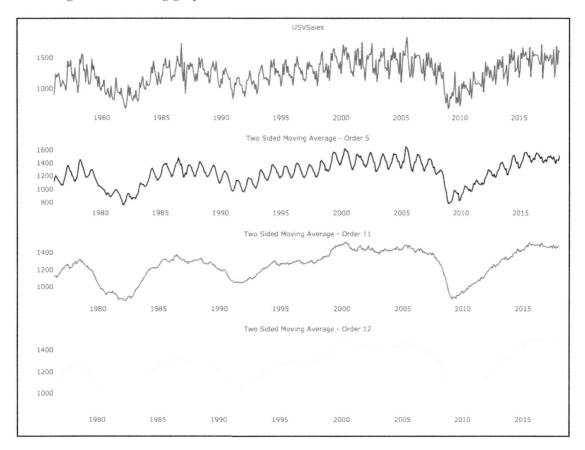

As you can see from the preceding graphs, the behavior of the two-sided MA is relatively similar to the one of the SMA, as we saw earlier.

The higher the order of the function, the smoother the output. Of course, the smoothing effect comes at the cost of losing observations from both the start and end of the series. The loss of observations is a function of the order of the function, since the higher the order of the MA function, the higher the loss of observations.

In the case of the US vehicle sales series, the fifth order function performed well on smoothing some of the series oscillation and left the seasonal and trend patterns. While both the eleventh and twelfth order functions successfully removed the seasonal pattern, some of the noise that was left on the eleventh one was smoothed by the twelfth one.

In this case, the selection of the order of the functions depends on the level of smoothing you want and the cost you are willing to pay.

A simple MA versus a two-sided MA

The selection of a specific type of MA method depends on the aim of the transformation. Moreover, the use of a different range of order, as we saw in the preceding examples, may change the outcome significantly. Generally, when applying both simple and two-sided MAs with arithmetic average using the same order, as in the following example, the output of both methods will be identical but lagged. The two-sided window at time t will group observations $t-n_1$ until $t+n_2$ inclusively, which is the same group of observations when using the one-sided window at time $t+n_2$ (assuming that both windows have the same order):

```
# Creating one-sided and two-sided moving average with an order of 12
  one_sided_12 <- ts_ma(USVSales, n = NULL, n_left = 11, plot = FALSE)
  two_sided_12 <- ts_ma(USVSales, n = NULL, n_left = 6, n_right = 5,plot =
FALSE)
  one_sided <- one_sided_12$unbalanced_ma_12
  two_sided <- two_sided_12$unbalanced_ma_12
```

We will now bind the output of the one-sided and two-sided MA functions with the USVSales series and plot it with the ts_plot function:

```
ma <- cbind(USVSales, one_sided, two_sided)
 p <- ts_plot(ma,
          Xgrid = TRUE,
          Ygrid = TRUE,
          type = "single",
          title = "One-Sided vs. Two-Sided Moving Average - Order 12")
```

Next, we will use the layout function from the **plotly** package to set the plot legend and labels:

```
library(plotly)
 p <- p %>% layout(legend = list(x = 0.05, y = 0.95),
                   yaxis = list(title = "Thousands of Units"),
                   xaxis = list(title = "Year"))
```

We will get the following graph:

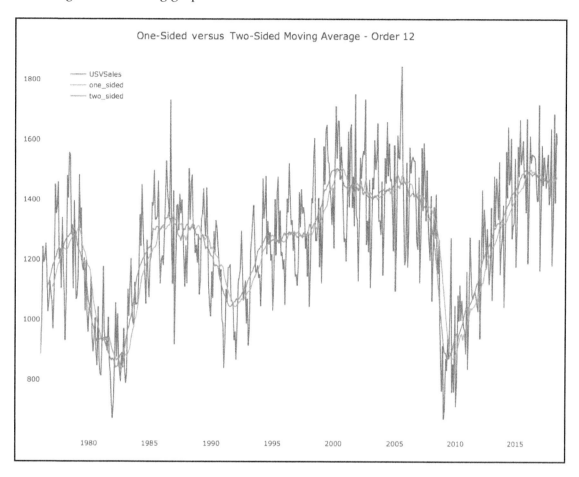

Typically, time series data describes a continuous phenomenon over time, where each observation is relatively close in value or highly correlated to a certain degree with its past and future consecutive observations. Therefore, the use of a centered two-sided MA function (or close to centered when the order of the function is even) is generally more appropriate to apply as a smoother or data filter method. In the case of the one-sided MA function, it would make sense to use it when you need to have the most recent observations (as the loss of observations, in this case, is from the beginning of the series).

The selection of a specific MA method depends primarily on the aim of the transformation and the cost that is associated with it. In the preceding example, you can see that the output of the two-sided MA function fits better with the overall changes in the series trend with respect to the one-sided function output. This is mainly due to the fact that there is a delay of five periods between the two methods.

On the other hand, this comes at the cost of losing the series' last 5 observations in addition to the first 6 (as opposed to the last of the first 11 observations of the one-sided function). While the loss of observations by both functions is equal to 11 (as the order of both functions is equal to 12), typically, the value of the last observations is higher than the first observations in the series. This makes the use of the two-sided function more expensive when you care about the most recent observations of the series.

The time series components

Patterns in time series data are the backbone of the analysis of it. As with other fields of statistics and, in particular, the field of machine learning, one of the primary goals of time series analysis is to identify patterns in data. Those patterns can then be utilized to provide meaningful insights about both past and future events such as seasonal, outliers, or unique events. Patterns in time series analysis can be categorized into one of the following:

- **Structural patterns**: These are also known as series components, which represent, as the name implies, the core structure of the series. There are three types of structural patterns—trend, cycle, and seasonal. You can think about those patterns as binary events, which may or may not exist in the data. This helps to classify the series characteristics and identify the best approach to analyze the series.
- **Non-structural**: This is also known as the irregular component, and refers to any other types of patterns in the data that are not related to the structural patterns.

We can use these two groups of patterns (structural and non-structural) to express time series data using the following equation, when the series has an additive structure:

$$Y_t = T_t + S_t + C_t + I_t$$

And when the series has a multiplicative structure:

$$Y_t = T_t \times S_t \times C_t \times I_t$$

Where Y_t represents the series observation at time t and T_t, S_t, C_t, and I_t represent the value of the trend, seasonal, cycle, and irregular components of the series at time t, respectively. Don't worry if you are not familiar with the terms additive and multiplicative models; we will define these later on in the chapter.

The cycle component

The definition of the cycle in a time series is derived from the broad definition of a cycle in macroeconomics. A cycle can be described as a sequence of repeatable events over time, where the starting point of a cycle is at a local minimum of the series and the ending point is at the next one, and the ending point of one cycle is the starting point of the following cycle.

Moreover, unlike the seasonal pattern, cycles do not necessarily occur at equally spaced time intervals, and their length could change from cycle to cycle. The US monthly unemployment rate series is an example of a series with a cycle pattern. Let's load the series from the **TSstudio** package and review its main characteristics with the `ts_info` function:

```
data(USUnRate)

ts_info(USUnRate)

##   The USUnRate series is a ts object with 1 variable and 853 observations
##   Frequency: 12
##   Start time: 1948 1
##   End time: 2019 1
```

The `USUnRate` series is a `ts` object with a monthly frequency, and it starts in January 1948. As we do not need the full length of the series to view its cycles, we will use the `window` function to subset the series using January 1990 as the starting point, and plot it with the `ts_plot` function:

```
unemployment <- window(USUnRate, start = c(1990,1))
ts_plot(unemployment,
        title = "US Monthly Unemployment Rate",
        Ytitle = "Unemployment Rate (%)",
        Xtitle = "Year",
        Xgrid = TRUE,
        Ygrid = TRUE)
```

We will get the following graph:

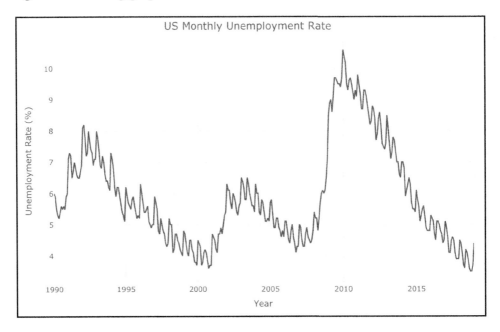

Looking at the preceding series plot, you can easily observe that the series has had three cycles since 1990:

- The first cycle occurred between 1990 and 2000, which was close to an 11-year cycle
- The second cycle started in 2000 and ended in 2007, which was a 7-year cycle
- A third cycle, which began in 2007 and as of May 2019 has not been completed yet, which means that this has continued for more than 12 years

As you can see in the preceding graph, the three cycles of the unemployment rate series have a different length.

Just a word of caution about the `cycle` function in R. The usage of the `cycle` function from the **stats** package is completely different from the definition of the preceding cycle.

The `cycle` function, as introduced in `Chapter 3`, *The Time Series Object*, retrieves the frequency units from the `ts` object and should not be confused with the preceding `cycle` definition.

The trend component

A trend, if it exists in time series data, represents the general direction of the series, either up or down, over time. Furthermore, a trend could have either linear or exponential growth (or close to either one), depending on the series characteristics. We will use simulated data to demonstrate different types of trends, before starting to work with real-life data.

First, let's create a non-trend series as our baseline data. We will use the `runif` function to generate a monthly series with 200 uniform observations distributed between 5 and 5.2. To be able to reproduce this plot with the same value, we will set the seed to 1234 with the `set.seed` function:

```
set.seed(1234)

ts_non_trend <- ts(runif(200, 5,5.2),
                   start = c(2000,1),
                   frequency = 12)
```

The non-trending series will be used as a baseline for the following series:

```
ts_linear_trend_p <- ts_non_trend + 1:length(ts_non_trend) / (0.5 *
length(ts_non_trend))

ts_linear_trend_n <- ts_non_trend - 1:length(ts_non_trend) / (0.5 *
length(ts_non_trend))

ts_exp_trend <- ts_non_trend + exp((1:length(ts_non_trend) -1 ) / (0.5 *
length(ts_non_trend))) - 1
```

The series mentioned in the preceding code are explained as follows:

- `ts_linear_trend_p`: This is a series with a positive linear trend, which adds an increasing arithmetic progression sequence as a function of time
- `ts_linear_trend_n`: This is a series with a negative linear trend, which adds a decreasing arithmetic progression sequence as a function of time
- `ts_exp_trend`: This is a series with an exponential trend, which adds an increasing geometric progression sequence as a function of time

Let's plot the series and review the different types of trends. For convenience, we will first merge the four series to multiple time series objects with the **xts** package:

```
library(xts)

merged_series <- merge(Baseline_No_Trend = as.xts(ts_non_trend),
                       Positive_Linear_Trend = as.xts(ts_linear_trend_p),
```

```
                            Negative_Linear_Trend = as.xts(ts_linear_trend_n),
                            Exponential_Trend = as.xts(ts_exp_trend))
```

Next, we will plot the output with the **TSstudio** and **plotly** packages:

```
ts_plot(merged_series,
                type = "single",
                Xgrid = TRUE,
                Ygrid = TRUE,
                title = "Different Types of Trends",
                Ytitle = "The Values of the Series",
                Xtitle = "Year") %>%
    layout(legend = list(x = 0.1, y = 0.9))
```

We will get the following graph:

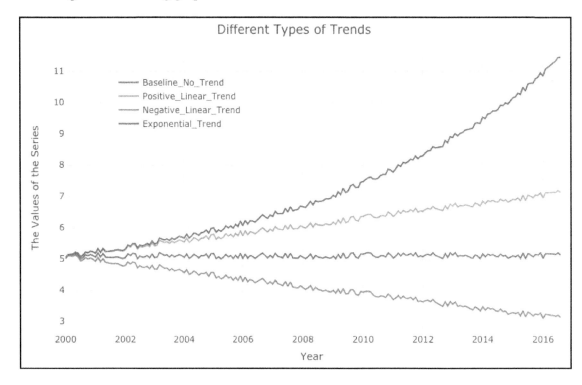

Those simple examples represent non-complex time series data with a clear trend component, and it is therefore simple to identify the trend and classify its growth type. Typically, your data could have additional components and patterns, such as seasonality, as we saw in the natural gas consumption series in `Chapter 4`, *Working with zoo and xts Objects*. Next, we will introduce the seasonal component and see how the two (trend and seasonal components) combine together.

The seasonal component

The seasonal component (or seasonality) is another common pattern in time series data. If this exists, it represents a repeated variation in the series, which is related to the frequency units of the series (for example, the months of the year for a monthly series). One of the common examples for a series with a strong seasonality pattern is the demand for electricity or natural gas. In those cases, the seasonal pattern is derived from a variety of seasonal events, such as weather patterns, the season of the year, and sunlight hours.

In addition, a series could have more than one seasonal pattern. A classic example of this is the hourly demand for electricity, which could potentially have three different seasonality patterns:

- Hourly seasonality, which is derived from parameters such as sunlight hours and temperatures throughout the day
- Weekly seasonality, which depends on the day of the week (weekdays versus the weekend)
- Monthly seasonality, which is related to the season of the year (high consumption during the winter months versus low consumption during the summer months, assuming that the heating system is powered by electricity)

We will focus on tools for seasonality analysis in the next chapter.

Let's simulate a seasonal pattern by using a `sin` function as a function of the series frequency units, along with some random noise. We will utilize the non-trending (`ts_non_trend`) series we created earlier as the random noise and plot it with the `ts_plot` function:

```
seasonal_pattern <- sin(2*pi * (1:length(ts_non_trend)) /
frequency(ts_non_trend))

ts_seasonal <- ts_non_trend + seasonal_pattern

ts_plot(ts_seasonal,
        title = "Seasonal Pattern without Trend",
```

```
                Xgrid = TRUE,
                Ygrid = TRUE,
                Ytitle = "The Values of the Series",
                Xtitle = "Year")
```

We get the following output graph:

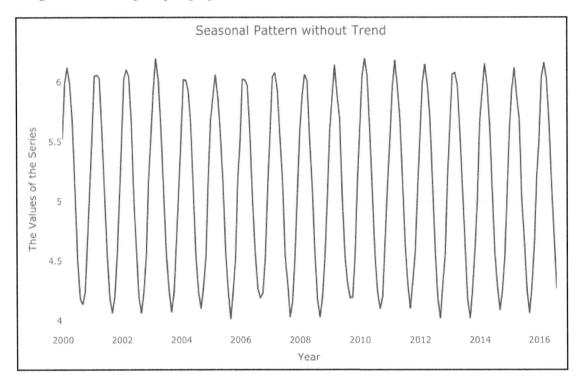

This is a simplistic example of a series with a seasonal pattern. However, unless you are very lucky, it is most likely that your series will be a combination of multiple patterns, which will create a more complex data structure.

A common example of a mixture of patterns is a series with both seasonal and trend patterns. In a similar manner to how we added the seasonal pattern to the non-trending series, let's add the patterns to the rest of the trend series we created before (both linear and exponential) and merge it to a single `xts` object:

```
seasonal_with_Ptrend <- ts_linear_trend_p + seasonal_pattern
seasonal_with_Ntrend <- ts_linear_trend_n - seasonal_pattern
seasonal_with_Etrend <- ts_exp_trend + seasonal_pattern

merged_series_seasonal <- merge(Positive_Linear_Trend =
```

```
as.xts(seasonal_with_Ptrend),
                                Negative_Linear_Trend =
as.xts(seasonal_with_Ntrend),
                                Exponential_Trend =
as.xts(seasonal_with_Etrend))
```

Let's now generate the graph by using the following code snippet:

```
ts_plot(merged_series_seasonal,
        type = "single",
        Xgrid = TRUE,
        Ygrid = TRUE,
        title = "Seasonal Pattern with Trend",
        Ytitle = "The Values of the Series",
        Xtitle = "Year") %>%
   layout(legend = list(x = 0.1, y = 0.9))
```

We will get the following output graph:

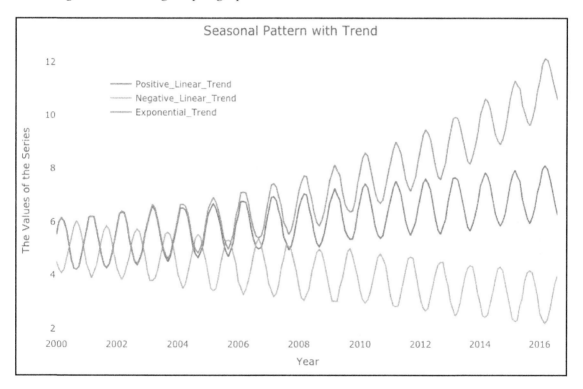

Let's now look at the difference between the seasonal component versus the cycle component.

The seasonal component versus the cycle component

The seasonal and cycle components both describe cyclic events over time, where the length of their cycle distinguish the two. As defined previously, the seasonal component has a constant cycle, which is derived and tied to the series frequency. On the other hand, the cycle length of the cycle component is not necessarily constant and can typically vary from one cycle to the next one. A simplistic way to identify whether a cycle pattern exists in a series is with the use of a heatmap for the time series data.

A time series heatmap is a three-dimensional plot, where the *y*-axis and *x*-axis represent the frequency units and year respectively, and the color represents the magnitude of the observation value. We will use the `ts_heatmap` function from the **TSstudio** package to plot the heatmap of the monthly natural gas consumption (`USgas`) and the unemployment rate (`USUnRate`) in the US. While the first series (`USgas`) represents a time series with a strong seasonal pattern, the second (`USUnRate`), as we saw before, represents a series with a strong cycle pattern:

```
ts_heatmap(USgas,
          title = "Heatmap - the US Natural Gas Consumption")
```

We will get the following output heatmap:

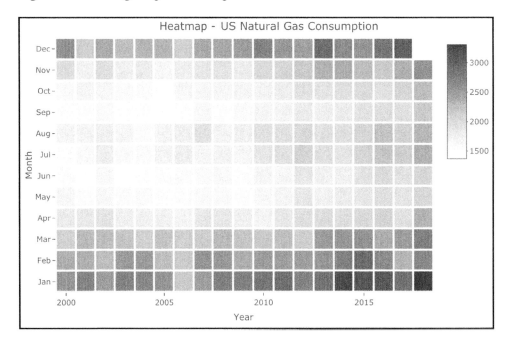

As you can see from the heatmap plot of the `USgas` series, the color flow derives from the frequency units. In this case, the winter months, December and January, usually have the darkest color with respect to the rest of the months of the year. On the other hand, the months of May, June, and September consistently have the brightest color:

```
ts_heatmap(USUnRate,
            title = "Heatmap - The US Unemployment Rate")
```

We will get the following output heatmap:

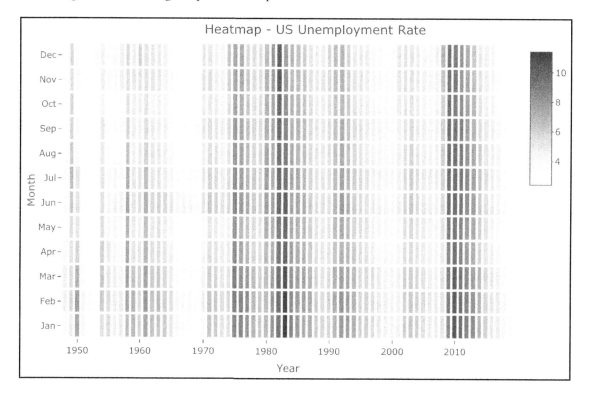

In this example, the color flow of USUnRate is vertical, which indicates the state of the cycle. In this case, the brightest vertical strips represent the ending of one cycle and the beginning of the following one. Likewise, the darkest vertical strips represent the cycle peaks.

White noise

Paradoxically, the main pattern of a white noise series is the lake of patterns. A series is defined as white noise when there is no correlation between the series observations or patterns. In other words, the relationship between different observations is random. In many of the applications of white noise in time series, there are some assumptions made about the distribution of the white noise series. Typically, unless mentioned otherwise, we assume that white noise is an **independent and identically distributed random variables (i.i.d)**, with a mean of 0 and a variance of σ^2. For instance, we can simulate white noise with the rnorm function and generate random numbers with a normal distribution of mean of 0 and variance of 1:

```
set.seed(1234)

white_noise <- ts(rnorm(12*10, mean =  0, sd = 1),
                  start = c(2008, 1),
                  frequency = 12)
```

Again, as we are generating a sequence of random numbers, we will set the seed number. Let's plot the series as follows:

```
ts_plot(white_noise, title = "White Noise ~ N(0, 1)",
        line.mode = "lines+markers",
        Xgrid = TRUE,
        Ygrid = TRUE,
        Ytitle = "The Values of the Series")
```

We will get the following output:

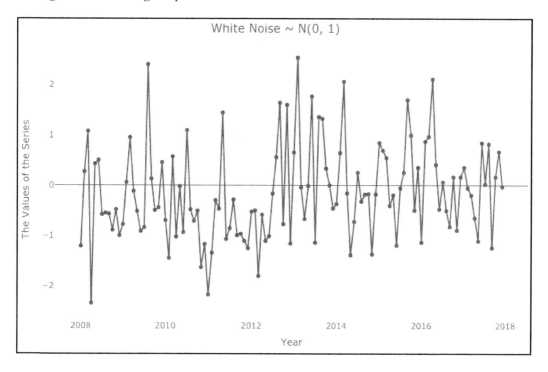

There are a few methods for testing whether a time series is white noise:

- The basic method is carried out by plotting and eyeballing the series to identify whether the variation of the series appears to be random or not.

- We can measure the correlation between the series and its lags with the **autocorrelation function** (**ACF**). A series is considered to be white noise whenever there is no correlation between the series and its lag. The `acf` function from the **stats** package calculates the level of correlation between a series and its lags. We will use the `acf` function to calculate and plot the level of correlation of the `white_noise` series we created previously:

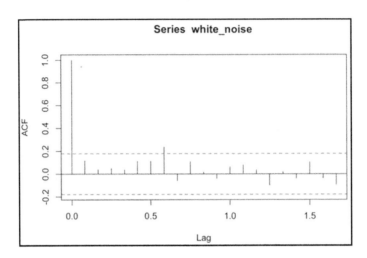

The plot of the `acf` function describes the level of correlation between the series and its lags, where the x-axis represents the lag number and the y-axis represents the level of correlation between the series and the lags. The two dotted blue lines represent the null hypothesis that the level of correlation between the series and a lag is zero using a chi-square statistical test. Therefore, we would consider a lag to have some degree of correlation with the series only if the level of correlation is either above the upper or below the lower dotted line (that is, fails to reject the null hypothesis). In the case of the preceding `white_noise` series, there is only one significant lag with a relatively low level of correlation, and we can therefore conclude that the series is white noise. We will come back to the ACF function in `Chapter 7`, *Correlation Analysis* in order to go into more detail.

- The Ljung-Box test is another statistical test to evaluate whether the series is correlated with its lags. In this case, the null hypothesis assumes that the lags are not correlated. Therefore, lags with lower p-values (with respect to the level of significance of the test) would be considered as being correlated with the series. The `Box.test` function, another **stats** package function, performs a Ljung-Box test on a series and a specific lag.

In the following example, we will use the `lapply` function with the `Box.test` function to apply a Ljung-Box test to the `white_noise` series and its first 24 lags:

```
library(dplyr)
x <- lapply(1:24, function(i){
    p <- Box.test(white_noise, lag = i, type = "Ljung-Box")
    output <- data.frame(lag = i, p_value = p$p.value)
  return(output) }) %>% bind_rows
```

Next, we will plot the results using the `plot` function and add a horizontal line with the `abline` function to define the level of significance of 0.05:

```
plot(x = x$lag,
     y = x$p_value, ylim = c(0,1),
     main = "Series white_noise - Ljung-Box Test",
     xlab = "Lag", ylab = "P-Value")

abline(h = 0.05, col="red", lwd=3, lty=2)
```

We will get the following plot:

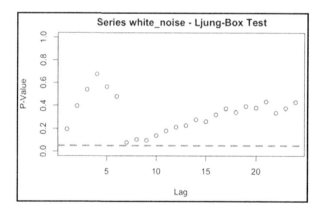

You can see in the preceding Ljung-Box test summary that the p-value of all the lags is above the red dotted line, which indicates that we failed to reject the null hypothesis for a level of significance of 0.05. This indicates that the series is not correlated with its first 24 lags and is, therefore, a white noise series.

The irregular component

Now that we have defined white noise, we can introduce the fourth component of the series—the irregular component. This component, which is the remainder between the series and structural components, provides an indication of irregular events in the series. This includes non-systematic patterns or events in the data, which cause irregular fluctuation. In addition, the irregular component could provide some indication of the appropriate fit of the other components when using a decomposing method. A high correlation in this component is an indication that some patterns related to one of the other components were leftover due to an inaccurate estimate.

On the other hand, if the irregular component is not correlated with its lags (that is, a white noise), we can assume (depending on the series structure) that the estimation of the trend and seasonal components captured the majority of the information about the series structure. Later on in this chapter, we will see an example of the irregular component and its applications.

The additive versus the multiplicative model

Now that we have defined the series components, and before we continue onto our next topic, the decomposition of time series, it is time to introduce the additive and multiplicative models. These terms describe the model structure. As the name implies, a model is defined as additive whenever we add together its components:

$$Y_t = T_t + S_t + C_t + I_t$$

Similarly, a model is defined as multiplicative whenever we multiply its components:

$$Y_t = T_t \times S_t \times C_t \times I_t$$

Here, as before, Y_t represents the series observation at time t and T_t, S_t, C_t, and I_t represent the value of the trend, seasonal, cycle, and irregular components of the series at time t, respectively.

We classify a series as additive whenever there is a growth in the trend (with respect to the previous period), or if the amplitude of the seasonal component roughly remains the same over time. On the other hand, we classify a series as multiplicative whenever the growth of the trend or the magnitude of the seasonal component increases or decreases by some multiplicity from period to period over time.

The US monthly natural gas consumption series is an example of an additive series. You can easily notice that the amplitude of the seasonal component remains the same (or close to the same) over time:

```
ts_plot(USgas,
        title = "US Monthly Natural Gas consumption",
        Ytitle = "Billion Cubic Feet",
        Xtitle = "Year",
        Xgrid = TRUE,
        Ygrid = TRUE)
```

We will get the following graph:

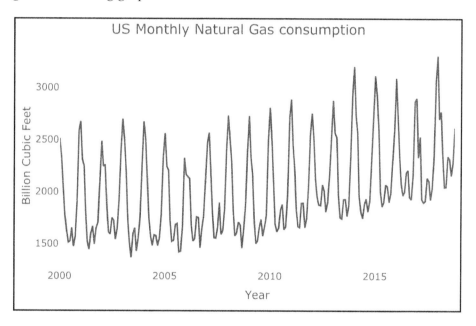

As you can see, the amplitude of the USgas series seasonal component over the past 20 years did not change by much (apart from some years, which may be related to some unusual weather patterns). In addition, the series trend seems to be linear, with some structural breaks during 2010. On the other hand, the famous AirPassengers dataset (available in the **dataset** package), which describes the total monthly international airline passengers between the years 1949 and 1960, is an excellent example for multiplicative series. During those years, right after World War II, the improvement in aviation technology contributed to the fast growth in the airline industry. As you can see in the following data, the amplitude of the seasonal component increases from year to year:

```
data(AirPassengers)
```

We will then plot this with the `ts_plot` function:

```
ts_plot(AirPassengers,
        title = "Monthly Airline Passenger Numbers 1949-1960",
        Ytitle = "Thousands of Passengers",
        Xtitle = "Years",
        Xgrid = TRUE,
        Ygrid = TRUE)
```

We will then get the following graph:

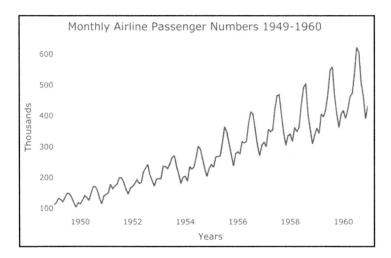

Let's now learn how to handle multiplicative series.

Handling multiplicative series

Most forecasting models assume that the variation of the input series remains constant over time. This assumption typically holds for a series with an additive structure. However, it fails when the series has a multiplicative structure. The typical approach for handling a series with a multiplicative structure is by applying a data transformation on the input series. The most common data transformation approaches for time series data are the following:

- **Log transformation**: This applies a *log* on both sides of the series equation:

$$log(Y_t) = log(T_t \times S_t \times C_t \times I_t)$$

Using the mathematical characteristics of the *log* function—*log(a × b) = log(a) + log(b)*, we can transform the equation into a new series with an additive structure:

$$log(Y_t) = log(T_t) + log(S_t) + log(C_t) + log(I_t)$$

This new structure of the series allows us to treat it as a normal additive series.

- **Box-Cox transformation**: This is based on applying power on the input series using the following formula:

$$Y_t'|\lambda = \begin{cases} \frac{Y_t^\lambda - 1}{\lambda} & \lambda \neq 0 \\ log(Y_t) & \lambda = 0 \end{cases}$$

As you can see from the preceding Box-Cox equation, for $\lambda = 0$, the transformation is a *log* transformation.

The **forecast** package provides several tools for applying a Box-Cox transformation on time series data. The BoxCox.lambda function estimates the value of λ, which minimizes the coefficient variation of the input series. For example, we will use this function to identify the λ value for the AirPassenger series:

```
library(forecast)

AirPassenger_lamda <- BoxCox.lambda(AirPassengers)

AirPassenger_lamda

## [1] -0.2947156
```

We can then use this λ value to transform the input series with the BoxCox function and plot it with the ts_plot function:

```
AirPassenger_transform <- BoxCox(AirPassengers, lambda =
AirPassenger_lamda)

ts_plot(AirPassenger_transform,
        title = "Monthly Airline Passenger Numbers 1949-1960 with Box-Cox
Transformation",
        Ytitle = "Number of Passengers - Scaled",
        Xtitle = "Years",
        Xgrid = TRUE,
        Ygrid = TRUE)
```

We will get the following graph:

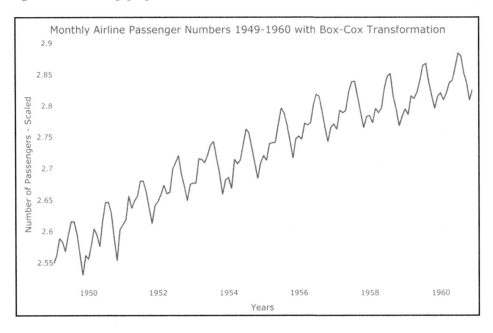

As you can see from the transformation plot of the `AirPassenger` series, the values of the series are scaled. Most of the forecasting models in the **forecast** package automatically transform the series before applying the model, and then re-transform the forecast output back to the original scale.

The decomposition of time series

Once the data has been cleaned and reformatted, one of the first steps of the analysis is to identify the structure of the series components. The decomposition of time series is a generic name for the process of separating a series into its components. This process provides insights into the structural patterns of the series. Typically, those insights utilize and identify the most appropriate approaches to handle the series, based on the aim of the analysis (for example, seasonality analysis, and forecasting). For example, if you identify in this process that the series has a strong seasonality pattern, you should select models that have the ability to handle this pattern. Although there are multiple decomposition methods, in this chapter, we will focus on the classical seasonal decomposition method, as most methods are based on a type of extension of this method.

Classical seasonal decomposition

Classical decomposition (or classical seasonal decomposition by MA) is one of the most common methods of decomposing a time series down to its components. This simplistic method for estimating the three components is based on the use of an MA function followed by simple arithmetic calculations.

This is a three-step process, where each step is dedicated to the estimation of one of the components in sequential order (hence, the calculation of each component is derived from the estimate of the previous component):

1. **Trend estimation**: This is the first step of the decomposing process, by using the MA function to remove the seasonal component from the series. The order of the MA function is defined by the frequency of the series. For instance, if the frequency of the input series is monthly (or 12), then the order of the MA should be set to 12. Since we are using a two-sided MA, some of the first and last observations of the trend estimation will be missing. You may recall that the loss of observations in this process depends on the order of the MA function.

2. **Seasonal component estimation**: A two-step process, starting with detrending the series by subtracting the trend estimation from the previous step from the series, where:

   - You can use $Y_t - \hat{T}_t$ when using the additive model, and $Y_t/\hat{T}_t$ when the model is multiplicative. Here, Y_t is the original series observation at time t and $\hat{T}_t$ is the corresponding trend estimation.

   - After the series is detrended, the next step is to estimate the corresponding seasonal component for each frequency unit (for example, for a monthly series, the seasonal component for January, February, and so on). This simple calculation is done by grouping the observations by their frequency unit and then averaging each group. The output of this process is a new series with a length that is equal to the series frequency and is ordered accordingly. This series represents the seasonal component of each frequency unit, so this estimation is one-to-many (one estimation for multiple observations). For example, if the input series has a monthly frequency, the seasonal component of observations that occurred during January will be the same across the series.

2. **Irregular component estimation**: This is a straightforward calculation, subtracting the estimation of the trend and seasonal components from the original series. This is $\hat{I}_t = Y_t - \hat{T}_t - \hat{S}_t$ for an additive series, and $\hat{I}_t = Y_t / (\hat{T}_t \times \hat{S}_t)$ for a multiplicative series. Here, Y_t represents the original series at time t, and $\hat{T}_t$, $\hat{S}_t$, and $\hat{I}_t$ represent the corresponding trend and seasonal and irregular components estimate.

The `decompose` function from the **stats** package is an implementation of this method. The following code is an example of the use of the `decompose` function to decompose the US monthly vehicle sales series down to its components. By default, this function is set to an additive model:

```
data(USVSales)

usv_decompose <- decompose(USVSales)
```

Let's review the class and structure of the decompose output function:

```
str(usv_decompose)
```

We will get the following output:

```
## List of 6
##  $ x       : Time-Series [1:517] from 1976 to 2019: 885 995 1244 1191
1203 ...
##  $ seasonal: Time-Series [1:517] from 1976 to 2019: -223.5 -100.3 142.4
37.6 147.7 ...
##  $ trend   : Time-Series [1:517] from 1976 to 2019: NA NA NA NA NA ...
##  $ random  : Time-Series [1:517] from 1976 to 2019: NA NA NA NA NA ...
##  $ figure  : num [1:12] -223.5 -100.3 142.4 37.6 147.7 ...
##  $ type    : chr "additive"
##  - attr(*, "class")= chr "decomposed.ts"
```

Let's review the class of the decompose output using the `class` function:

```
class(usv_decompose)

## [1] "decomposed.ts"
```

As you can see from the preceding output, the function returns a list of six objects:

- x: This is the original series, a `ts` object.
- `seasonal`: This is the estimate of the seasonal component, a `ts` object.

- `trend`: This is the estimate of the series trend, a `ts` object. You can se[e] first (and also the last) observations are missing due to the use of th[e] MA function. The number of missing values is defined by the order of the M[A] function.
- `random`: This is the estimate of the irregular component, a `ts` object. This output is nothing but the remainder of the series and the preceding two components. The `random` object is missing whenever the `trend` estimation is missing.
- `figure`: This is the estimated seasonal figure only.
- `type`: This is the type of decomposition, either an additive (the default), or multiplicative model.

R's built-in `plot` function can plot the output of the `decompose` function in a straightforward way as it supports the `decomposed.ts` class (as is defined in the function methods; see `methods(plot)`):

```
plot(usv_decompose)
```

We will get the following graph for the additive time series:

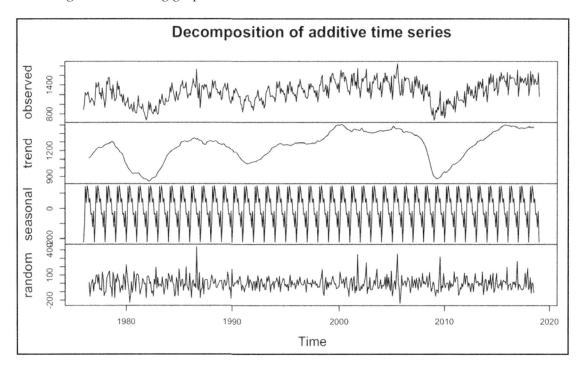

Similarly, if the series has multiplicative growth, like the `AirPassengers` series, you can set the decomposition process with a multiplicative model:

```
air_decompose <- decompose(AirPassengers, type = "multiplicative")

plot(air_decompose)
```

We will get the following graph for the multiplicative time series:

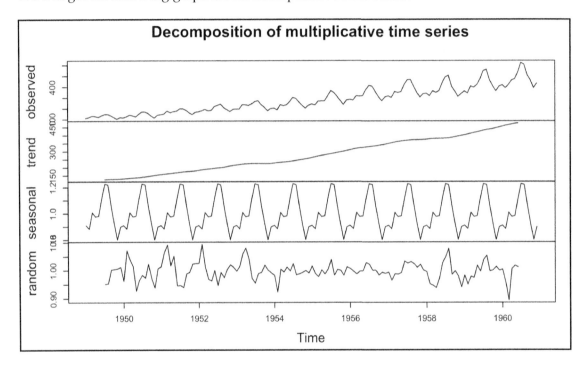

One of the downsides of the classical decomposition method is that seasonal component estimation is based on the arithmetic average, which results in a one-to-many estimation, so there is a single seasonal component estimation for each cycle unit (for example, all observations of the series that occurred in January will have the same seasonal component estimation if the series is monthly).

This is not problematic when applying this method to an additive series, such as the US vehicle sales or the monthly natural gas consumption datasets, as the magnitude of the seasonal oscillation remains the same (or close to the same) over time. On the other hand, this not the case for a series with multiplicative growth, as the magnitude of the seasonal oscillation grows over time. An excellent example of this is the preceding `AirPassengers` dataset, as the magnitude of the seasonal component increases over time. An average would not represent the seasonal oscillation at the beginning and end of the series, as it would both over and underestimate them respectively. On the other hand, it would have a good fit somewhere in the middle, where it is close to the mean. A good indication of this can be found in the irregular component, which, in the case of the `AirPassengers` data, is relatively high at the beginning and end of the series and low in the middle.

> This, of course, should not come as a surprise, as the irregular component represents the remainder between the series and the trend and the seasonal estimation.

Seasonal adjustment

Seasonal adjustment is the process of removing the seasonal fluctuation from a series. The use of this process is popular in the field of economic research, as it provides a better overview of series changes over time. A common example is the **Gross Domestic Production** (**GDP**) index, one of the main indicators of economic health. This indicator has a strong seasonal pattern, as the majority of production in most sectors is affected by seasonal events through the calendar year, such as weather (for example, the agriculture sector) or holidays (for example, the retail and airline sectors). As a result, in a calendar year, some calendar quarters (for example, the first quarter of the year) will be higher (or lower) than others.

The US GDP is a good example as, historically, the growth in the first quarter is the lowest and highest in the second quarter, due to those seasonal patterns. In this case, the removal of the seasonal pattern from the GDP allows us to estimate the real growth of the GDP between the first and the second quarter of the year. The transformation process of the seasonal adjustment method is straightforward:

1. Estimate the seasonal component using a decomposition process
2. Remove the seasonal component from the series, which leaves the series with only the trend and the irregular component
3. Optionally, you can apply a smoothing function to remove noise and outliers

Typically, most of the economic data that you hear about in the news, such as GDP, unemployment rate, and consumption indices, are seasonally adjusted.

Summary

The decomposition of time series data down to its components is one of the core methods in time series analysis. The use of this method is part of descriptive analysis, as it can provide some useful insights into series patterns and structures. Those insights can be utilized to identify the best approaches and models to be used with a series.

The focus of this chapter has been on the classical seasonal decomposition process with MA, one of the most common decomposition methods. Although this method is not the most advanced or accurate, it is the basis of most advanced methods. Therefore, understanding the mechanisms of this process, such as the role of the MA, means that you can apply more sophisticated methods with minimum effort.

In the next chapter, we will focus on the analysis of the seasonal component of time series data.

6
Seasonality Analysis

Seasonality, as we saw in the previous chapter, is one of the main components of time series data. Furthermore, this component, when existing in a series, plays a pivotal role in the forecasting process of the future values of the series, as we will see in the coming chapters, since it contains structural patterns. In this chapter, we will focus on methods and approaches for identifying and then classifying the seasonal patterns of a series. This includes the use of descriptive statistics tools, such as summary statistics, as well as data visualization methods, utilizing packages such as **dplyr**, **ggplot2**, **plotly**, **forecast**, and **TSstudio**.

In this chapter, we will cover the following topics:

- Single and multiple seasonality patterns
- Descriptive statistic methods to identify seasonality patterns
- Data visualization tools to explore and identify seasonality patterns

Technical requirement

The following packages will be used in this chapter:

- **forecast**: Version 8.5 and above
- **TSstudio**: Version 0.1.4 and above
- **plotly**: Version 4.8 and above
- **ggplot2**: Version 3.1.1 and above
- **dplyr**: Version 0.8.1 and above
- **UKgrid**: Version 0.1.1 and above

You can access the codes for this chapter from the following link:

```
https://github.com/PacktPublishing/Hands-On-Time-Series-Analysis-with-R/tree/
master/Chapter06
```

Seasonality types

The series frequency, as we saw in the preceding chapters, defines the amounts of intervals in a single cycle unit of the series. The term **cycle** here refers to constant cycles, and should not be confused with the term **cycle component**, which was introduced in the previous chapter. In addition, the frequency units are ordered and repeated in the same order. For example, January and December would always be the first and last units, respectively, for a calendric series with a monthly frequency. A seasonal pattern exists in a time series whenever we can tie a repeated event in the series to a specific frequency unit, for example, the average temperature in New York during the month of January, or the average number of passengers in the London underground between 8 a.m. and 9 a.m. Hence, there is a strong relationship between seasonal pattern and the frequency of the series.

Furthermore, as funny as it may sound, most of the seasonal patterns in nature are related to two astrophysical phenomena:

- The orbit of Earth around the Sun (also known as the orbital period of Earth), which is defined as 365 days
- The rotation of Earth (or solar day) with a length of 86,400 seconds or 24 hours

For instance, the seasonality patterns of natural phenomena such as weather (temperature, rain, and snow fall), sunrise and sunset times, or the tide level are dictated directly from the orbital period and the solar time of Earth. This, of course, triggers a sequence of sub-events, which automatically change the seasonal pattern from the original phenomena; for example, the demand for electricity or the consumption of natural gas derived from the weather. When seasonality exists in the time series data, we can classify this into one of the following categories:

- **Single seasonal pattern**: Whenever there is only one dominant seasonal pattern in the series
- **Multiple seasonal patterns**: If more than one dominant seasonal pattern exists in the series

Typically, multiple seasonal patterns are more likely to occur whenever the series has a high frequency (for example, daily, hourly, half-hourly, and so on), as there are more options to aggregate the series to a lower frequency. A typical example of multiple seasonality is the hourly demand for electricity, which could have multiple seasonal patterns, as the demand is derived from the hour of the day, the day of the week, or the yearly patterns, such as weather or the amount of daylight throughout the day. On the other hand, as the frequency of the series is lower (for example, monthly, quarterly, and so on), it is more likely to have only one dominant seasonal pattern as opposed to a high-frequency series, as there are fewer aggregation options for another type of frequencies.

Throughout the examples in this chapter, we will continue to use the USgas dataset and will introduce the UKgrid dataset as an example of a time series with single and multiple seasonal patterns, respectively.

You may recall that the USgas dataset represents the total monthly consumptions of natural gas in the US since January 2000, and this is available in the **TSstudio** package:

```
library(TSstudio)

data(USgas)

ts_info(USgas)
## The USgas series is a ts object with 1 variable and 223 observations
## Frequency: 12
## Start time: 2000 1
## End time: 2018 7
```

Let's use the ts_plot function to plot and review the series structure:

```
ts_plot(USgas,
        title = "US Monthly Natural Gas consumption",
        Ytitle = "Billion Cubic Feet",
        Xtitle = "Year",
        Xgrid = TRUE,
        Ygrid = TRUE)
```

The output is as follows:

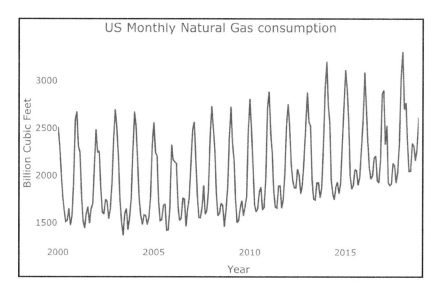

The UKgrid dataset represents the national demand in the UK high-voltage electric power transmission network since 2011 in a half-hourly frequency. This dataset is available on the **UKgrid** package. For convenience reasons, we will transform the series from a half-hourly frequency to hourly and will use an xts format. We will use the extract_grid function from the **UKgrid** package for this transformation:

```
library(UKgrid)

UKgrid_xts <- extract_grid(type = "xts",
                           columns = "ND",
                           aggregate = "hourly",
                           na.rm = TRUE)
## The UKgrid series is a xts object with 1 variable and 69720 observations
## Frequency: hourly
## Start time: 2011-01-01
## End time: 2018-12-14 23:00:00
```

Let's review the structure of the UKgrid series:

```
ts_plot(UKgrid,
        title = "National Hourly Demand UK Grid",
        Ytitle = "Megawatts",
        Xtitle = "Year",
        Xgrid = TRUE,
        Ygrid = TRUE)
```

The output is as follows:

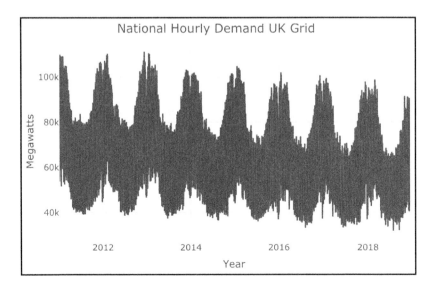

As you can see in the preceding plot, the national demand of the UK high-voltage electric power transmission network (or the UKgrid series), similar to the USgas series, has a strong seasonal pattern. The main difference between the two series is their density (or granularity) per cycle unit (which, in this case, is a calendar year), as the UKgrid series has 8,760 observations per cycle unit (or 24 × 365) as opposed to 12 observations of the USgas series. Having more observations per cycle unit, that is, high-frequency time series data, could potentially provide more insightful information about the series behavior as opposed to a lower frequency time series data. However, this comes with the price of additional complexity, which therefore requires more effort in the analysis process.

Seasonal analysis with descriptive statistics

Descriptive statistics are a simple yet powerful method to describe the key statistical characteristics of the data. This method is based on the use of summary statistics tables and is a summary of the key statistical indicators, such as the mean, median, quantile, and standard deviation, and data visualization tools, such as box plots and bar charts. Descriptive statistics can be used to describe the characteristics of the frequency units of a series. This allows us to identify whether we can segment each period of the series by some statistical criteria, for example, the mean, the quantile range, and so on.

 The applications of the descriptive statistics methods are different from the ones of the statistical inference methods. While the first provides descriptions and insights on the data, the second offers conclusive insights about relations and causation in the data.

Summary statistics tables

The **dplyr** package, one of the most popular packages in R, provides a set of tools for working and seamlessly summarizing data frame objects. In the following example, we will use the **dplyr** package to group the USgas series by its frequency units (the months of the year), and then summarize the mean and standard deviation of each frequency unit. Before starting the process, we will transform the USgas series (and later on the UKgrid series) into a data frame object:

```
# Transforming the ts object to data.frame object
USgas_df <- data.frame(year = floor(time(USgas)), month = cycle(USgas),
USgas = as.numeric(USgas))

# Setting the month abbreviation and transforming it to a factor
USgas_df$month <- factor(month.abb[USgas_df$month], levels = month.abb)
```

```
head(USgas_df)##    year month   USgas
## 1 2000    Jan 2510.5
## 2 2000    Feb 2330.7
## 3 2000    Mar 2050.6
## 4 2000    Apr 1783.3
## 5 2000    May 1632.9
## 6 2000    Jun 1513.1
```

Next, we will use the `group_by` and `summaries` functions to group, summarize the data by its frequency units, and then plot the results with the **plotly** package:

```
# Summarized the series by its frequency units
 library(dplyr)

 USgas_summary <- USgas_df %>%
   group_by(month) %>%
   summarise(mean = mean(USgas),
             sd = sd(USgas))

 USgas_summary## # A tibble: 12 x 3
##    month mean    sd
##    <fct> <dbl> <dbl>
##  1 Jan   2773.  281.
##  2 Feb   2474.  193.
##  3 Mar   2294.  201.
##  4 Apr   1869.  162.
##  5 May   1686.  172.
##  6 Jun   1669.  197.
##  7 Jul   1830.  223.
##  8 Aug   1836.  180.
##  9 Sep   1633.  182.
## 10 Oct   1723.  172.
## 11 Nov   1976.  234.
## 12 Dec   2517.  261.
library(plotly)

plot_ly (data = USgas_summary, x = ~ month, y = ~ mean, type = "bar", name
= "Mean") %>%
layout (title = "USgas - Monthly Average", yaxis = list(title = "Mean",
range = c(1500, 2700)))
```

The output is shown in the following graph:

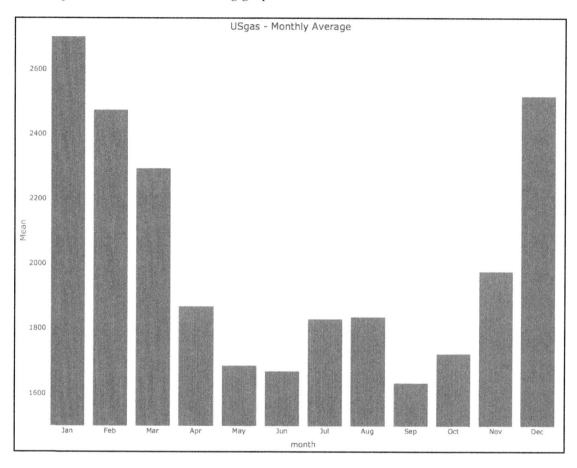

You can see from the summary statistic table of the series that, on average, each month is different from the next consecutive month by its standard deviation with the exception of the two pairs May/June and July/August, which are relatively close to each other. This allows us to characterize some months with a distinct behavior from the rest, such as January, February, March, and November. It is worth mentioning that the variation in the monthly averages mainly results in the series trend as we saw in the previous chapter, with the decomposing function that shifts up the series from year to year. In the case of a linear trend, detrending the series won't change the monthly difference by much as it will shift the series down in the same proportion. On the other hand, it will reduce the variation (that is, the standard deviation) of the monthly average, as it will be aligning each observation closer to its frequency unit peers.

The first indication for the potential existence of multiple seasonal patterns in the series is a high frequency, such as daily, hourly, and minutely. In those cases, there is more than one way to set the frequency of the series. For example, if we capture a time series in a daily interval, the series frequency can be set as follows:

- Daily (or 365), assuming that the most appropriate cycle is a full year
- Weekdays (or 7) whenever the weekday oscillation is more dominant than the one of the full-year cycle

When using a descriptive statistics process with this type of series, it will make sense to apply this method for each potential frequency of the series (or at least the main ones) in order to examine whether there is an indication for the seasonal pattern. For example, UKgrid is an hourly time series, which marks it automatically as a *suspect* of having multiple seasonal patterns. Potentially, as mentioned previously, the hourly demand for electricity could have three different seasonal patterns:

- **Hourly**: This is probably the main seasonal pattern in the series, as there is a direct relationship between the demand for electricity and the hour of the day (there is high demand during the day and low demand during the night).
- **Weekday**: The demand for electricity throughout the day is, potentially, derived from the day of the week. It would make sense to expect a high consumption during working days and a lower rate of consumption throughout the weekend.
- **Monthly**: As weather patterns vary throughout the year, the amount of daylight and other seasonal factors could impact the demand for electricity.

As with the USgas series, we will first transform the UKgrid series into data.frame format:

```
library(xts)
UKgrid_df <- data.frame(time = index(UKgrid_xts), UKgrid =
as.numeric(UKgrid_xts))
str(UKgrid_df)## 'data.frame': 66456 obs. of 2 variables:
##  $ time  : POSIXct, format: "2011-01-01 00:00:00" "2011-01-01 01:00:00"
...
##  $ UKgrid: num  69698 68374 64736 60975 56892 ...
```

The next step is to create seasonal features based on the periods we wish to check. For this, we will use the **lubridate** package to create indicators for the hour of the day, the day of the week, and the month by using the hour, wday, and month functions respectively. This will allow us to group and summarize the series based on each periodicity:

```
library(lubridate)
 UKgrid_df$hour <- hour(UKgrid_df$time)
 UKgrid_df$weekday <- wday(UKgrid_df$time, label = TRUE, abbr = TRUE)
```

```
UKgrid_df$month <- factor(month.abb[month(UKgrid_df$time)], levels =
month.abb)

head(UKgrid_df)
##                     time UKgrid hour weekday month
## 1 2011-01-01 00:00:00   69698    0     Sat   Jan
## 2 2011-01-01 01:00:00   68374    1     Sat   Jan
## 3 2011-01-01 02:00:00   64736    2     Sat   Jan
## 4 2011-01-01 03:00:00   60975    3     Sat   Jan
## 5 2011-01-01 04:00:00   56892    4     Sat   Jan
## 6 2011-01-01 05:00:00   54751    5     Sat   Jan
```

It will be more efficient to start to explore the most granular layer of the series first, as it could indicate the direction of the aggregations of the series. Therefore, we will first summarize the series by its hourly cycle:

```
UKgrid_hourly <- UKgrid_df %>%
  dplyr::group_by(hour) %>%
  dplyr::summarise(mean = mean(UKgrid, na.rm = TRUE), sd = sd(UKgrid, na.rm
= TRUE))
```

We can now use the summary statistics table to plot both the hourly mean and its standard deviation. Since those two variables are not on the same scale, we will use a two *y* axes plot, where the left-hand side represents the hourly mean and the right-hand side represents the hourly mean standard deviation:

```
# Plotting the mean and the standard deviation
plot_ly(UKgrid_hourly) %>%
  add_lines(x = ~ hour, y = ~ mean, name = "Mean") %>%
  add_lines(x = ~ hour, y = ~ sd, name = "Standard Deviation", yaxis =
"y2",
            line = list(color = "red", dash = "dash", width = 3)) %>%
  layout(
    title = "The UK Grid National Demand - Hourly Average vs. Standard
Deviation",
    yaxis = list(title = "Mean"),
    yaxis2 = list(overlaying = "y",
                  side = "right",
                  title = "Standard Deviation"
    ),
    xaxis = list(title="Hour of the day"),
    legend = list(x = 0.05, y = 0.9),
    margin = list(l = 50, r = 50)
  )
```

The output is shown in the following graph:

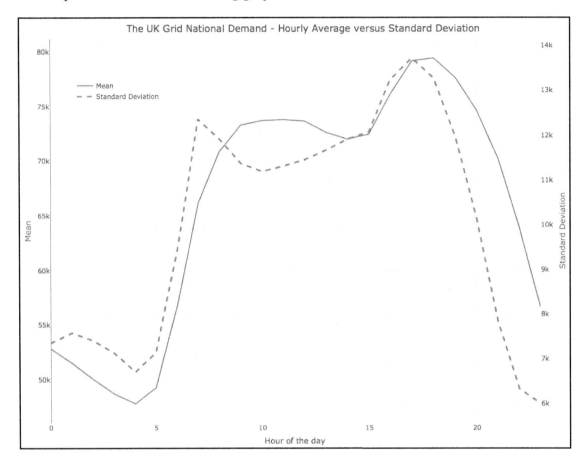

Looking at the plot of the preceding summary statistic table, we can see the following behavior of the series:

- There is low demand during the nighttime (between midnight and 6 a.m.) and high demand between the morning hours and early evening.
- There is a strong correlation between the average demand and its standard deviation.
- The relatively low standard deviation of the demand average during the nighttime could indicate that there is strong sub-seasonal effect during those hours beside the hourly seasonality. This should make sense, as those are normal sleep hours, and therefore, on average, the demand is reasonably the same throughout the weekdays.
- On the other hand, the high standard deviation throughout the high-demand hours could indicate that the demand is distributed differently on different periodicity views (such as weekday or month of the year).

To examine the last point, we will subset the series into two groups representing the demand in the middle of the night and the demand throughout the day (3 a.m. and 9 a.m., respectively), and then we will group them by the weekday:

```
UKgrid_weekday <- UKgrid_df %>%
    dplyr::filter(hour == 3 | hour == 9) %>%
  dplyr::group_by(hour, weekday) %>%
  dplyr::summarise(mean = mean(UKgrid, na.rm = TRUE),
                   sd = sd(UKgrid, na.rm = TRUE))

UKgrid_weekday$hour <- factor(UKgrid_weekday$hour)

plot_ly(data = UKgrid_weekday, x = ~ weekday, y = ~ mean, type =
"bar",color = ~ hour) %>%
  layout(title = "The Hourly Average Demand by Weekday",
         yaxis = list(title = "Mean", range = c(30000, 75000)),
         xaxis = list(title = "Weekday"))
```

The following plot shows the output:

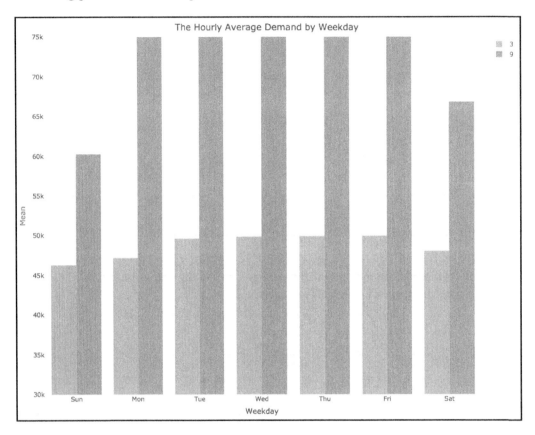

You will see in the preceding bar chart that the demand for electricity at 3 a.m. is relatively stable throughout all the days of the week, with a slight difference between the average during the weekdays and the days in the weekend (about 2% different). On the other hand, there is a significant difference between the weekday and weekend demand at 9 a.m. (that is, the demand on Monday is higher on average by 28% from the one on Sunday). Not surprisingly, those results aligned with our earlier expectations. We can now leverage those insights to examine whether a monthly seasonal pattern exists in the series. We will now select the same hours (3 a.m. and 9 a.m.); however, this time we will group this data by month (instead of weekdays):

```
UKgrid_month <- UKgrid_df %>%
    dplyr::filter(hour == 3 | hour == 9) %>%
  dplyr::group_by(hour, month) %>%
  dplyr::summarise(mean = mean(UKgrid, na.rm = TRUE),
                   sd = sd(UKgrid, na.rm = TRUE))
```

```
UKgrid_month$hour <- factor(UKgrid_month$hour)

plot_ly(data = UKgrid_month, x = ~ month, y = ~ mean, type = "bar",color =
~ hour) %>%
    layout(title = "The Hourly Average Demand by Weekday",
            yaxis = list(title = "Mean", range = c(30000, 75000)),
            xaxis = list(title = "Month"))
```

The output is as follows:

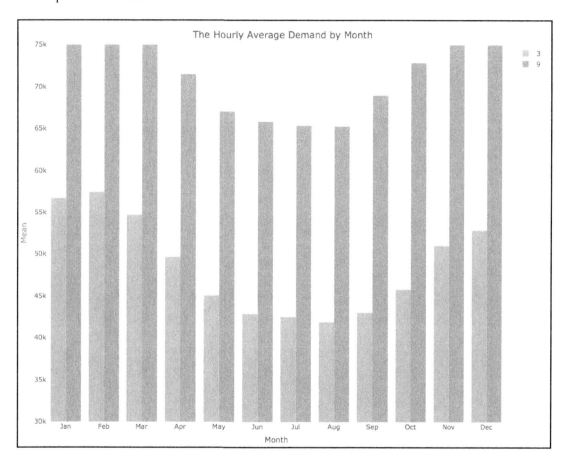

We can see from the bar plot of the monthly aggregation summary that, on average, the demand during both the night (3 a.m.) and morning (9 a.m.) vary throughout the months of the year. Moreover, there is a significant change in demand during the nighttime as opposed to the weekday aggregation. The variation of the series from month to month indicates the existence of monthly seasonality in the series.

Seasonal analysis with density plots

Another approach for analyzing seasonal patterns in time series data is by plotting the distribution of the frequency units by using histogram or density plots. This will allow us to examine whether each frequency unit has a unique distribution that can distinguish it from the rest of the units. In the following examples, we will use the **ggplot2** package to plot the density plot of each frequency unit using the `geom_density` **geometric object (geom)**. This geom is using the kernel density estimation method to smooth the histogram plot. We will start by plotting the density of each of the `USgas` months:

```
# Plotting the density of each frequency unit
library(ggplot2)
ggplot(USgas_df, aes(x = USgas)) +
   geom_density(aes(fill = month)) +
   ggtitle("USgas - Kernel Density Estimates by Month") +
   facet_grid(rows = vars(as.factor(month)))
```

The output is in the following plot:

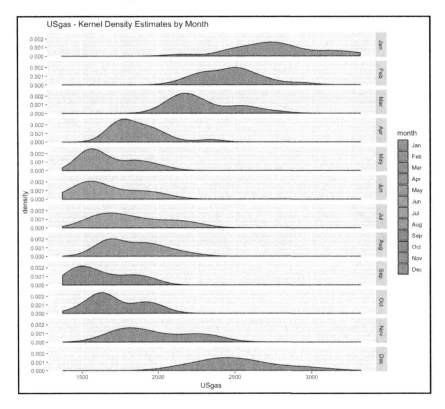

This plot is an excellent example of the use of data visualization tools for storytelling. The shape of the density plot of each month provides us with insights about the characteristics of each month (or frequency unit). We can see some indication of a seasonal pattern in the series, as the density plots are not overlapping on each other (with the exception of some consecutive months, such as May and June). In addition, we can see that, for some months, the shape of the distributions is flatter with long tails (mainly during the winter months—November, December, and January). This could be a result of the volatility in some of the exogenous factors; for instance, a combination of weather patterns along with the elasticity or sensitivity of the series for changes in weather. For example, in the case of natural gas consumption, there is a higher elasticity during the winter months due to the dependency of the heating systems for this resource, which does not exist during summer time.

Nevertheless, don't forget the effect of the trend or the growth from year to year (as we know from the previous chapter, the USgas series had a linear trend since the year 2010) as we did not remove it from the series. Let's repeat this process; this time we will detrend the USgas series before plotting it. We will apply a simple method for detrending the series by using the decompose function to compute the series trend and then subtract it from the series:

```
USgas_df$USgas_detrend <- USgas_df$USgas - decompose(USgas)$trend

ggplot(USgas_df, aes(x = USgas_detrend)) +
  geom_density(aes(fill = month)) +
  ggtitle("USgas - Kernel Density Estimates by Month") +
  facet_grid(rows = vars(as.factor(month)))
```

The output is as follows:

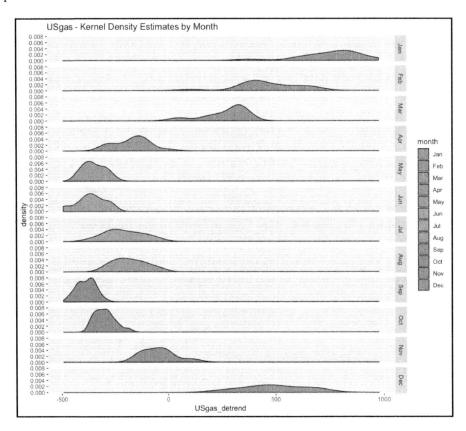

As you can notice, the removal of the series trend sharpens the seasonal effect as the tail of all the distribution become shorter. Although, in the case of the USgas series, the indication of the existence of seasonal pattern was very clear before removing the trend, in other cases it may not be as clear. Therefore, it is recommended that you remove the series trend whenever the trend is non-linear or when there is distribution that has a long tail.

In the case where the distribution of most of the frequency units is flat with a long tail, it could be an indication of multiple seasonal patterns in the series. Let's return to the UKgrid series and plot the 24-hour density plots:

```
# Density plot - 24 hour frequency
UKgrid_df$hour <- as.factor(UKgrid_df$hour)
ggplot(UKgrid_df, aes(x = UKgrid)) +
  geom_density(aes(fill = hour)) +
  ggtitle("UKgrid - Kernel Density Estimates by Hour of the day") +
  facet_grid(rows = vars(as.factor(hour)))
```

The output is as follows:

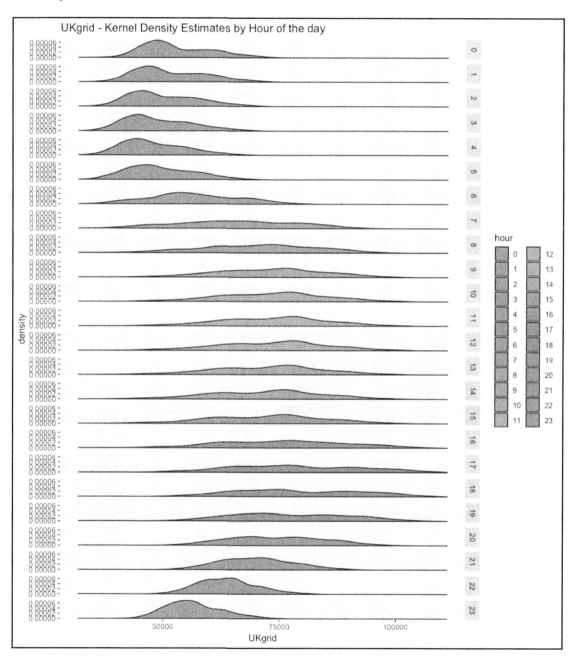

As we observed earlier with the summary statistics tables, the distribution of the net demand for electricity during the nighttime is relatively stable (hence the non-flat distribution with short tails as opposed to flat with long tail distribution during the daytime). If we subset one of the hours during the day and plot its distribution by the day of the week, we should expect an overlapping during the nighttime and be able to distinguish between the distribution during the weekdays and weekend, as opposed to just the weekday.

For example, the following plot represents the distribution of the demand at 9 a.m. throughout the days of the week. You can see that the distribution during the weekdays is distinguished from the one at the weekend:

```
UKgrid_df$weekday <- as.factor(UKgrid_df$weekday)

UKgrid_df %>% dplyr::filter(hour == 0) %>%
ggplot(aes(x = UKgrid)) +
   geom_density(aes(fill = as.factor(weekday))) +
   ggtitle("UKgrid - Kernel Density Estimates by Hour of the day") +
   facet_grid(rows = vars(as.factor(weekday)))
```

The output is shown in the following plot:

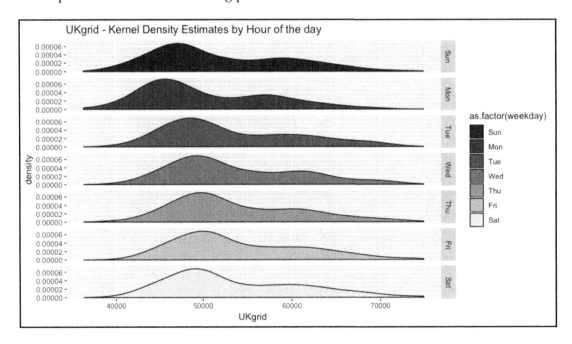

Let's now look at the structural tools for seasonal analysis.

Structural tools for seasonal analysis

Data visualization methods have a pivotal role in time series analysis, and in particular with seasonal analysis. As we saw in the preceding examples, the use of data visualization tools allows us to communicate statistical results in an intuitive and insightful way. In the coming sections, we will introduce built-in tools for seasonal analysis with the **forecast** and **TSstudio** packages.

Seasonal analysis with the forecast package

The **forecast** package provides several functions for seasonal analysis based on the **ggplot2** package graphics engine (and the `base plot` function) and it supports the `ts` objects. The `ggseasonplot` function creates a seasonal plot of the series by splitting and plotting each year as a separate line. This allows the user to obtain the changes in the series from year to year. Let's use this function to create the seasonal plot of the `USgas` series:

```
library(forecast)
ggseasonplot(USgas,year.labels=TRUE,continuous=TRUE)
```

The output is as follows:

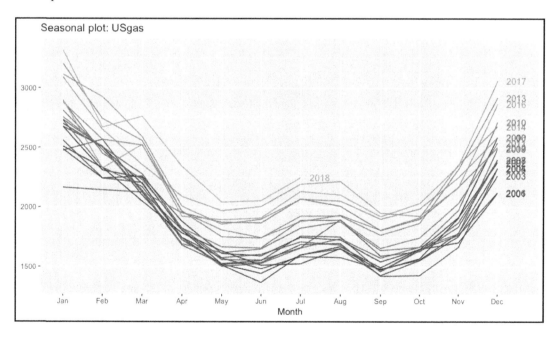

We can easily learn from this simple representation of the `USgas` series that the series has a strong repeated pattern, which indicates the existence of the monthly seasonal pattern. Furthermore, as you can see from the color scale and the `years` labels, the series is growing from year to year.

Another intuitive way to represent a series by its frequency cycle is with the polar plot. The polar plot spreads the frequency units across 360 degrees, depending on the number of frequency units (here this is *360/frequency*), where the distance from the polar center represents the magnitude of the observations. `ggseasonplot` provides a polar representation of the time series data by setting the polar argument to `TRUE`:

```
ggseasonplot(USgas, polar = TRUE)
```

The output is as follows:

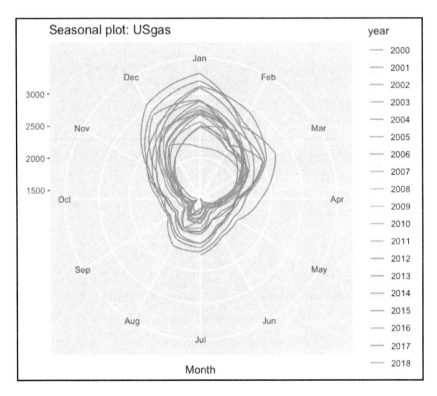

Likewise, in the normal preceding seasonal plot, you can see in the polar representation of the `USgas` series that the series has repeated seasonal patterns along with a year-to-year growth or trend.

Seasonal analysis with the TSstudio package

The **TSstudio** package provides a set of interactive data visualization functions based on the **plotly** package engine for seasonal analysis. It supports multiple time series objects, such as `ts`, `xts`, `zoo`, and data frame objects (`data.frame`, `data.table`, and `tbl`).

The `ts_seasonal` function provides several types of seasonal plots. The `type` argument sets the type of plot. The default option of the type argument is `normal`, which provides a similar seasonal plot as the `ggseasonplot` function:

```
ts_seasonal(USgas,type ="normal")
```

The output is as follows:

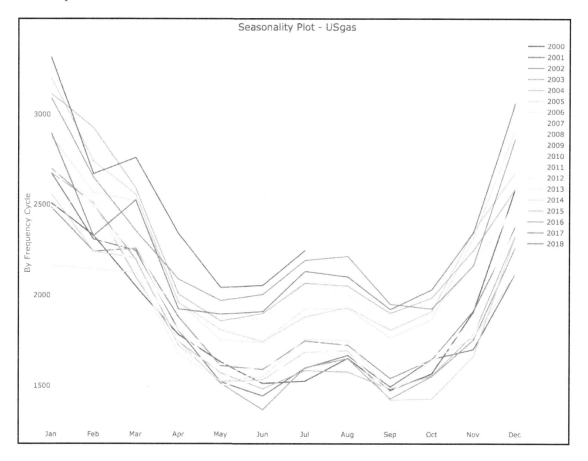

The `cycle` option group plots the series frequency units over time in chronological order; for example, all the observations that occurred during January over a certain amount of time for a monthly series. This allows us to identify seasonal pattern without detrending the series. For instance, in the following plot of the `USgas` series, you can see that, despite the growth from year to year, in most of the cases the order of the months (from high to low) remains the same:

```
ts_seasonal(USgas, type = "cycle")
```

The output is as follows:

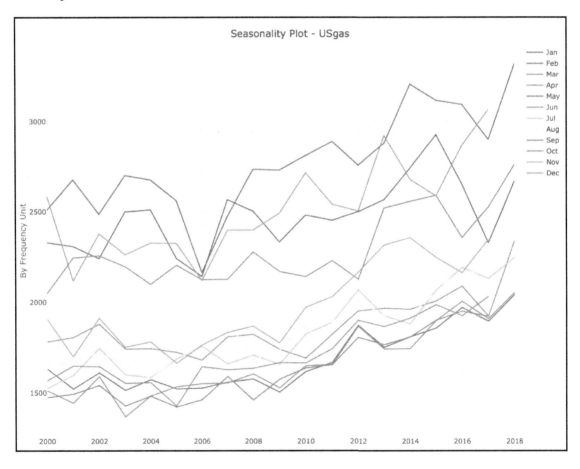

The `box` option provides a box plot representation for each frequency unit:

```
ts_seasonal(USgas, type = "box")
```

The output is as follows:

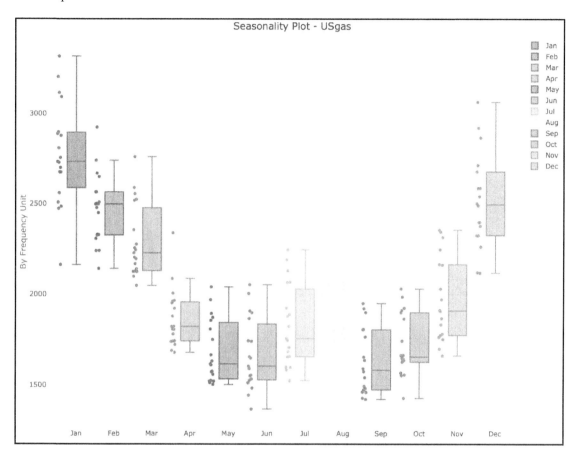

The box plot can be very informative plot, as it provides the range and quartile representation of the observations of each frequency unit. On the other hand, some of the oscillation in the box plot representation may occur as results of the series trend. Therefore, it is always recommended that you use a combination of different views of the series seasonality to get the full picture. The `all` option returns a plot of all of the three plots (`normal`, `cycle`, and `box`) side by side. This allows you to connect the information from the three different representations of the series to get a better understanding of the patterns (if any exist) and characteristics of the series:

```
ts_seasonal(USgas, type = "all")
```

The output is as follows:

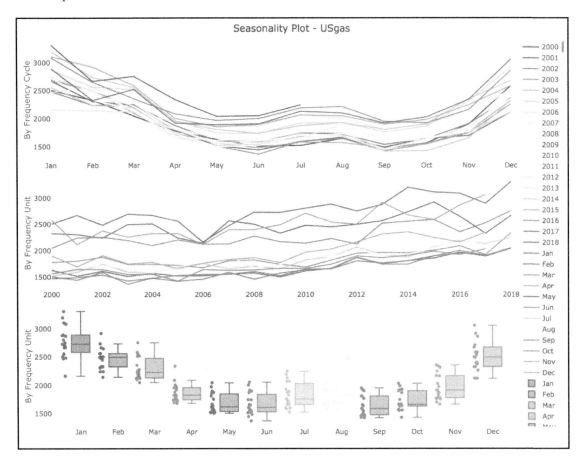

A time series heat map is another informative way to explore seasonality in time series data. The `ts_heatmap` function returns a `heatmap` plot of the time series object where the *y*-axis represents the frequency units (the months, for example, in the case of a monthly series) and the *x*-axis represents the cycle units of the series (the years, for example, in the case of a monthly series). The magnitude of each observation is represented by the color scale of the map, so the darker it is, the higher the value of the observation with respect to the overall values of the series:

```
ts_heatmap(USgas, color = "Reds")
```

The output is shown in the following graph:

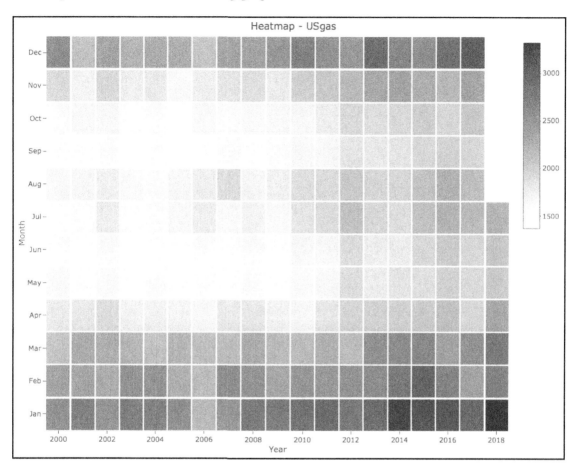

Last but not least, we will look at the `ts_quantile` function for visualizing the quantile plot of time series data. This function supports time series objects with a time or date index (such as the `xts`, `zoo`, and `data.frame` objects), and it's mainly useful on high-frequency time series data, such as hourly or daily. By default, the function returns a quantile plot of the series frequency units, where the middle line represents the median and the lower and upper lines represent the 25th and 75th percentiles. For instance, we will use this function to visualize the 24 cycles of the `UKgrid` dataset:

```
ts_quantile(UKgrid)
```

The output is as follows:

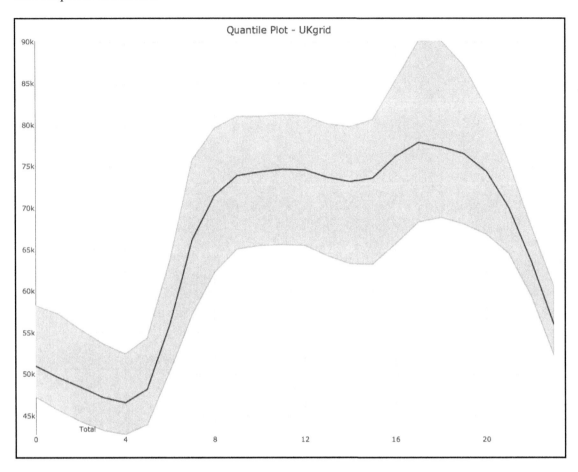

The `period` argument allows you to examine whether the seasonal patterns of the series are changing when using a different subset of time. This allows you to examine whether the series has additional seasonal patterns. For example, we can plot the 24-hour cycle of the `UKgrid` series by the day of the week by setting the period argument to weekdays:

```
ts_quantile(UKgrid, period = "weekdays", n = 2)
```

The output is as follows:

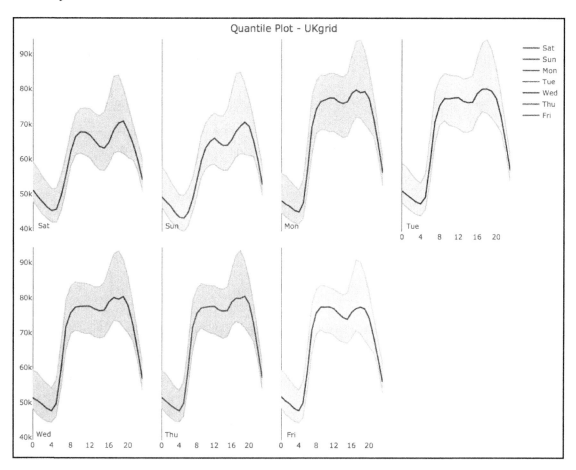

As we saw earlier with the density plots, the demand for electricity during the daytime is relatively higher throughout the weekdays in comparison to during the weekends. In the same way, you can plot the 24-hour cycle by month:

```
ts_quantile(UKgrid, period = "monthly", n = 2)
```

The output is as follows:

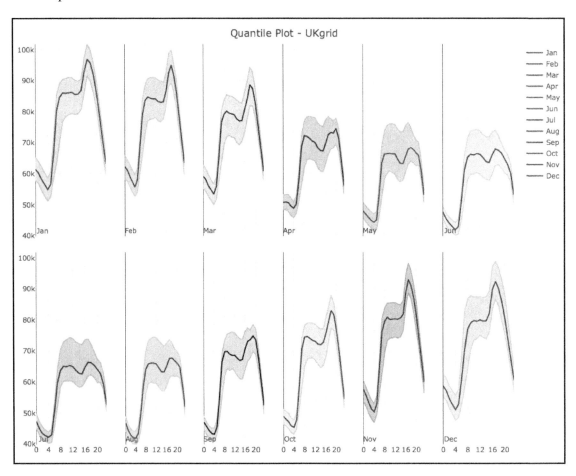

The main advantage of the quantile plots of multiple periods (for example, days of the week, months, and so on) over the density plot we used earlier is that the first represents all the frequency units (and, in the case of the UKgrid series, with a 24-hour frequency), while the second represents a single frequency unit (for example, the density of 9 a.m. throughout the weekdays).

Summary

The use of descriptive statistics and data visualization tools plays a pivotal role in the seasonality analysis of time series data. As we saw in this chapter, there is a close relationship between the frequency of the series and the type of seasonal patterns. A series with a lower frequency (such as monthly or quarterly) would potentially have a single dominant seasonal pattern. On the other hand, if the series frequency is higher, the probability is that multiple seasonal patterns exist in the series. This, of course, should help you to determine which tools or approaches to use in the analysis process. Last but not least, in some instances, you should consider removing exogenous factors (such as the series trend) to get a clear picture of the seasonal patterns and to avoid misleading results.

In the next chapter, we will focus on the correlation analysis of time series data.

Correlation Analysis

7

Due to the continuous and chronologically ordered nature of time series data, there is a likelihood that there will be some degree of correlation between the series observations. For instance, the temperature in the next hour is not a random event since, in most cases, it has a strong relationship with the current temperature or the temperatures that have occurred during the past 24 hours. In many cases, the series of past observations contains predictive information about future events, which can be utilized to forecast the series' future observations. Throughout this chapter, we will focus on identifying and revealing those relationships with the use of correlation analysis techniques, such as the autocorrelation and cross-correlation functions, along with the data visualization tools.

This chapter will cover the following topics:

- Causality versus correlation
- The autocorrelation and partial autocorrelation functions
- Data visualization tools for correlation analysis

Technical requirement

The following packages will be used in this chapter:

- **TSstudio**: Version 0.1.4 and above
- **plotly**: Version 4.8 and above
- **stats**: Version 3.6.0 and above

You can access the codes for this chapter from the following link:

```
https://github.com/PacktPublishing/Hands-On-Time-Series-Analysis-with-R/tree/master/Chapter07
```

Correlation between two variables

One of the main goals of correlation analysis is to identify and quantify the relationship between two variables. This relationship could vary from having a full dependency or linear relationship between the two, to complete independence. One of the most popular methods for measuring the level of correlation between two variables is the Pearson correlation coefficient. Although this method is not necessarily the most appropriate one for time series data, it is a simple and intuitive representative of the statistical logic beyond most of the methods for measuring correlation. This method, also known as the population correlation coefficient, is a ratio between the covariance of two variables and the multiplication of their standard deviation:

$$\rho_{X,Y} = \frac{COV(X,Y)}{\sigma_X \sigma_Y}, \; where \; -1 \leq \rho_{X,Y} \leq 1$$

The values of the correlation coefficient segment the level of correlation into three main groups:

- **Positively correlated**: This is where the value of the coefficient is greater than 0. This indicates some degree of a positive linear relationship between the variables, depending on the value of the coefficient. As the value of $\rho_{X,Y}$, the correlation coefficient, grows closer to 1, the linear relationship between the two variables grows stronger; 1 indicates a perfect linear dependency.
- **Negatively correlated**: This is where the value of the coefficient is lower than 0. This is the reflection of the positive correlation, and it is an indication for an inverse linear relationship. In this case, as the value of $\rho_{X,Y}$ is closer to -1, the negative linear relationship of the two variables (for example, when one variable goes up the other goes down); -1 represents a perfect inverse linear dependency between the two variables.
- **Not correlated**: This is where the value of the coefficient is equal to 0, which indicates that the two variables are independent.

This interpretation of the correlation values can easily be derived from the formula mentioned previously. You may remember from your `stats` class that two random variables are entirely independent of each other when the covariance of the two is equal to 0 (or $COV(X, Y) = 0$), therefore the correlation coefficient will be equal to 0 in those cases.

If two random variables are independent, you can conclude that the correlation between the two variables is zero. On the other hand, if the correlation between two random variables is zero, we cannot conclude by default that the variables are independent, as a non-linear relationship may exist.

Similarly, when a variable is a linear combination of another variable, the covariance of the two is equal to the multiplication of their standard deviation (or $COV(X,Y) = \sigma_X\sigma_Y$). A special case is a correlation of a variable with itself, which is the variance divided by its square standard deviation:

$$\rho_{X,X} = \frac{COV(X,X)}{\sigma_X\sigma_X} = \frac{VAR(X)}{\sigma_X^2} = 1$$

Typically, we would consider the correlation between two variables to be strong if the value of the correlation coefficient is higher than 0.75 or lower than -0.75 (but this, of course, could change according to the field of research).

Measuring and analyzing the correlation between two variables, in the context of time series analysis, can be categorized in the following two categories:

- Analyzing the correlation between a series and its lags, as some of the past lags may contain predictive information, which can be utilized to forecast future events of the series. One of the most popular methods for measuring the level of correlation between a series and its lags is the autocorrelation function.
- Analyzing the correlation between two series in order to identify exogenous factors or predictors, which can explain the variation of the series over time (for example, the effect of weather patterns such as rainfall or temperature on taxi rides in New York City). In this case, the measurement of correlation is typically done with the cross-correlation function.

In the context of time series analysis, the first method (also know as lags analysis) is an integrated part of the analysis, whereas the use of the second method (also known as causality analysis) is less common. This is mainly related to the cost associated with each method. While in lags analysis we extract the required data (the series lags) from the series itself, causality analysis requires additional effort, such as identifying and extracting external variables, which may not always available. We will start with the lags analysis methods and techniques and then generalize them to the causality analysis approaches.

Lags analysis

The goal of lags analysis is to identify and quantify the relationship between a series and its lags. This relationship is typically measured by calculating the correlation between the two and with the use of data visualization tools. The level of correlation between a series and its lags is derived from the series characteristics. For instance, you should expect the series to have a strong correlation with its seasonal lags (for example, lags 12, 24, and 36 when the series frequency is monthly) when the series has strong seasonal patterns. This should make sense, as the direction of the series is impacted by its seasonal pattern. Another example is the price of a stock over time, which, in this case, should be correlated with the most recent lags. In the following examples, we will use the USgas, EURO_Brent, and USVSales series, each with different characteristics to demonstrate the correlation pattern that is associated with each type. Before continuing to the autocorrelation function, let's load the three series from the **TSstudio** package and review their main characteristics:

```
library(TSstudio)
```

We will start with the US monthly natural gas consumption:

```
data(USgas)
```

Let's generate a plot, as follows:

```
ts_plot(USgas,
        title = "US Monthly Natural Gas consumption",
        Ytitle = "Billion Cubic Feet",
        Xtitle = "Year")
```

We will get the following plot:

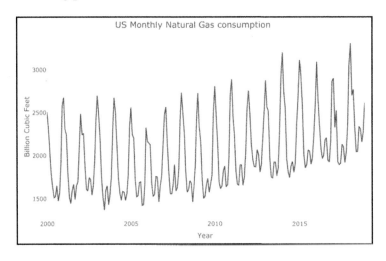

As we saw in the previous chapter, the main characteristic of the USgas series is the strong seasonal pattern. The second series is the EURO_Brent series, which represents the monthly prices of the Brent crude oil in USD. As you can observe in the following plot, the price of the oil does not have seasonal patterns or general trends:

```
data(EURO_Brent)

ts_plot(EURO_Brent,
        title = "Brent Crude Oil Prices",
        Ytitle = "US Dollars per Barrel",
        Xtitle = "Year")
```

We will get the following plot:

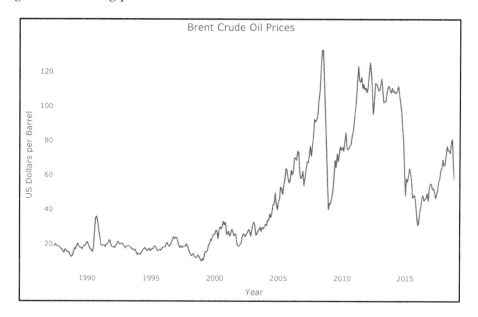

The last series that we will utilize in this chapter is USVSales, the US monthly total vehicle sales. This series, as can be seen in the following plot, is an example of a series with both seasonal and cycle patterns:

```
data(USVSales)

ts_plot(USVSales,
        title = "US Monthly Total Vehicle Sales",
        Ytitle = "Thousands of units",
        Xtitle = "Year")
```

We will get the following plot:

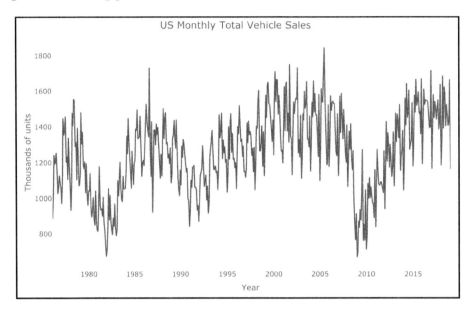

Let's now look at the autocorrelation function.

The autocorrelation function

The **autocorrelation function** (**ACF**) is the main method in time series analysis for quantifying the level of correlation between a series and its lags. This method is fairly similar (both mathematically and logically) to the Pearson correlation coefficient, which we saw earlier, and can be formalized with the following expression:

$$r_k = \frac{\sum_{t=k+1}^{n-k} (x_{t-k} - \overline{x})(x_t - \overline{x})}{\sum_{t=1}^{n} (x_t - \overline{x})^2}$$

Here, r_k represents the ACF correlation coefficient of the series with its k lag; and n, x_t, and $\overline{x}$ denote the number of observations of the series, the t observation of the series, and the mean, respectively. The acf function from the **stats** package is R's built-in ACF, which, by default, visualizes the results using a bar plot. Let's use this function to plot the correlation of the USgas series and its first 60 lags (by setting the lag.max argument to 60):

```
acf(USgas, lag.max = 60)
```

We will get the following plot:

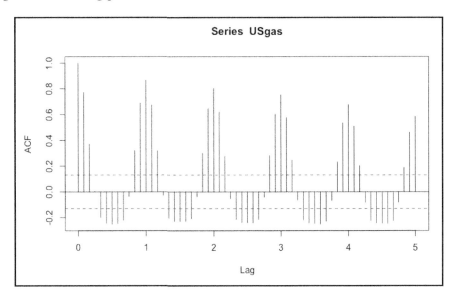

Each bar in the ACF plot represents the level of correlation between the series and its lags in chronological order. Note that the *x*-axis notation is a bit misleading, as the units represent the seasonal lags (for example, lags 1 and 2 represent the 12 and 24 lags). The blue dotted lines indicate whether the level of correlation between the series and each lag is significant or not. By testing the null hypothesis that the correlation of the lag with the series is equal to zero, we can reject it whenever the level of correlation is either above or below the upper and lower dotted lines, respectively, with a level of significance of 5%. Otherwise, whenever the correlation is between the upper and lower dotted lines, we fail to reject the null hypothesis, and we can therefore ignore those lags (or assume that there is no significant correlation between the two).

As you can see from the preceding ACF plot of the USgas series, the series has a strong positive correlation with the seasonal lags (which decay over time) along with negative correlation with the mid-seasonal lags (for example, lags 6, 18, and 30). This should not come as a surprise, as this behavior is aligned with the strong seasonal pattern of the series. Similarly, we can plot the correlation of the EURO_Brent and USVSales series and review how their unique correlation pattern aligns with their characteristics:

```
acf(EURO_Brent, lag.max = 60)
```

We will get the following plot:

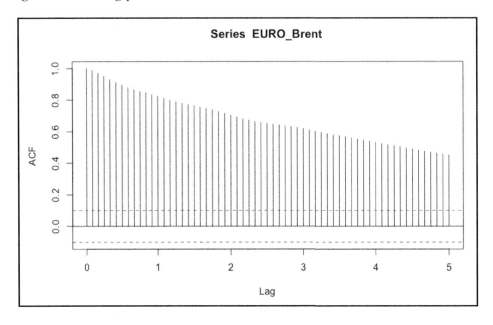

In the case of the EURO_Brent series, you can see that the correlation of the series with its lags is decaying over time, whereas the closer the lag is, chronologically to the series, the stronger the relationship with the series.

This type of correlation is also an indication that the series is not stationary and a differencing of the series is required. Do not worry if you are not familiar with those terms (stationary and differencing); in Chapter 11, *Forecasting with ARIMA models*, we will introduce the stationary state of time series data and its applications.

Let's now generate a plot for USVSales:

```
acf(USVSales, lag.max = 60)
```

We get the following plot:

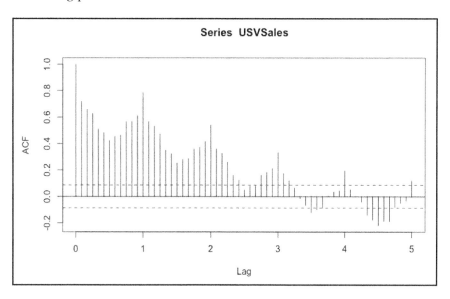

The correlation pattern of USVSales has a unique shape, which is a result of the combination of seasonal and cycle patterns of the series. Similarly to USgas, the correlation plot has a cyclic shape as a result of the seasonal pattern of the series. On the other hand, the decay rate of USVSales is faster compared to the rate of USgas due to the cycle pattern of the series, which shifts the series direction over time. As a result, the series is mainly correlated with the first seasonal lag. That being said, if we remove the series cycle (or detrend it) we will probably have a similar correlation pattern as USgas.

The partial autocorrelation function

One of the downsides of the autocorrelation function is that it does not remove the effect of lags *1* up to *k-1* on the series when calculating the correlation of the series with the *k* lag. The **partial autocorrelation function (PACF)**, the sister function of the ACF, provides a solution for this by computing the conditional correlation of the series with the *k* lag given the relationship of the *1, 2, ...,* and *k-1* lags with the series. In other words, the PACF provides an estimation for the direct correlation of the series with the *k* lag after removing the correlation of the *k* lag with the previous lags. The pacf function from the **stats** package provides an estimation for the PACF values for a given input. Let's review the PACF output for the first 60 lags of the USgas dataset:

```
pacf(USgas, lag.max = 60)
```

We will get the following plot:

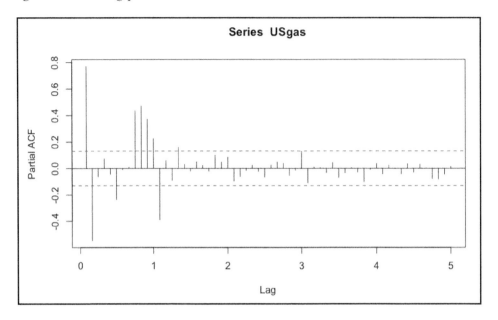

Both the ACF and PACF values play a pivotal role in the tuning process of the **AutoRegressive Integrated Moving Average** (**ARIMA**) family of models (for example, AutoRegressive or Moving Average). Don't worry if you are not familiar with those terms, as we will discuss them in detail in `Chapter 11`, *Forecasting with ARIMA Models*.

Lag plots

A lag plot is a simplistic and non-statistical approach for analyzing the relationship between a series and its lags. As the name indicates, this method is based on data visualization tools, with the use of two-dimensional scatter plots for visualizing the series (typically on the *y*-axis) against the *k* lag of the series. Hence, each pair of points represents a combination of the series observations and their corresponding lagged values. As more points on the lag plot are closer to the 45 degree line, the higher the correlation will be between the series and the corresponding lag. The **TSstudio** package provides a customized function, `ts_lags`, for creating multiple lag plots. Let's use the function to plot the USgas series against its lags:

```
ts_lags(USgas)
```

We will get the following plot:

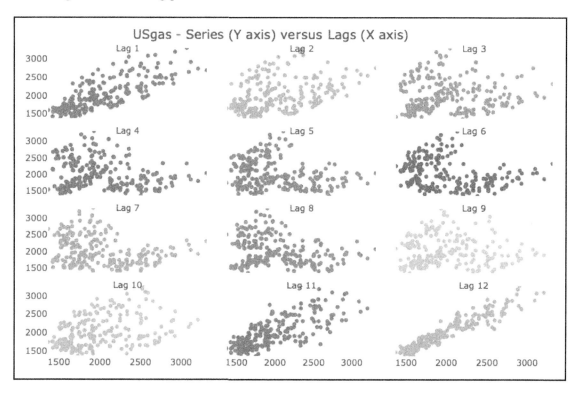

Looking at the lag plots of the USgas series, you can see that, moving along from the first lag up to the sixth lag, the relationship between the series and its lags become less linear. This process starts to reverse from the seventh lag as the relationship gradually becomes more linear, where the seasonal lag (or lag 12) has the strongest relationship with the series. Those results are aligned with the ones we saw earlier with the ACF plot. By default, the ts_lags function plots the first 12 lags of the series, where the lag argument allows you to set the number of lags.

For example, we can plot the most recent seasonal lags (that is, lags 12, 24, 36, and 48) by setting the lags number with the lags argument to the corresponding lags:

```
ts_lags(USgas, lags = c(12, 24, 36, 48))
```

We will get the following plot:

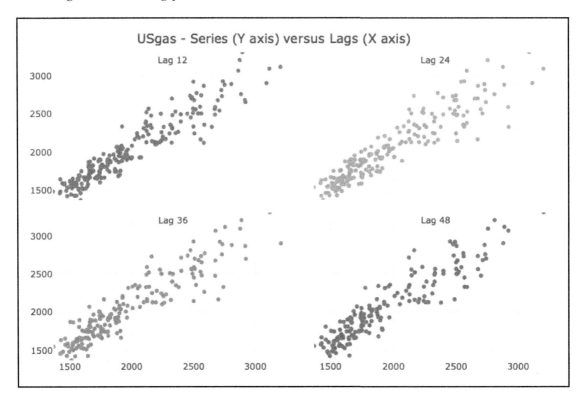

Similarly, we can plot the lag plots for the EURO_Brent and USVSales series. As you can see in the following plot, the results in both cases are aligned with the ones we received before with the ACF:

```
ts_lags(EURO_Brent)
```

We will get the following plot:

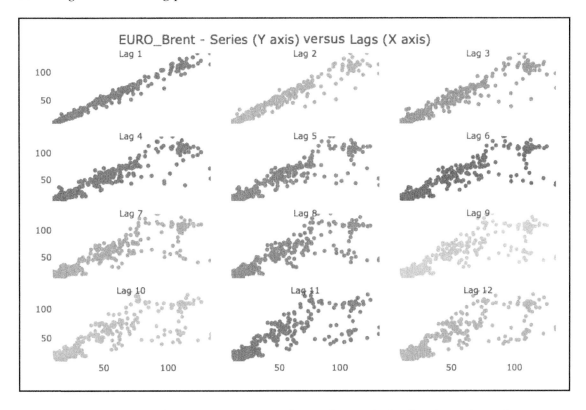

The EURO_Brent series has a strong linear relationship with the first lag, where the strength of that relationship decays as the distance of the lag from the series is higher:

```
ts_lags(USVSales)
```

We will get the following plot:

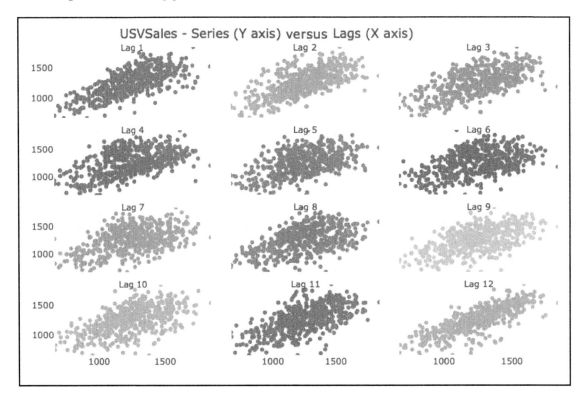

In the case of USVSales, the 12 lag has the closest linear relationship with the series (as we observed before with the ACF plot).

Causality analysis

The use of the series lags to forecast the future value of the series is beneficial whenever the series has stable repeated patterns over time. An excellent example of this type of series is the US natural gas consumption, as it has a strong seasonal pattern along with a consistent trend (or growth) pattern. Yet, the main pitfall of this method is that it will fail whenever the changes in the series derive from exogenous factors. In these cases, using only past lags could potentially lead to misleading results, as the lags do not necessarily drive the changes in the series. The goal of causality analysis, in the context of time series analysis, is to identify whether a causality relationship exists between the series we wish to forecast and other potential exogenous factors. The use of those external factors as drivers of the forecasting model (whenever exists) could potentially provide accurate and robust forecast (as oppose of using only the past observation of the series). Before diving into the details of causality analysis, let's pause and define causality and its characteristics and the distinctions between causality and correlation.

Causality versus correlation

Two variables will have a causality relationship whenever the change of one variable triggers a direct change of the second variable. This is also known as a cause-and-effect relationship. For instance, the temperatures in Chicago have a direct impact on the consumption of natural gas throughout the year (as most of the heating systems operate with natural gas) and we can therefore assume that there is a causality relationship between the two. One of the main characteristics of causality is a high correlation between the two variables. This should make sense, as there is a high dependency between the two variables. On the other hand, this could be misleading in some cases, as high correlation by itself between two variables should not instantly imply the existence of a causality relationship, as the two may have a high dependency on a third variable.

For example, you should expect to have a high correlation between the sales of ice cream and bathing suits (high demand during the summer and low throughout the winter). However, there is no causal relationship between the two besides the fact that both are highly correlated with the same factor—the season of the year (or weather patterns).

The following diagram describes this type of relationship:

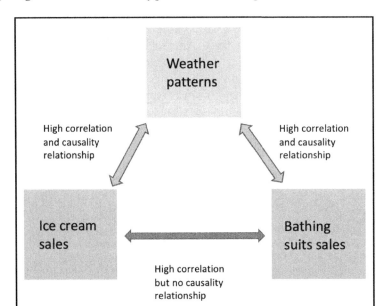

In the context of time series analysis, the causality between two time series can be categorized into the following two types:

- **Direct causality**: This is where series *B* reacts immediately to the changes of series *A* at time *t*. For example, the speed of the wind will have a direct impact on the level of electricity production of a wind turbine.
- **In-direct causality**: This is where the change of series *A* at time *t* triggers a change of series *B* at time *t + n* (where *n > 0*). This lag effect is common in economic indicators, such as **Gross Domestic Product** (**GDP**) and consumption or the unemployment rate, where the change in the first triggers a gradual change in the other over time (for example, a drop in the GDP this quarter will impact the employment rate in the next quarter).

Typically, a series from the first type will have a stronger dependency and a higher level of correlation compared to the second type. Yet, it is harder (or even not practical in some cases) to utilize series *A* as a predictor of series *B*, as the future values of series *A* are unknown and therefore need to be forecast as well (unless the future values are deterministic).

This could potentially increase the level of uncertainty of the model output, due to the fact that the input values are forecasted and will therefore come with some degree of uncertainty (as opposed to the actual input values of series *A* that were used in the training process).

For example, if you wish to forecast the level of electricity production of a wind turbine during the next 10 days by using the wind speed as a predictor, you will have to forecast the wind speed in the next 10 days as well. The forecast of wind speed by itself could be a challenging process. On the other hand, it is more common to use the *n* lag of series *A* as a predictor of series *B* (when applicable), as in this case, the input is the actual values of the series (assuming the length of *n* is equal to or less than the forecast horizon). Don't worry if at this point you are not familiar with the training process of the forecasting model. We will discuss this in detail in the next chapter.

Analyzing and identifying causality between two series is based on the use of correlation measurement and lag plots, along with some intuition and common sense (as mentioned previously, high correlation by itself is not necessarily an indication for causality). In the next section, we will introduce the cross-correlation function for measuring the correlation between two time series.

The cross-correlation function

The **cross-correlation function (CCF)** is the sister function of the ACF and it measures the level of correlation between two series and their lags in a fairly similar way. In the coming example, we will analyze the relationship between the total vehicle sales (USVSales) and the unemployment rate (USUnRate) in the US to understand whether there is a cause and effect relationship between the two. The monthly unemployment rate in the US is available in the **TSstudio** package, so let's load the series and review it with the ts_plot function:

```
data(USUnRate)

ts_plot(USUnRate,
        title = "US Monthly Civilian Unemployment Rate",
        Ytitle = "Unemployment Rate (%)",
        Xtitle = "Year")
```

We will get the following plot:

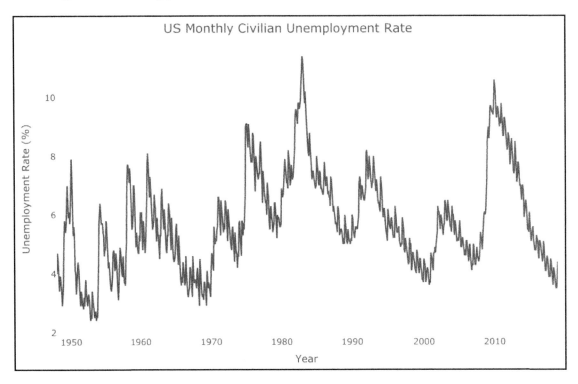

As you can observe in the preceding plot, the USUnRate series starts during the 1950s, as opposed to the USVSales series, which began in 1976. Therefore, before starting, let's align the two series to the same time frame using the window function:

```
us_vsales <- window(USVSales, start = c(1976,1), end = c(2018,6))
us_unrate <- window(USUnRate, start = c(1976,1), end = c(2018,6))
```

Next, we will plot the two series on a two-*y*-axis plot (as the units of the two series are different) using the **plotly** package:

```
library(plotly)

plot_ly(x = time(us_vsales),
        y = us_vsales,
        type = "scatter",
        mode = "line",
        name = "Total Vehicle Sales") %>%
   add_lines(x = time(us_unrate),
             y = us_unrate,
```

```
          name = "Unemployment Rate",
          yaxis = "y2") %>%
layout(
  title = "Total Monthly Vehicle Sales vs Unemployment Rate in the US",
  yaxis2 =  list(
    overlaying = "y",
    side = "right",
    title = "Percentage",
    showgrid = FALSE
  ),
  yaxis = list(title = "Thousands of Units",
              showgrid = FALSE),
  legend = list(orientation = 'h'),
  margin = list(l = 50, r = 50, b = 50, t = 50, pad = 2)
)
```

We will get the following plot:

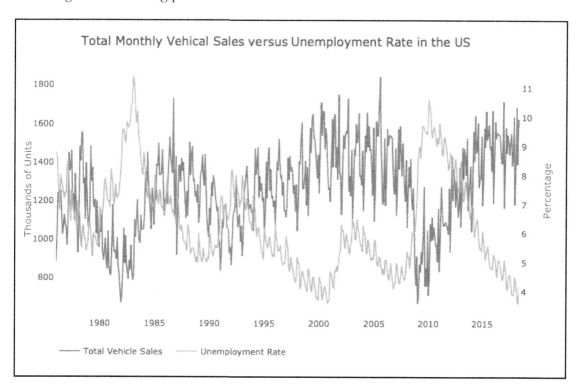

It is pretty clear from the preceding plot that the two series move to the opposite direction, so when the vehicle sales increase, the unemployment rate decreases and the other way around. You can also see that, in most of the cases, the changes in the vehicle sales series are leading to the changes in the unemployment rate. In order to explore this assumption further, we can measure the level of correlation between the unemployment rate and the vehicle sales and its lags using the `ccf` function from the **stats** package as well:

```
ccf(x = us_vsales, y = us_unrate, lag.max = 36)
```

We will get the following plot:

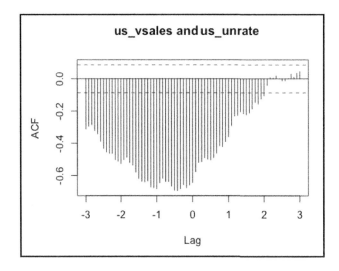

Similarly to the ACF output, each bar in the CCF plot represents the level of correlation between the main series and the lags of the secondary. Lag 0 represents the direct correlation between the two series, where the negative and positive lags represent the correlation between the unemployment rate and the past and leading lags of the vehicle sales series, respectively. The main thing to note from the preceding plot is that the unemployment rate is correlated more to the past lags as opposed to the leading lags of the vehicle sales.

The highest correlation between the two series was observed with the 5 lag of the vehicle sales and was not far away from the seasonal lag as well (that is, lag 12). It is difficult (and probably even wrong) to conclude from the results that the vehicle sales explicitly drive the changes in the unemployment rate (and it is definitely not in the scope of this book). However, there is some indication of a causality relationship, which can be derived from the level of correlation along with common sense, given the size of the vehicle industry in the US and its historical impact on the economy.

Alternatively, you can plot the relationship between US vehicle sales and the lags of the unemployment rate with the `ccf_plot` function from the **TSstudio** package. This function works similarly to the `ts_lags` function we previously introduced:

```
ccf_plot(x = USVSales, y = USUnRate, lags = 0:12)
```

We will get the following plot:

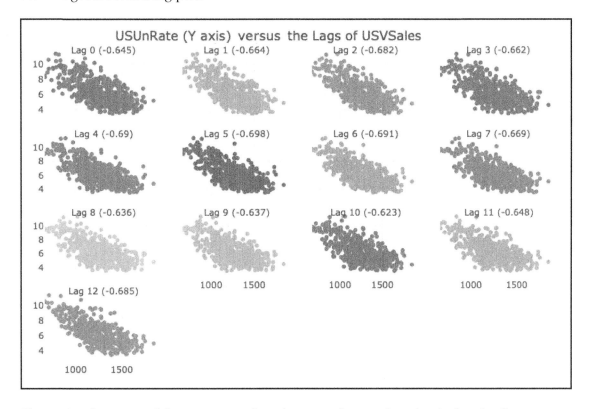

The main advantage of the `ccf_plot` function over the `ccf` function is that the first automatically aligns the two series according to their chronological order, whereas the `ccf` function does not have this automatic functionality, and therefore requires a preprocessing step (as we used previously with the `window` function).

Summary

Correlation analysis of time series data is one of the main steps of the analysis process. Throughout this chapter, we introduced different approaches for identifying the correlation between a series and its lags and causality between two time series. Those approaches include the use of both statistical methods, such as the ACF and PACF, and data visualization methods. The application of the correlation analysis plays a pivotal role in many time series applications, from the descriptive analysis of a series, as we saw in this chapter, to tuning time series forecasting models, such as the ARIMA model.

In the next chapter, we will introduce strategies for training, testing, benchmarking, and evaluating forecasting models.

8
Forecasting Strategies

So far, we have mainly been focusing on the first two components of the time series analysis workflow—data preprocessing and descriptive analysis. Starting from this chapter, we will shift gear and move on to the third and last component of the analysis—the forecast. Before we dive into different forecasting models in the upcoming chapters, we will introduce the main elements of the forecasting workflow. This includes approaches for training a forecasting model, performance evaluation, and benchmark methods. This will provide you with a set of tools for designing and building a forecasting model according to the goal of the analysis.

This chapter covers the following topics:

- Training and testing approaches for a forecasting model
- Performance evaluation methods and error measurement matrices
- Benchmark methods
- Quantifying forecast uncertainty with confidence intervals and simulation

Technical requirement

The following packages will be used in this chapter:

- **forecast**: Version 8.5 and above
- **TSstudio**: Version 0.1.4 and above
- **plotly**: Version 4.8 and above

You can access the codes for this chapter from the following link:

```
https://github.com/PacktPublishing/Hands-On-Time-Series-Analysis-with-R/tree/
master/Chapter08
```

The forecasting workflow

Traditional time series forecasting follows the same workflow as most of the fields of predictive analysis, such as regression or classification, and typically includes the following steps:

1. **Data preparation**: Here, we prepare the data for the training and testing process of the model. This step includes splitting the series into training (in-sample) and testing (out-sample) partitions, creating new features (when applicable), and applying a transformation if needed (for example, log transformation, scaling, and so on).

2. **Train the model**: Here, we used the training partition to train a statistical model. The main goal of this step is to utilize the training set to train, tune, and estimate the model coefficients that minimize the selected error criteria (later on in this chapter, we will discuss common error metrics in detail). The fitted values and the model estimation of the training partition observations will be used later on to evaluate the overall performance of the model.

3. **Test the model**: Here, we utilize the trained model to forecast the corresponding observations of the testing partition. The main idea here is to evaluate the performance of the model with a new dataset (that the model did not *see* during the training process).

4. **Model evaluation**: Last but not least, after the model was trained and tested, it is time to evaluate the overall performance of the model on both the training and testing partitions.

Based on the evaluation process of the model, if the model meets a certain threshold or criteria, then we either retain the model using the full series in order to generate the final forecast or select a new training parameter/different model and repeat the training process.

One of the main pitfalls when training a statistical model is overfitting the model to the training set. Overfitting occurs when the model is *overlearning* the data that the model trained with and fails to generalize the model's performance on the training set on other datasets. One of the main signs for overfitting is a high ratio between the error rate on the testing set and training set (for example, a high error on the training partition versus a low error on the training partition). Therefore, the evaluation of the model's performance on both the training and testing partitions is essential to identify overfitting. Generally, overfitting is caused by incorrectly tuning the model parameters or by using a model with high complexity.

On the other hand, this process has its own unique characteristics, which distinguish it from other predictive fields:

- The training and testing partitions must be ordered in chronological order, as opposed to random sampling.
- Typically, once we have trained and tested the model using the training and testing partitions, we will retrain the model with all of the data (or at least the most recent observation in chronological order). At first glance, this might be shocking and terrifying for people with a background in traditional machine learning or supervised learning modeling, as typically it leads to overfitting and other problems. We will discuss the reason behind this and how to avoid overfitting later.

The following diagram demonstrates the forecasting workflow:

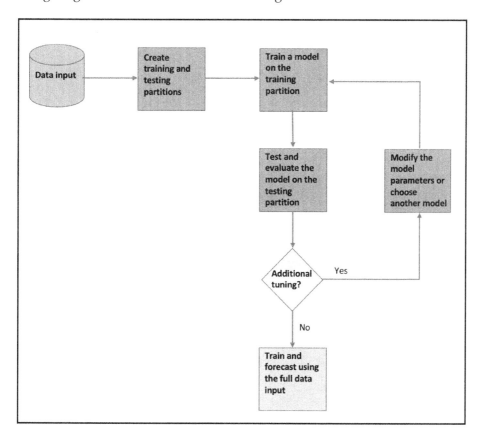

Now, we will take a look at the different training approaches.

Training approaches

One of the core elements of the forecasting workflow is the model training process. The quality of the model's training will have a direct impact on the forecast output. The main goals of this process are as follows:

- Formalize the relationship of the series with other factors, such as seasonal and trend patterns, correlation with past lags, and external variables in a predictive manner
- Tune the model parameters (when applicable)
- The model is scalable on new data, or in other words, avoids overfitting

As we mentioned previously, prior to the training process, the series is split into training and testing partitions, where the model is being trained on the training partition and tested on the testing partition. These partitions must be in chronological order, regardless of the training approach that has been used. The main reason for this is that most of the time series models establish a mathematical relationship between the series in terms of its past lags and error terms.

Training with single training and testing partitions

One of the most common training approaches is using single training and testing (or single out-of-sample) partitions. This simplistic approach is based on splitting the series into training and testing partitions (or in-sample and out-sample partitions, respectively), training the model on the training partition, and testing its performance on the testing set:

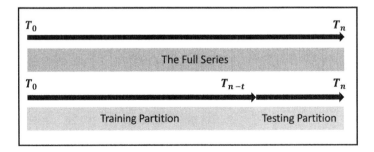

As you can see in the preceding diagram, the training and testing partitions are ordered and organized in chronological order. This approach has a single parameter—the length of the out-of-sample (or the length of the testing partition). Typically, the length of the testing partition is derived from the following rules of thumb:

- The length of the testing partition should be up to 30% of the total length of the series in order to have enough observation data for the training process.
- The length of the forecasting horizon (as long it is not violating the previous term). This is mainly related to the fact that the level of uncertainty increases as the forecast horizon increases. Therefore, aligning the testing set to the forecast horizon could, potentially, provide a closer estimate of the forecast's expected error.

For example, if we have a monthly series with 72 observations (or 6 years) and the goal is to forecast the next year (or 12 months), it would make sense to use the first 60 observations for training and test the performance using the last 12 observations. Creating partitions in R can be done manually with the `window` function from the **stats** package. For instance, let's split the `USgas` series into partitions, leaving the last 12 observations of the series as the testing partition and the rest as training:

1. First, let's load the `USgas` series from the **TSstudio** package into the environment:

```
library(TSstudio)

data(USgas)
```

2. We can observe the main characteristics of the `USgas` series with the `ts_info` function:

```
ts_info(USgas)
```

We get the following output:

```
##   The USgas series is a ts object with 1 variable and 227
observations
##   Frequency: 12
##   Start time: 2000 1
##   End time: 2018 11
```

3. Let's use the `window` function to split the series into training and testing partitions:

```
train <- window(USgas,
                start = time(USgas)[1],
```

```
                    end = time(USgas)[length(USgas) - 12])

      test <- window(USgas,
                      start = time(USgas)[length(USgas) - 12 + 1],
                      end = time(USgas)[length(USgas)])
```

4. The summary of the testing and testing partition can be seen in the following output:

```
ts_info(train)
```

We get the following output:

```
##   The train series is a ts object with 1 variable and 215
observations
##   Frequency: 12
##   Start time: 2000 1
##   End time: 2017 11
```

5. Now, let's take a look at the `test` partition:

```
ts_info(test)
```

We get the following output:

```
##   The test series is a ts object with 1 variable and 12
observations
##   Frequency: 12
##   Start time: 2017 12
##   End time: 2018 11
```

6. Alternatively, the `ts_split` function from the **TSstudio** package provides a customized way for creating training and testing partitions for time series data:

```
# The sample.out argument set the size of the testing partition
(and therefore the training partition)
USgas_partitions <- ts_split(USgas, sample.out = 12)

train <- USgas_partitions$train
test <- USgas_partitions$test
```

7. You can observe from the following output that we received the same execute results that we received previously:

```
ts_info(train)
```

We get the following output:

```
##   The train series is a ts object with 1 variable and 215
observations
##   Frequency: 12
##   Start time: 2000 1
##   End time: 2017 11
```

8. Now, let's look at the `test` partition:

```
ts_info(test)
```

We get the following output:

```
##   The test series is a ts object with 1 variable and 12
observations
##   Frequency: 12
##   Start time: 2017 12
##   End time: 2018 11
```

The simplicity of this method is its main advantage, as it is fairly fast to train and test a model while using (relatively) *cheap* compute power. On the other hand, it isn't possible to come to a conclusion about the stability and scalability of the model's performance based on a single test unit. It is feasible that a model, only by chance, will have relatively good performance on the testing set but do poorly on the actual forecast as it isn't stable over time. One way to mitigate that risk is with the backtesting approach, which is based on training a model with multiple training and testing partitions.

Forecasting with backtesting

The backtesting approach for training a forecasting model is an advanced version of the single out-of-sample approach we saw previously. It is based on the use of a rolling window to split the series into multiple pairs of training and testing partitions. A basic backtesting training process includes the following steps:

1. **Data preparation**: Create multiple pairs of training and testing partitions.
2. **Train a model**: This is done on each one of the training partitions.
3. **Test the model**: Score its performance on the corresponding testing partitions.

4. **Evaluate the model**: Evaluate the model's accuracy, scalability, and stability based on the testing score. Based on the evaluation, you would do one of the following:

- Generate the final forecast to check whether the model score meets a specific threshold or criteria
- Apply additional tuning and optimization for the model and repeat the training and evaluations steps

The use of scoring methodology allows us to assess the model's stability by examining the model's error rate on the different testing sets. We would consider a model as stable whenever the model's error distribution on the testing sets is fairly narrow. In this case, the error rate of the actual forecast should be within the same range of the testing sets (assuming there are no abnormal events that impact the forecast error rate).

This method is, conceptually, similar to the cross-validation approach for training machine learning models. The main distinction between the two approaches is related to how their partitions are set. While the backtesting partitions are ordered chronologically, the ones of the cross-validation approach are based on random sampling.

The main setting parameters of a backtesting training model are as follows:

- **The length of the training partitions**: It is set by the window setting. There are two common types of rolling windows:
  - **Expanding window**: Using the first N observations as the initial training partition, add the following n observations to create the following training partition. The length of the training partition grows as the window rolls over the series.
  - **Sliding window**: Set the first N observations as the initial training partition and shift the window by n observations to create the following training partition. The length of the training partitions remains the same as the window rolls over the series:
    - The length of the testing partitions—a constant value, typically aligned with the length of the forecasting horizon (under the limitation of the minimum number of observations required to train the model)
    - The space between each training partition—defines the pace of the rolling window
    - The number of training and testing partitions

The following diagram demonstrates the structure of the backtesting with an expanding window:

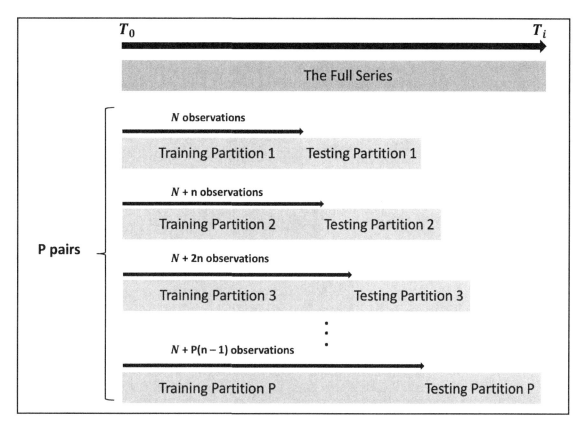

As you can see in the preceding diagram, all of the training partitions of the expanding window method start at the same index point, T_0, where each training partition is a combination of the previous training partition with the following n observations (where n is a constant that represents the expanded rate of the window). It would make sense to use this method when the series has a strong seasonal pattern and stable trend. In this case, the first observations of the series could, potentially, have predictive information that can be utilized by the model. The downside of this method is training the model with different length partitions, as typically a model tends to *learn* more and therefore perform better when more data is available. Therefore, we may observe that the performance of models that are trained on the latest partitions perform better than the ones that are trained with the first partitions.

This bias does not exist in the second training approach—the sliding window, as all of the training partitions, are of the same length, as you can see in the following diagram:

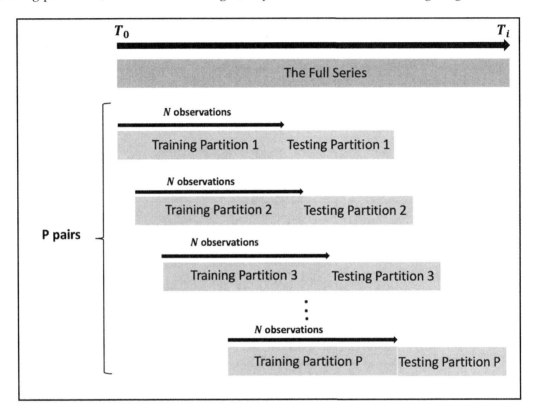

It would make more sense to use the sliding window whenever the input series has structural change or high volatility, or when most of the predictive power is linked to the most recent history (or high correlation with the most recent lags of the series). For example, as we saw in the previous chapter, monthly crude oil prices have a strong relationship with the most recent lags of the series, and the far history doesn't contain powerful predictive information about the series' future direction.

While the backtesting approach provides us with intuitive information about the stability and scalability of the model, it comes with a higher computation cost compared to the single training and testing partition approach. Hence, this trade-off between the two approaches should be taken into consideration when selecting the training approach.

Forecast evaluation

The primary goal of the evaluation step is to assess the ability of the trained model to forecast (or based on other criteria) the future observations of the series accurately. This process includes doing the following:

- **Residual analysis**: This focuses on the quality of the model, with fitted values in the training partition
- **Scoring the forecast**: This is based on the ability of the model to forecast the actual values of the testing set

Residual analysis

Residual analysis tests how well the model captured and identified the series patterns. In addition, it provides information about the residuals distributions, which are required to build confidence intervals for the forecast. The mathematical definition of a residual is the difference between the actual observation and the corresponding fitted value of the model, which was observed in the training process, or as the following equation:

$$\epsilon_t = Y_t - \hat{Y}_t$$

Here, ϵ_t, Y_t, and $\hat{Y}_t$ represent the residual, actual, and fitted values, respectively, at time t.

This process includes the use of data visualizations tools and statistical test to assess the following:

- **Test the goodness of the fit against the actual values**: You do this by plotting the residuals values over time in chronological order. The plot indicates how well the model was able to capture the oscillation of the series in the training partition. Residuals with random oscillation around the zero and with constant variation (white noise) indicate that the model is able to capture the majority of the series variation. On the other hand, if the residual oscillation does not have the white noise characteristics, it is an indication that the model failed to capture the series patterns. Here are some potential interpretations of the possible output:
    - **All or most of the residuals are above the zero lines**: This is an indication that the model tends to underestimate the actual values
    - **All or most of the residuals are below the zero lines**: This is an indication that the model tends to overestimate the actual values

- **Random spikes**: This is an indication for potential outliers in the training partition:
    - **The residual autocorrelation**: This indicates how well the model was able to capture the patterns of the series. Non-correlated lags indicate that there were no patterns that the model did not capture. Similarly, the existence of correlated lags indicates patterns that the model did not capture.
    - **The residuals distribution**: This is required to conclude about the reliability of the forecast confidence interval. If the residuals are not normally distributed, we cannot use it to create confidence intervals as it is based on the assumption that the residuals are normally distributed.

- To demonstrate the residual analysis process, we will train an ARIMA model on the training partition we created earlier for the USgas series. Don't worry if you're not familiar with the ARIMA model—we will discuss it in detail in Chapter 11, *Forecasting with the ARIMA Model*. We will train the model with the auto.arima function from the **forecast** package:

```
library(forecast)

md <- auto.arima(train)
```

To examine the residuals, we will use the checkresiduals function from the **forecast** package, which returns the following four outputs:

- Time series plot of the residuals
- ACF plot of the residuals
- Distribution plot of the residuals
- The output of the Ljung-Box test

The Ljung-Box test is a statistical method for testing whether the autocorrelation of a series (which, in this case, is the residuals) is different from zero and uses the following hypothesis:

- H_0: The level of correlation between the series and its lag is equal to zero, and therefore the series observations are independent
- H_1: The level of correlation between the series and its lag is different from zero, and therefore the series observations are not independent

Let's use the `checkresiduals` function to evaluate the trained model's performance on the training partition:

```
checkresiduals(md)
```

We get the following residuals from the ARIMA model:

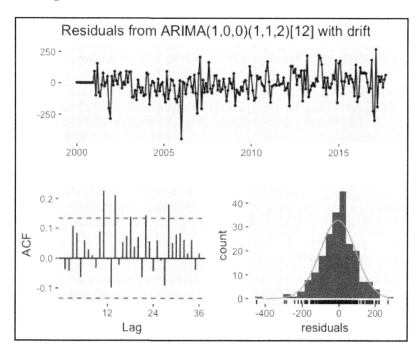

The output is as follows:

```
##
##   Ljung-Box test
##
## data:  Residuals from ARIMA(1,0,0)(1,1,2)[12] with drift
## Q* = 48.345, df = 19, p-value = 0.0002287
##
## Model df: 5.    Total lags used: 24
```

Starting with the output of the Ljung-Box test output, you will notice that, based on the *P*-value results, we can reject the null hypothesis with a level of significate of 0.01. Hence, there is an indication that the correlation between the residual series and its lags are different from zero. The ACP plot provides additional support for that as well. This indicates that the model did not fully capture all of the series patterns, and you may want to modify the model tuning parameters. The residual time series plot oscillates around the *x*-axis, with the exception of a few residuals, which cross the value of $\pm$ 250. This could indicate that some outliers occur during these periods, and you should check those data points in the series (later on in this chapter, we will look at a more intuitive method to compare the fitted values with the actual values using the `test_forecast` function from the **TSstudio** package). Last but not least is the distribution plot of the residuals, which seem to be a fairly good representation of a normal distribution.

 In an ideal world, you should end this process with white noise and independent residuals. Yet, in reality, in some cases, it will be harder to achieve this goal due to the series' structure (outliers, structural breaks, and so on), and you may have to select a model that brings you closer to this goal.

Scoring the forecast

Once you finalize the model tuning, it is time to test the ability of the model to predict observations that the model didn't see before (as opposed to the fitted values that the model saw throughout the training process). The most common method for evaluating the success of the forecast in order to predict the actual values is to use accuracy or error metrics. The most common method for evaluating the forecast's success is to predict the actual values with the use of an error metric to quantify the forecast's overall accuracy. The selection of a specific error metric depends on the forecast accuracy's goals. An example of common error metrics are as follows:

- **Mean Squared Error (MSE)**: This quantifies the average squared distance between the actual and forecasted values:

$$MSE = \frac{1}{n} \sum_{t=1}^{n} (Y_t - \hat{Y}_t)^2$$

The squared effect of the error prevents positive and negative values from cancelling each other out and panelize the error score as the error rate increases.

- **Root Mean Squared Error (RMSE)**: This is the root of the average squared distance of the actual and forecasted values:

$$RMSE = \sqrt{MSE} = \sqrt{\frac{1}{n} \sum_{t=1}^{n} (Y_t - \hat{Y}_t)^2}$$

Like *MSE*, the *RMSE* has a large error rate due to the squared effect and is therefore sensitive to outliers.

- **Mean Absolute Error (MAE)**: This measures the absolute error rate of the forecast:

$$MAE = \frac{|Y_t - \hat{Y}_t|}{n}$$

Similarly to *MSE* and *RMSE*, this method can only have positive values. This is so that is can avoid the cancellation of positive and negative values. On the other hand, there is no error penalization, and therefore this method is not sensitive to outliers.

- **Mean Absolute Percentage Error (MAPE)**: This measures the average percentage absolute error:

$$MAPE = \frac{1}{n} \sum_{t=1}^{n} |\frac{Y_t - \hat{Y}_t}{Y_t}|$$

It is easier to compare, benchmark, or communicate with non-technical people due to the percentage representative.

For example, let's use the model we trained earlier to forecast the 12 observations we left for testing and score its performance. We will use the `forecast` function from the **forecast** package to forecast the following `12` mounts (with respect to the end point of the training partition):

```
fc <- forecast(md, h = 12)
```

Now that we've assigned the forecast to the `fc` object, we will use the accuracy function from the **forecast** package to score the model's performance with respect to the actual values in the testing partition:

```
accuracy(fc, test)
##                       ME       RMSE       MAE        MPE       MAPE      MASE
 ## Training set   -7.049742   98.39066   72.24738  -0.584141  3.525916
0.6760411
 ## Test set       192.851978  208.01192  192.85198   7.840542  7.840542
1.8045758
 ##                           ACF1   Theil's U
 ## Training set   -0.03702499         NA
 ## Test set       -0.29130569   0.658966
```

The `accuracy` function, which we will use intensively in the upcoming chapters, returns several error metrics for both the fitted values (the `Training set` row) and the actual forecast (the `Test set` row). You will notice that the model MAPE results are 3.52% and 7.84% on the training and testing partitions, respectively. A higher error rate on the testing partition compared to the training partition should not come as a surprise, as typically the model saw the training partition data throughout the training process. A fairly low error rate in the training set, along with the high error rate in the testing set, is a clear indication of overfitting in the model.

An alternative approach to evaluating the fit of the model on both the training and testing is with the `test_forecast` function from the **TSstudio** package. This function visualizes the actual series, the fitted values on the training partition, and the forecasted values on the testing set. Hovering over the fitted or forecasted values makes a textbox pop up with the RMSE and MAPE results on both the training and testing partitions (which, unfortunately, cannot transfer to the book itself):

```
test_forecast(actual = USgas,
              forecast.obj = fc,
              test = test)
```

The output is as follows:

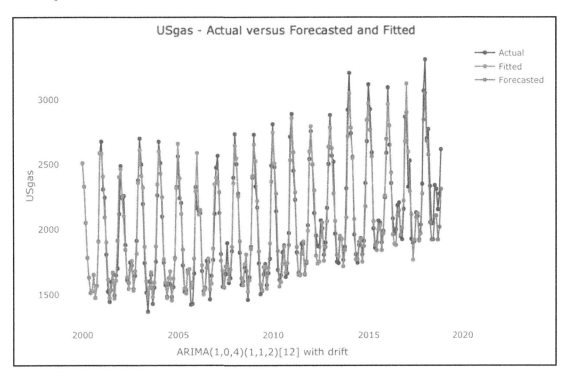

It is easier and faster to identify insights about the goodness of the fit of both the fitted and forecasted values when plotting those values against the actual values of the series. For instance, you will immediately notice that the residual peak during 2006 is caused by outliers (or lower consumption than the normal pattern of the series). In addition, the actual forecast missed the 2018 yearly peak. Those insights cannot be observed with error metrics.

Forecast benchmark

According to the error metrics, the trained model scored a MAPE of 7.84% or RMSE of 208.01. How can we assess whether these results are too high or low? The most common method is to benchmark the model's performance to some baseline forecast or to some legacy method that we wish to replace. A popular benchmark approach would be to use a simplistic forecasting approach as a baseline. For instance, let's forecast the series with a naive approach and use it as a benchmark for the previous forecast we created with the ARIMA model.

A simple naive approach typically assumes that the most recently observed value is the true representative of the future. Therefore, it will continue with the last value to infinity (or as the horizon of the forecast). We can create a naive forecast with the `naive` function from the **forecast** package and use the training set as the model input:

```
library(forecast)
```

We can review the performance of the model on the training and testing partitions using the following `test_forecast` function:

```
naive_model <- naive(train, h  = 12)
test_forecast(actual = USgas,
              forecast.obj = naive_model,
              test = test)
```

We get the following output:

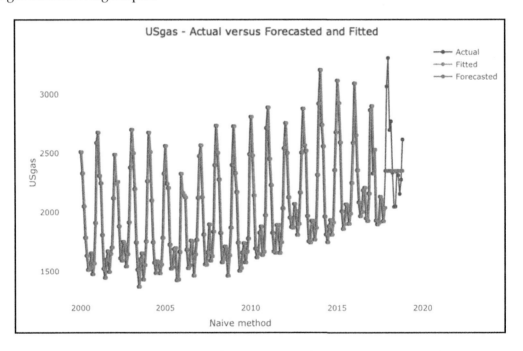

Similarly, we can utilize the `accuracy` function to evaluate the model's performance on both the training and testing partitions:

```
accuracy(naive_model, test)
##                    ME      RMSE      MAE        MPE      MAPE     MASE
 ## Training set  -2.223474 281.3634 225.4507 -0.9763903 10.96819 2.109612
 ## Test set     432.466667 580.8980 432.4667 15.6592587 15.65926 4.046725
```

```
##                       ACF1  Theil's U
## Training set 0.3893404          NA
## Test set     0.6063137   1.637631
```

In the case of the naive model, there is no training process, and the fitted values are set as the actual values (as you can see from the preceding plot). Since USgas has a strong seasonal pattern, it would make sense to use a seasonal naive model that takes into account seasonal variation. snaive_model from the **forecast** package uses the last seasonal point as a forecast of all of the corresponding seasonal observations. For example, if we are using monthly series, the value of the most recent January in the series will be used as the point forecast for all future January months:

```
snaive_model <- snaive(train, h = 12)
 test_forecast(actual = USgas,
               forecast.obj = snaive_model,
               test = test)
```

The output is shown in the following screenshot:

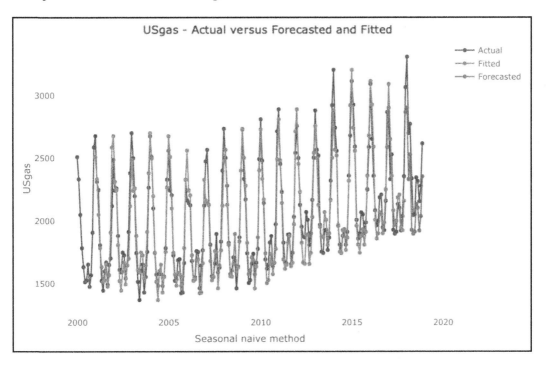

Let's use the `accuracy` function once more to review the seasonal naive performance on the training and testing partitions:

```
accuracy(snaive_model, test)
##                      ME     RMSE      MAE       MPE     MAPE     MASE
## Training set   20.69505 138.1953 106.8683 0.8499305 5.216692 1.000000
## Test set      242.78333 260.0920 242.7833 9.7342130 9.734213 2.271799
##                    ACF1 Theil's U
## Training set  0.4089415        NA
## Test set      0.1542089 0.7419918
```

It seems that the seasonal naive model has a better fit for the type of series we are forecasting, that is, USgas, due to its strong seasonal pattern (compared to the naive model). Therefore, we will use it as a benchmark for the ARIMA model. By comparing both the MAPE and RMSE of the two models in the testing partition, it is clear that the ARIMA model provides a lift (in terms of accuracy) with respect to the benchmark model:

Model	MAPE	RMSE
ARIMA	7.84%	208.01
snaive	9.73%	250.09

Finalizing the forecast

Now that the model has been trained, tested, tuned (if required), and evaluated successfully, we can move forward to the last step and finalize the forecast. This step is based on recalibrating the model's weights or coefficients with the full series. There are two approaches to using the model parameter setting:

- If the model was tuned manually, you should use the exact tuning parameters that were used on the trained model
- If the model was tuned automatically by an algorithm (such as the `auto.arima` function we used previously), you can do either of the following:
  - Extract the parameter setting that was used by with the training partition
  - Let the algorithm retune the model parameters using the full series, under the assumption that the algorithm has the ability to adjust the model parameters correctly when training the model with new data

The use of algorithms to automate the model tuning process is recommended when the model's ability to tune the model is tested with backtesting. This allows you to review whether the algorithm has the ability to adjust the model parameters correctly, based on the backtesting results. For simplicity reasons, we will keep using the `auto.arima` model to train the final model:

```
md_final <- auto.arima(USgas)

fc_final <- forecast(md_final, h = 12)
```

We will use the `plot_forecast` function from the **TSstudio** package to plot the final forecast:

```
plot_forecast(fc_final,
              title = "The US Natural Gas Consumption Forecast",
              Xtitle = "Year",
              Ytitle = "Billion Cubic Feet")
```

The output is as follows:

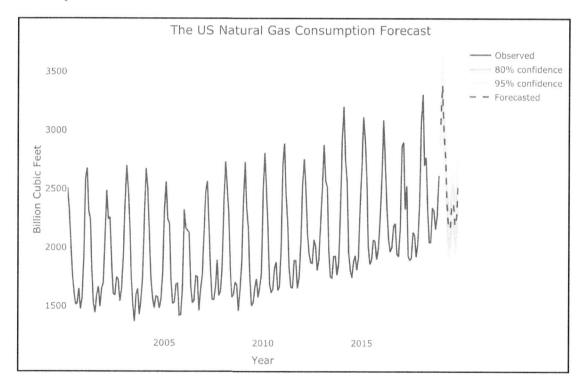

Handling forecast uncertainty

The main goal of the forecasting process, as we saw previously, is to minimize the level of uncertainty around the future values of the series. Although we cannot completely eliminate this uncertainty, we can quantify it and provide some range around the point estimate of the forecast (which is nothing but the model's expected value of each point in the future). This can be done by using either the confidence interval (or a credible interval, when using the Bayesian model) or by using simulation.

Confidence interval

The confidence interval is a statistical approximation method that's used to express the range of possible values that contain the true value with some degree of confidence (or probability). There are two parameters that determine the range of confidence interval:

- The level of confidence or the probability that the true value will be in that range. The higher the level of confidence is, the wider the interval range.
- The estimated standard deviation of the forecast at time $T+i$, where T represents the length of the series and i represents the i forecasted value. The lower the error rate, the shorter the range of the prediction interval.

By default, the `forecast` function generates a prediction interval with a level of confidence of 80% and 95%, but you can modify it using the level argument. For example, let's use the trained model's `md_final` and `forecast` functions for the next 60 months using the prediction interval with confidence levels of 80% and 90%:

```
fc_final2 <- forecast(md_final,
                 h = 60,
                 level = c(80, 90))

plot_forecast(fc_final2,
          title = "The US Natural Gas Consumption Forecast",
          Xtitle = "Year",
          Ytitle = "Billion Cubic Feet")
```

The output is shown in the following screenshot:

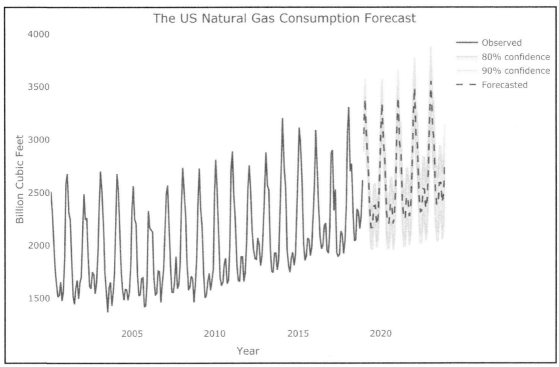

Simulation

An alternative approach is to use the model distribution to simulate possible paths for the forecast. This method can only be used when the model distribution is available. The `forecast_sim` function from the **TSstudio** package provides a built-in function for simulating possible forecasting paths. This estimate can be used to calculate the forecast point estimate (for example, using the mean or median of all of the paths), or to calculate probabilities of getting different values. We will feed the same model to the function and run `100` iterations:

```
fc_final3 <- forecast_sim(model = md_final,
                          h = 60,
                          n = 500)
```

The output of the preceding function contains all of the calculate simulations and the simulated paths. Let's extract the simulation plot (and use the **plotly** package to add titles for the plot):

```
library(plotly)

fc_final3$plot %>%
  layout(title = "US Natural Gas Consumption – Forecasting Simulation",
         yaxis = list(title = "Billion Cubic Feet"),
         xaxis = list(title = "Year"))
```

The output is as follows:

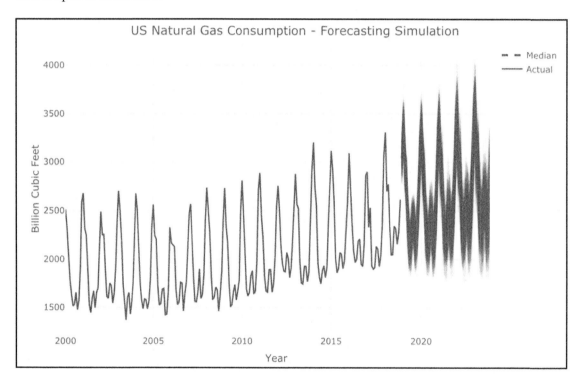

Now, let's take a look at the horse race approach.

Horse race approach

Last but not least, we will end this chapter with a robust forecasting approach that combines what we've learned so far in this chapter. The *horse race* approach is based on training, testing, and evaluating multiple forecasting models and selecting the model that performs the best on the testing partitions. In the following example, we will apply horse racing between seven different models (we will review the models in the upcoming chapters; for now, don't worry if you are not familiar with them) using six periods of backtesting. The `ts_backtesting` function from the **TSstudio** package conducts the full process of training, testing, evaluating, and then forecasting, using the model that performed the best on the backtesting testing partitions. By default, the model will test the following models:

- `auto.arima`: Automated ARIMA model
- `bsts`: Bayesian structural time series model
- `ets`: Exponential smoothing state space model
- `hybrid`: An ensemble of multiple models
- `nnetar`: Neural network time series model
- `tbats`: Exponential smoothing state space model, along with Box-Cox transformation, trend, ARMA errors, and seasonal components
- `HoltWinters`: Holt-Winters filtering

Before we run the function, let's set the seed value with the `set.seed` function so that we're able to reproduce the results:

```
set.seed(1234)
```

Now, let's run the `ts_backtesting` function and see its output:

```
USgas_forecast <- ts_backtesting(ts.obj = USgas,
                                 periods = 6,
                                 models = "abehntw",
                                 error = "MAPE",
                                 window_size = 12,
                                 h = 60,
                                 plot = FALSE)
```

The output of the `ts_backtesting` function is as follows:

```
##    Model_Name  avgMAPE    sdMAPE    avgRMSE    sdRMSE
## 1        bsts 6.341667 0.5825261 184.9650 19.414553
## 2         ets 6.721667 0.5984786 176.9167 12.839003
## 3  auto.arima 6.908333 0.9675416 192.2400 17.169408
```

```
## 4        hybrid 6.930000 0.6554998 190.9467  7.320794
## 5 HoltWinters 7.308333 0.3264608 204.8283  8.812086
## 6        tbats 7.986667 0.9594721 215.8633 18.279782
## 7       nnetar 8.508333 1.2979587 268.6117 23.842204
```

The model provides a leaderboard (as we can see in the preceding output) that's ordered based on the error criteria that's set. In this case, the `bsts` model had the lowest error rate, and therefore the function recommended that we use it (although all of the models and their forecasts are available for extraction from the function output). We can plot the error rate and the suggested forecast using the model stored in the output object:

```
USgas_forecast$summary_plot
```

The output is shown as follows:

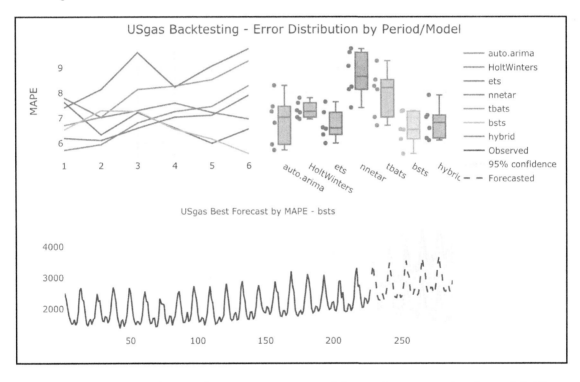

Those error plots provide an informative overview of the performance of each model. We consider a model good if the error distribution is both narrow and low with respect to the rest of the tested models (such as the `bsts` model).

Summary

The training process of a forecasting model is the final step of the time series analysis. The focus of this chapter was to introduce the principle of the forecasting workflow. As we saw, there are several methods that we can use to train a forecasting model, and the method selection process should align with the forecasting goals and available resources. In the following chapters, you will see these applications in practice.

In the next chapter, we will use the applications of the linear regression model to forecast time series data.

Forecasting with Linear Regression

9

The linear regression model is one of the most common methods for identifying and quantifying the relationship between a dependent variable and a single (univariate linear regression) or multiple (multivariate linear regression) independent variables. This model has a wide range of applications, from causal inference to predictive analysis and, in particular, time series forecasting.

The focus of this chapter is on methods and approaches for forecasting time series data with linear regression. That includes methods for decomposing and forecasting the series components (for example, the trend and seasonal patterns), handling special events (such as outliers and holidays), and using external variables as regressors.

This chapter covers the following topics:

- Forecasting approaches with linear regression models
- Extracting and estimating the series components
- Handling structural breaks, outliers, and special events
- Forecasting series with multiseasonality

Technical requirement

The following packages will be used in this chapter:

- **TSstudio**: Version 0.1.4 and above
- **plotly**: Version 4.8 and above
- **dplyr**: Version 0.8.1 and above
- **lubridate**: Version 1.7.4 and above
- **forecast**: Version 8.5 and above

You can access the codes for this chapter from the following link:

```
https://github.com/PacktPublishing/Hands-On-Time-Series-Analysis-with-R/tree/
master/Chapter09
```

The linear regression

The primary usage of the linear regression model is to quantify the relationship between the dependent variable Y (also known as the response variable) and the independent variable/s X (also known as the predictor, driver, or regressor variables) in a linear manner. In other words, the model expresses the dependent variable as a linear combination of the independent variables. A linear relationship between the dependent and independent variables can be generalized by the following equations:

- In the case of a single independent variable, the equation is as follows:

$$Y_i = \beta_0 + \beta_1 * X_{1,i} + \epsilon_i$$

- For n independent variables, the equation looks as follows:

$$Y_i = \beta_0 + \beta_1 X_{1,i} + \beta_2 X_{2,i} + \ldots + \beta_n X_{n,i} + \epsilon_i$$

The model variables for these equations are as follows:

- i represents the observations index, $i = 1,..., N$
- Y_i represents the i observation of the dependent variable
- $X_{j,i}$ represents the i value of the j independent variable, where $j = 1,..., n$
- β_0 represents the value of the constant term (or intercept)
- β_j represents the corresponded parameters (or coefficients) of the j independent variables
- ε_i defines the error term, which is nothing but all the information that was not captured by independent variables for the i observation

 The term linear, in the context of regression, referred to the model coefficients, which must follow a linear structure (as this allows us to construct a linear combination from the independent variables). On the other hand, the independent variables can follow both a linear and non-linear formation.

Assuming the preceding equations represent the true nature of the linear relationship between the dependent and independent variables, then the linear regression model provides an estimation for those coefficients (that is, $\hat{\beta}_0, \hat{\beta}_1, \ldots, \hat{\beta}_n$), which can be formalized by the following equations:

- For the univariate linear regression model, the equation is as follows:

$$\hat{Y}_i = \hat{\beta}_0 + \hat{\beta}_1 X_{1,i}$$

- For the multivariate linear regression model, the equation is as follows:

$$\hat{Y}_i = \hat{\beta}_0 + \hat{\beta}_1 X_{1,i} + \hat{\beta}_2 X_{2,i} + \ldots + \hat{\beta}_n X_{n,i}$$

The variables for these equations are as follows:

- i represents the observation's index, $i = 1,\ldots, N$
- $\hat{Y}_i$ represents the estimate of the dependent variable i observation
- $X_{j,i}$ represents the i value of the j independent variable, where $j = 1,\ldots, n$
- $\hat{\beta}_0$ represents the estimate of the constant term (or intercept)
- $\hat{\beta}_1, \ldots, \hat{\beta}_n$ are the estimate of the corresponded parameters (or coefficients) of the n independent variables

The estimation of the model's coefficients is based on the following two steps:

- Define a cost function (also known as loss function)—setting some error metric to minimize
- Apply mathematical optimization for minimizing the cost function

The most common estimation approach is applying the **Ordinary Least Squares (OLS)** method as an optimization technique for minimizing the residuals sum of squares ($\sum_{i=1}^{N} \hat{\epsilon}_i^2$).

Squaring the residuals has two effects:

- It prevents positive and negative values canceling each other when summing them together
- The square effect provides an exponential penalization for residuals with longer distance, as their cost becomes higher

There are multiple estimation techniques besides the **OLS**, such as the maximum likelihood, method of moments, and Bayesian. Although those methods are not in the scope of the book, it is highly recommended to read and learn about alternative approaches.

Coefficients estimation with the OLS method

The OLS is a simple optimization method that is based on basic linear algebra and calculus, or matrix calculus. (This section is for general knowledge—if you are not familiar with matrix calculus you can skip this section.) The goal of the OLS is to identify the coefficients that minimize the residuals sum of squares. Suppose the residual of the i observation defines as the following:

$$\hat{\epsilon}_i = Y_i - \hat{Y}_i$$

We can then set the cost function with the following expression:

$$\sum_{i=1}^{N} \hat{\epsilon}_i^2 = (Y_1 - \hat{Y}_1)^2 + (Y_2 - \hat{Y}_2)^2 + \ldots + (Y_n - \hat{Y}_n)^2$$

Before applying the OLS method for minimizing the residuals sum of squares, for simplicity reasons, we will transform the representative of the cost function into a matrix formation:

$$Y = \begin{bmatrix} Y_1 \\ Y_2 \\ \cdot \\ \cdot \\ \cdot \\ Y_N \end{bmatrix}, \quad X = \begin{bmatrix} 1 & X_{1,1} & \cdots & X_{1,n} \\ \cdot & & & \\ \cdot & & & \\ \cdot & & & \\ 1 & X_{N,1} & \cdots & X_{N,n} \end{bmatrix}, \quad \beta = \begin{bmatrix} \beta_0 \\ \beta_1 \\ \cdot \\ \cdot \\ \cdot \\ \beta_n \end{bmatrix}, \quad \epsilon = Y - X\beta = \begin{bmatrix} \epsilon_1 \\ \epsilon_2 \\ \cdot \\ \cdot \\ \cdot \\ \epsilon_N \end{bmatrix}$$

Those sets of matrices represent the following:

- Vector Y (or $N \times 1$ matrix), representing a dependent variable with N observations
- X, a $N \times n + 1$ dimensions matrix, representing the corresponding n independent variables and a scalar of 1's for the intercept component (β_0)

- β, an $(n+1) \times 1$ dimensions matrix, representing the model coefficients
- ϵ, an $N \times 1$ dimensions matrix, representing the corresponding error (or the difference between) the actual value Y and its estimate βX

 The residual term $\hat{\epsilon}_t$ should not be confused with the error term ϵ_i. While the first represents the difference between the series Y and its estimate $\hat{Y}$, the second (error term) represents the difference between the series and its expected value

Let's set the cost function using the matrix form as we defined it previously:

$$\sum \epsilon^2 = \sum \epsilon^T \epsilon$$

We will now start to expand this expression by using the formula of ϵ as we outlined previously:

$$\epsilon^T \epsilon = (Y - X\beta)^T (Y - X\beta)$$

Next, we will multiply the two components (ϵ^T and ϵ) and open the brackets:

$$\epsilon^T \epsilon = Y^T Y - 2Y^T X\beta + \beta^T X^T X\beta$$

Since our goal is to find the β that minimizes this equation, we will differentiate the equation with respect to β and then set it to zero:

$$\frac{\partial \epsilon^T \epsilon}{\partial \beta} = \frac{\partial (Y^T Y - 2Y^T X\beta + \beta^T X^T X\beta)}{\partial \beta} = 0$$

Solving this equation will yield the following output:

$$X^T X\beta = X^T Y$$

Manipulating this equation allows us to extract $\hat{\beta}$ matrix, the estimate of the coefficient matrix β:

$$\hat{\beta} = (X^T X)^{-1} X^T Y$$

Note that we changed the notation of β to $\hat{\beta}$ on the final output as it represents the estimate of the true value of β.

The key properties of the OLS coefficients estimation are as follows:

- The main feature of the OLS coefficients estimation method is the unbiasedness of the estimation of the coefficients with respect to the actual values. In other words, for any given, $\hat{\beta}_i$, $E(\hat{\beta}_i) = \beta_i$
- The sample regression line will always go through the mean of X and Y
- The mean of $\hat{Y}$, the OLS estimation of the dependent variable Y, is equal to $\overline{Y}$, the mean the dependent variable
- The mean of the residuals vector $\hat{\epsilon}$ is equal to zero, or $\dfrac{\sum_{i=1}^{N} \hat{\epsilon}_i}{N} = 0$

The OLS assumptions

The OLS model's main assumptions are the following:

- The model coefficients must follow a linear structure (for example, $Y = \hat{\beta}_0 + \hat{\beta}_1 e^{X}$ is a linear model but $Y = \hat{\beta}_0 + X_1^{\hat{\beta}_1}$ is not).
- There is no perfect collinearity between independent variables $X_1, X_2, \ldots, X_n$. In other words, none of the independent variables are a linear combination of any of the other independent variables.
- All the independent variables must be a non-zero variance (or non-constant).
- The error term ϵ, conditioned on the matrix of independent variables X, is an **independent and identically distributed (i.i.d)** variable with mean 0 and constant variance σ^2.
- Both the dependent and independent variables draw from the population in a random sample. This assumption does not hold when regressing time series data, as typically the observations have some degree of correlation. Therefore, this assumption is relaxed when regressing time series data.

The OLS assumption about the error term ϵ—i.i.d. with mean *0* and variance σ^2 is in many cases violated when working with time series data, as, typically, some degree of correlation exists in the model residuals. This is mainly an indication that the regression model didn't capture all the patterns or information of the series. In `Chapter 11`, *Forecasting with ARIMA Models*, we will introduce a method for handling this type of case, by modeling the error term with ARIMA model.

Forecasting with linear regression

The linear regression model, unlike the traditional time series models such as the **ARIMA** or **Holt-Winters**, was not designed explicitly to handle and forecast time series data. Instead, it is a generic model with a wide range of applications from causal inference to predictive analysis.

Therefore, forecasting with a linear regression model is mainly based on the following two steps:

1. Identifying the series structure, key characteristics, patterns, outliers, and other features
2. Transforming those features into input variables and regressing them with the series to create a forecasting model

The core features of a linear regression forecasting model are the trend and seasonal components. The next section focuses on identifying the series trend and seasonal components and then transforming them into input variables of the regression model.

Forecasting the trend and seasonal components

In `Chapter 5`, *Decomposition of Time Series Data*, we introduced the series structural components: the trend, cycle, seasonal and irregular components, and methods for decomposing them with the decompose function.

Recall that the decomposition of a series can be defined by one of the following expressions:

- $Y_t = T_t + S_t + C_t + I_t$, when the series has an additive structure
- $Y_t = T_t \times S_t \times C_t \times I_t$, when the series has a multiplicative structure

The explanation is as follows:

- **Trend**: Represents the series' growth over time after adjusting and removing the seasonal effects
- **Seasonal**: A recurring cyclical pattern that derived directly from the series frequency units (for example, the month of the year for a series with a monthly frequency)
- **Cycle**: A cyclical pattern that is not related to the series frequency unit
- **Irregular**: Any other patterns that are not captured by the trend, seasonal, and cycle components

For the sake of simplicity, we can drop the cycle component as it typically merged into the trend component (or ignored the cycle component). Therefore, we can update and replace the preceding equations with the following:

- $Y_t = T_t + S_t + I_t$, when the series has an additive structure
- $Y_t = T_t \times S_t \times I_t$, when the series has a multiplicative structure

We can now transform those equations for a linear regression model, by modifying the equations notation:

$$Y_t = \beta_0 + \beta_1 T_t + \beta_2 S_t + \epsilon_t$$

Where:

- Y represents a time series with n observations
- T, an independent variable with n observations, represents the series trend component
- S, an independent variable with n observations, represents the series seasonal component
- ϵ_t, the regression error term, represents the irregular component or any pattern that is not captured by the series trend and seasonal component
- β_0, β_1, and β_2, represent the model intercept, and coefficients of the trend and seasonal components, respectively

For the sake of convenience and in the context of working with time series, we will change the observations notation from *i* to *t*, as it represents the time dimension of the series.

The transformation of a series with a multiplicative structure into linear regression formation required a transformation of the series into an additive structure. This can be done by applying *log* transformation for both sides of the equations:

$$\log(Y_t) = \log(T_t) + \log(S_t) + \log(l_t)$$

Once the series transformed into an additive structure, the transformation to a linear regression formation is straightforward and follows the same process as described previously:

$$\log(Y_t) = \beta_0 + \beta_1 \log(T_t) + \beta_2 \log(S_t) + \epsilon_t$$

Features engineering of the series components

Before creating the regression inputs that represent the series trend and seasonal components, we first have to understand their structure. In the following examples, we will demonstrate the process of creating new features from existing series using the `USgas` series.

Let's load the series from the **TSstudio** package again and plot it with the `ts_plot` function:

```
library(TSstudio)

data(USgas)

ts_plot(USgas,
        title = "US Monthly Natural Gas consumption",
        Ytitle = "Billion Cubic Feet",
        Xtitle = "Year")
```

The output is shown as follows:

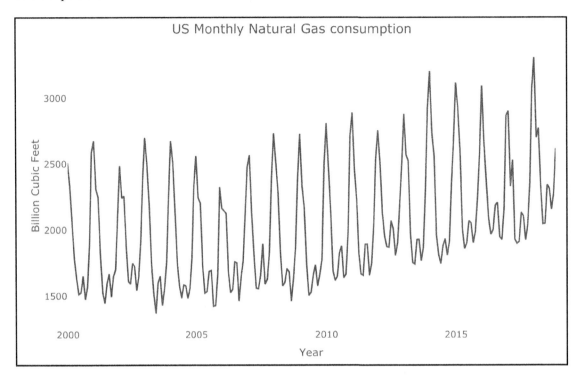

Also, let's review the main characteristics of the series using the `ts_info` function:

```
ts_info(USgas)
##   The USgas series is a ts object with 1 variable and 227 observations
##   Frequency: 12
##   Start time: 2000 1
##   End time: 2018 11
```

As you can see in the series plot, and as we saw on the previous chapters, USgas is a monthly series with a strong monthly seasonal component and fairly stable trend line. We can explore the series components structure with the `ts_decompose` function further:

```
ts_decompose(USgas)
```

The output is shown as follows:

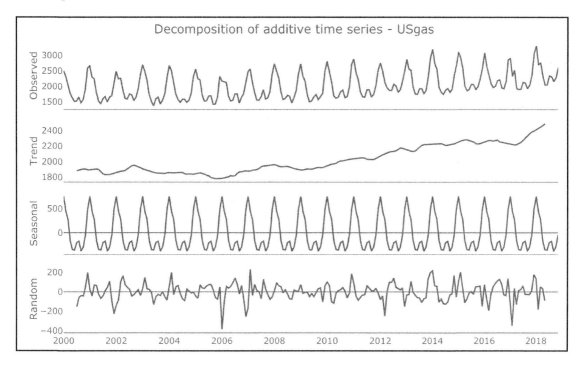

You can see in the preceding plot that the trend of the series is fairly flat between **2000** and **2010**, and has a fairly linear growth moving forward. Therefore, the overall trend between **2000** and **2018** is not strictly linear. This is an important insight that will help us to define the trend input for the regression model.

Before using the `lm` function, the built-in R linear regression function from the **stats** package, we will have to transform the series from a `ts` object to a `data.frame` object. Therefore, we will utilize the `ts_to_prophet` function from the **TSstudio** package:

```
USgas_df <- ts_to_prophet(USgas)
```

The function transforms the `ts` object into two columns of `data.frame`, where the two columns represent the time and numeric components of the series, respectively:

```
head(USgas_df)
```

We get the following output:

```
##            ds      y
## 1 2000-01-01 2510.5
## 2 2000-02-01 2330.7
## 3 2000-03-01 2050.6
## 4 2000-04-01 1783.3
## 5 2000-05-01 1632.9
## 6 2000-06-01 1513.1
```

After we transform the series into a `data.frame` object, we can start to create the regression input features. The first feature we will create is the series trend. A basic approach for constructing the trend variable is by indexing the series observations in chronological order:

```
USgas_df$trend <- 1:nrow(USgas_df)
```

Regressing the series with the series index provides an estimate of the marginal growth from month to month, as the index is in chronological order with constant increments.

The second feature we want to create is the seasonal component. Since we want to measure the contribution of each frequency unit to the oscillation of the series, we will use a categorical variable for each frequency unit. In the case of the USgas series, the frequency units represent the months of the year, and, therefore, we will create a categorical variable with 12 categories, each category corresponding to a specific month of the year. We will use the `month` function from the **lubridate** package to extract the month of the year from the `ds` date variable:

```
library(lubridate)

USgas_df$seasonal <- factor(month(USgas_df$ds, label = T), ordered = FALSE)
```

We used the `factor` function to convert the output of the `month` function into no ordered categorical variable. Let's now review the data frame after adding the new features:

```
head(USgas_df)
```

We get the following output:

```
##             ds        y trend seasonal
## 1 2000-01-01 2510.5     1      Jan
## 2 2000-02-01 2330.7     2      Feb
## 3 2000-03-01 2050.6     3      Mar
## 4 2000-04-01 1783.3     4      Apr
## 5 2000-05-01 1632.9     5      May
## 6 2000-06-01 1513.1     6      Jun
```

Last but not least, before we start to regress the series with those features, we will split the series into a training and testing partition. We will set the last 12 months of the series as a testing partition:

```
h <- 12 # setting a testing partition length

train <- USgas_df[1:(nrow(USgas_df) - h), ]

test <- USgas_df[(nrow(USgas_df) - h + 1):nrow(USgas_df), ]
```

Now, after we created the training and testing data frames, let's review how the regression model captures each one of the components separately and all together.

Modeling the series trend and seasonal components

We will first model the series trend by regressing the series with the trend variable, on the training partition:

```
md_trend <- lm(y ~ trend, data = train)
```

We will use the `summary` function to review the model details:

```
summary(md_trend)
##
## Call:
## lm(formula = y ~ trend, data = train)
##
## Residuals:
##     Min      1Q  Median      3Q      Max
```

```
## -537.6 -305.3 -150.1  317.1 1067.7
##
## Coefficients:
##              Estimate Std. Error t value            Pr(>|t|)
## (Intercept) 1772.2648    53.3781  33.202 < 0.0000000000000002 ***
## trend          2.1548     0.4285   5.029          0.00000105 ***
## ---
## Signif. codes:  0 '***' 0.001 '**' 0.01 '*' 0.05 '.' 0.1 ' ' 1
##
## Residual standard error: 390 on 213 degrees of freedom
## Multiple R-squared:  0.1061, Adjusted R-squared:  0.1019
## F-statistic: 25.29 on 1 and 213 DF,  p-value: 0.000001048
```

As you can see from the preceding regression output, the coefficient of the trend variable is statistically significant to a level of 0.001. However, the adjusted R-squared of the regression is fairly low, which generally makes sense, as most of the series variation of the series is related to the seasonal pattern as we saw in the plots previously.

 As you can note from the preceding regression output, the fourth column represents the *p*-value of each one of the model coefficients. The *p*-value provides the probability that we will reject the null hypothesis given it is actually true, or the type I error. Therefore, for the *p*-value smaller than α, the threshold value, we will reject the null hypothesis with a level of significance of α, where typical values of α are 0.1, 0.05, 0.01, and so on.

As always, it is recommended that you put some context to the numbers with data visualization. Therefore, we will use the model we created to predict the fitted values on the training partition and the forecasted values on the testing partition. The predict function from the **stats** package, as the name implies, predicts the values of an input data based on a given model.

We will use it to predict both the fitted and forecasted values of the trend model we trained before:

```
train$yhat <- predict(md_trend, newdata = train)

test$yhat <- predict(md_trend, newdata = test)
```

We will create a utility function that plots the series and the model output, utilizing the **plotly** package:

```
library(plotly)

plot_lm <- function(data, train, test, title = NULL){
 p <- plot_ly(data = data,
         x = ~ ds,
         y = ~ y,
         type = "scatter",
         mode = "line",
         name = "Actual") %>%
   add_lines(x =  ~ train$ds,
           y = ~ train$yhat,
           line = list(color = "red"),
           name = "Fitted") %>%
   add_lines(x =  ~ test$ds,
           y = ~ test$yhat,
           line = list(color = "green", dash = "dot", width = 3),
           name = "Forecasted") %>%
   layout(title = title,
         xaxis = list(title = "Year"),
         yaxis = list(title = "Billion Cubic Feet"),
         legend = list(x = 0.05, y = 0.95))
 return(p)
 }
```

The function arguments are as follows:

- data: The input data, a data.frame object following the same structure as the one of the USgas_df (including the yhat variable)
- train: The corresponding training set that was used to train the model
- test: Likewise, the corresponding testing set that was used to evaluate the forecast model
- title: The plot title, by default, set to NULL

Let's set the inputs of the plot_lm function with the model output:

```
plot_lm(data = USgas_df,
       train = train,
       test = test,
       title = "Predicting the Trend Component of the Series")
```

The output is shown as follows:

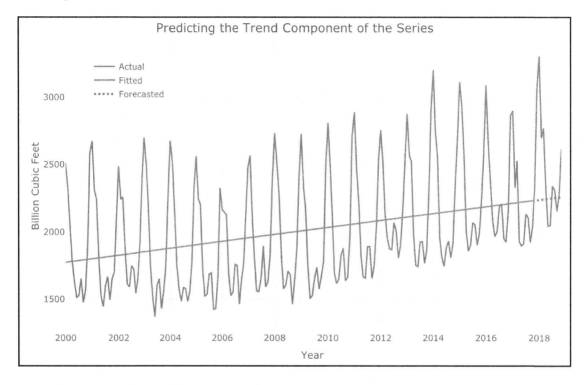

Overall, the model was able to capture the general movement of the trend, yet a linear trend may fail to capture the structural break of the trend that occurred around 2010. Later on, in this chapter, we will see an advanced method to capture a non-linear trend.

Last but not least, for comparison analysis, we want to measure the model error rate both in the training and the testing sets:

```
mape_trend <- c(mean(abs(train$y - train$yhat) / train$y),
                mean(abs(test$y - test$yhat) / test$y))
mape_trend
```

We get the following output:

```
## [1] 0.1646270 0.1201788
```

The process of modeling and forecasting the seasonal component follows the same process as we applied with the trend, by regressing the series with the seasonal variable we created before:

```
md_seasonal <- lm(y ~ seasonal, data = train)
```

Let's review the model details:

```
summary(md_seasonal)
```

We get the following output:

```
##
## Call:
## lm(formula = y ~ seasonal, data = train)
##
## Residuals:
##     Min      1Q Median     3Q     Max
## -577.1 -141.1  -41.9  130.0   462.2
##
## Coefficients:
##               Estimate Std. Error t value Pr(>|t|)
## (Intercept)    2742.4        45.3   60.52  < 2e-16 ***
## seasonalFeb    -279.4        64.1   -4.36  2.1e-05 ***
## seasonalMar    -474.5        64.1   -7.41  3.4e-12 ***
## seasonalApr    -900.2        64.1  -14.05  < 2e-16 ***
## seasonalMay   -1076.6        64.1  -16.80  < 2e-16 ***
## seasonalJun   -1095.2        64.1  -17.09  < 2e-16 ***
## seasonalJul    -936.3        64.1  -14.61  < 2e-16 ***
## seasonalAug    -906.5        64.1  -14.15  < 2e-16 ***
## seasonalSep   -1110.1        64.1  -17.32  < 2e-16 ***
## seasonalOct   -1019.3        64.1  -15.91  < 2e-16 ***
## seasonalNov    -766.0        64.1  -11.95  < 2e-16 ***
## seasonalDec    -258.1        65.0   -3.97  1.0e-04 ***
## ---
## Signif. codes:  0 '***' 0.001 '**' 0.01 '*' 0.05 '.' 0.1 ' ' 1
##
## Residual standard error: 192 on 203 degrees of freedom
## Multiple R-squared:  0.793,  Adjusted R-squared:  0.782
## F-statistic: 70.7 on 11 and 203 DF,  p-value: <2e-16
```

Since we regress the dependent variable with a categorical variable, the regression model creates coefficients for 11 out of the 12 categories, which are those embedded with the slope values. As you can see in the regression summary of the seasonal model, all the model's coefficients are statistically significant. Also, you can notice that the adjusted R-squared of the seasonal model is somewhat higher with respect to the trend model (0.78 as opposed to 0.1).

Before we plot the fitted model and forecast values with the `plot_lm` function, we will update the values of `yhat` with the `predict` function:

```
train$yhat <- predict(md_seasonal, newdata = train)
test$yhat <- predict(md_seasonal, newdata = test)
```

Now we can use the `plot_lm` function to visualize the fitted model and forecast values:

```
plot_lm(data = USgas_df,
        train = train,
        test = test,
        title = "Predicting the Seasonal Component of the Series")
```

The output is shown as follows:

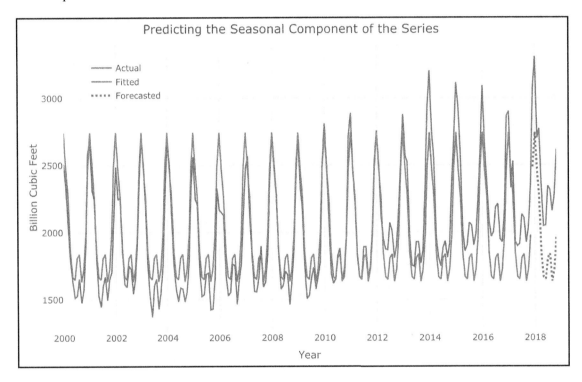

As you can see in the preceding plot, the model is doing a fairly good job of capturing the structure of the series seasonal pattern. However, you can observe that the series trend is missing. Before we add both the trend and the seasonal components, we will score the model performance:

```
mape_seasonal <- c(mean(abs(train$y - train$yhat) / train$y),
                   mean(abs(test$y - test$yhat) / test$y))

mape_seasonal
```

We get the following output:

```
## [1] 0.07786439 0.19906796
```

The high error rate on the testing set is related to the trend component that was not included in the model. The next step is to join the two components into one model and to forecast the feature values of the series:

```
md1 <- lm(y ~ seasonal + trend, data = train)
```

Let's review the model summary after regressing the series with both the trend and seasonal components:

```
summary(md1)
```

We get the following output:

```
##
## Call:
## lm(formula = y ~ seasonal + trend, data = train)
##
## Residuals:
##     Min      1Q  Median      3Q     Max
## -506.7   -71.2   -13.8    79.0   328.5
##
## Coefficients:
##               Estimate Std. Error t value Pr(>|t|)
## (Intercept)   2500.682     31.620   79.09  < 2e-16 ***
## seasonalFeb   -281.769     40.302   -6.99  3.9e-11 ***
## seasonalMar   -479.227     40.303  -11.89  < 2e-16 ***
## seasonalApr   -907.201     40.304  -22.51  < 2e-16 ***
## seasonalMay  -1085.948     40.305  -26.94  < 2e-16 ***
## seasonalJun  -1106.933     40.307  -27.46  < 2e-16 ***
## seasonalJul   -950.374     40.310  -23.58  < 2e-16 ***
## seasonalAug   -922.932     40.312  -22.89  < 2e-16 ***
## seasonalSep  -1128.862     40.316  -28.00  < 2e-16 ***
## seasonalOct  -1040.442     40.319  -25.81  < 2e-16 ***
## seasonalNov   -789.461     40.324  -19.58  < 2e-16 ***
## seasonalDec   -269.863     40.895   -6.60  3.6e-10 ***
## trend            2.347      0.133   17.64  < 2e-16 ***
## ---
## Signif. codes:  0 '***' 0.001 '**' 0.01 '*' 0.05 '.' 0.1 ' ' 1
##
## Residual standard error: 121 on 202 degrees of freedom
## Multiple R-squared:  0.919,  Adjusted R-squared:  0.914
## F-statistic:  190 on 12 and 202 DF,  p-value: <2e-16
```

Regressing the series with both the trend and the seasonal components together provides additional lift to the adjusted R-squared of the model from 0.78 to 0.91. This can be seen in the plot of the model output:

```
train$yhat <- predict(md1, newdata = train)
test$yhat <- predict(md1, newdata = test)

plot_lm(data = USgas_df,
        train = train,
        test = test,
        title = "Predicting the Trend and Seasonal Components of the
Series")
```

The output is shown as follows:

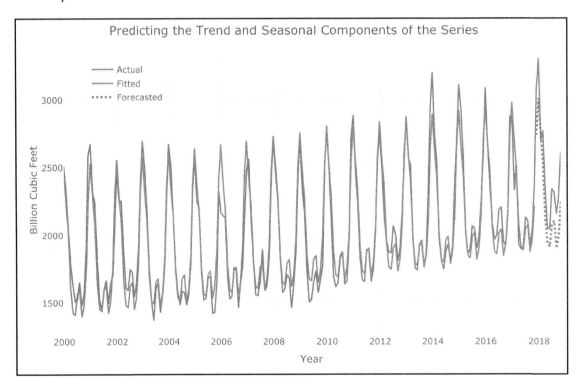

Let's measure the model's MAPE score on both the training and testing partitions:

```
mape_md1 <- c(mean(abs(train$y - train$yhat) / train$y),
              mean(abs(test$y - test$yhat) / test$y))

mape_md1
```

We get the following output:

```
## [1] 0.04501471 0.09192438
```

Regressing the series with both the trend and the seasonal components provides a significant lift in both the quality of fit of the model and with the accuracy of the model. However, when looking at the plot of the model fit and forecast, you can notice that the model trend is *too* linear and missing the structural break of the series trend. This is the point where adding a polynomial component for the model could potentially provide additional improvement for the model accuracy.

A simple technique to capture a non-linear trend is to add a polynomial component to the series trend in order to capture the trend curvature over time. We will use the I argument, which allows us to apply mathematical operations on any of the input objects. Therefore, we will use this argument to add a second degree of the polynomial for the trend input:

```
md2 <- lm(y ~ seasonal + trend + I(trend^2), data = train)
```

The summary of the model can be seen as follows:

```
summary(md2)
```

We get the following output:

```
## 
## Call:
## lm(formula = y ~ seasonal + trend + I(trend^2), data = train)
## 
## Residuals:
##     Min      1Q  Median      3Q     Max
## -466.5   -55.5    -5.1    60.1   309.5
## 
## Coefficients:
##                  Estimate  Std. Error  t value  Pr(>|t|)
## (Intercept)    2617.20174    33.00223    79.30   < 2e-16 ***
## seasonalFeb    -281.63380    36.26107    -7.77   4.0e-13 ***
## seasonalMar    -478.98651    36.26167   -13.21   < 2e-16 ***
## seasonalApr    -906.88591    36.26267   -25.01   < 2e-16 ***
## seasonalMay   -1085.58755    36.26406   -29.94   < 2e-16 ***
## seasonalJun   -1106.55810    36.26584   -30.51   < 2e-16 ***
```

```
## seasonalJul   -950.01422    36.26801   -26.19   < 2e-16 ***
## seasonalAug   -922.61703    36.27057   -25.44   < 2e-16 ***
## seasonalSep  -1128.62207    36.27352   -31.11   < 2e-16 ***
## seasonalOct  -1040.30714    36.27686   -28.68   < 2e-16 ***
## seasonalNov   -789.46112    36.28061   -21.76   < 2e-16 ***
## seasonalDec   -263.18413    36.80761    -7.15   1.6e-11 ***
## trend           -0.89541     0.48054    -1.86     0.064 .
## I(trend^2)       0.01501     0.00215     6.97   4.5e-11 ***
## ---
## Signif. codes:   0 '***' 0.001 '**' 0.01 '*' 0.05 '.' 0.1 ' ' 1
##
## Residual standard error: 109 on 201 degrees of freedom
## Multiple R-squared:  0.934,  Adjusted R-squared:  0.93
## F-statistic:  220 on 13 and 201 DF,  p-value: <2e-16
```

Adding the second-degree polynomial to the regression model did not lead to a significant improvement of the goodness of fit of the model. On the other model, as you can see in the following model output plot, this simple change in the model structure allows us to capture the structural break of the trend over time:

```
train$yhat <- predict(md2, newdata = train)
test$yhat <- predict(md2, newdata = test)


 plot_lm(data = USgas_df,
         train = train,
         test = test,
         title = "Predicting the Trend (Polynomial) and Seasonal Components
of the Series")
```

The output is shown as follows:

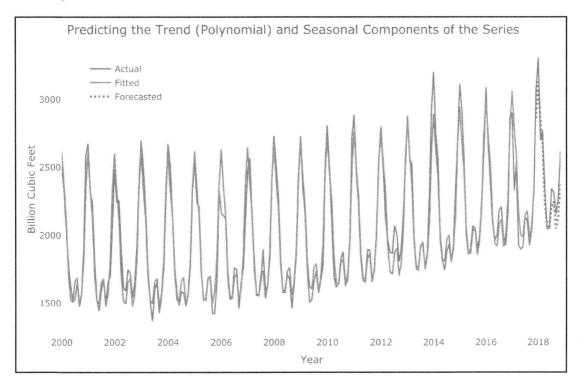

As we can see from the model following the MAPE score, the model accuracy significantly improved from adding the polynomial trend to the regression model, as the error on the testing set dropped from 9.2% to 4.5%:

```
mape_md2 <- c(mean(abs(train$y - train$yhat) / train$y),
              mean(abs(test$y - test$yhat) / test$y))

mape_md2
```

We get the following output:

```
## [1] 0.03706897 0.04559134
```

The tslm function

So far, we have seen the manual process of transforming a `ts` object to a linear regression forecasting model format. The `tslm` function from the **forecast** package provides a built-in function for transforming a `ts` object into a linear regression forecasting model. Using the `tslm` function, you can set the regression component along with other features.

We will now repeat the previous example and forecast the last 12 observations of the `USgas` series with the `tslm` function using the trend, square of the trend, and the seasonal components. First, let's split the series to training and testing partitions using the `ts_split` function:

```
USgas_split <- ts_split(USgas, sample.out = h)

train.ts <- USgas_split$train

test.ts <- USgas_split$test
```

Next, we will apply the same formula we used to create the preceding md2 forecasting model using the `tslm` function:

```
library(forecast)

md3 <- tslm(train.ts ~ season + trend + I(trend^2))
```

Let's now review md3, the output of the `tslm` function, and compare it with the output of md2:

```
summary(md3)
```

We get the following output:

```
##
## Call:
## tslm(formula = train.ts ~ season + trend + I(trend^2))
##
## Residuals:
##     Min      1Q   Median      3Q     Max
## -466.52  -55.46    -5.13   60.06  309.53
##
## Coefficients:
##                  Estimate   Std. Error t value            Pr(>|t|)
## (Intercept)   2617.201742    33.002235  79.304 < 0.0000000000000002 ***
## season2       -281.633803    36.261068  -7.767    0.000000000000404 ***
## season3       -478.986514    36.261672 -13.209 < 0.0000000000000002 ***
## season4       -906.885912    36.262671 -25.009 < 0.0000000000000002 ***
```

```
## season5       -1085.587550      36.264062 -29.936 < 0.0000000000000002 ***
## season6       -1106.558097      36.265843 -30.512 < 0.0000000000000002 ***
## season7        -950.014218      36.268012 -26.194 < 0.0000000000000002 ***
## season8        -922.617026      36.270570 -25.437 < 0.0000000000000002 ***
## season9       -1128.622074      36.273520 -31.114 < 0.0000000000000002 ***
## season10      -1040.307142      36.276865 -28.677 < 0.0000000000000002 ***
## season11       -789.461118      36.280610 -21.760 < 0.0000000000000002 ***
## season12       -263.184126      36.807605  -7.150   0.000000000015734 ***
## trend            -0.895408       0.480540  -1.863             0.0639 .
## I(trend^2)        0.015010       0.002155   6.966   0.000000000045450 ***
## ---
## Signif. codes:  0 '***' 0.001 '**' 0.01 '*' 0.05 '.' 0.1 ' ' 1
##
## Residual standard error: 108.8 on 201 degrees of freedom
## Multiple R-squared:  0.9344, Adjusted R-squared:  0.9301
## F-statistic: 220.1 on 13 and 201 DF,  p-value: < 0.00000000000000022
```

As you can observe from the preceding output, both models (`md2` and `md3`) are identical.

There are several advantages to using the `tslm` function, as opposed to manually setting a regression model for the series with the `lm` function:

- Efficiency—does not require transforming the series to a `data.frame` object and feature engineering
- The `output` object supports all the functionality of the `forecast` (such as the `accuracy` and `checkresiduals` functions) and **TSstudio** packages (such as the `test_forecast` and `plot_forecast` functions)

Modeling single events and non-seasonal events

In some cases, time series data may contain unusual patterns that are either re-occurring over time or not. The following are examples of such events:

- **Outliers**: A single event or events that are out of the normal patterns of the series.
- **Structural break**: A significant event that changes the historical patterns of the series. A common example is a change in the growth of the series.
- **Non-seasonal re-occurring events**: An event that repeats from cycle to cycle, but the time at which they occur changes from cycle to cycle. A common example of such an event is the Easter holidays, which occur every year around March/April.

By not expressing in the regression model, this type of events will bias the estimated coefficients, as the model will weight those types of events along with the regular events of the series. The use of hot encoding, binary, or flag variables could help the model to either ignore this type of events or adjust the model coefficients accordingly.

For instance, you can observe in the decompose plot of the USgas series shown previously that the series trend had a structural break around the year 2010. While growth before the year 2010 was relatively flat, the slope of the trend changed afterwards, with positive growth. In this case, we can use a binary variable that equals zero for observations before the year 2010 and one year afterwards.

Regressing a tslm model with external variables requires a separated data.frame object with the corresponding variables. The following example demonstrates the creation process of an external binary variable that equals 0 before the year 2010 and 1 afterward, using the USgas_df table:

```
r <- which(USgas_df$ds == as.Date("2014-01-01"))

USgas_df$s_break <- ifelse(year(USgas_df$ds) >= 2010, 1, 0)

USgas_df$s_break[r] <- 1
```

We will now use the new feature to remodel the USgas series:

```
md3 <- tslm(USgas ~ season + trend + I(trend^2) + s_break, data = USgas_df)
```

Let's use the summary function to review the model output:

```
summary(md3)

## 
## Call:
## tslm(formula = USgas ~ season + trend + I(trend^2) + s_break,
##     data = USgas_df)
## 
## Residuals:
##     Min      1Q  Median      3Q     Max
## -461.4   -55.9    -6.4    67.4   285.8
## 
## Coefficients:
##                 Estimate  Std. Error t value Pr(>|t|)
## (Intercept)   2647.44816    32.30603   81.95  < 2e-16 ***
## season2       -298.73237    35.05548   -8.52  2.9e-15 ***
## season3       -481.80356    35.05753  -13.74  < 2e-16 ***
## season4       -910.06095    35.06096  -25.96  < 2e-16 ***
## season5      -1094.53085    35.06576  -31.21  < 2e-16 *
```

```
## season6      -1114.15537     35.07195   -31.77   < 2e-16 ***
## season7       -950.33977     35.07952   -27.09   < 2e-16 ***
## season8       -925.83668     35.08849   -26.39   < 2e-16 ***
## season9      -1129.21978     35.09886   -32.17   < 2e-16 ***
## season10     -1039.14697     35.11065   -29.60   < 2e-16 ***
## season11      -783.59194     35.12386   -22.31   < 2e-16 ***
## season12      -256.28337     35.59344    -7.20   1.0e-11 ***
## trend           -1.67443      0.46052    -3.64   0.00035 ***
## I(trend^2)       0.01678      0.00188     8.91   2.4e-16 ***
## s_break         74.57388     28.93187     2.58   0.01063 *
## ---
## Signif. codes:  0 '***' 0.001 '**' 0.01 '*' 0.05 '.' 0.1 ' ' 1
##
## Residual standard error: 108 on 212 degrees of freedom
## Multiple R-squared:  0.939,  Adjusted R-squared:  0.935
## F-statistic:  234 on 14 and 212 DF,  p-value: <2e-16
```

As can see in the summary of the preceding model, the structural break variable is statistically significant, with a level of 0.01. Likewise, in the case of outliers or holidays, hot encoding can be applied by setting a binary variable that equals 1 whenever an outlier or non-seasonal re-occurring event occurs, and 0 otherwise.

 Note that, once you have trained a forecasting model with the tslm function with the use of external variables, you will have to produce the future values of those variables as they are going to be used as input of the forecast.

Forecasting a series with multiseasonality components – a case study

One of the main advantages of the regression model, as opposed to the traditional time series models such as ARIMA or Holt-Winters, is that it provides a wide range of customization options and allows us to model and forecast complex time series data such as series with multiseasonality.

In the following examples, we will use the UKgrid series to demonstrate the forecasting approach of a multiseasonality series with a linear regression model.

The UKgrid series

The UKgrid series represents the national grid demand for electricity in the UK, and it is available in the **UKgrid** package. This series represents a high-frequency time series data with half-hourly frequency. We will utilize the extract_grid function from the **UKgrid** package to define the series, main characteristics (for example, data format, variables, frequency, and so on). This transformation function allows us to aggregate the series frequency from half-hourly to a lower frequency such as hourly, daily, or monthly. As our goal here is to forecast the daily demand in the next 365 days, we will set the series to daily frequency using the data.frame structure:

```
library(UKgrid)

UKdaily <- extract_grid(type = "data.frame",
                        columns = "ND",
                        aggregate = "daily")
```

We will use the head function to review the series variables:

```
head(UKdaily)
```

We get the following output:

```
##    TIMESTAMP         ND
## 1 2011-01-01 1671744
## 2 2011-01-02 1760123
## 3 2011-01-03 1878748
## 4 2011-01-04 2076052
## 5 2011-01-05 2103866
## 6 2011-01-06 2135202
```

As you can see, this series has two variables:

- TIMESTAMP: A date object used as the series timestamp or index
- ND: The net demand of electricity

We will use the ts_plot function to plot and review the series structure:

```
ts_plot(UKdaily,
        title = "The UK National Demand for Electricity",
        Ytitle = "MW",
        Xtitle = "Year")
```

The following shows the output:

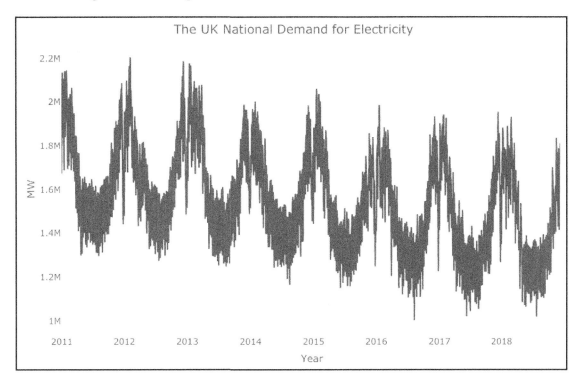

As you can see in the preceding plot, the series has a clear downtrend and has a string seasonal pattern. As we saw in Chapter 6, *Seasonality Analysis*, this series has multiple seasonality patterns:

- **Daily**: A cycle of 365 days a year
- **Day of the week**: A 7-day cycle
- **Monthly**: Effected from the weather

Evidence for those patterns can be seen in the following heatmap of the series since 2016 using the ts_heatmap function from the **TSstudio** package:

```
ts_heatmap(UKdaily[which(year(UKdaily$TIMESTAMP) >= 2016),],
           title = "UK the Daily National Grid Demand Heatmap")
```

The following shows the output:

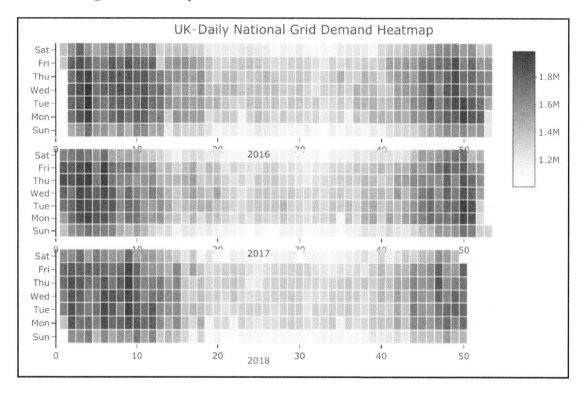

As you can see in the series heatmap, the overall demand increases throughout the winter weeks (for example, calendar weeks 1 to 12 and weeks 44 to 52). In addition, you can observe the change of the series during the days of the weeks, as the demand increases during the working days of the week, and decreases over the weekend.

Preprocessing and feature engineering of the UKdaily series

In order to capture the seasonal components of the series, we will set the series as daily frequency and create the following two features:

- Day of the week indicator
- Month of the year indicator

In addition, as it is reasonable to assume (we will confirm this assumption with the ACF function once we have transformed the series into a `ts` object) that the series has a strong correlation with the seasonal lags, we will create a lag variable with a lag of 365 observations. We will utilize the **dplyr** package for creating those features:

```
library(dplyr)

UKdaily <- UKdaily %>%
  mutate(wday = wday(TIMESTAMP, label = TRUE),
         month = month(TIMESTAMP, label = TRUE),
         lag365 = dplyr::lag(ND, 365)) %>%
  filter(!is.na(lag365)) %>%
  arrange(TIMESTAMP)
```

 Recall that the cost of using a lag variable with a length of *N* is the loss of the first *N* observations (as the lags of those observations cannot be generated from the series). Therefore, we used the filter functions for removing the rows of the table that the `lag365` variable is missing (that is, the first 365 observations).

Let's review the structure of the `UKdaily` table after adding those new features:

```
str(UKdaily)
```

We get the following output:

```
## 'data.frame':    2540 obs. of  5 variables:
## $ TIMESTAMP: Date, format: "2012-01-01" "2012-01-02" ...
## $ ND       : int  1478868 1608394 1881072 1956360 1936635 1939424
1698505 1679311 1898593 1922898 ...
## $ wday     : Factor w/ 7 levels "Sun","Mon","Tue",..: 1 2 3 4 5 6 7 1 2
3 ...
## $ month    : Factor w/ 12 levels "Jan","Feb","Mar",..: 1 1 1 1 1 1 1 1
1 1 ...
## $ lag365   : int  1671744 1760123 1878748 2076052 2103866 2135202
2121523 1861515 1837427 2093269 ...
```

As the `tslm` function input must be in a `ts` format (at least for the series), we will convert the series to a `ts` object. We will use the first timestamp of the series and the `year` and `yday` (the day of the year) functions from the **lubridate** package to set the object starting point:

```
start_date <- min(UKdaily$TIMESTAMP)

start <- c(year(start_date), yday(start_date))
```

As we saw in Chapter 3, *The Time Series Object*, we will use the ts function from the **stats** package to set the ts object:

```
UK_ts <- ts(UKdaily$ND,
            start = start,
            frequency = 365)
```

After we transform the series into a ts object, we can go back and confirm the assumption we made about the correlation level between the series and its seasonal lags with the ts_acf function (an interactive version of the acf function from the **TSstudio** package). We will review the correlation of the series with its lags from the past four years:

```
ts_acf(UK_ts, lag.max = 365 * 4)
```

We get the following output:

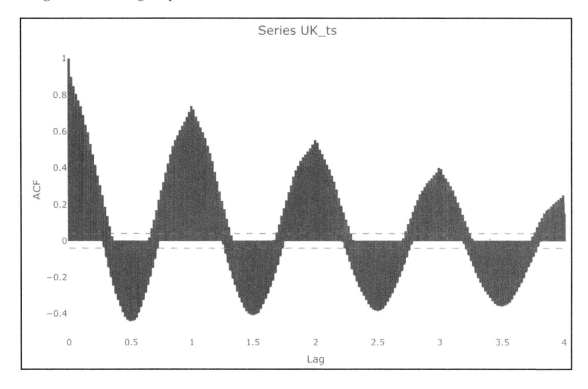

The preceding ACF plot confirms our assumption, and the series has a strong relationship with the seasonal lags, in particular lag 365, the first lag.

As a side note, you can be sure that the series also has a strong correlation with the weekly lags (that is, lag 7, 14, 21, and so on). However, generally, it is not recommended that you use lags that are smaller than the forecast horizon (for example, lag 7, when the forecast horizon is 365), as you will have to forecast those lags as well to be able to use them as an input in the model. This involves additional effort, as you will have to forecast those lags. Furthermore, it may increase the forecast bias as we are using forecasted values as inputs.

Now, after we have created the new features for the model and set the `ts` object, we are ready to split the input series and the corresponding external features object we created (`UKdaily`) into a training and testing partition. As our goal is to forecast the next 365 observations, and the length of the series is large enough (2,540 observations), we can afford to set the testing partition to the length of the forecasting horizon—365 observations. We will set `h`, an indicator variable, to `365` and use it to define the partitions and, later on, the forecast horizon:

```
h <- 365
```

As before, we will split the series into a training and testing partitions with the `ts_split` function:

```
UKpartitions <- ts_split(UK_ts, sample.out = h)

train_ts <- UKpartitions$train
test_ts <- UKpartitions$test
```

In a similar manner, we have to split the features we created for the regression model (the seasonal and lag features) into a training and testing partition following the exact same order as we used for the corresponding `ts` object. We will use the `data.frame` index functionality to set the `UKdaily` table to training and testing partitions:

```
train_df <- UKdaily[1:(nrow(UKdaily) - h), ]
test_df <- UKdaily[(nrow(UKdaily) - h + 1):nrow(UKdaily), ]
```

Training and testing the forecasting model

After we have created the different features for the model, we are ready to start the training process of the forecasting model. We will use the training partition and start to train the following three models:

- **Baseline model**: Regressing the series with the seasonal and trend component using the built-in features of the `tslm` function. As we set the series frequency to `365`, the seasonal feature of the series refers to the daily seasonality.
- **Multiseasonal model**: Adding the day of the week and month of the year indicators for capturing the multiseasonality of the series.
- **A multiseasonal model with a seasonal lag**: Using, in addition to the seasonal indicators, the seasonal lag variable.

The comparison of these three models will be based on the following criteria:

- Performance of the model on the training and testing set using the MAPE score
- Visualizing the fitted and forecasted values versus the actual values of the series using the `test_forecast` function

 Starting with a simplistic model (baseline model) will allow us to observe whether adding new features contributes to the model performance or whether we should avoid it, as adding more features or complexity to the model does not always yield better results.

We will start with the baseline model, regressing the series with its seasonal and trend components:

```
md_tslm1 <- tslm(train_ts ~ season + trend)
```

Next, we will utilize the trained model, `md_tslm1`, to forecast the next 365 days of the series, corresponding to the observations of the testing partition, using the `forecast` function:

```
fc_tslm1 <- forecast(md_tslm1, h = h)
```

Let's compare the model performance on the training and testing sets using the `test_forecast` function:

```
test_forecast(actual = UK_ts,
              forecast.obj = fc_tslm1,
              test = test_ts)
```

The output is shown as follows:

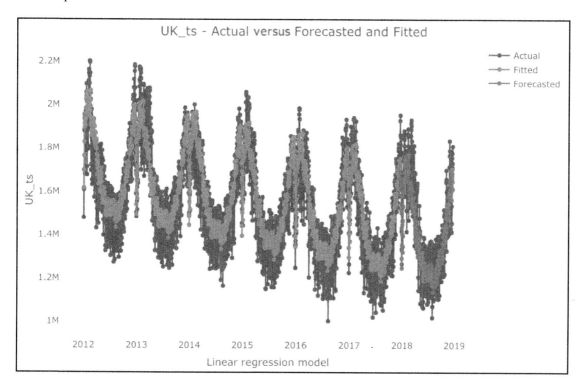

We can observe from the preceding performance plot that the baseline model is doing a great job of capturing both the series trend and the day of the year seasonality. On the other hand, it fails to capture the oscillation that related to the day of the week. The MAPE score of the model, as we can see in the output of the following `accuracy` function, is 6.09% and 7.77% on the training and testing partitions, respectively:

```
accuracy(fc_tslm1, test_ts)
```

We get the following output:

```
##                                     ME      RMSE       MAE         MPE
## Training set  -0.0000000000007315552  112133.5  92602.47  -0.5399055
## Test set       48298.6969219034435809590  135141.0  113146.70  2.6201812
##                  MAPE       MASE      ACF1  Theil's U
## Training set  6.097994  0.7644557  0.502279        NA
## Test set      7.777603  0.9340533  0.508189  1.136721
```

We will now try improve the model accuracy, by adding the day of the week and month of the year features to the model:

```
md_tslm2 <- tslm(train_ts ~ season + trend + wday + month,
                data = train_df)
```

As we are now using features from an external data source, we have to specify the input data with the `data` argument. We will now repeat the same process as before, by using a forecast with the trained model and evaluating the model performance:

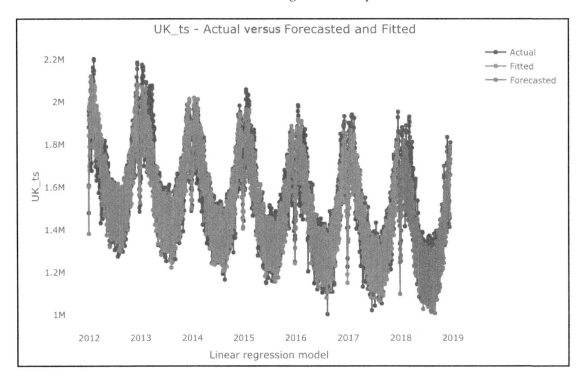

Looking at the preceding performance plot of the second model, we can observe the contribution of the seasonal features on the forecast, as the second model was able to capture both the trend and the multiseasonal patterns of the series. This can also be observed on the model MAPE score, which dropped to 2.87% and 5.23% in the training and testing partitions, respectively:

```
accuracy(fc_tslm2, test_ts)
```

We get the following output:

```
##                                    ME      RMSE       MAE        MPE
## Training set    -0.000000000001671321 61384.46 45614.64 -0.1462402
## Test set      48475.302282246622780804 98603.29 77795.70  3.1031691
##                   MAPE       MASE      ACF1 Theil's U
## Training set 2.874880 0.3765599 0.7127754        NA
## Test set     5.236208 0.6422223 0.6565167 0.8053068
```

Last but not least, let's add the lag variable to the model, and repeat the same process as before:

```
md_tslm3 <- tslm(train_ts ~ season + trend + wday + month + lag365,
  data = train_df)

fc_tslm3 <- forecast(md_tslm3, h = h, newdata = test_df)
```

The performance of the third model can be seen in the following plot:

```
test_forecast(actual = UK_ts,
              forecast.obj = fc_tslm3,
              test = test_ts)
```

We get the plot as seen in the following graph:

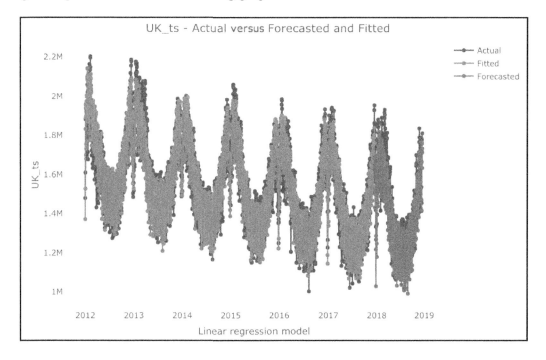

It is hard to observe from the performance plot of the third model, if there is a significant difference from the second model. Therefore, let's review the MAPE score of the third model:

```
accuracy(fc_tslm3, test_ts)
```

We get the following output:

```
##                                     ME      RMSE      MAE       MPE
MAPE
## Training set     0.000000000003641324 59271.32 44457.55 -0.137529
2.814302
## Test set     44255.320284163266478572 96357.83 75372.88  2.795172
5.078317
##                     MASE       ACF1 Theil's U
## Training set 0.3670078 0.7020265          NA
## Test set     0.6222213 0.6245326 0.7888625
```

The results of the third model show a small improvement in the model accuracy with 2.81% on the training set and 5.07% on the testing set.

Model selection

Now it's time to select a model. At this point, it is clear that the second and third models perform better than the first model. As both the second and third model achieved a fairly similar MAPE score, with a small advantage for the third model, we should ask ourselves whether an improvement of less than 0.2% on the error rate of the testing set is worth the cost of using the lag variable (that is, the loss of 365 observations and additional cost of a degree of freedom for the model).

It depends.

There is no straightforward answer to this question. Furthermore, it depends on the goal of the forecast. It is recommended that you consider the following test:

- **The first question you should ask in this case**: Is the lag variable statistically significant? If the variable is not statistically significant, there is no point in continuing the discussion, and it is better to drop the variable. In the case of the third model, we can use the summary function to observe the level of significance of the lag365 variable:

  ```
  summary(md_tslm3)$coefficients %>% tail(1)
  ```

We get the following output:

```
##          Estimate Std. Error t value Pr(>|t|)
## lag365    -0.251      0.022   -11.4 4.06e-29
```

The *p*-value of the `lag365` variable indicated that the variable is statistically significant at a level of 0.001.

- Similarly, we can apply a single ANOVA test with the `anova` function from the **stats** package, and check if the additional variable is significant:

```
anova(md_tslm3)
```

We get the following output:

```
## Analysis of Variance Table
##
## Response: train_ts
##               Df   Sum Sq  Mean Sq F value Pr(>F)
## season       364 6.70e+13 1.84e+11   43.12 <2e-16 ***
## trend          1 1.53e+13 1.53e+13 3595.90 <2e-16 ***
## wday           6 1.91e+13 3.18e+12  745.71 <2e-16 ***
## month         11 6.42e+10 5.84e+09    1.37   0.18
## lag365         1 5.55e+11 5.55e+11  129.98 <2e-16 ***
## Residuals   1791 7.64e+12 4.27e+09
## ---
## Signif. codes:  0 '***' 0.001 '**' 0.01 '*' 0.05 '.' 0.1 ' ' 1
```

The ANOVA test also indicated that the `lag365` variable is statistically significant.

- **Backtesting**: It might be the case that the third model is more accurate just by chance and not because the lag variable contributes to the model accuracy, as the difference is relatively small. Therefore, the backtesting of both models could help to validate whether the contribution of the lag variable is consistent over several testing periods. I will leave it to you to conduct backtesting for both of the models as a fun exercise.

 More robust methods can apply for feature selection such as stepwise, ridge, or lasso regression. Although those methods are not in the scope of this book, it is recommended that you read about them. In Chapter 12, *Forecasting with Machine Learning Models*, we will explore advanced regression approaches with machine learning models, which include feature selection methods.

For the sake of simplicity, we will go with the accuracy criteria and select the third model to forecast the series. The next step is to retrain the model on all series and forecast the next 365 days:

```
final_md <- tslm(UK_ts ~ season + trend + wday + month + lag365,
  data = UKdaily)
```

Residuals analysis

Just before we finalize the forecast, let's do some analysis of the selected model residuals using the checkresiduals function:

```
checkresiduals(final_md)
```

We get the following output:

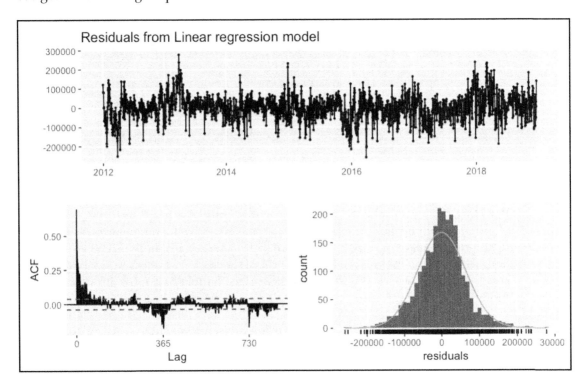

As you can see from the preceding residual summary plot, the residuals are not white noise, as some autocorrelation exists between the residuals series and their lags. This is technically an indication that the model did not capture all the patterns or information that exists in the series. One way to address this issue is to identify additional variables that can explain the variation in the residuals. The main challenge with this approach is that it is hard to identify external variables that can explain the variation of the residuals, and are also feasible to forecast. For example, it is reasonable to assume that weather patterns affect the demand for electricity, yet it is hard to predict those weather patterns a year ahead.

An alternative approach, when patterns *leftover* in the residuals of the model is to treat the model's residuals as a separate time series data and to model it with other time series forecasting model. A common approach is a regression with ARIMA error, which we will introduce in `Chapter 11`, *Forecasting with ARIMA Models*.

Finalizing the forecast

Let's finalize the process and utilize the selected trained model to forecast the future 365 observations. Since we used external variables with the `tslm` function, we will have to generate their future values. This is relatively simple, as we used deterministic variables. Therefore, we will create a `data.frame` object with the values of `wday`, `month`, and `lag365` for the next 365 future observations. A simplistic approach is to first create the corresponding dates of the forecasted observations, and then extract from this object the day of the week and month of the year:

```
UK_fc_df <- data.frame(date = seq.Date(from = max(UKdaily$TIMESTAMP) +
days(1),

                                       by = "day",
                                       length.out = h))
```

Next, we can utilize the `date` variable for creating the `wday` and `month` variables with the **lubridate** package:

```
UK_fc_df$wday <- factor(wday(UK_fc_df$date, label = TRUE), ordered = FALSE)

UK_fc_df$month <- factor(month(UK_fc_df$date, label = TRUE), ordered =
FALSE)

UK_fc_df$lag365 <- tail(UKdaily$ND, h)
```

Let's use the `forecast` function to create the forecast:

```
UKgrid_fc <- forecast(final_md, h = h, newdata = UK_fc_df)
```

Last but not least, we will plot the final forecast with the `plot_forecast` function from the **TSstudio** package:

```
plot_forecast(UKgrid_fc,
              title = "The UK National Demand for Electricity Forecast",
              Ytitle = "MW",
              Xtitle = "Year")
```

We get the following output:

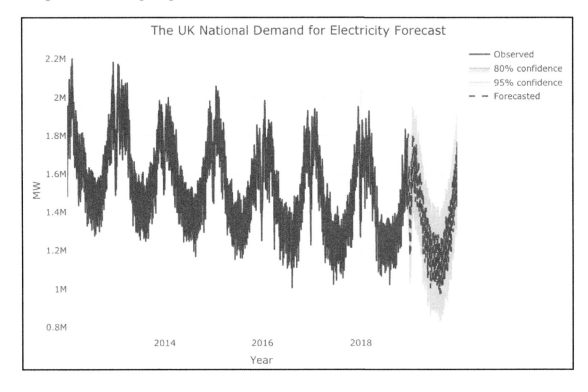

Summary

In this chapter, we introduced the forecasting applications of the linear regression model. Although the linear regression model was not designed to handle time series data, with simple feature engineering we can transform a forecasting problem into a linear regression problem. The main advantage of the linear regression model with respect to other traditional time series models is the ability of the model to incorporate external variables and factors. Nevertheless, this model can handle time series with multiseasonality patterns, as we saw with the UK demand for electricity forecast. Last but not least, the forecasting approaches we demonstrated in this chapter will be the base for advanced modeling with machine learning models that we will discuss in `Chapter 12`, *Forecasting with Machine Learning Models*.

In the next chapter, we will introduce the exponential smoothing methods, a family of forecasting models based on a weighted moving average approach.

10
Forecasting with Exponential Smoothing Models

In `Chapter 5`, *Decomposition of Time Series Data*, we looked at the application of smoothing functions for noise reduction in time series data and trend estimation. In this chapter, we will expand on the use of smoothing functions and introduce their forecasting applications. This family of forecasting models can handle a variety of time series types, from series with neither trends nor seasonal components to series with both trends and seasonal components. We will start with the basic moving average model and simple exponential smoothing models, and then add more layers to the model, as well as the model's ability to handle complex time series data.

In this chapter, we will cover the following topics:

- Forecasting with moving average models
- Forecasting approaches with smoothing models
- Tuning parameters for smoothing models

Technical requirement

The following packages will be used in this chapter:

- **forecast**: Version 8.5 and above
- **h2o**: Version 3.22.1.1 and above and Java version 7 and above
- **TSstudio**: Version 0.1.4 and above
- **plotly**: Version 4.8 and above
- **dplyr**: Version 0.8.1 and above
- **tidyr**: Version 0.8.3 and above
- **Quandl**: Version 2.9.1 and above

You can access the codes for this chapter from the following link:

```
https://github.com/PacktPublishing/Hands-On-Time-Series-Analysis-with-R/tree/ma
ster/Chapter10
```

Forecasting with moving average models

In Chapter 5, *Decomposition of Time Series Data*, we looked at the application of the moving average functions to smooth time series data. Those functions, with a small tweak, can be used as a forecasting model. In the upcoming section, we will introduce two of the most common moving average forecasting functions—the simple and weighted moving average. These models, as you will see later on in this chapter, are the foundation for the exponential smoothing forecasting models.

The simple moving average

The **simple moving average (SMA)** function, which we used in Chapter 5, *Decomposition of Time Series Data*, for smooth time series data can be utilized, with some simple steps, as a forecasting model. First, let's recall the structure of the SMA function for smoothing time series data:

$$Y'_{\,t} = \frac{Y_{t-\frac{m-1}{2}} + \ldots + Y_t + \ldots + Y_{t+\frac{m-1}{2}}}{m}$$

This occurs when we use a two-sided rolling window. Let's take a look at the following equation:

$$Y'_{\,t} = \frac{Y_{t-m+1} + \ldots + Y_{t-1} + Y_t}{m}$$

This occurs when we use a left tail rolling window. Here the following applies:

- Y_t represents the t observation of series Y with T observations, where $1 \leq t \leq T$
- Y'_t represents the smoothed value of Y_t
- m represents the length of the rolling window, where $m \leq T$

As you can see, in both cases (and generally with any other type of rolling window), the rolling window includes the t observation of the series. Converting an SMA smoothing function into a forecasting model is based on averaging the past consecutive m observations of the series. For example, $\hat{Y}_{t+1|t=T}$, which is the value of the first forecasting observation of the series (that is, observation $T+1$) is equal to the average of the past m observations:

$$\hat{Y}_{t+1|t=T} = \frac{Y_{t-m+1} + \ldots + Y_{t-1} + Y_t}{m}$$

Where, the following terms are used in the preceding equation:

- $Y_{t-m+1} + \ldots + Y_{t-1} + Y_t$ are the past last m observations of series Y with T observations, given $t = T$
- $\hat{Y}_{t+1|t=T}$ represents the first forecasted value of a series with T observations (that is, given t is equal to the last observation of the series T)
- Like the previous equation, m represents the length of the rolling window

You can observe from the preceding formulas of both the smoothing function (Y'_t) and forecasting functions ($\hat{Y}_{t+1|t=T}$) that the smoothed value of the last observation of the series (observation T) is the forecasted value of observation $T+1$. Moreover, only the first forecasted value (observation $T+1$) is constructed by averaging only actual values of the series (for example, $Y_{t-m+1} + \ldots + Y_{t-1} + Y_t$). As we shift the rolling window to forecast the following observations of the series, the actual values are replaced with the previously forecasted values. For instance, the calculation of the second forecasted value on-line, $T+2$, is defined by the following expression:

$$\hat{Y}_{t+2|t=T} = \frac{Y_{t-m+2} + \ldots + Y_{t-1} + Y_t + \hat{Y}_{t+1}}{m}$$

In this case, the function inputs are the last $m-1$ observations of the series, along with the first forecasted value, $\hat{Y}_{t+1|t=T}$. From the $T + m + 1$ observation and onward, the function inputs are the last m forecasted values.

Forecasting with the SMA function is recommended when the input series has no structural patterns, such as trend and seasonal components. In this case, it is reasonable to assume that the forecasted values are relatively close to the last observations of the series.

In the following example, we will create a customized SMA function and use it to forecast the monthly prices of the Robusta coffee prices in the next 12 months. The Robusta coffee prices (USD per kg) are an example of time series data that has no specific trend or seasonal patterns. Rather, this series has a cycle component, where the magnitude and length of the cycle keep changing from cycle to cycle. This series is part of the `Coffee_Prices` dataset and is available on the **TSstudio** package:

```
library(TSstudio)

data(Coffee_Prices)
```

Let's review the properties of the `Coffee_Prices` dataset with the `ts_info` function:

```
ts_info(Coffee_Prices)
```

We get the following output:

```
## The Coffee_Prices series is a mts object with 2 variables and 1402
observations
## Frequency: 12
## Start time: 1960 1
## End time: 2018 5
```

This dataset is an `mts` object and contains both the monthly prices (USD per kg) of the Robusta and Arabica coffee prices between 1960 and 2018. We will extract the monthly prices of the Robusta coffee from the `Coffee_Prices` object:

```
robusta <- Coffee_Prices[,1]
```

Let's review the series:

```
ts_plot(robusta,
        title = "The Robusta Coffee Monthly Prices",
        Ytitle = "Price in USD",
        Xtitle = "Year")
```

The output is as follows:

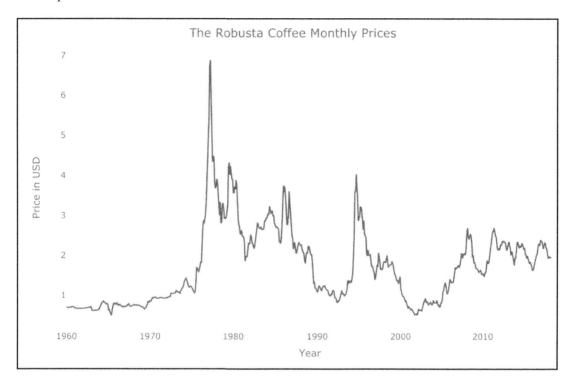

Next, we will create a basic SMA function using some of the functionality of the **tidyr** package:

```
library(tidyr)

sma_forecast <- function(df, h, m, w = NULL){
  # Error handling
  if(h > nrow(df)){
    stop("The length of the forecast horizon must be shorter than the
length of the series")}
  if(m > nrow(df)){
    stop("The length of the rolling window must be shorter than the length
of the series")}
  if(!is.null(w)){
    if(length(w) != m){
      stop("The weight argument is not aligned with the length of the
rolling window")
    } else if(sum(w) !=1){
      stop("The sum of the average weight is different than 1")
    }}
```

```
# Setting the average weigths
if(is.null(w)){
  w <- rep(1/m, m)
}
### Setting the data frame ###
# Changing the Date object column name
names(df)[1] <- "date"
# Setting the training and testing partition
# according to the forecast horizon
df$type <- c(rep("train", nrow(df) - h), rep("test", h))
# Spreading the table by the partition type
df1 <- df %>% spread(key = type, value = y)
# Create the target variable
df1$yhat <- df1$train
# Simple moving average function
for(i in (nrow(df1) - h + 1):nrow(df1)){
  r <- (i-m):(i-1)
  df1$yhat[i] <- sum(df1$yhat[r] * w)
}
# dropping from the yhat variable the actual values
# that were used for the rolling window
df1$yhat <- ifelse(is.na(df1$test), NA, df1$yhat)
df1$y <- ifelse(is.na(df1$test), df1$train, df1$test)
return(df1)
}
```

The function arguments are as follows:

- df: The input series in a two-column data frame format, where the first column is a Date object and the second one is the actual values of the series.
- h: The horizon of the forecast. For the purpose of the following example, the function set the last h observations as a testing set. This allows us to compare model performance.
- m: The length of the rolling window.
- w: The weights of the average, by default, using equal weights (or arithmetic average).

The `sma_forecast` function has the following components:

- **Error handling**: Test and verify whether the input arguments of the function are valid. If one of the defined tests isn't true, it will stop the function from running and trigger an error message.
- **Data preparation**: This defines the `data.frame` object based on the window length and the forecast horizon.
- **Data calculation**: Calculates the simple moving average and return the results.

Let's utilize this function to demonstrate the performance of the SMA function. We will forecast the last 24 months of the Robusta series using a rolling window of 3, 6, 12, 24, and 36 months:

```
robusta_df <- ts_to_prophet(robusta)

robusta_fc_m1 <-  sma_forecast(robusta_df, h = 24, m = 1)
robusta_fc_m6 <-  sma_forecast(robusta_df, h = 24, m = 6)
robusta_fc_m12 <- sma_forecast(robusta_df, h = 24, m = 12)
robusta_fc_m24 <- sma_forecast(robusta_df, h = 24, m = 24)
robusta_fc_m36 <- sma_forecast(robusta_df, h = 24, m = 36)
```

We will use the **plotly** package to plot the results of the different moving average functions:

```
library(plotly)

plot_ly(data = robusta_df[650:nrow(robusta_df),], x = ~ ds, y = ~ y,
        type = "scatter", mode = "lines",
        name = "Actual") %>%
  add_lines(x = robusta_fc_m1$date, y = robusta_fc_m1$yhat,
            name = "SMA - 1", line = list(dash = "dash")) %>%
  add_lines(x = robusta_fc_m6$date, y = robusta_fc_m6$yhat,
            name = "SMA - 6", line = list(dash = "dash")) %>%
  add_lines(x = robusta_fc_m12$date, y = robusta_fc_m12$yhat,
            name = "SMA - 12", line = list(dash = "dash")) %>%
  add_lines(x = robusta_fc_m24$date, y = robusta_fc_m24$yhat,
            name = "SMA - 24", line = list(dash = "dash")) %>%
  add_lines(x = robusta_fc_m36$date, y = robusta_fc_m36$yhat,
            name = "SMA - 36", line = list(dash = "dash")) %>%
  layout(title = "Forecasting the Robusta Coffee Monthly Prices",
         xaxis = list(title = ""),
         yaxis = list(title = "USD per Kg."))
```

We get the following plot:

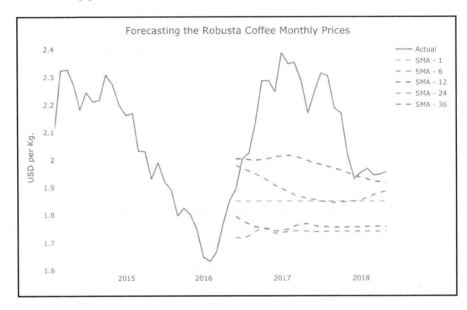

The main observations from the preceding plot are as follows:

- If the length of the rolling window is shorter:
    - The range of the forecast is fairly close to the most recent observations of the series
    - The faster the forecast converges to some constant value
- If the window length is longer:
    - The longer it takes until the forecast converges to some constant value
    - It can handle better shocks and outliers
- An SMA forecasting model with a rolling window of a length of 1 is equivalent to the Naïve forecasting model

While the SMA function is fairly simple to use and cheap on compute power, it has some limitations:

- The forecasting power of the SMA function is limited to a short horizon and may have poor performance in the long run.
- This method is limited for time series data, with no trend or seasonal patterns. This mainly effects the arithmetic average that smooths the seasonal pattern and becomes flat in the long run.

Weighted moving average

The **weighted moving average (WMA)** is an extended version of the SMA function, and it is based on the use of the weighted average (as opposed to arithmetic average). The main advantage of the WMA function, with respect to the SMA function, is that it allows you to distribute the weight of the lags on the rolling window. This can be useful when the series has a high correlation with some of its lags. The WMA function can be formalized by the following expression:

$$Y\hat{}_{T+n} = w_1 Y_{T+n-m} + \ldots + w_m Y_{T+n-1}$$

Here, $Y\hat{}_{T+n}$ is the n forecasted value of the series at time $T + n$, and w is a scalar of a size m which defines the weight of each observation in the rolling window. The use of the weighted average provides more flexibility as it can handle series with a seasonal pattern. In the following example, we will use the `sma_forecast` function we created previously to forecast the last 24 months of the `USgas` dataset. In this case, we will utilize the w argument to set the average weight and therefore transform the function from SMA to WMA. Like we did previously, we will first transform the series into `data.frame` format with the `ts_to_prophet` function:

```
data(USgas)

USgas_df <- ts_to_prophet(USgas)
```

In the following example, we will use the following two strategies:

- The WMA model for applying all the weight on the seasonal lag (lag `12`):

```
USgas_fc_m12a <- sma_forecast(USgas_df,
                              h = 24,
                              m = 12,
                              w = c(1, rep(0,11)))
```

- The WMA model for weighting the first lag with `0.2` and the seasonal lag (lag `12`) with `0.8`:

```
USgas_fc_m12b <- sma_forecast(USgas_df,
                              h = 24,
                              m = 12,
                              w = c(0.8, rep(0,10), 0.2))
```

Let's utilize the **plotly** package to plot the output of both of the WMA models:

```
plot_ly(data = USgas_df[190:nrow(USgas_df),],
        x = ~ ds,
        y = ~ y,
        type = "scatter",
        mode = "lines",
        name = "Actual") %>%
  add_lines(x = USgas_fc_m12a$date,
            y = USgas_fc_m12a$yhat,
            name = "WMA - Seasonal Lag",
            line = list(dash = "dash")) %>%
  add_lines(x = USgas_fc_m12b$date,
            y = USgas_fc_m12b$yhat,
            name = "WMA - 12 (0.2/0.8)",
            line = list(dash = "dash")) %>%
  layout(title = "Forecasting the Monthly Consumption of Natural
Gas in the US",
         xaxis = list(title = ""),
         yaxis = list(title = "Billion Cubic Feet"))
```

We get the following output:

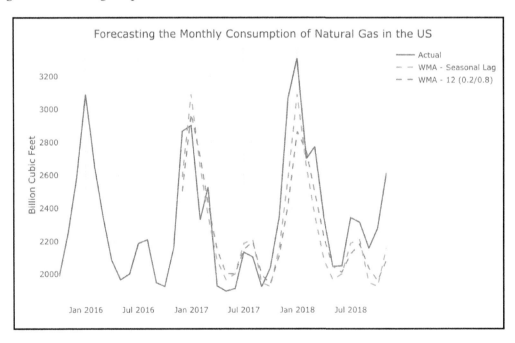

As you can see in the preceding plot, both models captured the seasonal oscillation of the series to some extent. Setting the full weight on the seasonal lag is equivalent to the seasonal Naïve model. This strategy could be useful for a series with a dominant seasonal pattern, such as USgas. In the second example, we weighted the average between the most recent lag and the seasonal lag. It would make sense to distribute the weights between the different lags when the series has a high correlation with those lags.

While WMA can capture the seasonal component of a series, it cannot capture the series trend (due to the average effect). Therefore, this method will start to lose its effectiveness once the forecast horizon crosses the length of the series frequency (for example, more than a year for monthly series). Later on in this chapter, we will introduce the Holt-Winters model, which can handle time series with both seasonal and trend components.

Forecasting with exponential smoothing

Among the traditional time series forecasting models, the exponential smoothing functions are one of the most popular forecasting approaches. This approach, conceptually, is close to the moving average approach we introduced previously, as both are based on forecasting the future values of the series by averaging the past observations of the series. The main distinction between the exponential smoothing and the moving average approaches is that the first is averaging all series observations, as opposed to a subset of *m* observations by the latter.

Furthermore, the advance exponential smoothing functions can handle series with a trend and seasonal components. In this section, we will focus on the main exponential smoothing forecasting models:

- Simple exponential smoothing model
- Holt model
- Holt-Winters model

Simple exponential smoothing model

The **Simple exponential smoothing** (SES) as its name implies, is the simplest forecasting model among the exponential smoothing family. The main assumption of this model is that the series stays at the same level (that is, the local mean of the series is constant) over time, and therefore, this model is suitable for series with neither trend nor seasonal components. The SES model shares some of the attributes of the WMA model, as both models forecast the future values of the series by a weighted average of the past observations of the series.

On the other hand, the main distinction between the two is that the SES model is utilizing all the previous observations, whereas the WMA model is using only the most recent m observations (for a model with a rolling window of a length of m). The main attribute of the SES model is the weighted average technique, which is based on the exponential decay of the observation weights according to their chronological distance (that is, series index or timestamp) from the first forecasted values. The decay rate of the observation weights is set by α, the smoothing parameter of the model.

In addition, the SES function is a step function, where the n forecasted value of the model becomes the input of the next forecast of the next observations, $n+1$. We can formalize this relationship by using the following equations:

$$\hat{Y_{T+1}} = \alpha Y_T + (1 - \alpha)\hat{Y_T}$$

Where, the following terms are used in the preceding equation:

- $\hat{Y_{T+1}}$ is the forecasted value of the observation $T+1$ for a series with n observations (for example, $T = 1,...,n$)
- Y_T is the T observation of the series
- α is the smoothing parameter of the model, where $0 < \alpha \leq 1$
- $\hat{Y_T}$ is the forecasted value of observation T at step $T-1$

Since the model assumes that the level of the model doesn't change over time, we can generalize the preceding equation for the forecast of the $T+n$ observation of the series (where $n \geq 1$):

$$\hat{Y_{T+n}} = \hat{Y_{T+1}} = \alpha Y_T + (1 - \alpha)\hat{Y_T}$$

Hence, the goal of the model is to calculate the series level based on the input data. This results in a flat forecast.

The process of identifying the model level is relatively simple and can be obtained from the preceding model equation. Since this is a recursive equation, we can expand this equation by assigning the value of $\hat{Y_{T-1}}$ the forecasted value of the previous period, $T-1$:

$$\hat{Y_{T+1}} = \alpha Y_T + (1 - \alpha)[\alpha Y_{T-1} + (1 - \alpha)\hat{Y_{T-1}}] = \alpha Y_T + \alpha(1 - \alpha)Y_{T-1} + (1 - \alpha)^2 \hat{Y_{T-1}}$$

In the same manner, we can keep expanding this equation by recursively assigning the formulas of all the previous observation's forecasts. This expansion process continues all the way to the first forecasted value of the series (in chronological order) $\hat{Y}_2$:

$$\hat{Y_{T+1}} = \alpha Y_T + \alpha(1-\alpha)Y_{T-1} + \alpha(1-\alpha)^2 Y_{T-1} + \ldots + \alpha(1-\alpha)^{T-2}Y_3 + (1-\alpha)^{T-1}\hat{Y}_2$$

Chronologically, the first observation that can be forecast is Y_2 (since there are no available observations to forecast Y_1, the first observation of the series). Therefore, the preceding equation can be expanded to the forecast value of the second observation, or as follows:

$$\hat{Y}_2 = \alpha Y_1 + (1-\alpha)\hat{Y}_1$$

Since there is no supporting data to forecast Y_1 (since this is the first available observation of the series), we need to initialize the value of $\hat{Y}_1$. This is typically done by assigning the actual value of the first observation (that is, $\hat{Y}_1 = Y_1$), or by estimating it. We can simplify this equation further by assigning the equation of $\hat{Y}_2$ and rearranging the right-hand side of this equation:

$$\hat{Y_{T+1}} = \alpha Y_T + \alpha(1-\alpha)Y_{T-1} + \alpha(1-\alpha)^2 Y_{T-1} + \ldots + \alpha(1-\alpha)^{T-1}Y_1 + (1-\alpha)^T \hat{Y}_1$$

This can simplify the preceding equation so that it now looks as follows:

$$\hat{Y_{T+1}} = \alpha[(1-\alpha)^0 Y_T + (1-\alpha)^1 Y_{T-1} + (1-\alpha)^2 Y_{T-1} + \ldots + (1-\alpha)^T Y_1] + (1-\alpha)^T \hat{Y}_1$$

This can be compressed further into the following expression:

$$\hat{Y_{T+1}} = \sum_{i=1}^{T} \alpha(1-\alpha)^{i-1}Y_i + (1-\alpha)^T \hat{Y}_1$$

Another interpretation of the forecast equation of the SES model can be observed by manipulating the forecast equation, as follows:

$$\hat{Y_{T+1}} = \alpha Y_T + (1-\alpha)\hat{Y}_T = \alpha Y_T + \hat{Y}_T - \alpha \hat{Y}_T.$$

As we saw in the previous chapter, $Y_t - \hat{Y}_t$ denote the error term of the fitted value of observation t. Therefore, the forecast value of the observation $T+1$ by the SES model is nothing but the forecasted value of the previous observation, $\hat{Y}_t$, and the proportion of the forecast error term as a function of α, or as follows:

$$\hat{Y_{T+1}} = \hat{Y}_T + \alpha e_T, \quad where$$

e_T is defined as the forecast error for T observation of the series (for example, the last observation of a series with T observations), or as follows:

$$e_T = Y_T - \hat{Y}_T$$

A more common form for this equation is the component form, which in the case of the SES model is the estimation of $\hat{Y}_{T+1}$ and $\hat{Y}_T$ to denote the model estimation of the series level at time T and *T-1*, respectively. The preceding equation can be rewritten like so:

$$\hat{Y_{T+1}} = l_T = \alpha Y_T + (1 - \alpha)l_{T-1}$$

The smoothing parameter of the model, α, defines the rate of the model weight's decay. Since α is closer to *1*, the weights of the most recent observations are higher. On the other hand, the decay rate, in this case, is faster. A special case is a SES model with $\alpha = 1$, which is equivalent to a naive forecasting model:

$$\hat{Y}_{T+1|\alpha=1} = Y_T$$

This is also equivalent to the *n* forecasted value:

$$\hat{Y}_{T+n|\alpha=1} = Y_T$$

The following example demonstrates the decay of the weights of the observations on the most recent 15 observations, for α values between 0.01 to 1:

```
alpha_df <- data.frame(index = seq(from = 1, to = 15, by = 1),
                       power = seq(from = 14, to = 0, by = -1))

alpha_df$alpha_0.01 <- 0.01 * (1 - 0.01) ^ alpha_df$power
alpha_df$alpha_0.2 <- 0.2 * (1 - 0.2) ^ alpha_df$power
alpha_df$alpha_0.4 <- 0.4 * (1 - 0.4) ^ alpha_df$power
alpha_df$alpha_0.6 <- 0.6 * (1 - 0.6) ^ alpha_df$power
alpha_df$alpha_0.8 <- 0.8 * (1 - 0.8) ^ alpha_df$power
alpha_df$alpha_1 <- 1 * (1 - 1) ^ alpha_df$power
```

Let's plot the results:

```
plot_ly(data = alpha_df) %>%
  add_lines(x = ~ index, y = ~ alpha_0.01, name = "alpha = 0.01") %>%
  add_lines(x = ~ index, y = ~ alpha_0.2, name = "alpha = 0.2") %>%
  add_lines(x = ~ index, y = ~ alpha_0.4, name = "alpha = 0.4") %>%
  add_lines(x = ~ index, y = ~ alpha_0.6, name = "alpha = 0.6") %>%
  add_lines(x = ~ index, y = ~ alpha_0.8, name = "alpha = 0.8") %>%
```

```
add_lines(x = ~ index, y = ~ alpha_1, name = "alpha = 1") %>%
layout(title = "Decay Rate of the SES Weights",
       xaxis = list(title = "Index"),
       yaxis = list(title = "Weight"))
```

We get the following output:

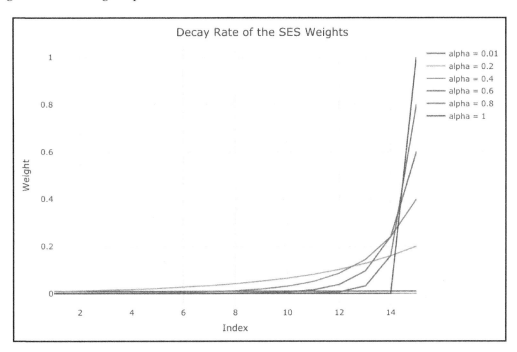

We can transform the preceding equations into component from, which describes the model by its components. In the case of the SES model, we have a single component—the model level. As we mentioned previously, the model's main assumption is that the series level remains the same over time, and therefore we can rewrite the model equation using the following notations:

$$\hat{Y_{T+1}} = l_T$$

Here, l_T defines the model level at time T, which is a weighted average of Y_T and the level of the previous period, l_{T-1}:

$$\hat{Y_{T+1}} = l_T = \alpha Y_T + (1 - \alpha)l_{T-1}$$

Forecasting with the ses function

The **forecast** package provides a customized SES model with the `ses` function. The main arguments of this function are as follows:

- `initial`: Defines the method for initializing the value of $\hat{Y}_1$, which can be calculated by using the first few observations of the series by setting the argument to simple, or by estimating it with `ets` model (an advanced version of the Holt-Winters model from the **forecast** package) when setting it to optimal.
- `alpha`: Defines the value of the smoothing parameter of the model. If set to `NULL`, the function will estimate it.
- `h`: Sets the forecast horizon.

Let's use the `ses` function to forecast the monthly prices of the Robusta coffee again. We will leave the last `12` months of the series as a testing set for benchmarking the model's performance. We will do this using the `ts_split` function from the **TSstudio** package:

```
robusta_par <- ts_split(robusta, sample.out = 12)
train <- robusta_par$train
test <- robusta_par$test
```

After we set the training and testing partition, we will use the training partition to train a SES model with the `ses` function:

```
library(forecast)
fc_ses <- ses(train, h = 12, initial = "optimal")
```

Let's review the model details:

```
fc_ses$model

## Simple exponential smoothing
##
## Call:
##  ses(y = train, h = 12, initial = "optimal")
##
##   Smoothing parameters:
##     alpha = 0.9999
##
##   Initial states:
##     l = 0.6957
##
##   sigma:  0.161
##
##       AIC      AICc      BIC
## 1989.646 1989.681 2003.252
```

As you can see from the output of the model, the `ses` function set the initial value to 0.69, which is fairly close to the value of the first observations ($Y_1 = 0.696$), and set the `alpha` parameter to `0.9999` (which technically is fairly close to the NAIVE forecast). We can review the model's performance by using the `test_forecast` function:

```
test_forecast(actual = robusta,
              forecast.obj = fc_ses,
              test = test) %>%
  layout(title = "Robusta Coffee Prices Forecast vs. Actual",
         xaxis = list(range = c(2010, max(time(robusta)))),
         yaxis = list(range = c(1, 3)))
```

We get the following output:

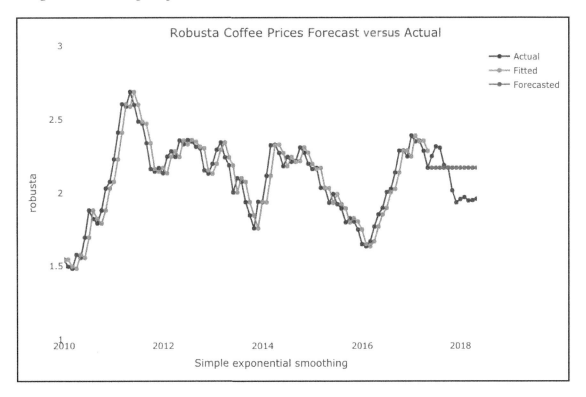

As we can see from the preceding forecast plot, the `ses` function is utilizing the training set to identify the series level by estimating the `alpha` parameter and the initial level of the model (or $\hat{Y}_1$). The forecast value level is fairly close to the value of the last observation of the series since the α value, in this case, is close to *1*. Since the goal of the SES model is to forecast the level of the series, the model won't capture any short-term oscillation.

In the case of a flat forecast, the confidence intervals of the model play a critical role, since the level of uncertainty is higher. Therefore, it will be useful to evaluate whether the forecast values are within the model confidence interval bounds. We will use the `plot_forecast` function from the **TSstudio** package to create an interactive plot for the `fs_ses` model we created and plot the testing set:

```
plot_forecast(fc_ses) %>%
  add_lines(x = time(test) + deltat(test),
            y = as.numeric(test),
            name = "Testing Partition") %>%
  layout(title = "Robusta Coffee Prices Forecast vs. Actual",
         xaxis = list(range = c(2010, max(time(robusta)) +
deltat(robusta))),
         yaxis = list(range = c(0, 4)))
```

The output is as follows:

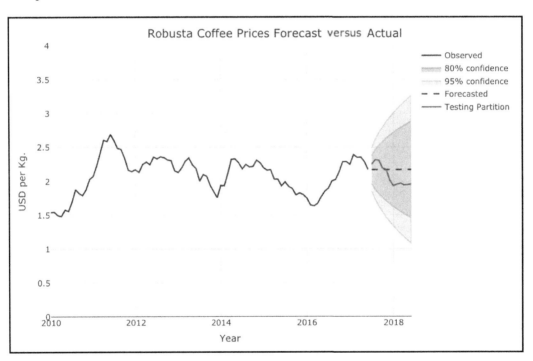

As you can see from the preceding forecast plot, the testing set is within the range of the **80% confidence** interval.

Model optimization with grid search

The `ses` function optimizes the values of the model parameters (α and l_0) that minimize the **sum of squared errors** (**SSE**) of the model on the training set. An alternative optimization approach is to use a grid search. A grid search is a simplistic but powerful approach that's used to identify the values of the model's parameters that minimize the model error. In the case of the SES model, we will apply a grid search to identify the optimal value of α that minimizes some error metric of the model (for example, MAPE, RMSE, and so on).

In the following example, we will use a grid search to tune the model parameters α and l_0, which minimize the model's MAPE for the Robusta prices series. As we saw in the preceding performance plot of the Robusta forecast, there is a gap between the structure of the fitted values (marked in red) and the forecasted value (marked in green) since the SES model has a flat forecast. Therefore, we will split the model into training, testing, and validation partitions, and for each value of α, we will apply the following steps:

1. Train the SES model using the training partition and forecast the observations of the testing partition
2. Evaluate the performance of the model on both the training and testing partition
3. Append the training and testing partitions (in chronological order) and retrain the model on the new partition (training and testing) before forecasting the values of the validation partition
4. Evaluate the performance of the second model on the validation partition

These steps will allow us to select the alpha value that minimizes the MAPE on the testing partition and use the validation set to validate the performance of the model. Before we set the function, let's set the training, testing, and validation partitions using the `ts_split` function:

```
robusta_par1 <- ts_split(robusta, sample.out = 24)

train1 <- robusta_par1$train
test1 <- ts_split(robusta_par1$test, sample.out = 12)$train

robusta_par2 <- ts_split(robusta, sample.out = 12)

train2 <- robusta_par2$train
valid <- robusta_par2$test
```

We will use the `train1` and `test1` variables for training and testing partition, and `train2` for retraining the model and validating the results on the `valid` partition. The following `alpha` variable defines the search range. We will assign a sequence of values between 0 and 1 with an increment of 0.01 using the `seq` function:

```
alpha <- seq(from = 0, to = 1, by = 0.01)
```

Since the value of `alpha` must be greater than zero, we will replace 0 with a small number that's fairly close to zero:

```
alpha[1] <- 0.001
```

We will use the `lapply` function to iterate on the model using the different values of α:

```
library(dplyr)

ses_grid <- lapply(alpha, function(i){
  md1 <- md_accuracy1 <- md2 <- md_accuracy2 <- results <-   NULL
  md1 <- ses(train1, h = 12, alpha = i, initial = "simple")
  md_accuracy1 <- accuracy(md1, test1)
  md2 <- ses(train2, h = 12, alpha = i, initial = "simple")
  md_accuracy2 <- accuracy(md2, valid)

  resutls <- data.frame(alpha = i,
                        train = md_accuracy1[9],
                        test = md_accuracy1[10],
                        valid = md_accuracy2[10])

}) %>% bind_rows()
```

As you can see in the following testing results, while α = 1 minimizes the MAPE on the training partition, α = 0.03 minimizes the error rate on the testing partition. The results on the validation partition are following the same pattern as the testing partition, with an MAPE score of 9.98% on the testing partition and 6.60% on the validation partition:

```
plot_ly(data = ses_grid, x = ~ alpha, y = ~ train,
        line = list(color = 'rgb(205, 12, 24)'),
        type = "scatter",
        mode = "lines",
        name = "Training") %>%
  add_lines(x = ~ alpha, y = ~ test, line = list(color = "rgb(22, 96,
167)", dash = "dash"), name= "Testing") %>%
  add_lines(x = ~ alpha, y = ~ valid, line = list(color = "green", dash =
"dot"), name = "Validation") %>%
  layout(title = "SES Model Grid Search Results",
         yaxis = list(title = "MAPE (%)"))
```

The output is shown in the following screenshot:

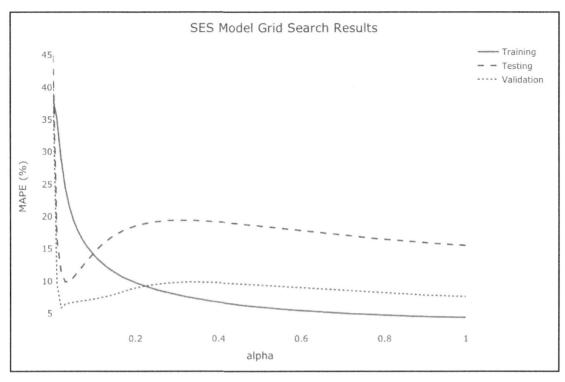

Now, let's take a look at the Holt method.

Holt method

The Holt method, also known as the double exponential smoothing model, is an expanded version of the SES model. It's based on estimating the most recent level and trend with the use of two smoothing parameters, α and β. Once the model estimates the most recent level and trend (L_T, and T_T, respectively), it utilizes them to construct the series forecast using the following equation:

- For a series with additive trend, $\hat{Y_{T+h}} = L_T + hT_T$
- For a series with multiplicative trend, $\hat{Y_{T+1}} = L_T \times hT_T$

Here, the variables of those equations are as follows:

- $Y_{\hat{T+h}}$ is the forecast value of the h forecasted value of a series with T observations
- L_T is the estimate of the series level at time T
- T_T is the estimate of the marginal impact of the series trend at time T (for example, the added value from advance series by one frequency unit)
- h is the number of forecasting steps since time T

Similar to the SES model, the calculation of the series level and trend by the Holt model is based on a weighted average with the use of two smoothing parameters, α and β. For a series with an additive trend, the calculation of the most recent level and trend of the series can be obtained with the following equations:

$$L_T = \alpha Y_T + \alpha(1 - \alpha)(L_{T-1} + T_{T-1})$$

$$T_T = \beta(L_T - L_{T-1}) + (1 - \beta)T_{T-1}$$

The following equations can be used for a series with a multiplicative trend:

$$L_T = \alpha Y_T + \alpha(1 - \alpha)(L_{T-1} \times T_{T-1})$$

$$T_T = \beta(\frac{L_T}{L_{T-1}}) + (1 - \beta)T_{T-1}$$

 As we saw in the previous chapters, a multiplicative model can transform into an additive model if we apply *log* transformation on both sides of the equation.

The Holt model estimates the values of L_T and T_T, the series level and trend at time T, using a weighted average of all the series observations. In a similar manner to the SES model estimation process, this recursive process starts with the forecast of the second observation of the model:

$$\hat{L}_2 = \alpha Y_1 + \alpha(1 - \alpha)(\hat{L}_1 + \hat{T}_1)$$

$$\hat{T}_2 = \beta(\hat{L}_2 - \hat{L}_1) + (1 - \beta)\hat{T}_1$$

Where, the following terms are used in the preceding equation:

- $\hat{L}_1$ and $\hat{L}_2$ are the forecast of the level of the first and second observations of the series, respectively
- $\hat{T}_1$ and $\hat{T}_2$ are the trend forecast of the first and second observations of the series, respectively

Since we cannot forecast the level and trend value for the first observation of the series, we will have to approximate $\hat{L}_1$ and $\hat{T}_2$ (similar to the $\hat{L}_1$ approximation process of the SES model). The forecast of the next observations in line (for example, 3 to T) are recursively created using the level and trend estimation, as well as the actual values of the preceding observations.

Forecasting with the holt function

The **forecast** package provides an implementation of the Holt model with the `holt` function. This function automatically initializes the values of $\hat{L}_1$ and $\hat{T}_1$, and identifies the values of α and β that minimize the SSE of the model on the training set. In the following example, we will retrieve the US **Gross Domestic Product (GDP)** quarterly data from the **Federal Reserve Economic Data (FRED)** API using the **Quandl** package:

```
library(Quandl)

gdp <- Quandl("FRED/GDP", start_date = "2010-01-01", type = "ts")

ts_info(gdp)
##   The . series is a ts object with 1 variable and 37 observations
##   Frequency: 4
##   Start time: 2010 1
##   End time: 2019 1
```

You will notice in the following plot that the GDP series has a strong linear trend and no seasonal component (since the series is seasonally adjusted):

```
ts_plot(gdp,
         title = "US Gross Domestic Product",
         Ytitle = "Billions of Dollars",
         Xtitle = "Source: U.S. Bureau of Economic Analysis /
fred.stlouisfed.org")
```

The output is as follows:

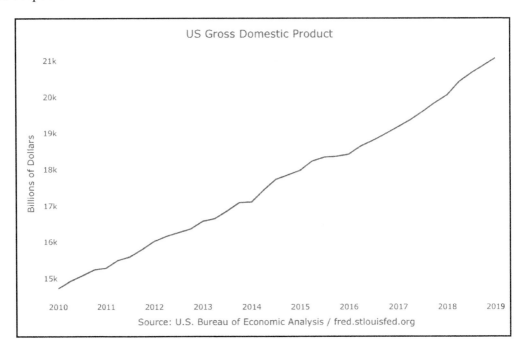

Like we did previously, we will leave the last eight quarters for testing and train the model with the rest of the observations of the series with the `holt` function:

```
gdp_par <- ts_split(gdp, sample.out = 8)

train <- gdp_par$train
test <- gdp_par$test

fc_holt <- holt(train,  h = 8, initial = "optimal")
```

Let's review the model's parameters:

```
fc_holt$model
```

We get the following output:

```
## Holt's method
##
## Call:
##   holt(y = train, h = 8, initial = "optimal")
##
##    Smoothing parameters:
```

```
##      alpha = 0.7418
##      beta  = 0.0001
##
##    Initial states:
##      l = 14583.6552
##      b = 157.8047
##
##    sigma:   80.2774
##
##        AIC      AICc      BIC
## 357.7057 360.3144 364.5422
```

The initialized values of $\hat{L}_1$ and $\hat{T}_1$ of the function are relatively close to the values of the first observation of the series ($Y_1 = 14721.35$) and the average difference between each quarter. In addition, the selected α of 0.74 indicated that the model heavily weighed the last observation of the series, Y_T. On the other hand, the value of β is fairly close to zero, which indicates that updating the trend value from period to period doesn't take into account the change in the level and carries the initial value of the trend, $\hat{T}_1$, forward.

Let's compare the model's performance in the training and testing partitions with the accuracy function:

```
accuracy(fc_holt, test)
```

We get the following output:

```
##                      ME       RMSE       MAE         MPE      MAPE
## Training set  -0.2600704   74.53567  58.08445 -0.004075414 0.3403528
## Test set     362.8135830  423.92339 362.81358  1.764266683 1.7642667
##
##                    MASE       ACF1 Theil's U
## Training set 0.09300079 0.04713728        NA
## Test set     0.58091192 0.67212430  1.776891
```

As you can see from the output of the accuracy function, the ratio between the error rate on the testing and training set is more than 5 times for the RMSE and 4.5 for the MAPE. This large ratio in the error metrics is mainly derived from the following two reasons:

- The fitted values of the model on the training set are not bound by a linear line (as opposed to the forecast output)
- The growth of the trend in the last few quarters shift from a linear rate of growth to an exponential rate

The changes in the trend growth and the forecast can be observed with the test_forecast function:

```
test_forecast(gdp, forecast.obj = fc_holt, test = test)
```

The output is shown in the following screenshot:

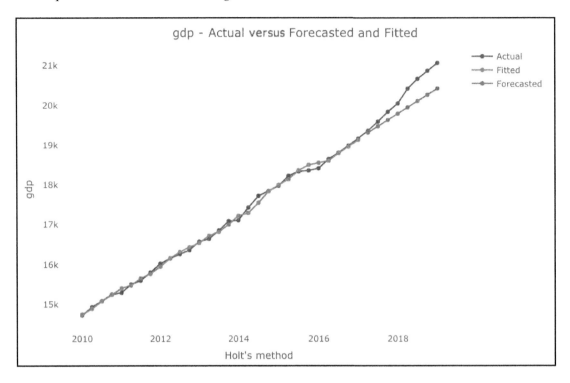

While the Holt model was designed to handle time series with the linear trend, the `exponential` argument of the `holt` function provides the option to handle series with exponential or decaying trends when set to TRUE. For the preceding example, we can utilize the exponential argument to modify the growth pattern of the trend.

In this case, we would like to have a higher weight for the trend, and we will set β to 0.75 (a more robust approach for identifying the optimal value of β would be to use a grid search):

```
fc_holt_exp <- holt(train,
                    h = 8,
                    beta = 0.75,
                    initial = "optimal",
                    exponential = TRUE)
```

The output of this model is as follows:

```
fc_holt_exp$model
```

We get the following output:

```
## Holt's method with exponential trend
##
## Call:
##  holt(y = train, h = 8, initial = "optimal", exponential = TRUE,
##
##  Call:
##      beta = 0.75)
##
##    Smoothing parameters:
##      alpha = 0.75
##      beta  = 0.75
##
##    Initial states:
##      l = 14586.0855
##      b = 1.0117
##
##    sigma:  0.0064
##
##      AIC      AICc       BIC
## 358.7179 360.4570 364.0467
```

Let's review the model's accuracy on the training and testing set with the `accuracy` function:

```
accuracy(fc_holt_exp, test)
```

We get the following output:

```
##                       ME      RMSE       MAE         MPE      MAPE
MASE
## Training set   -1.637148  100.0329   83.38575 -0.01160733  0.489303
0.1335115
## Test set      210.935365  255.0026  210.93537  1.02384022  1.023840
0.3377351
##                     ACF1  Theil's U
## Training set -0.2076372         NA
## Test set      0.6778485   1.069639
```

Similarly, we can plot the fitted and forecasted values against the actual data with the `test_forecast` functions:

```
test_forecast(gdp, forecast.obj = fc_holt_exp, test = test)
```

The output is as follows:

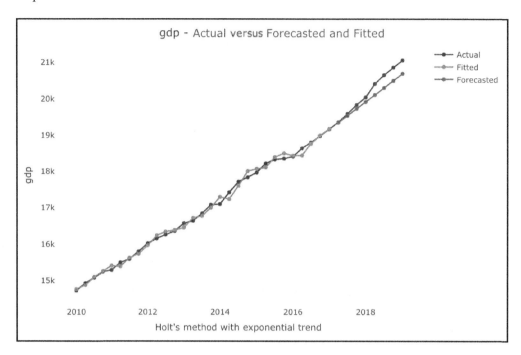

As you can see, the error rate of the second Holt model is more balanced, where the ration between the error on the testing and training set is 2.5 and 2.1 for the RMSE and MAPE metrics, respectively.

The use of the exponential or damped arguments required some prior knowledge or assumption on the future growth rate of the trend.

Holt-Winters model

We will close this chapter with the third and most advanced model among the exponential smoothing family of forecasting models—the Holt-Winters model. The **Holt-Winters (HW)** model is an extended version of the Holt model and can handle time series data with both trend and seasonal components. Forecasting the seasonal component required a third smoother parameter and equation, in addition to the ones of the level and trend.

Both of the trend and seasonal components could have either an additive or multiplicity structure, which adds some complexity to the model as there are multiple possible combinations:

- Additive trend and seasonal components
- Additive trend and multiplicative seasonal components
- Multiplicative trend and additive seasonal components
- Multiplicative trend and seasonal components

Therefore, before building an HW model, we need to identify the structure of the trend and the seasonal components. The following equations describe the HW model for a series with additive seasonal component:

$$\hat{Y}_{T+1} = L_T + hT_T + S_{T+h-m}$$

$$L_T = \alpha(Y_T - S_{T-m}) + (1 - \alpha)(L_{T-1} + T_{T-1})$$

$$T_T = \beta(L_T - L_{T-1}) + (1 - \beta) + (1 - \beta)T_{T-1}$$

$$S_T = \gamma(Y_T - L_T) + (1 - \gamma)S_{T-m}$$

The following equations describe the HW model for a series with a multiplicative seasonal structure:

$$\hat{Y}_{T+1} = (L_T + kT_T)S_{T+k-m}$$

$$L_T = \frac{\alpha Y_T}{S_{T-m}} + (1 - \alpha)(L_{T-1} + T_{T-1})$$

$$T_T = \beta(L_T - LT - 1) + (1 - \beta)T_{T-1}$$

$$S_T = \gamma\frac{Y_T}{L_T} + (1 - \gamma)S_{T-m}$$

The most common implementation of the HW model in R is the `HoltWinters` and `hw` functions from the **stats** and **forecast** packages. The main difference between the two functions is that the `hw` function can handle time series with an exponential or damped trend (similar to the Holt model). In the following example, we will use the `HoltWinters` function to forecast the last 12 months of the `USgas` series.

Let's use the decompose function to diagnose the structure of the trend and seasonal components of the series:

```
data(USgas)

decompose(USgas) %>% plot()
```

The output is as follows:

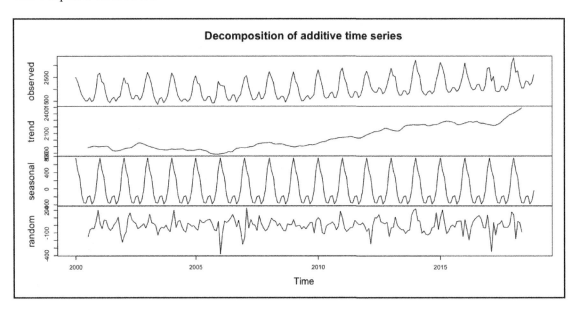

We can observe from the preceding plot that both the trend and seasonal components of the series have an additive structure. Like we did previously, we will create training and testing partitions using the last 12 months of the series to evaluate the performance of the model:

```
USgas_par <- ts_split(USgas, 12)

train <- USgas_par$train
test <- USgas_par$test
```

Next, we will use the HoltWinters model to forecast the last 12 months of the series (or the testing set):

```
md_hw <- HoltWinters(train)
```

Let's review the parameters of the trained model:

```
md_hw
```

We get the following output:

```
## Holt-Winters exponential smoothing with trend and additive seasonal
component.
 ##
## Call:
## HoltWinters(x = train)
 ##
## Smoothing parameters:
##   alpha: 0.3462899
##   beta : 0
##   gamma: 0.3766804
 ##
## Coefficients:
##            [,1]
## a    2299.3445761
## b      -0.1287005
## s1    516.2274996
## s2    788.9916937
## s3    396.5624290
## s4    285.0458175
## s5   -200.5519515
## s6   -311.8029253
## s7   -309.0225553
## s8   -133.0658271
## s9   -141.1034536
## s10 -339.8285611
## s11 -270.8429591
## s12   23.6032284
```

You will notice from the preceding model output that the model is mainly learning from the level and seasonal update (with $\alpha = 0.35$ and $\gamma = 0.37$). On the other hand, there is no learning from the trend initialized value $\beta = 0$. The next step is to forecast the next 12 months (or the values of the testing set) and evaluate the model's performance with the accuracy and test_forecast functions:

```
fc_hw <- forecast(md_hw, h = 12)

accuracy(fc_hw, test)
##                    ME      RMSE      MAE       MPE      MAPE      MASE
## Training set  6.08587  115.1122  86.92766 0.2617263 4.273029 0.8102333
## Test set    174.39927  194.4311 174.39927 6.9486812 6.948681 1.6255368
##                   ACF1 Theil's U
## Training set 0.2407121        NA
## Test set     0.1170619 0.7198667
```

The accuracy metrics of the model are fairly balanced, with an MAPE of 4.3% in the training set and 7% in the testing set. In the plot of the following model performance, you will notice that most of the forecast errors are related to the seasonal peak and the last observations of the series, which the model was underestimating:

```
test_forecast(actual = USgas,
              forecast.obj = fc_hw,
              test = test)
```

The output is as follows:

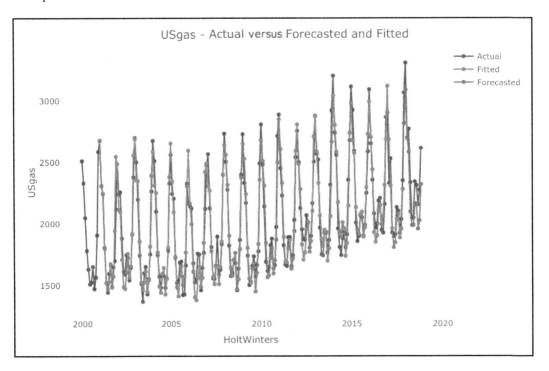

Plotting the fitted and forecasted values provides us with a better understanding of the model's performance. As we can see in the preceding plot, the HW model is doing a good job of capturing both the series seasonal patterns. On the other hand, the model is missing the peak of the year during the month of January in most cases.

Alternatively, the model can be trained with a grid search in a similar manner to what we did with the SES model. In this case, there are three parameters to optimize: α, β, and γ. The **TSstudio** package provides a customized grid search function based on the backtesting approach for training a HoltWinters function.

A grid search is a generic optimization approach for tuning models with multiple tuning parameters, such as tuning the α, β, and γ parameters of the HW model. This simple algorithm is based on setting (when applicable) a set of values for each parameter of the model and then iterating and testing the model with a different combination of the model's parameter values. Based on the selected error metric, the combination that minimizes the error criteria will be used with the final model. Generally, the main caveat of this approach is that it could be expensive to compute as the number of search combinations increase. In Chapter 12, *Forecasting with Machine Learning Models*, we will look at a more robust grid search algorithm with the **h2o** package.

For efficiency reasons, we will start with a shallow search that includes larger increments in the parameters' values. This will help us narrow down the search area and then apply a deeper search on those areas. The shallow search will include backtesting over 6 different periods using a sequence between 0 and 1 with an increment of 0.1:

```
shallow_grid <- ts_grid(train,
                    model = "HoltWinters",
                    periods = 6,
                    window_space = 6,
                    window_test = 12,
                    hyper_params = list(alpha = seq(0,1,0.1),
                                        beta = seq(0,1,0.1),
                                        gamma = seq(0,1,0.1)),
                    parallel = TRUE,
                    n.cores = 8)
```

The output of the following grid provides any combination of α, β, and γ with the error rate on each testing period and its overall mean. The table sorts the overall mean of the model from the best combination to the worst:

```
shallow_grid$grid_df[1:10,]
```

We get the following output:

```
##     alpha    beta gamma        1        2        3        4        5
## 1     0.4 0.00001   0.3 4.413769 2.605433 2.257627 3.725283 5.237407
## 2     0.3 0.00001   0.2 4.260377 2.632491 2.377467 3.922444 5.333127
## 3     0.3 0.10000   0.2 5.066178 2.548095 2.453950 3.743206 5.249969
## 4     0.3 0.00001   0.3 4.557990 2.455461 2.351108 4.313726 5.431035
## 5     0.4 0.00001   0.4 4.592116 2.311381 2.480636 4.241562 5.322397
## 6     0.2 0.00001   0.2 4.480924 2.962627 2.408871 4.231048 5.455692
## 7     0.4 0.00001   0.2 4.282419 2.688454 3.023123 3.872748 5.440050
## 8     0.5 0.00001   0.4 5.241874 3.425948 2.410089 3.373926 5.109618
## 9     0.1 0.00001   0.2 4.010023 3.321816 2.802651 4.507483 5.615869
```

```
## 10   0.1 0.10000   0.2 5.777916 2.320443 2.768832 4.249258 5.507453
##              6       mean
## 1   4.662878 3.817066
## 2   4.579267 3.850862
## 3   4.385781 3.907863
## 4   4.435515 3.924139
## 5   4.908380 3.976079
## 6   4.350566 3.981621
## 7   4.958675 4.044245
## 8   4.844823 4.067713
## 9   4.278671 4.089419
## 10  4.145535 4.128239
```

The `plot_grid` provides an intuitive view of the optimal range of values of each parameter by using a paracords plot. By default, the function is highlighting the top 10% models:

```
plot_grid(shallow_grid)
```

The output is as follows:

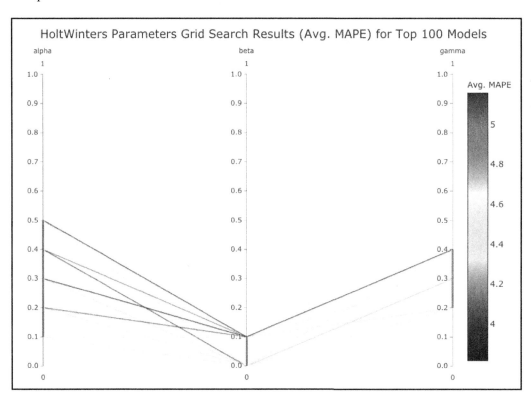

You will notice from the search plot output that the optimal range of α varies between 0.1 and 0.5, β is between 0 and 0.1, and γ is between 0.2 and 0.4. This will help us set the range of the hyperparameter search for the deeper grid search by narrowing down the range of search but using a more granular search:

```
deep_grid <-  ts_grid(train,
                      model = "HoltWinters",
                      periods = 6,
                      window_space = 6,
                      window_test = 12,
                      hyper_params = list(alpha = seq(0.1,0.5,0.01),
                                          beta = seq(0,0.1,0.01),
                                          gamma = seq(0.2,0.4,0.01)),
                      parallel = TRUE,
                      n.cores = 8)
```

As you can see in the following plot, the error range of the top 10% models has dropped with respect to the one of the shallow search:

```
plot_grid(deep_grid)
```

The output is as follows:

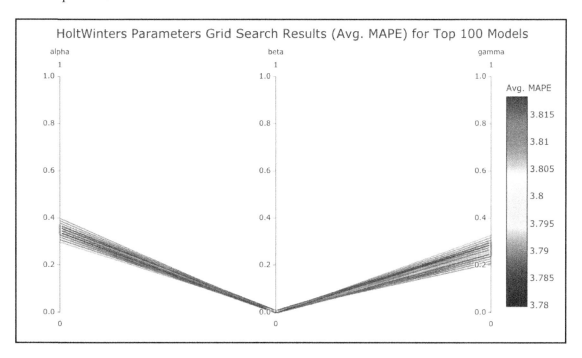

This plot can be viewed in a 3D view (when conducting a search for three parameters):

```
plot_grid(deep_grid, type = "3D", top = 250)
```

The output is shown in the following screenshot:

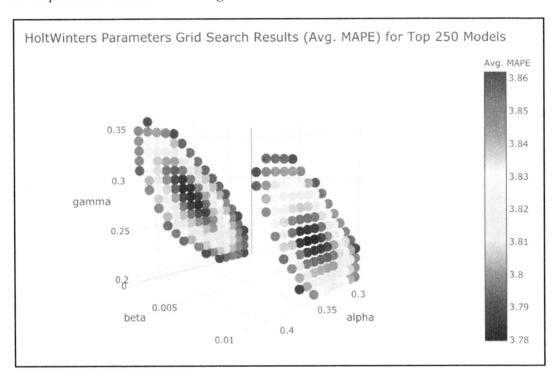

The last step of this process is to pull the values of the optimal smoothing parameters from the grid model based on the search, retrain the HW model, and utilize it to forecast the future values of the series:

```
md_hw_grid <- HoltWinters(train,
                          alpha = deep_grid$alpha,
                          beta = deep_grid$beta,
                          gamma = deep_grid$gamma)

fc_hw_grid <- forecast(md_hw_grid, h = 12)
```

We will use the `accuracy` and `test_forecast` functions in order to review the performance of the HW model that's been optimized by a grid search:

```
accuracy(fc_hw_grid, test)
##                        ME     RMSE      MAE       MPE     MAPE     MASE
## Training set    3.839412 116.7249  89.1783 0.2097637 4.401512 0.831211
## Test set      143.356247 171.8245 151.0337 5.6297541 5.914167 1.407751
##                     ACF1 Theil's U
## Training set 0.2560556        NA
## Test set     0.1230779 0.6220483
```

The plot of the fitted and forecasted values versus the actual values can be seen as follows:

```
test_forecast(actual = USgas,
forecast.obj = fc_hw_grid,
test = test)
```

The output is as follows:

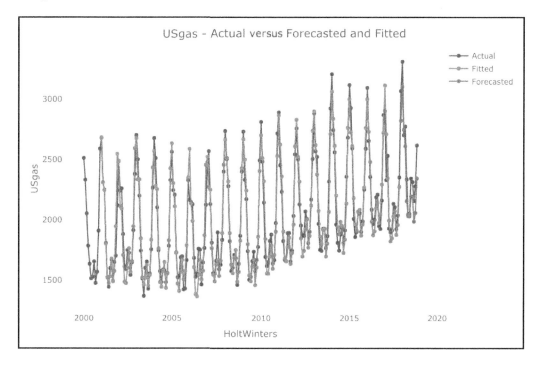

As you can see from the output of the `accuracy` and `test_forecast` functions, optimizing the model with grid search provides, in this case, a lift in the model's performance by reducing the MAPE score from 6.95% to 5.92%.

Summary

In this chapter, we introduced the use of a weighted average of past observations for forecast time series data. We started with a simplistic and naive forecasting approach with the moving average function. Although this function is limited to short-term forecasts and can only handle time series with no seasonal and trend components, it provides context for exponential smoothing functions. The exponential smoothing family of forecasting models is based on the use of different smoothing parameters, that is α, β, and γ, for modeling the main components of time series data—level, trend, and seasonal, respectively. The main advantages of exponential smoothing functions are their simplicity, they're cheap for computing, and their modularity, which allows them to handle different types of time series data, such as linear and exponential trends and seasonal components.

In the next chapter, we will learn about a more advanced forecasting approach with the ARIMA family of forecasting models.

11
Forecasting with ARIMA Models

The **Autoregressive Integrated Moving Average (ARIMA)** model is the generic name for a family of forecasting models that are based on the **Autoregressive (AR)** and **Moving Average (MA)** processes. Among the traditional forecasting models (for example, linear regression, exponential smoothing, and so on), the ARIMA model is considered as the most advanced and robust approach. In this chapter, we will introduce the model components—the AR and MA processes and the differencing component. Furthermore, we will focus on methods and approaches for tuning the model's parameters with the use of differencing, the **autocorrelation function (ACF)**, and the **partial autocorrelation function (PACF)**.

In this chapter, we will cover the following topics:

- The stationary state of time series data
- The random walk process
- The AR and MA processes
- The ARMA and ARIMA models
- The seasonal ARIMA model
- Linear regression with the ARIMA errors model

Technical requirement

The following packages will be used in this chapter:

- **forecast**: Version 8.5 and above
- **TSstudio**: Version 0.1.4 and above
- **plotly**: Version 4.8 and above
- **dplyr**: Version 0.8.1 and above
- **lubridate**: Version 1.7.4 and above
- **stats**: Version 3.6.0 and above
- **datasets**: Version 3.6.0 and above
- **base**: Version 3.6.0 and above

You can access the codes for this chapter from the following link:

```
https://github.com/PacktPublishing/Hands-On-Time-Series-Analysis-with-R/tree/
master/Chapter11
```

The stationary process

One of the main assumptions of the ARIMA family of models is that the input series follows the stationary process structure. This assumption is based on the Wold representation theorem, which states that any stationary process can be represented as a linear combination of white noise. Therefore, before we dive into the ARIMA model components, let's pause and talk about the stationary process. The stationary process, in the context of time series data, describes a stochastic state of the series. Time series data is stationary if the following conditions are taking place:

- The mean and variance of the series do not change over time
- The correlation structure of the series, along with its lags, remains the same over time

In the following examples, we will utilize the `arima.sim` function from the **stats** package to simulate a stationary and non-stationary time series data and plot it with the `ts_plot` function from the **TSstudio** package. The `arima.sim` function allows us to simulate time series data based on the ARIMA model's components and main characteristics:

- **An Autoregressive (AR) process**: Establish a relationship between the series and its past p lags with the use of a regression model (between the series and its p lags)
- **A Moving Average (MA) process**: Similar to the AR process, the MA process establishes the relationship with the error term at time t and the past error terms, with the use of regression between the two components (error at time t and the past error terms)
- **Integrated (I) process**: The process of differencing the series with its d lags to transform the series into a stationary state

Here, the model argument of the function defines p, q, and d, as well as the order of the AR, MA, and I processes of the model. For now, don't worry if you are not familiar with this function—we will discuss it in detail later in this chapter.

 The `arima.sim` function has a random component. Therefore, in order to be able to reproduce the examples throughout this chapter, we will use the `set.seed` function. The `set.seed` function allows you to create random numbers in a reproducible manner in R by setting the random generating seed value.

For instance, in the following example, we will simulate an AR process with one lag (that is, $p = 1$) and 500 observations with the `arima.sim` function. Before running the simulation, we will set the `seed` value to `12345`:

```
set.seed(12345)

stationary_ts <- arima.sim(model = list(order = c(1,0,0),
                                        ar = 0.5 ),
                           n = 500)
```

Now, let's plot the simulate time series with the `ts_plot` function:

```
library(TSstudio)

ts_plot(stationary_ts,
        title = "Stationary Time Series",
        Ytitle = "Value",
        Xtitle = "Index")
```

We get the following output:

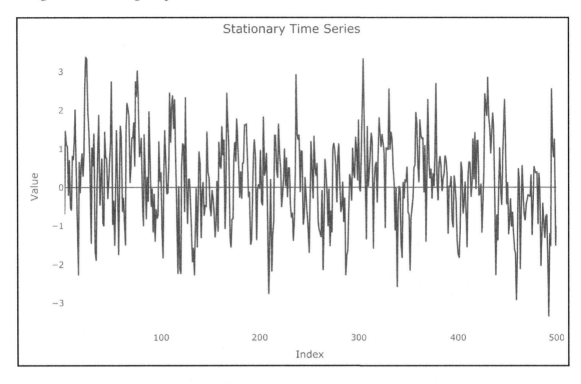

In this case, you can see that, overall, the mean of the series, over time, remains around the zero line. In addition, the series' variance does not change over time. Let's utilize the arima.sim function to create an example for non-stationary series:

```
set.seed(12345)

non_stationary_ts <- arima.sim(model = list(order = c(1,1,0),ar = 0.3),n =
500)

ts_plot(non_stationary_ts,
        title = "Non-Stationary Time Series",
        Ytitle = "Value",
        Xtitle = "Index")
```

We get the following output:

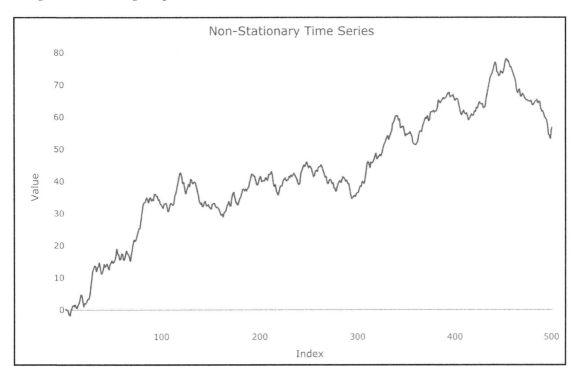

On the other hand, the second example violates the stationary condition as it is trending over time, which means it is changing over time.

We would consider a time series data as non-stationary whenever those conditions do not hold. Common examples of a series with a non-stationary structure are as follows:

- **A series with a dominant trend**: The series' mean changes over time as a function of the change in the series trend, and therefore the series is non-stationary
- **A series with a multiplicative seasonal component**: In this case, the variance of the series is a function of the seasonal oscillation over time, which either increases or decreases over time

The classic `AirPassenger` series (the monthly airline passenger numbers between 1949 and 1960) from the **datasets** package is a good example of a series that violates the two conditions of the stationary process. Since the series has both a strong linear trend and a multiplicative seasonal component, the mean and variance are both changing over time:

```
data(AirPassengers)

ts_plot(AirPassengers,
        title = "Monthly Airline Passenger Numbers 1949-1960",
        Ytitle = "Thousands of Passengers",
        Xtitle = "Year")
```

We get the following output:

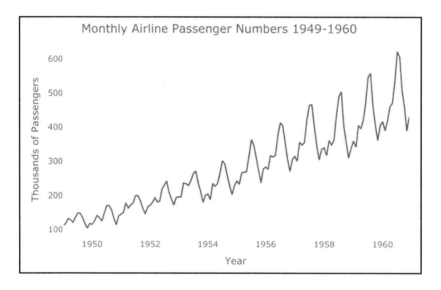

Transforming a non-stationary series into a stationary series

In most cases, unless you are very lucky, your raw data would probably come with a trend or other form of oscillation that violates the assumptions of the stationary process. Therefore, to handle this, you will have to apply some transformation steps in order to bring the series into a stationary state. Common transformations methods are differencing the series (or de-trending) and *log* transformation (or both). Let's review the applications of these methods.

Differencing time series

The most common approach to transforming a non-stationary time series data into a stationary state is by differencing the series with its lags. The main effect of differencing a series is the removal of the series trend (or detrending the series), which help to stabilize the mean of the series. We measured the degree or order of the series differencing by the number of times we difference the series with its lags. For example, the following equation defines the first order difference:

$$Y_t' = Y_t - Y_{t-1}$$

Here, Y_t' represents the first order difference of the series, and Y_t and Y_{t-1} represent the series itself and its first lag. In some cases, the use of the first order difference is not sufficient to bring the series to a stationary state, and you may want to apply second order differencing:

$$Y_t^* = Y_t' - Y_{t-1}' = (Y_t - Y_{t-1}) - (Y_{t-1} - Y_{t-2}) = Y_t - 2Y_{t-1} + Y_{t-2}$$

Another form of differencing is seasonal differencing, which is based on differencing the series with the seasonal lag:

$$Y_t' = Y_t - Y_{t-f}$$

Here, *f* represents the frequency of the series and Y_{t-f} represents the seasonal lag of the series. It is common to use seasonal differencing when a series has a seasonal component. The `diff` function from the **base** package differences the input series with a specific lag by setting the `lag` argument of the function to the relevant lag. Let's go back to the `AirPassenger` series and see how the first order and seasonal differencing affect the structure of the series. We will start with the first order difference:

```
ts_plot(diff(AirPassengers, lag = 1),
        title = "AirPassengers Series - First Differencing",
        Xtitle = "Year",
        Ytitle = "Differencing of Thousands of Passengers")
```

We get the following output:

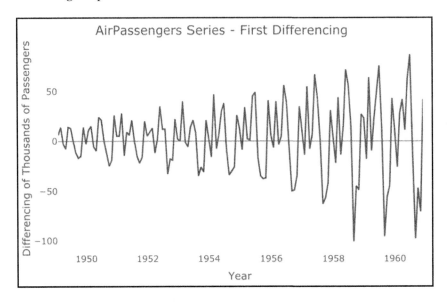

You can see that the first difference of the `AirPassenger` series removed the series trend and that the mean of the series is, overall, constant over time. On the other hand, there is clear evidence that the variation of the series is increasing over time, and therefore the series is not stationary yet. In addition to the first order difference, taking the seasonal difference of the series could solve this issue. Let's add the seasonal difference to the first order difference and plot it again:

```
ts_plot(diff(diff(AirPassengers, lag = 1), 12),
        title = "AirPassengers Series - First and Seasonal Differencing",
        Xtitle = "Year",
        Ytitle = "Differencing of Thousands of Passengers")
```

We get the following output:

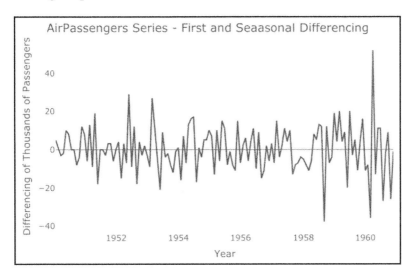

The seasonal difference did a good job of stabilizing the series variation, as the series now seems to be stationary.

Log transformation

In `Chapter 5`, *Decomposition of Time Series Data*, we saw the applications of the *log* transformation for handling multiplicative time series data. Likewise, we can utilize this approach to stabilize a multiplicative seasonal oscillation, if it exists. This approach is not a replacement for differencing, but an addition. For instance, in the example of the `AirPassenger` in the preceding section, we saw that the first differencing is doing a great job in stabilizing the mean of the series, but is not sufficient enough to stabilize the variance of the series. Therefore, we can apply a *log* transformation to transform the seasonal structure from multipliable to additive and then apply the first-order difference to stationarize the series:

```
ts_plot(diff(log(AirPassengers), lag = 1),
        title = "AirPassengers Series – First Differencing with Log
Transformation",
        Xtitle = "Year",
        Ytitle = "Differencing/Log of Thousands of Passengers")
```

We get the following output:

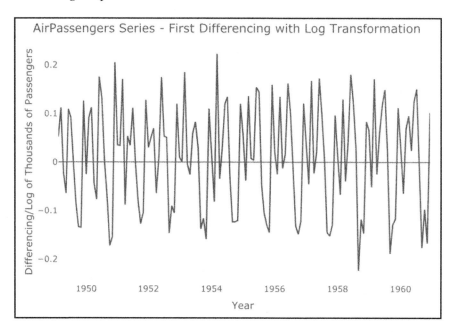

The *log* transformation with the first-order differencing is doing a better job of transforming the series into a stationary state with respect to the double differencing (first-order with seasonal differencing) approach we used prior.

The random walk process

The random walk, in the context of time series, describes a stochastic process of an object over time, where the main characteristics of this process are as follows:

- The starting point of this process at time *0* - Y_0 is known
- The movement (or the walk) of the series with random walk process from time *t-1* to time *t* are defined with the following equation:

$$Y_t = Y_{t-1} + \epsilon_t$$

Here, Y_{t-1} and Y_t represent the value of the series at time *t-1* and *t*, respectively, and ϵ_t represents a random number (or a white noise) with a mean of 0 and a variance of σ_ϵ^2. While the random walk process is not stationary, the first difference of a random walk represents a stationary process like so:

$$Y_t' = Y_t - Y_{t-1} = \epsilon_t$$

As we mentioned previously, ϵ_t has a constant mean and variance, and therefore Y_t' is a stationary process. A random walk is commonly used to simulate possible future paths of a series. For instance, we can simulate a random walk with the `arima.sim` function by setting the d parameter of the `order` argument to 1. This is equivalent to a non-stationary series with a first difference structure. The following code demonstrates the simulation of 20 different random walk paths of 500 steps, all starting at point 0 at time 0. We will create two plots: one for the random walk paths and another for their first-order difference. We will use the **plotly** package to do this:

```
library(plotly)

set.seed(12345)

p1 <- plot_ly()
p2 <- plot_ly()

for(i in 1:20){
    rm <- NULL
    rw <- arima.sim(model = list(order = c(0, 1, 0)), n = 500)
    p1 <- p1 %>% add_lines(x = time(rw), y = as.numeric(rw))
    p2 <- p2 %>% add_lines(x = time(diff(rw)), y = as.numeric(diff(rw)))
}
```

Here, p1 represents the plot of the random walk simulation:

```
p1 %>% layout(title = "Simulate Random Walk",
              yaxis = list(title = "Value"),
              xaxis = list(title = "Index")) %>%
    hide_legend()
```

We get the following output:

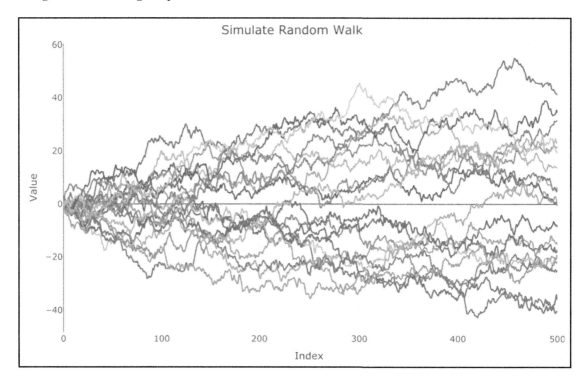

Here, p2 represents the corresponding plot of the first-order differencing of the random walk simulation:

```
p2 %>% layout(title = "Simulate Random Walk with First-Order Differencing",
             yaxis = list(title = "Value"),
             xaxis = list(title = "Index")) %>%
    hide_legend()
```

We get the following output:

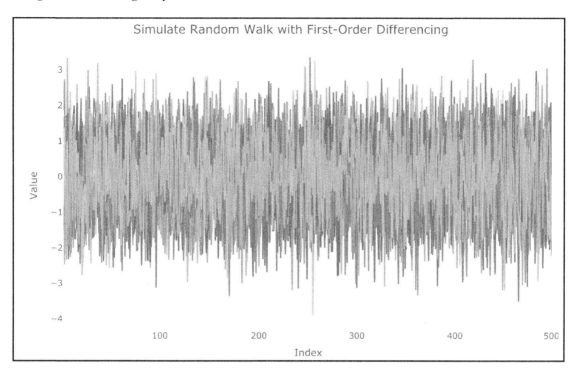

The AR process

The AR process defines the current value of the series, Y_t, as a linear combination of the previous p lags of the series, and can be formalized with the following equation:

$$AR(p) : Y_t = c + \sum_{i=1}^{p} \phi_i Y_{t-i} + \epsilon_t$$

Following are the terms used in the preceding equation:

- $AR(p)$ is the notation for an AR process with p-order
- c represents a constant (or drift)
- p defines the number of lags to regress against Y_t

- ϕ_i is the coefficient of the i lag of the series (here, ϕ_1 must be between -1 and 1, otherwise, the series would be trending up or down and therefore cannot be stationary over time)
- Y_{t-i} is the i lag of the series
- ϵ_t represents the error term, which is white noise

 An AR process can be used on time series data if, and only if, the series is stationary. Therefore, before applying an AR process on a series, you will have to verify that the series is stationary. Otherwise, you will have to apply some transformation method (such as differencing, *log* transformation, and so on) to transform the series into a stationary state. Later in this chapter, we will introduce the ARIMA model, which can handle non-stationary time series data.

For instance, *AR(1)*, the first-order AR process, is defined by the following equation:

$$AR(1) : Y_t = c + \phi_1 Y_{t-1} + \epsilon_t$$

 Note that in the case of the *AR(1)* process, if the value of $\phi_1 = 1$ or $\phi_1 = -1$, the series is a random walk (assuming ϵ_t is white noise). Whenever $\phi_1 > 1$ or $\phi_1 < -1$ the series is trending and therefore it cannot be stationary.

Similarly, *AR(2)*, the second-order AR process defines by the next equation:

$$AR(2) : Y_t = c + \phi_1 Y_{t-1} + \phi_2 Y_{t-2} + \epsilon_t, \ where \ -1 < \phi_1 + \phi_2 < 1$$

In the following example, we will utilize the `arima.sim` function again to simulate an *AR(2)* process structure time series data with 500 observations, and then use it to fit an AR model. We will use the model argument to set the AR order to 2 and set the lags coefficients $\phi_1 = 0.9$ and $\phi_2 = -0.3$:

```
set.seed(12345)

ar2 <- arima.sim(model = list(order = c(2,0,0),
                              ar = c(0.9, -0.3)),
                 n = 500)
```

Let's review the simulate time series:

```
ts_plot(ar2,
        title = "Simulate AR(2) Series",
        Ytitle = "Value",
        Xtitle = "Index")
```

We get the following output:

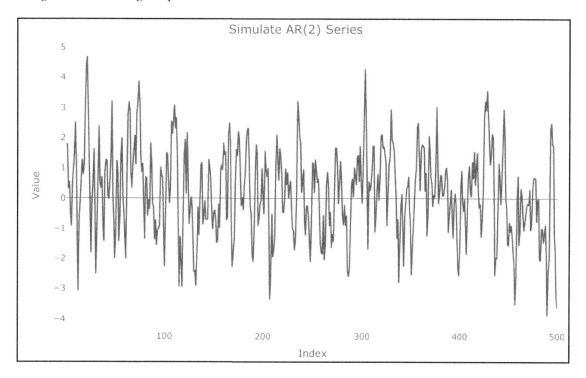

The `ar` function from the **stats** package allows us to fit an AR model on time series data and than forecast its future values. This function identifies the AR order automatically based on the **Akaike Information Criterion** (**AIC**). The `method` argument allows you to define the coefficients estimation method, such as the **ordinary least squares** (**OLS**) (which we saw in Chapter 9, *Forecasting with Linear Regression*), **maximum likelihood estimation** (**MLE**), and Yule-Walker (default). Let's apply the `ar` function to identify the AR order and estimate its coefficients accordingly:

```
md_ar <- ar(ar2)
```

Let's review the fitted model details:

```
md_ar
```

We get the following output:

```
##
## Call:
## ar(x = ar2)
##
## Coefficients:
## 1 2
## 0.8851 -0.2900
##
## Order selected 2 sigma^2 estimated as 1.049
```

As you can see from the preceding model summary, the `ar` function was able to identify that the input series is a second order AR process, and provided a fairly close estimate for the value of the actual coefficients, $\hat{\phi_1} = 0.88, \hat{\phi_2} = -0.29$ (as opposed to the actual coefficients' values, $\phi_1 = 0.9, \phi_2 = -0.3$).

Later on in this chapter, we will return to the AR model and discuss methods and approaches for identifying whether a series has an AR structure and its order.

Identifying the AR process and its characteristics

In the preceding example, we simulated an *AR(2)* series, and it was clear that we need to apply an AR model on the data. However, when working with real-time series data, you will have to identify the structure of the series before modeling it. In the world of the non-seasonal ARIMA family of models, a series could have one of the following structures:

- AR
- MA
- Random walk
- A combination of the preceding three (for example, AR and MA processes)

In this section, we will introduce the method for identifying the first case, that is, a series with only an AR structure. In the following sections, we will generalize this method to the rest of the cases (for example, MA, AR, MA, and so on).

Identifying the series structure includes the following two steps:

- Categorizing the type of process (for example, AR, MA, and so on)
- Once we have classified the process type, we need to identify the order of the process (for example, *AR(1)*, *AR(2)*, and so on)

Utilizing the **autocorrelation function** (**ACF**) and **partial autocorrelation function** (**PACF**), which we introduced in Chapter 7, *Correlation Analysis*, allows us to classify the process type and identify its order. If the ACF output tails off and the PACF output cuts off at lag *p*, this indicates that the series is an *AR(p)* process. Let's calculate and plot the ACF and PACF for the simulated *AR(2)* series we created previously with the ACF and PACF functions. First, we will use the par function to plot the two plots side by side by setting the mfrow argument to c(1,2) (one row, two columns):

```
par(mfrow=c(1,2))
```

Now, we will generate the plots with the acf and pacf functions:

```
acf(ar2)
pacf(ar2)
```

We get the following output:

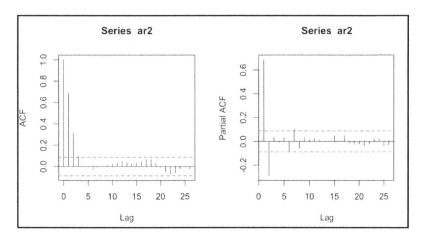

In the case of the `ar2` series, you can see that the ACF plot is tailing off and that the PACF plot is cut off at the second lag. Therefore, we can conclude that the series has a second order AR process.

The moving average process

In some cases, the forecasting model is unable to capture all the series patterns, and therefore some information is left over in model residuals (or forecasting error) ϵ_t. The goal of the moving average process is to capture patterns in the residuals, if they exist, by modeling the relationship between Y_t, the error term, ϵ_t, and the past q error terms of the models (for example, $\epsilon_{t-1}, \epsilon_{t-2}, \cdots, \epsilon_{t-q}$). The structure of the MA process is fairly similar to the ones of the AR. The following equation defines an MA process with a q order:

$$MA(q) : Y_t = \mu + \epsilon_t + \sum_{i=1}^{q} \theta_i \epsilon_{t-i}$$

The following terms are used in the preceding equation:

- $MA(q)$ is the notation for an MA process with q-order
- μ represents the mean of the series
- $\epsilon_{t-q}, \cdots, \epsilon_t$ are white noise error terms
- θ_i is the corresponding coefficient of ϵ_{t-i}
- q defines the number of past error terms to be used in the equation

 Like the AR process, the MA equation holds only if the series is a stationary process; otherwise, a transformation must be used on the series before applying the MA process.

For example, the second-order MA process is defined by the following equation:

$$MA(2) : Y_t = \mu + \epsilon_t + \theta_1 \epsilon_{t-1} + \theta_2 \epsilon_{t-2}$$

In a similar manner, since we simulated the *AR(2)* series in the previous section, we will utilize the `arima.sim` function to simulate a series with an *MA(2)* structure. In this case, we will set the q parameter in the `order` argument to 2 and set the MA coefficients to $\theta_1 = 0.5$ and $\theta_2 = -0.3$:

```
set.seed(12345)

ma2 <- arima.sim(model = list(order = c(0, 0, 2),
  ma = c(0.5, -0.3)),
  n = 500)
```

We will use the `ts_plot` function to plot the simulated series:

```
ts_plot(ma2,
        title = "Simulate MA(2) Series",
        Ytitle = "Value",
        Xtitle = "Index")
```

We get the following output:

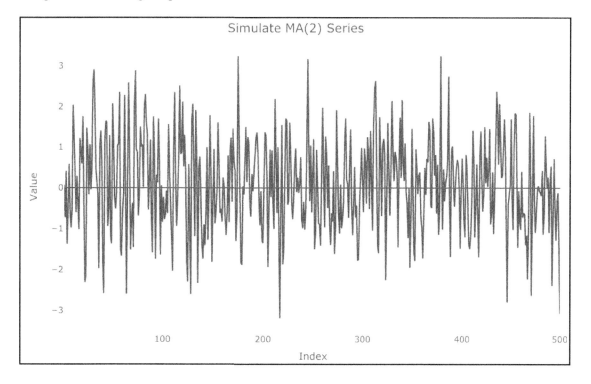

Modeling the MA process can be done with the `arima` function from the **stats** package. This function, when setting the order of the AR and the differencing components of the model to **0** with the order argument (that is, $p = 0$ and $d = 0$), is modeling only on the MA component. For instance, let's apply a second-order MA model with the `arima` function on the simulated *MA(2)* series:

```
md_ma <- arima(ma2, order = c(0,0,2), method = "ML")
```

 Similar to the `ar` function, you can select the coefficients estimation approach. In this case, there are three methods: **maximum likelihood** **(ML)**, minimize **conditional sum-of-squares** **(CSS)**, and the combination of the two, which is known as **CSS-ML**.

The output of the `arima` function is more detailed than the ones of the `ar` function, as it also provides the level of significance of each coefficient (the `s.e.`):

```
md_ma
```

We get the following output:

```
##
## Call:
## arima(x = ma2, order = c(0, 0, 2), method = "ML")
##
## Coefficients:
## ma1 ma2 intercept
## 0.530 -0.3454 0.0875
## s.e. 0.041 0.0406 0.0525
##
## sigma^2 estimated as 0.9829: log likelihood = -705.81, aic = 1419.62
```

Identifying the MA process and its characteristics

Similar to the AR process, we can identify an MA process and its order with the ACF and PACF functions. If the ACF is cut off at lag q and the PACF function tails off, we can conclude that the process is an *MA(q)*. Let's repeat the process we applied on the `ar2` series with the `ma2` series:

```
par(mfrow=c(1,2))
acf(ma2)
pacf(ma2)
```

We get the following output:

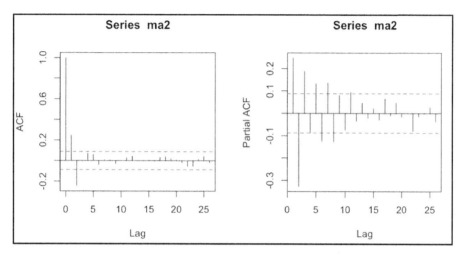

In the case of the `ma2` series, the ACF plot is cut off on the second lag (note that lag **0** is the correlation of the series with itself, and therefore it is equal to 1 and we can ignore it), and so the PACF tails off. Therefore, we can conclude that the `ma2` series is an MA(2) process.

The ARMA model

Up until now, we have seen how the applications of AR and MA are processed separately. However, in some cases, combining the two allows us to handle more complex time series data. The ARMA model is a combination of the AR(p) and *MA(q)* processes and can be written as follows:

$$ARMA(p, q) : Y_t = c + \sum_{i=1}^{p} \phi_i Y_{t-i} + \sum_{i=1}^{q} \theta_i \epsilon_{t-i} + \epsilon_t$$

The following terms are used in the preceding equation:

- *ARMA(p,q)* defines an ARMA process with a *p*-order AR process and *q*-order moving average process
- Y_t represents the series itself
- *c* represents a constant (or drift)
- *p* defines the number of lags to regress against Y_t
- ϕ_i is the coefficient of the *i* lag of the series
- Y_{t-1} is the *i* lag of the series
- *q* defines the number of past error terms to be used in the equation
- θ_i is the corresponding coefficient of ϵ_{t-i}
- $\epsilon_{t-q}, \cdots, \epsilon_t$ are white noise error terms
- ϵ_t represents the error term, which is white noise

For instance, an *ARMA(3,2)* model is defined by the following equation:

$$Y_t = c + \phi_1 Y_{t-1} + \phi_2 Y_{t-2} + \phi_3 Y_{t-3} + \theta_1 \epsilon_{t-1} + \theta_2 \epsilon_{t-2} + \epsilon_t$$

Let's simulate a time series data with an *ARMA(1,2)* structure with the `arima.sim` function and review the characteristics of the ARMA model. We will set the *p* and *q* parameters of the order argument to *1* and *2*, respectively, and set the AR coefficient as $\phi_1 = 0.7$, and the MA coefficients as $\theta_1 = 0.5$ and $\theta_2 = -0.3$:

```
set.seed(12345)

arma <- arima.sim(model = list(order(1,0,2),
                               ar = c(0.7),
                               ma = c(0.5,-0.3)),
                  n = 500)
```

Let's plot and review the series structure with the `ts_plot` function:

```
ts_plot(arma,
        title = "Simulate ARMA(1,2) Series",
        Ytitle = "Value",
        Xtitle = "Index")
```

We get the following output:

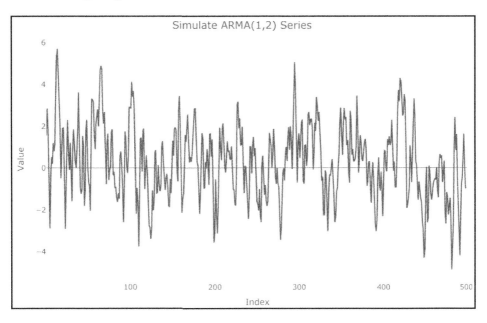

Fitting an ARMA model is straightforward with the `arima` function. In this case, we have to set the p and q parameters on the order argument:

```
arma_md <- arima(arma, order = c(1,0,2))
```

You can observe from the following output of the fitted model that the values of the model coefficients are fairly close to the one we simulated:

```
arma_md
```

We get the following output:

```
##
## Call:
## arima(x = arma, order = c(1, 0, 2))
##
## Coefficients:
##          ar1      ma1      ma2   intercept
##       0.7439   0.4785  -0.3954      0.2853
## s.e.  0.0657   0.0878   0.0849      0.1891
##
## sigma^2 estimated as 1.01:  log likelihood = -713.18,  aic = 1436.36
```

Here, as the coefficient's name implies, `ar1`, `ma1`, and `ma2` represent the estimation of the ϕ_1, θ_1, and θ_2 coefficients, respectively. You can note that the intercept parameter is not statistically significant, which should make sense as we didn't add an intercept to the simulated data.

Identifying an ARMA process

Identifying the ARMA process follows the same approach that we used previously with the AR and MA processes. An ARMA process exists in time series data if both the ACF and PACF plots tail off, as we can see in the following example:

```
par(mfrow=c(1,2))
acf(arma)
pacf(arma)
```

We get the following output:

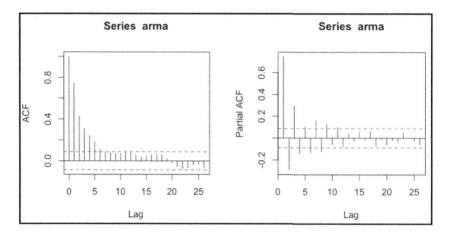

On the other hand, unlike the AR and MA processes, we cannot conclude the order of the ARMA process. There are several approaches for tuning the ARMA p and q parameters:

- **Manual tuning**: By starting with a combination of p and q and using some error criteria for identifying the model parameters.
- **Grid search**: By trying different combinations of the p and q parameters based on the grid matrix. Likewise, manual tuning and the selection of a specific combination of p and q parameters should be based on error criterion.
- **Algorithm-based search**: By using a function or algorithm for tuning the model parameters.

Later on in this chapter, we will introduce the `auto.arima` function from the **forecast** package, which is one of the most popular algorithms for the automation of the ARIMA family of models, including the ARMA model.

Manual tuning of the ARMA model

Manually tuning the ARMA model is mainly based on experimentation, intuition, common sense, and experience. The tuning process is based on the following steps:

1. Set some initial values for p and q. Typically, it is recommended to start with the minimum values of p and q (for example, $p = 1$ and $q = 1$).
2. Evaluate the fit of the model based on some error criterion. The most common error criteria are the **Akaike Information Criterion** (**AIC**) or **Bayesian information criterion** (**BIC**).
3. Adjust the values of either p and q.
4. Evaluate the change in the error metric.
5. Repeat the last two steps until you cannot achieve additional improvements of the error metric.

The main reasons for starting the tuning with minimum values of p and q is related to the following reasons:

- **Cost**: Since the order of the model is higher, the cost of the model is also higher and the degree of freedom of the model is reduced
- **Complexity**: Increases as the order of the model increases, which may result in overfitting

AIC and BIC are the most appropriate to use in this case since these two methods penalize models with higher order. This can be seen in the following formulas:

$$AIC = 2k - 2ln(\hat{L}), \; and$$

$$BIC = ln(n)k - 2ln(\hat{L})$$

Following are the terms used in the preceding equations:

- k represents the model number of parameters, or $p+q$
- $\hat{L}$ represents the maximum value of the likelihood function
- n is the number of input observations

The lower the AIC or BIC score, the better the model will fit. You can note that penalizing the BIC metric is higher with respect to AIC whenever $ln(n) > 2$, *or* $n > e^2$. Let's use the simulated ARMA series we created previously to apply this tuning approach. For simplicity reasons, we will not include an intercept and restrict the maximum value of k, that is, the model order (or $p+q$), to four. We will try the ARMA(1,1) model first:

```
arima(arma, order = c(1, 0, 1), include.mean = FALSE)
```

We get the following output:

```
##
## Call:
## arima(x = arma, order = c(1, 0, 1), include.mean = FALSE)
##
## Coefficients:
##          ar1     ma1
##       0.4144  0.8864
## s.e.  0.0432  0.0248
##
## sigma^2 estimated as 1.051:  log likelihood = -723,  aic = 1452
```

The AIC score of the initial model is 1452.

By default, the model output returns the AIC score of the model. If you wish to retrieve the BIC value, you can apply the BIC function, which returns the BIC value. For example, BIC(arima(arma, order = c(1, 0, 1), include.mean = FALSE)) will return 1441.73, which is the BIC score of the ARMA model we fit to the simulated data we created in the preceding example.

We will now start to increase the value of *p* and *q* while monitoring the change of the AIC score. The next model is the ARMA(2,1) model:

```
arima(arma, order = c(2, 0, 1), include.mean = FALSE)
```

We get the following output:

```
##
## Call:
## arima(x = arma, order = c(2, 0, 1), include.mean = FALSE)
##
## Coefficients:
##          ar1     ar2     ma1
##       0.3136  0.1918  0.9227
## s.e.  0.0486  0.0484  0.0183
##
## sigma^2 estimated as 1.019:  log likelihood = -715.26,  aic = 1438.52
```

Increasing *p* from 1 to 2 improves the AIC score, and therefore the ARMA(2,1) model is superior over the ARMA(1,1) model. Now, we will check ARMA(1,2):

```
arima(arma, order = c(1, 0, 2), include.mean = FALSE)
```

We get the following output:

```
##
## Call:
## arima(x = arma, order = c(1, 0, 2), include.mean = FALSE)
##
## Coefficients:
##           ar1      ma1       ma2
##        0.7602   0.4654   -0.4079
## s.e.   0.0626   0.0858    0.0832
##
## sigma^2 estimated as 1.014:  log likelihood = -714.27,  aic = 1436.54
```

The AIC score of ARMA(1,2) is even lower than the one of ARMA(2,1), and therefore it is now the superior model. Now, we will try the last combination of ARMA(2,2) and see if we can achieve additional improvements:

```
arima(arma, order = c(2, 0, 2), include.mean = FALSE)
```

We get the following output:

```
##
## Call:
## arima(x = arma, order = c(2, 0, 2), include.mean = FALSE)
##
## Coefficients:
##            ar1      ar2      ma1        ma2
##        0.7239   0.0194   0.4997   -0.3783
## s.e.   0.2458   0.1257   0.2427    0.2134
##
## sigma^2 estimated as 1.014:  log likelihood = -714.26,  aic = 1438.51
```

The AIC score of the ARMA(2,2) model is higher than the one of the ARMA(1,2), and so we will select the ARMA(1,2) model. The following table summarizes the AIC score of the four models we tested:

Model	AIC Score
ARMA(1,1)	1452.00
ARMA(2,1)	1438.52
ARMA(1,2)	**1436.54**
ARMA(2,2)	1438.51

The use of the AIC or BIC score as a model selection criterion does not guarantee that the selected model (by either AIC or BIC score) does not violate the model assumptions. Therefore, the next step is to apply a residual analysis in order to verify that, as we saw in `Chapter 8`, *Forecasting Strategies*, the residuals are as follows:

- Mean and variance are constant
- White noise or not correlated
- Normally distributed

For instance, we can use the `checkresiduals` function from the **forecast** package in order to validate those assumptions on the selected model:

```
library(forecast)

checkresiduals(arima(arma, order = c(1, 0, 2), include.mean = FALSE))
```

You can observe in the following `checkresiduals` output plot that the residuals of the ARMA(1,2) model satisfy the model assumptions that we defined previously:

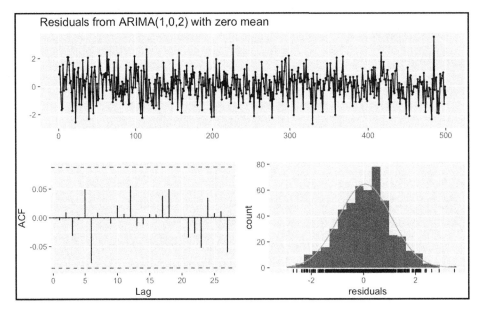

The `checkresiduals` function also returns the Ljung-Box test results, which suggests that the residuals are white noise:

```
##
##  Ljung-Box test
```

```
##
## data:  Residuals from ARIMA(1,0,2) with zero mean
## Q* = 5.3129, df = 7, p-value = 0.6218
##
## Model df: 3.   Total lags used: 10
```

Forecasting AR, MA, and ARMA models

Forecasting any of the models we saw until now was straightforward: we used the `forecast` function from the **forecast** package in a similar manner to how we used it in the previous chapter. For instance, the following code demonstrates the forecast of the next 100 observations of the AR model we trained previously in *The AR process* section with the `ar` function:

```
ar_fc <- forecast(md_ar, h = 100)
```

We can use `plot_forecast` to plot the forecast output:

```
plot_forecast(ar_fc,
  title = "Forecast AR(2) Model",
  Ytitle = "Value",
  Xtitle = "Year")
```

We get the following output:

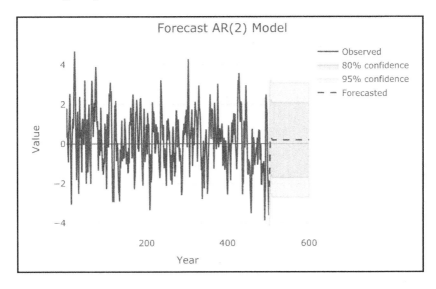

The ARIMA model

One of the limitations of the AR, MA, and ARMA models is that they cannot handle non-stationary time series data. Therefore, if the input series is non-stationary, a preprocessing step is required to transform the series from a non-stationary state into a stationary state. The ARIMA model provides a solution for this issue by adding the integrated process for the ARMA model. The **Integrated (I)** process is simply differencing the series with its lags, where the degree of the differencing is represented by the d parameter. The differencing process, as we saw previously, is one of the ways you can transform the methods of a series from non-stationary to stationary. For instance, $Y_t - Y_{t-1}$ represents the first differencing of the series, while $(Y_t - Y_{t-1}) - (Y_{t-1} - Y_{t-2})$ represents the second differencing. We can generalize the differencing process with the following equation:

$$Y_d = (Y_t - Y_{t-1}) - \ldots - (Y_{t-d+1} - Y_{t-d}), \ where$$

Y_d is the d differencing of the series. Let's add the differencing component to the ARMA model and formalize the ARIMA model:

$$ARIMA(p, d, q) : Y_d = c + \sum_{i=1}^{p} \phi_i Y_{d-i} + \sum_{i=1}^{q} \theta_i \epsilon_{t-i} + \epsilon_t$$

Following are the terms used in the preceding equation:

- *ARIMA(p,d,q)* defines an ARIMA process with a p-order AR process, d-degree of differencing, and q-order MA process
- Y_d is the d difference of series Y_t
- c represents a constant (or drift)
- p defines the number of lags to regress against Y_t
- ϕ_i is the coefficient of the i lag of the series
- Y_{d-i} is the d difference of the i lag of the series
- q defines the number of past error terms to be used in the equation
- θ_i is the corresponding coefficient of ϵ_{t-i}
- $\epsilon_{t-q}, \ldots, \epsilon_t$ are white noise error terms
- ϵ_t represents the error term, which is white noise

As you can see, both the AR and MA models can be represented with the ARMA model, you can also represent the AR, MA, or ARMA models with the ARIMA model, for example:

- The ARIMA(0, 0, 0) model is equivalent to white noise
- The ARIMA(0, 1, 0) model is equivalent to a random walk
- The ARIMA(1, 0, 0) model is equivalent to an AR(1) process
- The ARIMA(0, 0, 1) model is equivalent to an MA(1) process
- The ARIMA(1, 0, 1) model is equivalent to an ARMA(1,1) process

Identifying an ARIMA process

In this section, we will apply an ARIMA model, instead of the ARMA model, whenever the input series is not stationary. Differencing is required to transfer it into a stationary state. Identifying and setting the ARIMA model is a two-step process and is based on the following steps:

1. Identify the degree of differencing that is required to transfer the series into a stationary state
2. Identify the ARMA process (or AR and MA processes), as introduced in the previous section

Based on the findings of these steps, we will set the model parameters p, d, and q.

Identifying the model degree of differencing

Similar to the p and q parameters, setting the d parameter (the degree of differencing of the series) can be done with the ACF and PACF plots. In the following example, we will use the monthly prices of Robusta coffee since 2000. This series is part of the `Coffee_Prices` multiple time series objects from the **TSstudio** package. We will start by loading the `Coffee_Prices` series and subtracting the Robusta monthly prices since January 2010 using the `window` function:

```
data("Coffee_Prices")

robusta_price <- window(Coffee_Prices[,1], start = c(2000, 1))
```

Let's plot the `robusta_price` series and review its structure with the `ts_plot` function:

```
ts_plot(robusta_price,
        title = "The Robusta Coffee Monthly Prices",
        Ytitle = "Price in USD",
        Xtitle = "Year")
```

We get the following output:

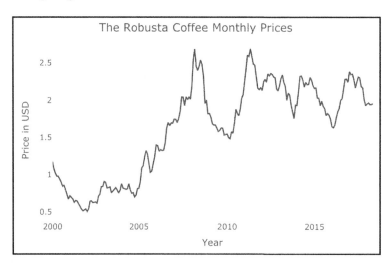

As you can see, the Robusta coffee prices over time are trending up, and therefore it is not in a stationary state. In addition, since this series represents continues prices, it is likely that the series has a strong correlation relationship with its past lags (as changes in price are typically close to the previous price). We will use the `acf` function again to identify the type of relationship between the series and it lags:

```
acf(robusta_price)
```

We get the following output:

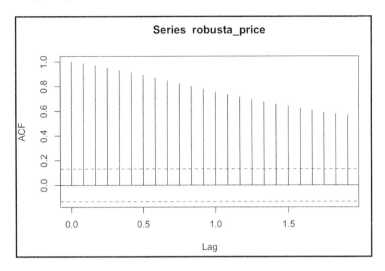

As you can see in the preceding output of the ACF plot, the correlation of the series with its lags is slowly decaying over time in a linear manner. Removing both the series trend and correlation between the series and its lags can be done by differencing the series. We will start with the first differencing using the `diff` function:

```
robusta_price_d1 <- diff(robusta_price)
```

Let's review the first difference of the series with the `acf` and `pacf` functions:

```
par(mfrow=c(1,2))
acf(robusta_price_d1)
pacf(robusta_price_d1)
```

We get the following output:

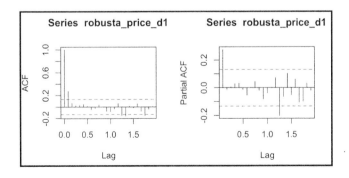

The ACF and PACF plots of the first difference of the series indicate that an AR(1) process is appropriate to use on the differenced series since the ACF is tailing off and the PACF cuts on the first lag. Therefore, we will apply an ARIMA(1,1,0) model on the robusta_price series to includes the first difference:

```
robusta_md <- arima(robusta_price, order = c(1, 1, 0))
```

We will use the summary function to review the model details:

```
summary(robusta_md)
```

We get the following output:

```
##
## Call:
## arima(x = robusta_price, order = c(1, 1, 0))
##
## Coefficients:
##          ar1
##       0.2780
## s.e.  0.0647
##
## sigma^2 estimated as 0.007142:  log likelihood = 231.38,  aic = -458.76
##
## Training set error measures:
##                      ME       RMSE        MAE        MPE      MAPE
## Training set 0.002595604 0.08432096 0.06494772 0.08104715 4.254984
##                   MASE        ACF1
## Training set 1.001542 0.001526295
```

You can see from the model summary output that the ar1 coefficient is statistically significant. Last but not least, we will check the model residuals:

```
checkresiduals(robusta_md)
```

We get the following output:

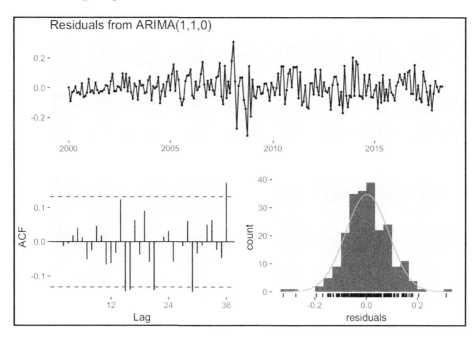

The Ljung-Box test suggested that the residuals are white noise:

```
##
##   Ljung-Box test
##
## data:  Residuals from ARIMA(1,1,0)
## Q* = 26.896, df = 23, p-value = 0.2604
##
## Model df: 1.    Total lags used: 24
```

Overall, the plot of the model's residuals and the Ljung-Box test indicate that the residuals are white noise. The ACF plot indicates that there are some correlated lags, but they are only on the border of being significant and so we can ignore them.

The seasonal ARIMA model

The **Seasonal ARIMA (SARIMA)** model, as its name implies, is a designated version of the ARIMA model for time series with a seasonal component. As we saw in `Chapter 6`, *Seasonality Analysis*, and `Chapter 7`, *Correlation Analysis*, a time series with a seasonal component has a strong relationship with its seasonal lags. The SARIMA model is utilizing the seasonal lags in a similar manner to how the ARIMA model is utilizing the non-seasonal lags with the AR and MA processes and differencing. It does this by adding the following three components to the ARIMA model:

- **SAR(P) process**: A seasonal AR process of the series with its past P seasonal lags. For example, a SAR(2) is an AR process of the series with its past two seasonal lags, that is, $Y_t = c + \Phi_1 Y_{t-f} + \Phi_2 Y_{t-2f} + \epsilon_t$, where Φ represents the seasonal coefficient of the SAR process, and f represents the series frequency.
- **SMA(Q) process**: A seasonal MA process of the series with its past Q seasonal error terms. For instance, a SMA(1) is a moving average process of the series with its past seasonal error term, that is, $Y_t = \mu + \epsilon_t + \Theta_1 \epsilon_{t-f}$, where Θ represents the seasonal coefficient of the SMA process, and f represents the series frequency.
- **SI(D) process**: A seasonal differencing of the series with its past D seasonal lags. In a similar manner, we can difference the series with its seasonal lag, that is, $Y_{D=1} = Y_t - Y_{t-f}$.

We use the following notation to denote the *SARIMA* parameters:

$$SARIMA(p, d, q) \times (P, D, Q)_s$$

Like before, the p and q parameters define the order of the AR and MA processes with its non-seasonal lags, respectively, and d defines the degree of differencing of the series with its non-seasonal lags. Likewise, the P and Q parameters represent the corresponding order of the seasonal AR and MA processes of the series with its seasonal lags, and D defines the degree of differencing of the series with its non-seasonal lags. For example, a $SARIMA(1, 0, 0) \times (1, 1, 0)_s$ model is a combination of an AR process of one non-seasonal and one seasonal lag, along with seasonal differencing.

Tuning the SARIMA model

The tuning process of the SARIMA model follows the same logic as one of the ARIMA models. However, the complexity of the model increases as there are now six parameters to tune, that is, p, d, q, P, D, and Q, as opposed to three with the ARIMA model. Luckily, the tuning of the P, D, and Q seasonal parameters follows the same logic as the ones of p, d, q, respectively, with the use of the ACF and PACF plots. The main difference between the tuning of these two groups of parameters (non-seasonal and seasonal) is that the non-seasonal parameters are tuned with the non-seasonal lags, as we saw previously with the ARIMA model. On the other hand, the tuning of the seasonal parameters are tuned with the seasonal lags (for example, for monthly series with lags 12, 24, 36, and so on).

Tuning the non-seasonal parameters

Applying the same logic that we used with the ARIMA model, tuning the non-seasonal parameters of the SARIMA model is based on the ACF and PACF plots:

- An $AR(p)$ process should be used if the non-seasonal lags of the ACF plot are tailing off, while the corresponding lags of the PACF plots are cutting off on the p lag
- Similarly, an $MA(q)$ process should be used if the non-seasonal lags of the ACF plot are cutting off on the q lag and the corresponding lags of the PACF plots are tailing off
- When both the ACF and PACF non-seasonal lags are tailing off, an ARMA model should be used
- Differencing the series with the non-seasonal lags should be applied when the non-seasonal lags of the ACF plot are decaying in a linear manner

Tuning the seasonal parameters

Tuning the seasonal parameters of the SARIMA model with ACF and PACF follows the same guidelines as the ones we used for selecting the ARIMA parameters:

- We will use a seasonal autoregressive process with an order of P, or SAR(P), if the seasonal lags of the ACF plot are tailing off and the seasonal lags of the PACF plot are cutting off by the P seasonal lag
- Similarly, we will apply a seasonal moving average process with an order of Q, or SMA(Q), if the seasonal lags of the ACF plot are cutting off by the Q seasonal lag and the seasonal lags of the PACF plot are tailing off

- An ARMA model should be used whenever the seasonal lags of both the ACF and PACF plots are tailing off
- Seasonal differencing should be applied if the correlation of the seasonal lags are decaying in a linear manner

Forecasting US monthly natural gas consumption with the SARIMA model – a case study

In this section, we will apply what we learned throughout this chapter and forecast the monthly consumption of natural gas in the US using the SARIMA model. Let's load the USgas series from the **TSstudio** package:

```
data(USgas)
```

Let's plot the series with the ts_plot function and review the main characteristics of the series:

```
ts_plot(USgas,
        title = "US Monthly Natural Gas consumption",
        Ytitle = "Billion Cubic Feet",
        Xtitle = "Year")
```

We get the following output:

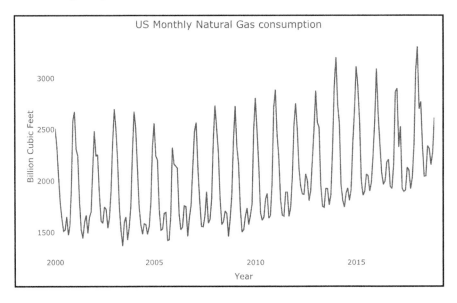

As we saw in the previous chapters, the USgas series has a strong seasonal pattern, and therefore among the ARIMA family of models, the SARIMA model is the most appropriate model to use. In addition, since the series is trending up, we can already conclude that the series is not stationary and some differencing of the series is required. We will start by setting the training and testing partitions with the ts_split functions, leaving the last 12 months of the series as the testing partition:

```
USgas_split <- ts_split(USgas, sample.out = 12)

train <- USgas_split$train
test <- USgas_split$test
```

Before we start the training process of the SARIMA model, we will conduct diagnostics in regards to the series correlation with the ACF and PACF functions. Since we are interested in viewing the relationship of the series with its seasonal lags, we will increase the number of lags to calculate and display by setting the lag.max argument to 60 lags:

```
par(mfrow=c(1,2))

acf(train, lag.max = 60)

pacf(train, lag.max = 60)
```

We get the following output:

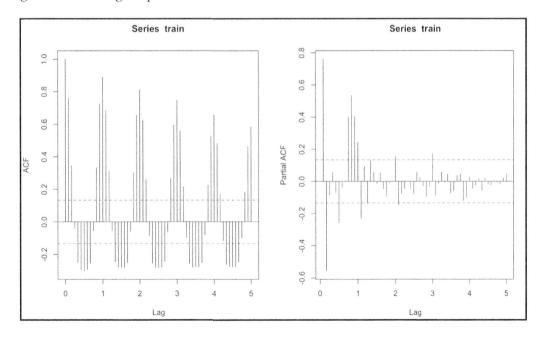

The preceding ACF plot indicates that the series has a strong correlation with both the seasonal and non-seasonal lags. Furthermore, the linear decay of the seasonal lags indicates that the series is not stationary and that seasonal differencing is required. We will start with a seasonal differencing of the series and plot the output to identify whether the series is in a stationary state:

```
USgas_d12 <- diff(train, 12)

ts_plot(USgas_d12,
        title = "US Monthly Natural Gas consumption - First Seasonal
Difference",
        Ytitle = "Billion Cubic Feet (First Difference)",
        Xtitle = "Year")
```

We get the following output:

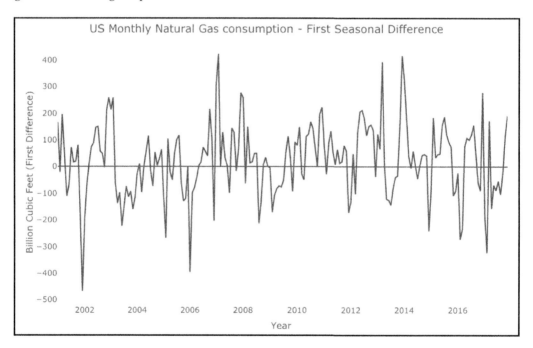

While we removed the series trend, the variation of the series is not stable yet. Therefore, we will also try to take the first difference of the series:

```
USgas_d12_1 <- diff(diff(USgas_d12, 1))

ts_plot(USgas_d12_1,
        title = "US Monthly Natural Gas consumption - First Seasonal and
Non-Seasonal Differencing",
```

```
                 Ytitle = "Billion Cubic Feet (Difference)",
                 Xtitle = "Year")
```

We get the following output:

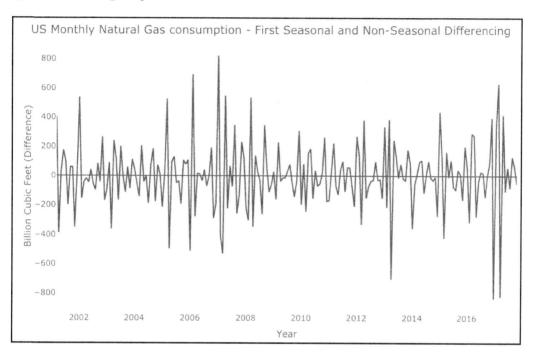

After taking the first order differencing, along with the first order seasonal differencing, the series seems to stabilize around the zero *x* axis line (or fairly close to being stable). After transforming the series into a stationary state, we can review the ACF and PACF functions again to identify the required process:

```
par(mfrow=c(1,2))

acf(USgas_d12_1, lag.max = 60)

pacf(USgas_d12_1, lag.max = 60)
```

We get the following output:

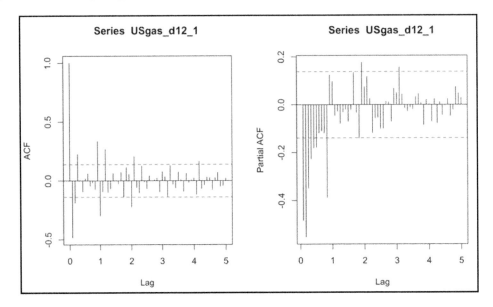

The main observation from the preceding ACF and PACF plots is that both the non-seasonal and seasonal lags (in both plots) are tailing off. Hence, we can conclude that after we difference the series and transform them into a stationary state, we should apply an ARMA process for both the seasonal and non-seasonal components of the SARIMA model.

The tuning process of the SARIMA model parameters follow the same steps that we applied previously with the ARMA model:

- We set the model maximum order (that is, the sum of the six parameters of the model)
- We set a range of a possible combination of the parameters' values under the model's maximum order constraint
- We test and score each model, that is, a typical score methodology with the AIC (which we used previously) or BIC
- We select a set of parameter combinations that give the best results

Now, we will start the tuning process for the USgas series by setting the model order to seven and setting the values of the model parameters to be in the range of 0 and 2. Given that we already identified the values of *d* and *D* (for example, *d = 1* and *D = 1*), which are the differencing parameters of the SARIMA model, we now can focus on tuning the remaining four parameters of the model, that is, p, q, P, and Q. Let's define those parameters and assign the search values:

```
p <- q <- P <- Q <- 0:2
```

Under the model's order constraint and the possible range of values of the model parameters, there are 66 possible combinations. Therefore, it will make sense, in this case, to automate the search process and build a grid search function to identify the values of the parameters that minimize the AIC score. We will utilize the expand.grid function in order to create a data.frame with all the possible search combinations:

```
arima_grid <- expand.grid(p,q,P,Q)

names(arima_grid) <- c("p", "q", "P", "Q")

arima_grid$d <- 1

arima_grid$D <- 1
```

Next, we will trim the grid search table by using combinations that exceed the order constraint of the model (for example, k ≤ 7). We will calculate and assign this to the k variable with the rowSums function:

```
arima_grid$k <- rowSums(arima_grid)
```

We will utilize the filter function from the **dplyr** package to remove combinations where the k value is greater than 7:

```
library(dplyr)

arima_grid <- arima_grid %>% filter(k <= 7)
```

Now that the grid search table is ready, we can start the search process. We will use the `lapply` function to iterate over the grid search table. This function will train the SARIMA model and score its AIC for each set of parameters in the grid search table. The `arima` function can train the SARIMA model by setting the `seasonal` argument of the model with the values of P, D, and Q:

```
arima_search <- lapply(1:nrow(arima_grid), function(i){
    md <- NULL
    md <- arima(train, order = c(arima_grid$p[i], 1, arima_grid$q[i]),
seasonal = list(order = c(arima_grid$P[i], 1, arima_grid$Q[i])))
    results <- data.frame(p = arima_grid$p[i], d = 1, q = arima_grid$q[i],
                          P = arima_grid$P[i], D = 1, Q = arima_grid$Q[i],
                          AIC = md$aic)
}) %>% bind_rows() %>% arrange(AIC)
```

We used the `bind_rows` and `arrange` functions to append the search results and arranged the table for the **dplyr** functions. Let's review the top results of the search table:

```
head(arima_search)
```

We get the following output:

```
##    p d q P D Q      AIC
## 1  1 1 1 1 2 1 1 2459.807
## 2  0 1 2 2 1 1 2461.229
## 3  1 1 1 0 1 1 2463.866
## 4  1 1 1 1 1 2 2464.550
## 5  1 1 1 0 1 2 2464.873
## 6  1 1 1 1 1 1 2465.310
```

The leading model based on the preceding search table is the $SARIMA(1,1,1)(2,1,1)_{12}$ model. Before we finalize the forecast, let's evaluate the selected model's performance on the testing set. We will retrain the model using the settings of the selected model:

```
USgas_best_md <- arima(train, order = c(1,1,1), seasonal = list(order = c(2,1,1)))
```

The model coefficients, as we can see in the following model summary, are all statistically significant at a level of 0.1:

```
USgas_best_md
```

We get the following output:

```
##
## Call:
## arima(x = train, order = c(1, 1, 1), seasonal = list(order = c(2, 1,
1)))
##
## Coefficients:
##           ar1      ma1     sar1     sar2      sma1
##        0.4143  -0.9244  -0.0216  -0.256   -0.7565
## s.e.   0.0733   0.0291   0.0956   0.088    0.0803
##
## sigma^2 estimated as 9837:   log likelihood = -1223.9,   aic = 2459.81
```

Let's use the `USgas_best_md` trained model to forecast the corresponding observations of the testing set:

```
USgas_test_fc <- forecast(USgas_best_md, h = 12)
```

Like we did previously, we will assess the model's performance with the accuracy function:

```
accuracy(USgas_test_fc, test)
```

We get the following output:

```
## ME RMSE MAE MPE MAPE MASE
## Training set 3.486041 96.13846 70.81773 0.03448147 3.445378 0.6600763
## Test set 173.187631 190.79318 180.62400 7.05220971 7.327692 1.6835560
## ACF1 Theil's U
## Training set 0.008556121 NA
## Test set -0.056179946 0.730488
```

We can use the performance of the seasonal naive model we used in `Chapter 8`, *Forecasting Strategies* (using the same training and testing set), as a benchmark for the SARIMA model's performance. Recall that the seasonal naive model's MAPE score was 5.2% on the training set and 9.7% on the testing set. Therefore, the SARIMA provides us with a lift in accuracy with a MAPE score of 3.4% and 7.3% on the training and testing partitions, respectively.

Now, we will use the `test_forecast` function to get a more intuitive view of the model's performance on the training and testing partitions:

```
test_forecast(USgas,
              forecast.obj = USgas_test_fc,
              test = test)
```

We get the following output:

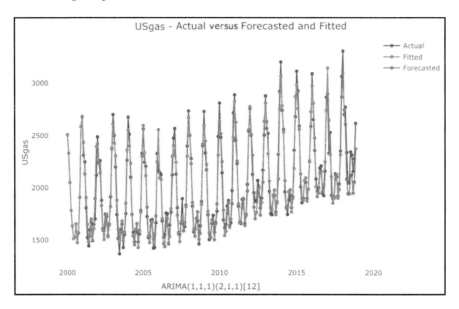

As you can see, the SARIMA model successfully captures the seasonal and trend pattern of the series. On the other hand, the model finds it challenging to capture the seasonal peaks (month of January) on the training partition and has 6.7% absolute error for the month of January (yearly peak) in the testing partition. This is the result of high fluctuation during the winter time. We can handle this uncertainty of the model during peak times with the model confidence intervals or path simulations the we looked at in Chapter 8, *Forecasting Strategies*.

At this point, you should pause and evaluate the general performance of the model thus far on the major metrics:

- AIC score on the training set
- The model coefficients significant
- MAPE score on both the training and testing set
- Benchmark the performance against other models (for example, a naive model)
- Fitted and forecasted plot

If you are satisfied with the results of the model on the different performance metrics, you should move forward and retrain the model with all the series and generate the final forecast. Otherwise, you should return the model parameters and repeat the evaluation process.

Now that we've satisfied the preceding conditions, we can move on to the last step of the forecasting process and generate the final forecast with the selected model. We will start by retraining the selected model on all the series:

```
final_md <- arima(USgas, order = c(1,1,1), seasonal = list(order =
c(2,1,1)))
```

Before we forecast the next 12 months, let's verify that the residuals of the model satisfy the model condition:

```
checkresiduals(final_md)
```

We get the following output:

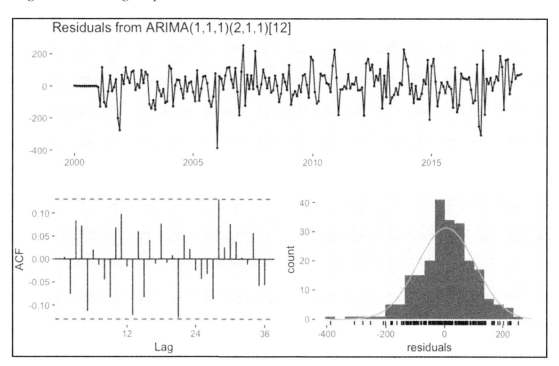

The output of the Ljung-Box test suggested that the residuals of the model are white noise:

```
## Ljung-Box test
##
## data: Residuals from ARIMA(1,1,1)(2,1,1)[12]
## Q* = 26.254, df = 19, p-value = 0.1233
##
## Model df: 5. Total lags used: 24
```

By looking at the preceding residuals plot, you can see that the residuals are white noise and normally distributed. Furthermore, the Ljung-Box test confirms that there is no auto-correlation left on the residuals—with a *p*-value of 0.12, we cannot reject the null hypothesis that the residuals are white noise. We are good to go! Let's use the `forecast` function to forecast the next 12 months of the USgas series:

```
USgas_fc <- forecast(final_md, h = 12)
```

We can plot the forecast with the `plot_forecast` function:

```
plot_forecast(USgas_fc,
              title = "US Natural Gas Consumption - Forecast",
              Ytitle = "Billion Cubic Feet",
              Xtitle = "Year")
```

We get the following output:

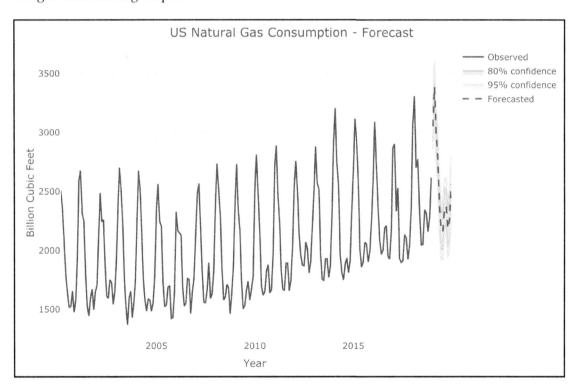

The auto.arima function

One of the main challenges of forecasting with the ARIMA family of models is the cumbersome tuning process of the models. As we saw in this chapter, this process includes many manual steps that are required for verifying the structure of the series (stationary or non-stationary), data transformations, descriptive analysis with the ACF and PACF plots to identify the type of process, and eventually tune the model parameters. While it might take a few minutes to train an ARIMA model for a single series, it may not scale up if you have dozens of series to forecast.

The `auto.arima` function from the **forecast** package provides a solution to this issue. This algorithm automates the tuning process of the ARIMA model with the use of statistical methods to identify both the structure of the series (stationary or not) and type (seasonal or not), and sets the model's parameters accordingly. For example, we can utilize the function to forecast `USgas`:

```
USgas_auto_md1 <- auto.arima(train)
```

Using the default arguments of the `auto.arima` function returns the ARIMA model that minimizes the AIC score. In this case, a $SARIMA(1, 0, 4)(1, 1, 2)_{12}$ model was selected with an AIC score of `2480.57`:

```
USgas_auto_md1
```

We get the following output:

```
## Series: train
## ARIMA(1,0,4)(1,1,2)[12] with drift
##
## Coefficients:
##          ar1     ma1     ma2     ma3     ma4     sar1     sma1     sma2
##       0.3405  0.1773  0.0473  0.1731  0.1617  -0.3743  -0.3040  -0.4527
## s.e.  0.2970  0.2984  0.1429  0.0854  0.1015   0.2831   0.2672   0.2022
##       drift
##       2.3219
## s.e.  0.3678
##
## sigma^2 estimated as 10537:  log likelihood=-1230.28
## AIC=2480.57   AICc=2481.71   BIC=2513.7
```

By default, the `auto.arima` function applies a shorter model search by using a step-wise approach for reducing the search time. The trade-off of this approach is that the model may miss some models that may achieve better results. This can be seen in the results of `USgas_auto_md1`, which achieved a higher AIC score than the model we tuned with the grid search we used previously (`2480.57` versus `2459.81` in the previous model).

We can improvise with the `auto.arima` results by setting the search argument of the model. The step-wise argument, when set to `FALSE`, allows you to set a more robust and thorough search, with the cost of higher search time. This trade-off between performance and compute time can be balanced whenever you have prior knowledge about the series' structure and characteristics. For example, let's retrain the training set of the `USgas` series again, this time using the following settings:

- Set the differencing parameters `d` and `D` to `1`.
- Limit the order of the model to seven by using the `max.order` argument. The `max.order` argument defines the maximum values of $p+q+P+Q$, hence we should set it to five (given that `d` and `D` are set to `1`).
- Under these constraints, search all possible combinations by setting the `stepwise` argument to `FALSE`.
- Set the `approximation` argument to `FALSE` for more accurate calculations of the information criteria:

```
USgas_auto_md2 <- auto.arima(train,
                             max.order = 5,
                             D = 1,
                             d = 1,
                             stepwise = FALSE,
                             approximation = FALSE)
```

You can see from the following results that with the robust search, the `auto.arima` algorithm returns the same model that was identified with the grid search we used in the *Seasonal ARIMA model* section:

```
USgas_auto_md2
```

We get the following output:

```
## Series: train
## ARIMA(1,1,1)(2,1,1)[12]
##
## Coefficients:
## ar1 ma1 sar1 sar2 sma1
## 0.4143 -0.9244 -0.0216 -0.256 -0.7565
## s.e. 0.0733 0.0291 0.0956 0.088 0.0803
##
## sigma^2 estimated as 10087: log likelihood=-1223.9
## AIC=2459.81 AICc=2460.24 BIC=2479.66
```

Linear regression with ARIMA errors

In Chapter 9, *Forecasting with Linear Regression*, we saw that with some simple steps, we can utilize a linear regression model as a time series forecasting model. Recall that a general form of the linear regression model can be represented by the following equation:

$$Y_t = \beta_0 + \beta X_t + \epsilon_t$$

One of the main assumptions of the linear regression model is that the error term of the series, ϵ, is the white noise series (for example, there is no correlation between the residuals and their lags). However, when working with time series data, this assumption is eased as, typically, the model predictors do not explain all the variations of the series, and some patterns are left on the model residuals. An example of the failure of this assumption can be seen while fitting a linear regression model to forecast the AirPassenger series.

Violation of white noise assumption

To illustrate this point, we will utilize the tslm function to regress the AirPassenger series with its trend, seasonal component, and seasonal lag (lag 12), and then evaluate the model residuals with the checkresiduals function. Before we start with the training process, let's prepare the data and create new features to represent the series trend and seasonal (using the month function from the **lubridate** package) components, as well as the seasonal lag:

```
df <- ts_to_prophet(AirPassengers)

names(df) <- c("date", "y")
```

```
df$lag12 <- dplyr::lag(df$y, n = 12)

library(lubridate)

df$month <- factor(month(df$date, label = TRUE), ordered = FALSE)

df$trend <- 1:nrow(df)
```

Here, the three variables represent the following:

- `lag12`: A numeric variable that represents the seasonal lag of the series (that is, lag 12)
- `month`: A categorical variable (12 categories, one for each month of the year) that represents the seasonal component of the series
- `trend`: A numeric variable that represents the marginal effect of moving in time by one index unit, which in this case is the marginal change of the series by moving in time by one month

Now, we will split the series into training and testing partitions, leaving the last 12 months for testing using the `ts_split` function:

```
par <- ts_split(ts.obj = AirPassengers, sample.out = 12)

train <- par$train

test <- par$test
```

For the regression of the time series object with an external `data.frame` object (`df`), we will apply the same split for training and testing partitions on the predictor's `data.frame` object:

```
train_df <- df[1:(nrow(df) - 12), ]
test_df <- df[(nrow(df) - 12 + 1):nrow(df), ]
```

Now, we can start to train the model with the `tslm` function:

```
md1 <- tslm(train ~ season + trend + lag12, data = train_df)
```

Let's use the `checkresiduals` function to review the model's residuals:

```
checkresiduals(md1)
```

We get the following output:

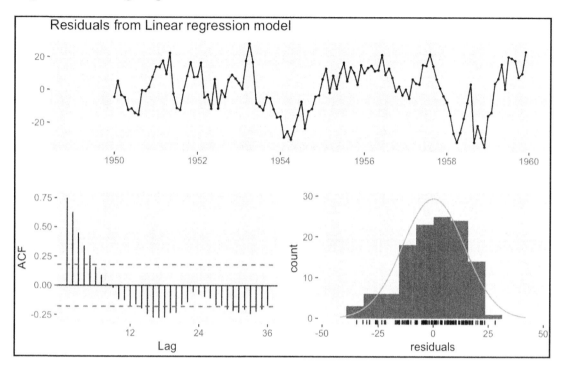

In the preceding ACF plot, the residuals series has a strong correlation with its past lags, and therefore the series is not white noise. We can conclude from the residuals plot that the regression model could not capture all the series patterns. Generally, this should not come as a surprise since the variation of the series could be affected by other variables, such as the ticket and oil prices, the unemployment rate, and other external factors.

A simple solution to this problem is to model the error terms with the ARIMA model and add it to the regression.

Modeling the residuals with the ARIMA model

As we saw in the preceding ACF plot, the `AirPassengers` residuals indicate that the model was unable to capture all the patterns of the series. Another way to think about this is that the modeling of the series is not complete yet, and additional modeling can be applied on the model residuals to reveal the true error term of the model. For instance, the following expression describes the linear relationship between the `AirPassengers` series and the *trend, month,* and *lag12* variables:

$$Y_t = \beta_0 + \beta_1 trend_t + \beta_2 month_t + \beta_3 lag12_t + \epsilon_t$$

Then, the correlated error term, ϵ_t, could be described by the following expression:

$$\epsilon_t = \beta_4 X_4 + \ldots + \beta_n X_n + \epsilon_t'$$

The following terms are used in the preceding equation:

- $X_4, \ldots, X_n$ are the additional variables that are required to explain the variation of the series that is not explained by the *trend, month,* and *lag12* variables
- $\beta_4, \ldots, \beta_n$ are the corresponding coefficients of the $X_4, \ldots, X_n$ variables
- ϵ_t' is white noise and the true error term of the model

In reality, finding additional predictors that can explain the remaining variation of the series is costly and time-consuming. Moreover, if variables such as ticket prices, economical indicators, and other factors are available, it is not easy to predict them (as they will be needed as inputs for the actual forecast). A simple solution is to utilize the auto-correlation relationship of the model residuals and model them with the ARIMA model. In other words, we can modify the `AirPassengers` linear regression and add *AR(p)* and *MA(p)* processes to the model:

$$Y_t = \beta_0 + \beta_1 trend_t + \beta_2 month_t + \beta_3 lag12_t + \sum_{i=1}^{p} \phi_i Y_{t-i} + \sum_{i=1}^{q} \theta_i \epsilon_{t-i} + \epsilon_t$$

The following terms are used in the preceding equation:

- $\sum_{i=1}^{p} \phi_i Y_{t-i}$ expresses an AR process with *p*-order
- $\sum_{i=1}^{q} \theta_i \epsilon_{t-i}$ expresses an MA process with *q*-order

The modified equation of the preceding `AirPassengers` model is a simplistic representation of the linear regression model with ARIMA errors (which in this case are ARMA errors). However, any of the ARIMA models we have looked at in this chapter, including the SARIMA model, can be used to model the residuals of the model.

Let's remodel the `AirPassengers` series, but this time with a linear regression model with ARIMA errors. While modeling the model's error term with an ARIMA model, we should treat the residuals as a series by itself and set the model components p, d, and q (and P, D, and Q if the residuals series has seasonal component) using any of the approaches we introduced in this chapter (for example, manual tuning, grid search, or automating the search process with the `auto.arima` process). For simplicity, we will utilize the `auto.arima` function.

The `auto.arima` function can be used to model a linear regression model with ARIMA errors via the use of the `xreg` argument:

```
md2 <- auto.arima(train,
             xreg = cbind(model.matrix(~ month,train_df)[,-1],
                          train_df$trend,
                          train_df$lag12),
             seasonal = TRUE,
             stepwise = FALSE,
             approximation = FALSE)
```

Note that the `auto.arima` and `arima` functions do not support categorical variables (that is, the `factor` class) with the `xreg` argument. Capturing the seasonal effect will require one-hot encoding (transforming each category into multiple binary variables) of the categorical variable. Therefore, we used the `model.matrix` function from the **stats** package on the `xreg` argument of the `auto.arima` function to transfer the `month` variable from a categorical variable into a binary variable. In addition, we dropped the first column, which represents the first category (in this case, the month of January), to avoid the dummy variable trap.

We set the `seasonal` argument to TRUE to include a search of both non-seasonal and seasonal models. The `auto.arima` function will conduct a full search when the step-wise and approximation arguments are set to FALSE. Let's use the `summary` function to review the model summary:

```
summary(md2)
```

We get the following output:

```
## Series: train
## Regression with ARIMA(2,0,0)(2,0,0)[12] errors
##
## Coefficients:
##           ar1      ar2      sar1     sar2   monthFeb   monthMar   monthApr
##        0.5849   0.3056   -0.4421  -0.2063    -2.7523     0.8231     0.2066
## s.e.   0.0897   0.0903    0.1050   0.1060     1.8417     2.3248     2.4162
##        monthMay monthJun monthJul monthAug  monthSep  monthOct
monthNov
##          2.8279   6.6057  11.2337  12.1909    3.8269    0.6350
-2.2723
## s.e.     2.5560   3.2916   4.2324   4.1198    2.9243    2.3405
2.4211
##        monthDec
##         -0.9918   0.2726   1.0244
## s.e.     1.9172   0.1367   0.0426
##
## sigma^2 estimated as 72.82:  log likelihood=-426.93
## AIC=889.86   AICc=896.63   BIC=940.04
##
## Training set error measures:
##                      ME      RMSE      MAE       MPE      MAPE      MASE
## Training set 0.4117147 8.353629 6.397538 0.2571543 2.549682 0.2100998
##                     ACF1
## Training set 0.005966714
```

The `auto.arima` function regresses the series with the `trend`, `month`, and `lag12` variables. In addition, the model used the AR(2) and SAR(2) processes for modeling the error term. We can now review the residuals of the modified `md2` model with the `checkresiduals` functions:

```
checkresiduals(md2)
```

We get the following output:

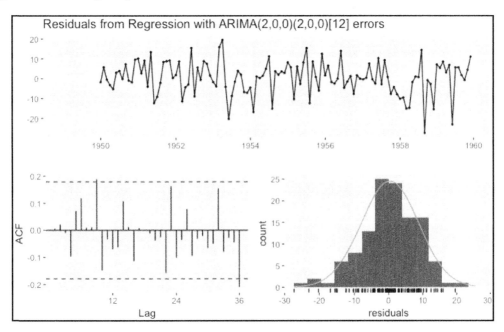

You can see the change in the ACF plot after applying the linear regression model with ARIMA errors as the majority of the lags are not statistically significant, as opposed to the preceding linear regression model (md1). Let's evaluate the performance of both models (md1 and md2) on the testing set:

```
fc1 <- forecast(md1, newdata = test_df)

fc2 <- forecast(md2, xreg = cbind(model.matrix(~ month,test_df)[,-1],
                                  test_df$trend,
                                  test_df$lag12))
```

When using the xreg argument with one of the **forecast** package functions, the corresponding inputs for the forecasting model should be fed to the xreg argument of the forecast function. Note that you have to execute the input variables in the same order that was used in the training model with the xreg argument of the **forecast** package!

Now, let's use the accuracy function to review the two model's performance on both the testing and training partitions:

```
accuracy(fc1, test)
```

We get the following output:

```
##                                  ME      RMSE      MAE       MPE
## Training set -0.00000000000001658222 13.99206 11.47136 -0.1200023
## Test set      10.796107235775016519597 20.82782 18.57391  1.9530865
##                 MAPE      MASE      ACF1 Theil's U
## Training set 4.472154 0.3541758 0.7502578        NA
## Test set     3.828115 0.5734654 0.1653119 0.4052175
```

Let's test the accuracy of the second model:

```
accuracy(fc2, test)
```

We get the following output:

```
##                    ME       RMSE       MAE       MPE      MAPE
MASE
## Training set   0.4117147   8.353629   6.397538   0.2571543 2.549682
0.2100998
## Test set      -11.2123707 17.928195 13.353910 -2.4898843 2.924174
0.4385521
##                   ACF1 Theil's U
## Training set  0.005966714        NA
## Test set     -0.325044930 0.3923795
```

You can see from the output of the accuracy function that the linear regression with the ARIMA model provides a significant improvement in the model's accuracy with a lift of 43% on the MAPE score on the training set (from 4.5% to 2.5%) and 31% on the testing set (from 3.8% to 2.9%).

Summary

In this chapter, we introduced the ARIMA family of models, one of the core approaches for forecasting time series data. The main advantages of the ARIMA family of models is their flexibility and modularity, as they can handle both seasonal and non-seasonal time series data by adding or modifying the model components. In addition, we saw the applications of the ACF and PACF plots for identifying the type of process (for example, AR, MA, ARMA, and so on) and its order.

While it is essential to be familiar with the tuning process of ARIMA models, in practice, as the number series to be forecast increase, you may want to automate this process. The `auto.arima` function is one of the most common approaches in R to forecast with ARIMA models as it can scale up when dozens of series need to be forecast.

Last but not least, we saw applications of linear regression with the ARIMA errors model in order to extract lost information from the model residuals.

In the next chapter, we will look at an advanced application of the regression models with machine learning models for forecasting time series data.

12
Forecasting with Machine Learning Models

In Chapter 9, *Forecasting with Linear Regression*, we saw how a basic regression model could utilize some simple steps to create a robust time series forecast. The use of a linear regression model for time series forecasting can be easily generalized to other regression approaches, in particular, machine learning-based regressions. In this chapter, we will focus on the use of machine learning models for time series forecasting using the **h2o** package. This chapter requires some basic knowledge of the training and tuning process of machine learning models.

In this chapter, we will cover the following topics:

- Introduction to the **h2o** package and its functionality
- Feature engineering of time series data
- Forecasting with the Random Forest model
- Forecasting with the gradient boosting machine learning model
- Forecasting with the automate machine learning model

Technical requirement

The following packages will be used in this chapter:

- **h2o**: Version 3.22.1.1 and above and Java version 7 and above
- **TSstudio**: Version 0.1.4 and above
- **plotly**: Version 4.8 and above
- **lubridate**: Version 1.7.4 and above

You can access the codes for this chapter from the following link:

```
https://github.com/PacktPublishing/Hands-On-Time-Series-Analysis-with-R/tree/
master/Chapter12
```

Why and when should we use machine learning?

In recent years, the use of **machine learning** (**ML**) models has become popular and accessible due to significant improvement in standard computation power. This led to a new world of methods and approaches for regression and classifications models. The process of creating time series forecasting with ML models follows the same process we used in `Chapter 9`, *Forecasting with Linear Regression*, with the linear regression model.

Before we start diving into the details, it is important to caveat the use of ML models in the context of time series forecasting:

- **Cost**: The use of ML models is typically more expensive than typical regression models, both in computing power and time.
- **Accuracy**: The ML model's performance is highly dependent on the quality (that is, strong casualty relationship with the dependent variable) of the predictors. It is likely that the ML models will over-perform, with respect to traditional methods such as linear regression when strong predictors are available.
- **Tuning**: Processing typical ML models is more complex than with common regression models, as those models have more tuning parameters and therefore, require some expertise.
- **Black-box**: Most of the ML models are considered black boxes, as it is hard to interrupt their output.
- **Uncertainty**: Generally, there is no straightforward method to quantify the forecasting uncertainty with confidence intervals like the traditional time series model does.

On the other hand, the main advantage of the ML models is their predictive power (when quality inputs are available), which, in many cases, is worth the effort and time involved in the process.

In the context of time series forecasting, it will be beneficial to forecast with ML models in the following cases:

- **Structural patterns**: Exits in the series, as those can produce new, predictive features
- **Multiple seasonality**: As a special case for structural patterns since, typically, the traditional time series models are struggling to capture those patterns when they exist

In this chapter, we will focus on the forecast of the US monthly vehicle sales using the following models:

- Random Forest
- Gradient boosting machine
- Auto ML model

 Note that the goals of this chapter are not to teach you the principles of ML (as it is a topic by itself and outside the scope of this book), but the principles of building forecasting models with the use of ML methods. Some basic background in training and tuning ML models is recommended for this chapter.

Why h2o?

In this chapter, we will use the **h2o** package to build and train forecasting models with the use of ML models. H2O is an open source, distributed, and Java-based library for machine learning applications. It has APIs for both R (the **h2o** package) and Python, and includes applications for both supervised and unsupervised learning models. This includes algorithms such as **deep learning** (DL), **gradient boosting machine** (GBM), XGBoost, **Distributed Random Forest** (RF), and the **Generalized Linear Model** (GLM).

The main advantage of the **h2o** package is that it is based on distributed processing and, therefore, it can be either used in memory or scaled up with the use of external computing power. Furthermore, the **h2o** package algorithms provide several methods so that we can train and tune machine learning models, such as the cross-validation method and the built-in grid search function.

Since the **h2o** package is using the Java language on the backhand, it is required that you install Java on your machine before loading the package. Additional information about the installation process of **h2o** is available in the platform documentation (`http://docs.h2o.ai/h2o/latest-stable/h2o-docs/downloading.html`).

Forecasting monthly vehicle sales in the US – a case study

In this chapter, we will focus on forecasting the total monthly vehicle sales in the US in the next 12 months with ML methods. The total monthly vehicle sales in the US series is available in the **TSstudio** package:

```
library(TSstudio)

data(USVSales)
```

Before we start preparing the series and create new features, we will conduct a short exploratory analysis of the series in order to identify the main characteristics of the series.

Exploratory analysis of the USVSales series

In this section, we will focus on exploring and learning about the main characteristics of the series. These insights will be used to build new features as inputs for the ML model. The exploratory analysis of the USVSales series will focus on the following topics:

- View the time series structure (frequency, start and end of the series, and so on)
- Explore the series components (seasonal, cycle, trend, and random components)
- Seasonality analysis
- Correlation analysis

The series structure

Let's start with `ts_info` and review the structure of the USVSales series:

```
ts_info(USVSales)
```

We get the following output:

```
##   The USVSales series is a ts object with 1 variable and 517 observations
##   Frequency: 12
##   Start time: 1976 1
##   End time: 2019 1
```

The USVSales series is a monthly ts object which represents the total vehicle sales in the US between 1976 and 2018 in thousands of units. Let's plot the series and review its structure with the ts_plot function:

```
ts_plot(USVSales,
        title = "US Total Monthly Vehicle Sales",
        Ytitle = "Thousands of Units",
        Xtitle = "Year")
```

We get the following output:

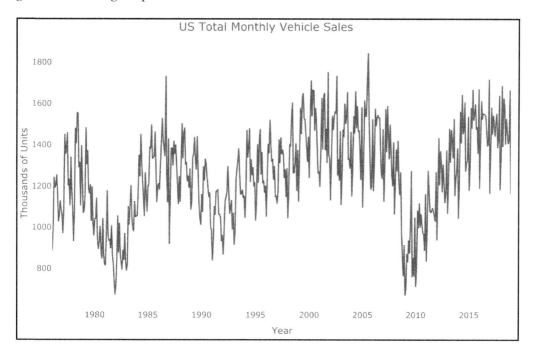

As you can see in the preceding plot, the series has cycle patterns, which is common for a macro economy indicator. In this case, it is a macro indicator of the US economy.

The series components

We can get a deeper view of the series components by decomposing the series into its components and plotting them with the `ts_decompose` function:

```
ts_decompose(USVSales)
```

We get the following output:

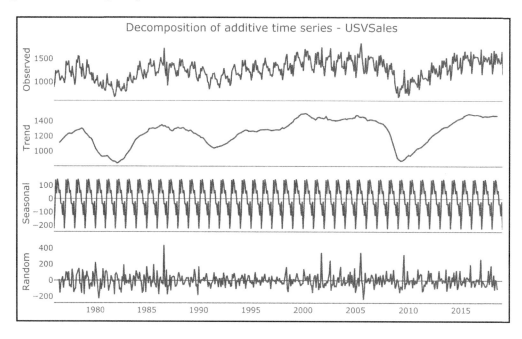

Beside the cycle-trend component, we can observe that the plot has a strong seasonal pattern, which we will explore next.

Seasonal analysis

To get a closer look at the seasonal component of the series, we will subtract from the series, decompose the trend we discussed previously, and use the `ts_seasonal` function to plot the box plot of the seasonal component of the detrend series:

```
USVSales_detrend <- USVSales - decompose(USVSales)$trend

ts_seasonal(USVSales_detrend, type = "box")
```

We get the following output:

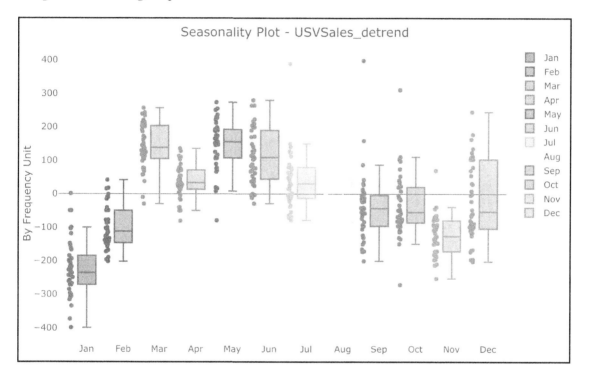

We can see from the preceding seasonal plot that, typically, the peak of the year occurred during the months of March, May, and June. In addition, you can see that the sales decay from the summer months and peak again in December during the holiday seasons. On the other hand, the month of January is typically the lowest month of the year in terms of sales.

Correlation analysis

As we saw in Chapter 7, *Correlation Analysis*, the USVSales series has a high correlation with its first seasonal lag. We can review this assessment with the use of the ts_acf function from the **TSstudio** package for reviewing the autocorrelation of the series:

```
ts_acf(USVSales)
```

We get the following output:

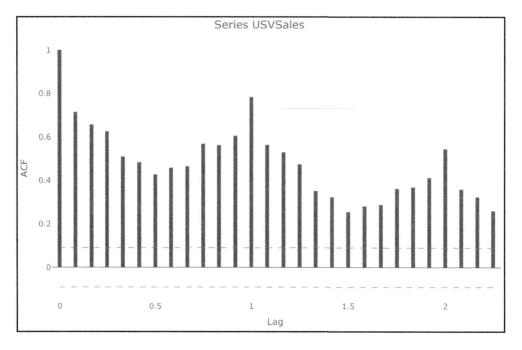

We can zoom in on the relationship of the series with the last three seasonal lags using the ts_lags function:

```
ts_lags(USVSales, lags = c(12, 24, 36))
```

We get the following output:

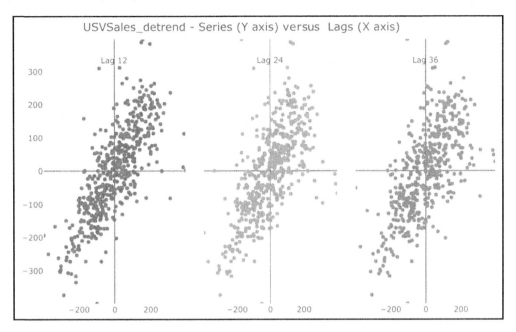

The relationship of the series with the first and also second seasonal lags has a strong linear relationship, as shown in the preceding lags plot.

Exploratory analysis – key findings

We can conclude our short exploratory analysis of the USVSales series with the following observations:

- The USVSales series is a monthly series with a clear monthly seasonality
- The series trend has a cyclic shape, and so the series has a cycle component embedded in the trend
- The series' most recent cycle starts right after the end of the 2008 economic crisis, between 2009 and 2010
- It seems that the current cycle reached its peak as the trend starts to flatten out
- The series has a strong correlation with its first seasonal lag

Moreover, as we intend to have a short-term forecast (of 12 months), there is no point in using the full series, as it may enter some noise into the model due to the change of the trend direction every couple of years. (If you were trying to create a long-term forecast, then it may be a good idea to use all or most of the series.) Therefore, we will use the model training observations from 2010 and onward. We will use the `ts_to_prophet` function from the **TSstudio** package to transform the series from a `ts` object into a `data.frame`, and the `window` function to subset the series observations since January 2010:

```
df <- ts_to_prophet(window(USVSales, start = c(2010,1)))

names(df) <-  c("date", "y")

head(df)
```

We get the following output:

```
##          date          y
## 1 2010-01-01  712.469
## 2 2010-02-01  793.362
## 3 2010-03-01 1083.953
## 4 2010-04-01  997.334
## 5 2010-05-01 1117.570
## 6 2010-06-01 1000.455
```

Before we move forward and start with the feature engineering stage, let's plot and review the subset series of `USVSales` with the `ts_plot` function:

```
ts_plot(df,
        title = "US Total Monthly Vehicle Sales (Subset)",
        Ytitle = "Thousands of Units",
        Xtitle = "Year")
```

We get the following output:

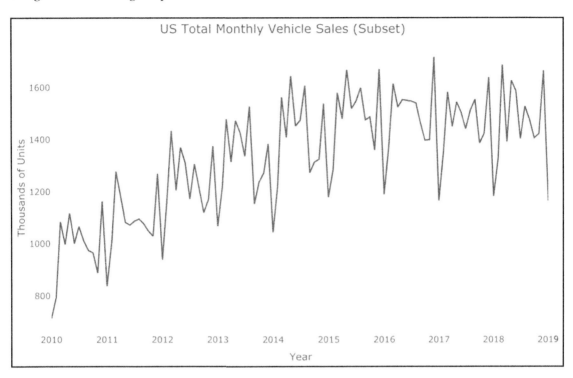

Feature engineering

Feature engineering plays a pivotal role when modeling with ML algorithms. Our next step, based on the preceding observations, is to create new features that can be used as informative input for the model. In the context of time series forecasting, here are some examples of possible new features that can be created from the series itself:

- **The series trend**: This uses a numeric index. In addition, as the series trend isn't linear, we will use a second polynomial of the index to capture the overall curvature of the series trend.
- **Seasonal component**: This creates a categorical variable for the month of the year to capture the series' seasonality.
- **Series correlation**: This utilizes the strong correlation of the series with its seasonal lag and uses the seasonal lag (`lag12`) as an input to the model.

We will use the **dplyr** and **lubridate** packages to create those features, as we can see in the following code:

```
library(dplyr)

library(lubridate)

df <- df %>% mutate(month = factor(month(date, label = TRUE), ordered =
FALSE),
                    lag12 = lag(y, n = 12)) %>%
        filter(!is.na(lag12))
```

We will then add the `trend` component and its second polynomial (trend squared):

```
df$trend <- 1:nrow(df)

df$trend_sqr <- df$trend ^ 2
```

Let's view the structure of the `df` object after adding the new features:

```
str(df)
```

We get the following output:

```
## 'data.frame':    97 obs. of  6 variables:
##  $ date     : Date, format: "2011-01-01" "2011-02-01" ...
##  $ y        : num  836 1007 1277 1174 1081 ...
##  $ month    : Factor w/ 12 levels "Jan","Feb","Mar",..: 1 2 3 4 5 6 7 8
9 10 ...
##  $ lag12    : num  712 793 1084 997 1118 ...
##  $ trend    : int  1 2 3 4 5 6 7 8 9 10 ...
##  $ trend_sqr: num  1 4 9 16 25 36 49 64 81 100 ...
```

There are additional feature engineering steps, which in the case of the `USVSales` series are not required, but may be required in other cases:

- **Scaling**: This may be required when the numeric inputs of the regression (either the series itself or at least one of the regression numeric predictors) are on a different numeric scale, for instance, regress revenue in billions of USD with a binary flag (for example, 0 or 1). Some models may fail to find coefficients or won't identify the true relationship between the variable. Some common scaling methods are as follows:
  - Log transformation
  - Normalize the series with Z-score
  - Scale the input between 0 and 1
  - Subtract the mean from the input

- **Hot encoding**: Categorical variables may be required when the algorithm does not support the use of factors (categorical variables) as input. In this case, for a variable with *N* categories, we will create new *N+1* variables—one variable for capturing the slope and *N* binary variables and one for each category.

Since the values of the input series are ranging between 800 to 1,700, there is no need to scale the series and its inputs. In addition, since the **h2o** package supports the inputs as R factors, there is no need to apply hot encoding.

Training, testing, and model evaluation

In order to compare the different models that we will be testing in this chapter, we will use the same inputs that we used previously. This includes executing same training and testing partitions throughout this chapter.

Since our forecast horizon is for 12 months, we will leave the last 12 months of the series as testing partitions and use the rest of the series as a training partition:

```
h <- 12

train_df <- df[1:(nrow(df) - h), ]

test_df <- df[(nrow(df) - h + 1):nrow(df), ]
```

Previously, the h variable represented the forecast horizon, which, in this case, is also equal to the length of the testing partition. We will evaluate the model's performance based on the MAPE score on the testing partition.

One of the main characteristics of ML models is the tendency to overfit on the training set. Therefore, you should expect that the ratio between the error score on the testing and training partition will be relatively larger than the corresponding results of traditional time series models, such as ARIMA, Holt-Winters, and time series linear regression.

In addition to the training and testing partitions, we need to create the inputs for the forecast itself. We will create a data.frame with the dates of the following 12 months and build the rest of the features:

```
forecast_df <- data.frame(date = seq.Date(from = max(df$date) + month(1),
length.out = h, by = "month"),
                          trend = seq(from = max(df$trend) + 1, length.out
= h, by = 1))

forecast_df$trend_sqr <- forecast_df$trend ^ 2
```

```
forecast_df$month <- factor(month(forecast_df$date, label = TRUE), ordered
= FALSE)
```

Last but not least, we will extract the last `12` observations of the series from the `df` object and assign them as the future lags of the series:

```
forecast_df$lag12 <- tail(df$y, 12)
```

Model benchmark

Introduced in `Chapter 8`, *Forecasting Strategies*, the performance of a forecasting model should be measured by the error rate, mainly on the testing partition, but also on the training partition. You should evaluate the performance of the model with respect to some baseline model. In the previous chapters, we benchmarked the forecast of the `USgas` series with the use of the seasonal naive model.

In this chapter, since we are using a family of ML regression models, it makes more sense to use a regression model as a benchmark for the ML models. Therefore, we will train a time series linear regression model, which we introduced in `Chapter 9`, *Forecasting with Linear Regression*. Using the training and testing partitions we created previously, let's train the linear regression model and evaluate its performance with the testing partitions:

```
lr <- lm(y ~ month + lag12 + trend + trend_sqr, data = train_df)
```

We will use the `summary` function to review the model details:

```
summary(lr)
```

We get the following output:

```
##
## Call:
## lm(formula = y ~ month + lag12 + trend + trend_sqr, data = train_df)
##
## Residuals:
##      Min       1Q   Median       3Q      Max
## -152.238  -38.412    1.175   34.471  119.947
##
## Coefficients:
##               Estimate Std. Error t value    Pr(>|t|)
## (Intercept)  533.54515   80.45593   6.632 0.00000000583 ***
## monthFeb     115.10262   36.87217   3.122       0.002614 **
## monthMar     287.20432   60.75992   4.727 0.00001142840 ***
## monthApr     189.81240   47.11880   4.028       0.000141 ***
## monthMay     258.85449   57.40489   4.509 0.00002550309 ***
```

```
## monthJun     212.14346     48.68294     4.358 0.00004414785 ***
## monthJul     181.74136     46.72620     3.889       0.000226 ***
## monthAug     239.95562     52.11112     4.605 0.00001797442 ***
## monthSep     148.28026     38.56246     3.845       0.000263 ***
## monthOct     118.08867     37.55868     3.144       0.002444 **
## monthNov     120.73354     36.01454     3.352       0.001295 **
## monthDec     267.91309     55.47217     4.830 0.00000777550 ***
## lag12           0.34120      0.11972     2.850       0.005740 **
## trend           8.68109      1.88781     4.598 0.00001838988 ***
## trend_sqr      -0.06869      0.01450    -4.738 0.00001096631 ***
## ---
## Signif. codes:  0 '***' 0.001 '**' 0.01 '*' 0.05 '.' 0.1 ' ' 1
##
## Residual standard error: 60.15 on 70 degrees of freedom
## Multiple R-squared:  0.9213, Adjusted R-squared:  0.9056
## F-statistic: 58.54 on 14 and 70 DF,  p-value: < 0.00000000000000022
```

Next, we will predict the corresponding values of the series on the testing partition with the `predict` function by using `test_df` as input:

```
test_df$yhat <- predict(lr, newdata = test_df)
```

Now, we can evaluate the model's performance on the testing partition:

```
mape_lr <- mean(abs(test_df$y - test_df$yhat) / test_df$y)

mape_lr
```

We get the following output:

```
## [1] 0.04041179
```

Hence, the MAPE score of the linear regression forecasting model is 4.04%. We will use this to benchmark the performance of the ML models.

Starting a h2o cluster

The **h2o** package is based on the use of distributed and parallel computing in order to speed up the compute time and be able to scale up for big data. All of this is done on either in-memory (based on the computer's internal RAM) or parallel distributed processing (for example, AWS, Google Cloud, and so on) clusters. Therefore, we will load the package and then set the in-memory cluster with the `h2o.init` function:

```
library(h2o)

h2o.init(max_mem_size = "16G")
```

We get the following output:

```
##
##
## Starting H2O JVM and connecting: ..... Connection successful!
##
## R is connected to the H2O cluster:
##     H2O cluster uptime:          5 seconds 370 milliseconds
##     H2O cluster timezone:        America/Los_Angeles
##     H2O data parsing timezone:   UTC
##     H2O cluster version:         3.22.1.1
##     H2O cluster version age:     4 months and 7 days !!!
##     H2O cluster name:            H2O_started_from_R_rami_izi146
##     H2O cluster total nodes:     1
##     H2O cluster total memory:    14.22 GB
##     H2O cluster total cores:     8
##     H2O cluster allowed cores:   8
##     H2O cluster healthy:         TRUE
##     H2O Connection ip:           localhost
##     H2O Connection port:         54321
##     H2O Connection proxy:        NA
##     H2O Internal Security:       FALSE
##     H2O API Extensions:          XGBoost, Algos, AutoML, Core V3, Core V4
##     R Version:                   R version 3.4.4 Patched (2018-03-19
## r74624)
```

`h2o.init` allows you to set the memory size of the cluster with the `max_mem_size` argument. The output of the function, as shown in the preceding code, provides information about the cluster's setup.

Any data that is used throughout the training and testing process of the models by the **h2o** package must load to the cluster itself. The `as.h2o` function allows us to transform any `data.frame` object into a `h2o` cluster:

```
train_h <- as.h2o(train_df)

test_h <- as.h2o(test_df)
```

In addition, we will transform the `forecast_df` object (the future values of the series inputs) into an `h2o` object, which will be used to generate, later on in this chapter, the final forecast:

```
forecast_h <- as.h2o(forecast_df)
```

For our convenience, we will label the names of the dependent and independent variables:

```
x <- c("month", "lag12", "trend", "trend_sqr")

y <- "y"
```

Now that the data has been loaded into the working cluster, we can start the training process.

Training an ML model

The **h2o** package provides a set of tools for training and testing ML models. The most common model training approaches are as follows:

- **Training/testing**: This is based on splitting the input data into training and testing partitions by allocating most of the input data to the training partition and leaving the rest to the testing partition. As the names of the partitions imply, the training set is used to train the model, while the testing partition is used to test its performance on new data. Typical allocations are 70/30 (that is, 70% of the data to the training partition and 30% to the testing partition), or roughly close to that ratio, where the data allocation between the two partitions must be random.
- **Training/testing/validation**: This is relatively similar to the previous approach, except with added validation partitions. The validation partition is used during the training process to evaluate the tuning of the model parameters. The tuned models are then tested on the testing partition.
- **Cross-validation**: This is one of the most popular training methods for ML models as it reduces the chance of overfitting of the model. This method is based on the following steps:
    1. Splitting the training set, randomly, into *K* folders
    2. Training the model *K* times, each time leaving a different folder out as a testing partition, and training the model with the remaining *K-1* folders
    3. Throughout the training process, the model tunes the model's parameters
    4. The final model is tested on the testing partition

Throughout this chapter, we will use the **cross-validation** (**CV**) approach to train these models.

Forecasting with the Random Forest model

Now that we have prepared the data, created new features, and launched a h2o cluster, we are ready to build our first forecasting model with the **Random Forest** (**RF**) algorithm. The RF algorithm is one of the most popular ML models, and it can be used for both classification and regression problems. In a nutshell, the RF algorithm is based on an ensemble of multiple tree models.

As its name implies, it has two main components:

- **Random**: The input for each tree model is based on a random sample, along with the replacement of both the columns and rows of the input data. This method is also known as bagging.
- **Forest**: The collection of tree-based models, which eventually creates the *forest*.

After the forest is built, the algorithm ensembles the prediction of all the trees in the forest into one output. This combination of randomizing the input for each tree model and then averaging their results reduces the likelihood of overfitting the model.

RF has several tuning parameters that allow you to control the level of randomization of the sampling process and how deep the forest is. The h2o.randomForest function from the **h2o** package provides the framework for training and tuning the RF model. The following are the main parameters of the h2o.randomForest function:

- x: A vector of characters with independent variable names
- y: A string, which is the name of the dependent variable
- training_frame: The input data must be a data.frame of **h20** package
- validation_frame: Optional; should be used when applying a training approach with the validation set
- nfolds: The number of *K*-folds for the CV process
- ntrees: Number of trees to be created
- sample_rate: Defines the number of rows to sample per tree
- max_depth: Sets the maximum tree depth (number of nodes); as the trees grow deeper, the complexity of the mode increases, as well as the risk for overfitting
- seed: Sets the seed value of the random numbers generator

In addition, this function has several control arguments, which allows you to control the running time of the model. Furthermore, they allow you to set a stop criteria for the model if adding additional trees doesn't improve the model's performance. These arguments are as follows:

- `stopping_metric`: Defines the type of error metric to be used for evaluating whether the model should stop and build new trees as there is no additional improvement
- `stopping_tolerance`: Sets the minimal improvement that is required to continue the training process
- `stopping_rounds`: Sets the number of rounds that should be used before stopping the training

We will start with a simplistic RF model by using 500 trees and 5 folder CV training. In addition, we will add a stop criteria to prevent the model from fitting the model while there is no significant change in the model's performance. In this case, we will set the stopping metric as RMSE, the stopping tolerance as 0.0001, and the stopping rounds to 10:

```
rf_md <- h2o.randomForest(training_frame = train_h,
                    nfolds = 5,
                    x = x,
                    y = y,
                    ntrees = 500,
                    stopping_rounds = 10,
                    stopping_metric = "RMSE",
                    score_each_iteration = TRUE,
                    stopping_tolerance = 0.0001,
                    seed = 1234)
```

The `h2o.randomForest` function returns an object with information about the parameter settings of the model and its performance on the training set (and validation, if used). We can view the contribution of the model inputs with the `h2o.varimp_plot` function. This function returns a plot with the ranking of the input variables' contribution to the model performance using a scale between 0 and 1, as shown in the following code:

```
h2o.varimp_plot(rf_md)
```

We get the following output:

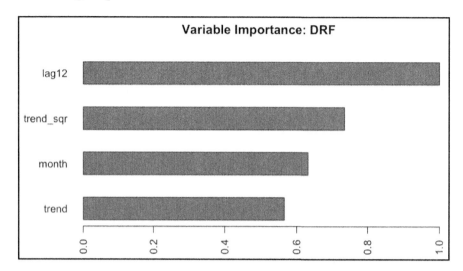

As we can see from the preceding variable importance plot, the lag variable, `lag12`, is the most important to the model. This shouldn't be a surprise as we saw the strong relationship between the series and its seasonal lag in the correlation analysis. Right after this, the most important variables are `trend_sqr`, `month`, and `trend`.

The output of the model contains (besides the model itself) information about the model's performance and parameters. Let's review the model summary:

```
rf_md@model$model_summary
```

We get the following output:

```
## Model Summary:
##   number_of_trees number_of_internal_trees model_size_in_bytes min_depth
## 1              42                       42               29398         7
##   max_depth mean_depth min_leaves max_leaves mean_leaves
## 1        13    9.80952         43         61    51.11905
```

We can see that we utilized only 42 trees out of the 500 that were set by the `ntrees` argument. This is as a result of the stopping parameters that were used on the model. The following plot demonstrates the learning process of the model as a function of the number of trees:

```
library(plotly)

tree_score <- rf_md@model$scoring_history$training_rmse
```

```
plot_ly(x = seq_along(tree_score), y = tree_score,
      type = "scatter", mode = "line") %>%
   layout(title = "The Trained Model Score History",
         yaxis = list(title = "RMSE"),
         xaxis = list(title = "Num. of Trees"))
```

We get the following output:

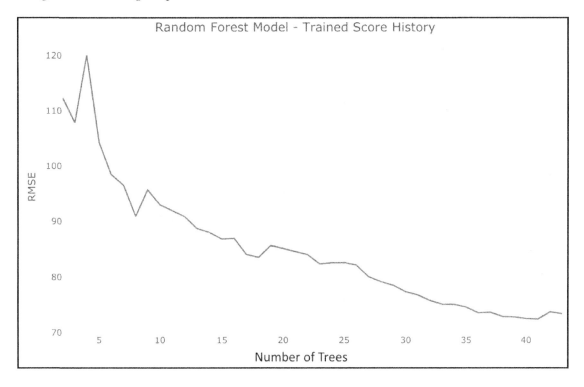

Last but not least, let's measure the model's performance on the testing partition. We will use the h2o.predict function to predict the corresponding values of the series on the testing partition:

```
test_h$pred_rf <- h2o.predict(rf_md, test_h)
```

Next, we will transfer the h2o data frame to a data.frame object with the as.data.frame function:

```
test_1 <- as.data.frame(test_h)
```

Now, we can calculate the MAPE score of the RF model on the test partition:

```
mape_rf <- mean(abs(test_1$y - test_1$pred_rf) / test_1$y)

mape_rf
```

We get the following output:

```
## [1] 0.03749611
```

As you can see from the model error score, the RF model with its default settings was able to achieve a lower error rate than our benchmark model, that is, the linear regression model, with a MAPE score of 3.7% as opposed to 4%.

Generally, when using the default option for the model's parameters, the model may perform well, but there might be some room left for additional optimization and improvement in regards to the performance of the model. There are a variety of techniques for model optimization and tuning parameters, such as manual tuning, grid search, and algorithm-based tuning. In the previous chapters, we looked at examples of these three approaches—we manually tuned the ARMA model in Chapter 11, *Forecasting with ARIMA Models*, we used the ts_grid function in Chapter 10, *Forecasting with Exponential Smoothing Models*, for tuning the Holt-Winters parameters with grid search, and automated the tuning of ARIMA model (again in Chapter 11, *Forecasting with ARIMA Models*) with the auto.arima algorithm.

We will demonstrate a grid search approach for tuning an ML model with the h2o.grid function. Later on in this chapter, we will look at an algorithm-based approach to tuning aN ML model with the h2o.automl function.

The h2o.grid function allows you to set a set of values for some selected parameters and test their performance on the model in order to identify the tuning parameters that optimize the model's performance. The main arguments of this function are as follows:

- algorithm: Defines the type of algorithm to use in the grid search
- hyper_params: Sets the search parameter's values
- search_criteria: Sets roles for the search, such as the stopping metric of the model, number of models, and runtime

Any of the training approaches of the **h2o** package (such as CV, training with validation) can be applied with the h2o.grid function.

We will start by setting the search parameters:

```
hyper_params_rf <-  list(mtries = c(2, 3, 4),
                         sample_rate = c(0.632, 0.8, 0.95),
                         col_sample_rate_per_tree = c(0.5, 0.9, 1.0),
                         max_depth = c(seq(1, 30, 3)),
                         min_rows = c(1, 2, 5, 10))
```

Here, the parameters we selected are as follows:

- `mtries`: Defines the columns to randomly select on each node of the tree
- `sample_rate`: Sets the row sampling for each tree
- `col_sample_rate_per_tree`: Defines the column sample rate per tree
- `max_depth`: Specifies the maximum tree depth
- `min_rows`: Sets the minimum number of observations for a leaf

The more parameters you add or define for a wide range of values, the larger the possible search combination. This could easily get to hundreds of combinations, which may run for a couple of hours (based on the available compute power). Therefore, setting the `search_criteria` argument is very important for efficiency reasons. The strategy argument of the `search_criteria` argument allows you to set either Cartesian (`Cartesian`) search or random (`RandomDiscrete`) search. The Cartesian search iterates and computes the models for all the possible search options in chronological order. On the other hand, the random search randomly selects a search combination from the grid search table.

It would make sense to use the Cartesian method when the number of search combinations is fairly small, or when you aren't limited in search time. On the other hand, for a large amount of search combinations, or when we have a time constraint, it is recommended to use random search. For efficiency reasons, we will set a random search and restrict the search time to 20 minutes with `max_runtime_sec`. We will use the same stopping metric that we used previously:

```
search_criteria_rf <- list(strategy = "RandomDiscrete",
                           stopping_metric = "rmse",
                           stopping_tolerance = 0.0001,
                           stopping_rounds = 10,
                           max_runtime_secs = 60 * 20)
```

After we set the search arguments for the `h2o.grid` function, we can start the search:

```
rf2 <- h2o.grid(algorithm = "randomForest",
                search_criteria = search_criteria_rf,
                hyper_params = hyper_params_rf,
```

```
        x = x,
        y = y,
        training_frame = train_h,
        ntrees = 5000,
        nfolds = 5,
        grid_id = "rf_grid",
        seed = 1234)
```

You will notice that we kept the same training approach, that is, 5 folders CV and the number of trees as 5000.

> Setting a large number of trees with a tree-based model such as RF or GBM, along with a stopping metric, will ensure that the model will keep building additional trees until it meets the stopping criteria. Therefore, setting the stopping criteria plays a critical roll in both the efficiency of the model and its results.

We will now extract the grid results, sort the models by their RMSE score, and pull the lead model:

```
rf2_grid_search <- h2o.getGrid(grid_id = "rf_grid",
                               sort_by = "rmse",
                               decreasing = FALSE)

rf_grid_model <- h2o.getModel(rf2_grid_search@model_ids[[1]])
```

Let's test the model on the testing partition and evaluate its performance:

```
test_h$rf_grid   <- h2o.predict(rf_grid_model, test_h)

mape_rf2 <- mean(abs(test_1$y - test_1$rf_grid) / test_1$y)

mape_rf2
```

We get the following output:

```
## [1] 0.03414109
```

The additional optimization step contributed to the lift in the model's accuracy, with a MAPE score of 3.33% compared to 3.7% and 4% for the first RF model we trained, and the linear regression model, respectively. The following plot provides an additional view of the model's performance:

```
plot_ly(data = test_1) %>%
    add_lines(x = ~ date, y = ~y, name = "Actual") %>%
    add_lines(x = ~ date, y = ~ yhat, name = "Linear Regression", line =
list(dash = "dot")) %>%
```

```
   add_lines(x = ~ date, y = ~ pred_rf, name = "Random Forest", line =
list(dash = "dash")) %>%
   add_lines(x = ~ date, y = ~ rf_grid, name = "Random Forest (grid)", line
= list(dash = "dash")) %>%
   layout(title = "Total Vehicle Sales - Actual vs. Prediction (Random
Forest)",
          yaxis = list(title = "Thousands of Units"),
          xaxis = list(title = "Month"))
```

We get the following output:

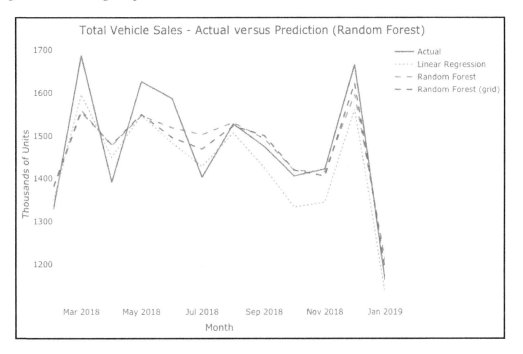

Now, let's look at the GBM model.

Forecasting with the GBM model

The GBM algorithm is another ensemble and tree-based model. It uses the *boosting* approach in order to train different subsets of the data, and repeats the training of subsets that the model had with a high error rate. This allows the model to learn from past mistakes and improve the predictive power of the model.

The main arguments of the GBM model are as follows

- x: A vector of characters with the independent variables names.
- y: A string, which is the name of the dependent variable.
- training_frame: The input data must be a data.frame of **h20** package.
- validation_frame: Optional; this should be used when we're applying a training approach with the validation set.
- nfolds: The number of *K*-fold for the CV process.
- ntrees: Number of trees to be created.
- sample_rate: Defines the number of rows to sample per tree.
- max_depth: Sets the maximum tree depth (number of nodes). As the trees grow deeper, the complexity of the mode increases, as well as the risk of overfitting.
- learn_rate: Defines the learning rate of the model with values between 0 and 1. The default rate is 0.1. As the learning rate comes closer to 0, the better the learning of the model will be, with the cost of longer compute time, along with a higher number of trees.
- seed: Sets the seed value of the random numbers generator.

The following example demonstrates the use of the h2o.gbm function for training the GBM model with the same input data we used previously:

```
gbm_md <- h2o.gbm(
    training_frame = train_h,
    nfolds = 5,
    x = x,
    y = y,
    max_depth = 20,
    distribution = "gaussian",
    ntrees = 500,
    learn_rate = 0.1,
    score_each_iteration = TRUE
)
```

Similar to the RF model, we can review the rank of the importance of the model's variables with the h2o.varimp_plot function:

```
h2o.varimp_plot(gbm_md)
```

We get the following output:

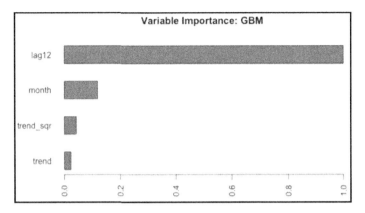

For RF, the GBM model ranks the **lag12** variable as the most important to the model. Let's test the model's performance on the testing set:

```
test_h$pred_gbm   <- h2o.predict(gbm_md, test_h)

test_1 <- as.data.frame(test_h)

mape_gbm <- mean(abs(test_1$y - test_1$pred_gbm) / test_1$y)

mape_gbm
```

We get the following output:

```
## [1] 0.02735553
```

The GBM model scored the lowest MAPE among the models we've tested so far with a 2.7% error rate, compared to 3.3% and 4% with the RF model (with grid search) and linear regression model, respectively. It would be a great exercise to apply a grid search on the GBM model and test whether any additional improvements can be achieved.

Let's visualize the results and compare the prediction with the actual and baseline prediction:

```
plot_ly(data = test_1) %>%
  add_lines(x = ~ date, y = ~y, name = "Actual") %>%
  add_lines(x = ~ date, y = ~ yhat, name = "Linear Regression", line =
list(dash = "dot")) %>%
  add_lines(x = ~ date, y = ~ pred_gbm, name = "Gradient Boosting Machine",
line = list(dash = "dash")) %>%
  layout(title = "Total Vehicle Sales - Actual vs. Prediction (Gradient
Boosting Machine)",
```

```
        yaxis = list(title = "Thousands of Units"),
        xaxis = list(title = "Month"))
```

We get the following output:

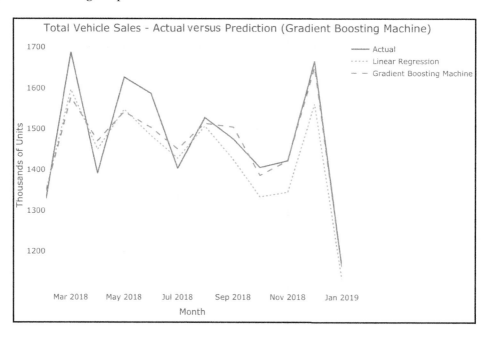

Forecasting with the AutoML model

So far, in this chapter, we have looked at two modeling approaches—the first using the algorithm's default setting with the RF and GBM models, and the second by applying a grid search with the RF model. Let's take a look at a third approach to tuning ML models. Here, we will use the h2o.automl function. The h2o.automl function provides an automated approach to training, tuning, and testing multiple ML algorithms before selecting the model that performed best based on the model's evaluation. It utilizes algorithms such as RF, GBM, DL, and others using different tuning approaches.

Similarly, the h2o.grid function can apply any of the training approaches (CV, training with validation, and so on) during the training process of the models. Let's use the same input as before, and train the forecasting model:

```
autoML1 <- h2o.automl(training_frame = train_h,
                      x = x,
                      y = y,
```

```
                              nfolds = 5,
                              max_runtime_secs = 60*20,
                              seed = 1234)
```

 We can set the runtime of the function. A longer running time could potentially yield better results.

In the preceding example, the function's running time was set to 20 minutes. The function returns a list with the `leaderboard` of all the tested models:

```
autoML1@leaderboard
```

We get the following output:

```
##                                                    model_id
## 1    DeepLearning_grid_1_AutoML_20190507_162701_model_1
## 2    DeepLearning_grid_1_AutoML_20190507_162701_model_12
## 3    DeepLearning_grid_1_AutoML_20190507_162701_model_9
## 4    DeepLearning_grid_1_AutoML_20190507_162701_model_2
## 5    DeepLearning_grid_1_AutoML_20190507_162701_model_5
## 6    DeepLearning_grid_1_AutoML_20190507_162701_model_4
##   mean_residual_deviance      rmse        mse        mae       rmsle
## 1               3977.890  63.07052   3977.890   49.20507  0.04897362
## 2               3986.516  63.13887   3986.516   48.95475  0.04908595
## 3               4121.476  64.19872   4121.476   50.80116  0.04983452
## 4               4289.938  65.49762   4289.938   51.64339  0.05128537
## 5               4440.572  66.63762   4440.572   50.27883  0.05153639
## 6               4441.784  66.64671   4441.784   52.11865  0.05229755
##
## [139 rows x 6 columns]
```

You can see that in this case, the top models are DL models with different tuning settings. We will select the leader model and test its performance on the testing set:

```
test_h$pred_autoML  <- h2o.predict(autoML1@leader, test_h)

test_1 <- as.data.frame(test_h)

mape_autoML <- mean(abs(test_1$y - test_1$pred_autoML) / test_1$y)

mape_autoML
```

We get the following output:

```
## [1] 0.03481595
```

The leader model of the output of `h2o.automl` achieved a MAPE score of 3.48%. Although the previous models achieved a higher score, it still provides a significant lift with respect to the baseline model. Let's visualize the prediction of the model on the testing partitions with respect to the actual and baseline prediction:

```
plot_ly(data = test_1) %>%
  add_lines(x = ~ date, y = ~y, name = "Actual") %>%
  add_lines(x = ~ date, y = ~ yhat, name = "Linear Regression", line =
list(dash = "dot")) %>%
  add_lines(x = ~ date, y = ~ pred_autoML, name = "autoML", line =
list(dash = "dash")) %>%
  layout(title = "Total Vehicle Sales - Actual vs. Prediction (Auto ML
Model)",
        yaxis = list(title = "Thousands of Units"),
        xaxis = list(title = "Month"))
```

We get the following output:

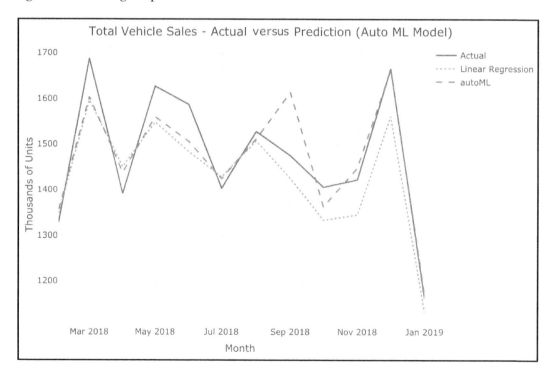

The main advantage of the `h2o.automl` function is that it can scale up while having multiple series to forecast with minimal intervention from the user. This, of course, comes with additional compute power and time cost.

Selecting the final model

Now that we've finished the training and testing process of the models, it's time to finalize the process and choose the model to forecast with the series. We trained the following models:

- **Baseline model**: Linear regression model with 4% MAPE score on the testing partition
- **RF**: Using default tuning parameters with 3.74% MAPE score on the testing partition
- **RF**: Using grid search for tuning the model parameters with 3.33% MAPE score on the testing partition
- **GBM**: Using the default tuning parameters with 2.75% MAPE score on the testing partition
- **AutoML**: Selecting a deep learning model with 3.48% MAPE score on the testing partition

Since all of these models achieved better results than the baseline, we can drop the baseline model. Also, since the second RF model (with grid search) achieved better results than the first, there is no point in keeping the first model. This leaves us with three forecasting models, that is, RF (with grid search), GBM, and AutoML. Generally, since the GBM model achieved the best MAPE results, we will select it. However, it is always nice to plot the actual forecast and check what the actual forecast looks like. Before we plot the results, let's use these three models to forecast the next 12 months using the data.frame forecast we created in the *Forecasting with the Random Forest model* and *Forecasting with the GBM model* sections:

```
forecast_h$pred_gbm <- h2o.predict(gbm_md, forecast_h)
forecast_h$pred_rf <- h2o.predict(rf_grid_model, forecast_h)
forecast_h$pred_automl <- h2o.predict(autoML1@leader, forecast_h)
```

We will transform the object back into a data.frame object with the as.data.frame function:

```
final_forecast <- as.data.frame(forecast_h)
```

Now, we can plot the final forecast with the **plotly** package:

```
plot_ly(x = df$date, y = df$y,
        type = "scatter",
        mode = "line",
        name = "Actual") %>%
  add_lines(x = final_forecast$date, y = final_forecast$pred_rf, name =
"Random Forest") %>%
```

```
  add_lines(x = final_forecast$date, y = final_forecast$pred_gbm, name =
"GBM") %>%
  add_lines(x = final_forecast$date, y = final_forecast$pred_automl, name =
"Auto ML") %>%
  layout(title = "Total Vehicle Sales - Final Forecast",
         yaxis = list(title = "Thousands of Units", range = c(1100, 1750)),
         xaxis = list(title = "Month", range = c(as.Date("2016-01-01"),
as.Date("2020-01-01"))))
```

We get the following output:

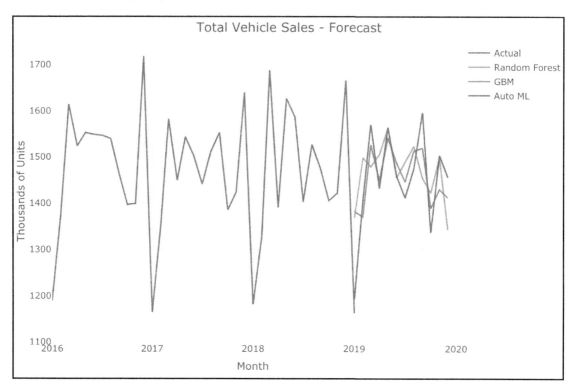

It seems that all three models capture the seasonality component of the vehicle sales series. However, it seems that the oscillation of AutoML is higher with respect to one of the RF and GBM models. Therefore, it would make sense to select either the GBM or RF models as the final forecast. A more conservative approach would be to create and ensemble the three forecasts by either weighted on regular average. For instance, you can use a simple function for testing the different average of different models and select the combination that minimizes the forecast error rate on the testing set.

Summary

In this chapter, we introduced the applications of ML models for forecasting time series data. Before we jumped into the modeling part, we looked at the usage of the major concepts we've learned about throughout this book. We started with an exploratory analysis of the US vehicle sales series using seasonality and correlation analysis. The insights from this process allowed us to build new features, which we then used as inputs for the ML models. Furthermore, we looked at the advantages of the grid search for tuning and optimizing ML models. Last but not least, we introduced the AutoML model from the **h2o** package in order to complete the automation, tuning, and optimization processes for ML models.

With that, I hope you have enjoyed the learning journey that we have been on throughout this book!

Other Books You May Enjoy

If you enjoyed this book, you may be interested in these other books by Packt:

R Machine Learning Projects
Sunil Kumar Chinnamgari

ISBN: 978-1-78980-794-3

- Explore deep neural networks and various frameworks that can be used in R
- Develop a joke recommendation engine to recommend jokes that match users' tastes
- Create powerful ML models with ensembles to predict employee attrition
- Build autoencoders for credit card fraud detection
- Work with image recognition and convolutional neural networks
- Make predictions for casino slot machine using reinforcement learning
- Implement NLP techniques for sentiment analysis and customer segmentation

Machine Learning with R
Brett Lantz

ISBN: 978-1-78829-586-4

- Discover the origins of machine learning and how exactly a computer learns by example
- Prepare your data for machine learning work with the R programming language
- Classify important outcomes using nearest neighbor and Bayesian methods
- Predict future events using decision trees, rules, and support vector machines
- Forecast numeric data and estimate financial values using regression methods
- Model complex processes with artificial neural networks — the basis of deep learning
- Avoid bias in machine learning models
- Evaluate your models and improve their performance
- Connect R to SQL databases and emerging big data technologies such as Spark, H2O, and TensorFlow

Leave a review - let other readers know what you think

Please share your thoughts on this book with others by leaving a review on the site that you bought it from. If you purchased the book from Amazon, please leave us an honest review on this book's Amazon page. This is vital so that other potential readers can see and use your unbiased opinion to make purchasing decisions, we can understand what our customers think about our products, and our authors can see your feedback on the title that they have worked with Packt to create. It will only take a few minutes of your time, but is valuable to other potential customers, our authors, and Packt. Thank you!

Index

Printed in Great Britain
by Amazon

49128163R00249